–1
RUGBY UNION
WHO'S WHO
1992/93

Compiled and edited by
ALEX SPINK

CollinsWillow

An Imprint of HarperCollins*Publishers*

First published in 1992 by
Collins Willow
an imprint of HarperCollins*Publishers*
London

© Alex Spink 1992

A CIP catalogue record for this book is available
from the British Library

ISBN 0 00 218392 7

Cover photographs of Gordon Hamilton and Phil Matthews,
Jean-Baptiste Lafond, Gary Armstrong, Emyr Lewis,
and Dewi Morris by AllSport
Portraits by AllSport and Mark Leech

Typeset in Plantin Light by Michael Mepham, Frome

Printed and bound in Great Britain by
Butler & Tanner Ltd, Frome and London

CONTENTS

Preface   v

Foreword   ix

The Captains review the 1991/92 Season   x

International Player's Player of the Year   xxxix

Key to statistics   xl

THE PLAYERS A TO Z   1

The French Captain reviews 1991/92   250

The French Players A to Z   255

Appendix   293

Retirees   308

World Cup results   330

Year in review   349

Major fixtures   379

Full list of entries   385

PEP TALK

If you're looking to improve your investment performance then Save & Prosper is the team to come to for a PEP talk. Because Save & Prosper's Personal Equity Plan is an excellent way of investing up to £6,000 (£12,000 for a couple) a year in the stock market, with all your investment returns tax-free. The tax exemption means the dividends are automatically increased by at least one third and you don't pay Capital Gains Tax on your profits – however big they are.

Save & Prosper, part of Flemings who manage £27 billion worldwide, are one of the leaders in the personal equity plan market with over 70,000 plans.

Talk to your financial adviser or ring us on our free Moneyline 0800 282 101 now.

CALL FREE 0800 282 101
9.00 a.m. – 5.30 p.m. ● 7 DAYS A WEEK

SAVE & PROSPER

■ THE INVESTMENT HOUSE ■
SPONSORS OF ENGLISH RUGBY

PREFACE

The Rugby Union Who's Who 1992/93 upholds the reputation set by its two predecessors as a voicepiece for the international playing fraternity. The long-held grievance is that the Game's administrators too often go about their business without bothering to consult the players. Now, though, the players' views cannot be ignored. Within the pages of this volume, they are given their own say.

The opinions expressed are motivated by genuine concern for the future of the game, not personal gain. There is undoubtedly a groundswell of feeling that those who take to the field on a Saturday afternoon, those whose blood, sweat and skill attract ever-increasing numbers through the turnstiles, those who have elevated the profile of the game to hitherto uncharted heights, at least deserve the courtesy of being heard.

Lions' captain Finlay Calder pleads for the powers-that-be to 'speak *with* the players, not *to* them'. Lions' hooker Brian Moore calls for 'player representation on all major decision and law-making committees... proper lines of communication are absolutely vital to the future of the game', and he points out that 'you cannot run a successful company without consulting your workforce'.

Many agree that the Unions are moving in the right direction, in terms of player welfare, but there remains no uniformity, and there will continue to be none as long as the game's governing body, the International Rugby Football Board, leave their member Unions free to interpret regulations as they see fit. 'Why is there no global uniformity?' asks Ireland's record try-scoring centre Brendan Mullin. 'The discretionary element handed to Unions by the IRB is ridiculous and has led to utter confusion. Rugby has outgrown what the archaic IRB was set up to administer.'

England, so we were told, received a £5, 000-per-squad member payment after the World Cup, while Scotland, according to John Jeffrey, collected £368. It is not the sum which bothers players so much as the discrepancy. What's good for the goose must be good enough for the gander.

The Southern Hemisphere nations are able to benefit from rugby-related activities, yet the four Home Unions cannot. As

England captain Will Carling argues: 'Players should be allowed to benefit from rugby-related activities because everything we do is naturally related to rugby.' He has a soul-mate in Scotland skipper David Sole, an intelligent and articulate man who, for the life of him, also cannot differentiate between the two. 'Surely there is no difference, ' he says.

For 99.9 per cent of rugby's worldwide playing community the opportunity to make money from rugby does not present itself. The opportunity to lose money does. For them, the worry concerns the amount of money leaving rather than entering their wallets as a result of increased commitments to the sport. England's World Cup final scrum-half Richard Hill highlights a vast lobby of opinion when he talks of the need for financial compensation to 'help players and employers cope with the staggering commitment expected of us'. He adds: 'Since 1988 we have knackered ourselves for work by becoming the fittest England side ever to take the field.'

There is, of course, a minority who would wish to see the game opened up to professionalism. In calling for players and coaches to be paid, erstwhile Ireland captain Phil Matthews explains that 'you have to take the extreme line to get any change at all'. He pleads with the authorities to 'remove the shackles of amateurism and take a realistic long-term view of what is happening in other sports'.

Speaking as both player and boss, Wales outside-half Mark Ring says: 'Look at me: I am retired at 29 with an old man's knee, having played solidly since I was seven. Top players should benefit for all the effort they put in, and their bosses should not lose out either. As an employer I could not afford to employ a rugby player who did nothing.'

There is hope. The call, in last year's edition, for the introduction of the five-point try, has been heeded. The players, without exception, want a more exciting product and the authorities have shown that they agree – although Wales scrum-half Robert Jones feels reducing the technical penalty to two points and not tampering with the try would have been a better plan. 'Increasing the try-value will make for a greater disparity between the major and the developing rugby nations, discouraging the latter, ' he says, citing the example of Wales, whose 63-6 loss to Australia would have been an even more demoralising 75-7 under the new scoring system.

Far and away the most unpopular of the new regulations is that which stipulates that 'when the ball becomes unplayable, or the ruck/maul becomes stationary, the team *not* in possession at the start of the ruck/maul will put the ball into an ensuing scrum'. Virtually universal condemnation rained down on that one. Brian Moore terms it 'a disaster – if you reward people who kill the ball, more will do it'. Others agree that cheats will be able to prosper.

There are those who believe that some of the new regulations will alter the face of the game... and not for the better. England prop Jeff Probyn, expressing his 'sadness' at the way things have changed, says: 'The need to be 100 per cent fitter to accommodate the new rule changes is taking away from the average player. That is not what I went into the game for.' Probyn's fear that almost gone are the days of rugby being a game for all shapes and sizes, is supported by his captain. Carling predicts that 'players will change to a more conformed 'flanker' body-type'.

Others would prefer the game to be left well alone. 'Stop messing about with the rules, ' demands Ireland flanker Pat O'Hara, while compatriot Mullin warns that 'changing the face of the game is no solution to its problems'. And Rob Andrew, the world's most-capped outside-half, says: 'Be careful not to go too far with rule changes designed to speed up the game and make it more entertaining. XV-a-side needs to maintain a distinct identity from Sevens.' On the subject of changing faces, Welsh reserve scrum-half Rupert Moon advocates 'cheap nose jobs for people with big noses' at the end of their careers!

For all these grievances, standards of refereeing has caused the greatest concern. 'Referees are not keeping up with the professional standards set by the players, ' considers England flanker Mickey Skinner, who adds: 'If they learned to play the advantage law we would have no need for half the new rules.'

John Olver, England's back-up hooker, asks for a few ex-forwards to become officials, because 'all referees seem to be backs who have no idea what is going on in the scrum'. Scotland flanker Ian Smith suggests setting up refereeing seminars 'where they can get together with players and coaches to work things out'.

There is no shortage of suggestions to improve rugby. Some are fanciful, others unworkable, yet many merit a hearing. Armchair quarterbacks these sources are not. These are the hands-on contributors to international rugby, the guys who captured everyone's imagination in the 1991 World Cup and the 1992 Five Nations' Championship.

Who can forget the month-long jamboree that was the Webb Ellis Cup, or the second leg of England's Grand Slam double? Not *The Rugby Union Who's Who 1992/93*. As in previous editions, this tome features a chronological reflection on the past international season (pp. 330–78), but this time the section is more comprehensive than ever. So, too, are the player biographies (pp. 1–249) which have been enlarged to give an even fuller picture of Saturday's heroes. Check out the Retirements (pp. 308–29) or the Appendix (pp. 293–307) if your personal favourite is not in the main body of the book.

For the first time, France is represented. Captain Philippe Sella has reviewed the international season from a Gallic perspective (p. 250) and there are biographies for every player who represented France in the period running from 22 June 1991 to the end of the 1992 Five Nations' season (pp. 255–92).

The book would not be complete without the Home Union captains recalling the past season (pp. x–xxxviii) and it is with Carling (England), Matthews and Phil Danaher (Ireland), Sole (Scotland) and Ieuan Evans (Wales) that I begin my vote of thanks. Without their co-operation, and the enthusiasm of all the players who appear, there would be no book.

I also extend my gratitude to the following: the AllSport photographic team, Westgate Sports (Rob Cole and Howard Evans), Chris Thau, the Rugby Football Union, the French Rugby Federation, the Irish Rugby Union, the Scottish Rugby Union, the Welsh Rugby Union, *Rugby World & Post*, the *Daily Telegraph* (for keeping me informed), and my family – Karen, Tom and Jenny (for keeping me sane).

Alex Spink
July 1992

FOREWORD

PAUL BATEMAN

Chief Executive, Save & Prosper Group

I am delighted to introduce this season's *Rugby Union Who's Who* – the third edition which Save and Prosper has sponsored.

The 1991/92 season was a memorable one for rugby fans. As sponsors of English rugby it was a great season for Save and Prosper too. England's performance in reaching the World Cup Final and then achieving a Grand Slam Double was an outstanding achievement.

However, this book recognises the skills and views of the top players from *all* the Home Countries and now, with the useful addition of the French players, across the Five Nations. It is these sportsmen who make rugby union such a wonderful game.

It will be interesting to see how the players featured here, and indeed those at the lower levels of the game, adapt to the new changes to the laws of the game. I am confident that there will once again be plenty of exciting rugby to enjoy.

THE CAPTAINS REVIEW
THE 1991/92 SEASON

 ## ENGLAND

Will Carling

WHEN we achieved the 1991 Grand Slam it was difficult to envisage a campaign more satisfying and more successful. Yet last season managed to outstrip its predecessor. As confidence spiralled so we became more professional in our approach, more disciplined in our performance, and ever less satisfied with imperfection.

We reached the World Cup final and achieved the first back-to-back Grand Slams since 1923-24. Critics were quick to query the strength of the Five Nations' opposition but, as Australia's Michael Lynagh pointed out: 'You've still got to score tries, you've still got to be able to play.' And to my mind we certainly did that.

Yet the season began on the wrong end of a 40-15 scoreline in Sydney – the second heaviest defeat ever suffered by an England side away from home. While obviously shocked to lose by such a margin I personally felt better because we had exposed ourselves to them, seen how good they were and given ourselves an idea of where we stood in the lead-in to the World Cup. Sure, we were Grand Slam champions but where did that put us in the world order?

> **❝ Had we not toured Australia prior to the World Cup I genuinely do not believe we would have been anything like as successful in the tournament ❞**

In spite of the fact that we lost so heavily, we actually felt we made enough chances to beat them, and that if we just put a bit of hard work into certain areas we would be in a position to compete come the autumn. It was most definitely a worthwhile tour, even if the results did not appear all that good. Indeed, had we not toured Australia prior to the World Cup I genuinely do not believe we would have been anything like as successful in the tournament.

Two months or so later the tournament kicked off at Twickenham with the defending champions New Zealand opposing us. In hindsight, we were far too tense in the build-up, with the result that we produced one of our worst performances for some time. We forgot to have a laugh in the week before, but at least we were quick to identify our failing. And we were both consoled and amazed by the realisation that we had played so poorly, by our standards, yet were still in touch with them at the end.

We reckoned that if we could settle down and get into a rhythm we were actually capable of beating these Southern Hemisphere sides later in the tournament. The defeat even helped us in a perverse kind of way as it lifted a little bit of pressure off the expectation. Had we beaten the All Blacks, people would have taken it as read that we would have no problems in going on to pick up the Cup. Mind you, we still believed we were good enough to triumph, and that belief was strengthened by the style in which we beat Italy (36-6) and the United States (37-9) to qualify for a quarter-final in France as Pool runners-up.

The Paris week was the hardest in the World Cup and, indeed, the hardest week we have had together as a team. Suddenly it was do or die. Had we lost that game, the World Cup would have been seen as a disaster after three years of preparation. So we felt under a lot of pre-match pressure and I think physically, and possibly mentally, it turned out to be the toughest game I have ever played. Some of the tackles, the general pace and ferocity was amazing. The steel in the team when France pegged the scores back to 10-10 could not be translated into words. There was just no way we were going to lose.

The pressure got to France even more than us. Serge Blanco's uncharacteristic reaction in the first few minutes showed to me the kind of emotion they let into their play and, as we have all learned, once emotion comes into the game you are on very dangerous ground. The result, 19-10 in our favour, supported that view.

The build-up to the Scotland semi-final was also incredibly tense. Being booked for a week in the same hotel where we had stayed the night we lost the 1990 Grand Slam decider only added to the tension. I remember vividly walking into it and thinking 'I really don't like this place.' We desperately did not want to get caught up in that past but, equally, we wanted to rid ourselves of the memory.

It was always going to be a hard week, with the Scots constantly telling us that we did not have a chance. But, on the day, we produced an incredibly disciplined performance. The first 20 minutes were frantic, but after that I felt we were in control. Our performance was not expansive, it was not pretty, but it was an amazingly controlled display. Scotland had a very good side, incredibly well motivated, yet we beat them and, although the score was not convincing, I thought the last 15 minutes belonged to us. Mind you, I thank God we won because to have walked away a loser, especially at Murrayfield again, having come so close to the final, would have been an awful feeling to carry for years and years to come.

> ❛ *We came to the conclusion that the way to beat Australia was by running at them in midfield, trying to win quick ball, hit again and then move it wide... We played just about as well as we could have, but lost out to a truly great side* ❜

So to the final where, contrary to one popular school of thought, we did not succumb to media pressure to throw the ball about. We did not sit down and massively alter our game-plan. We just thought, tactically, that we needed to run slightly more set-piece ball in order to minimise the influence of Australia's high-quality kickers and equally proficient line-out men. We realised that we were not going to dominate up front as we had in previous matches. As it turned out we actually did not run that much more set-piece ball than previously. What was different was the amazing amount of second-, third- and fourth-phase ball we were winning, which created the impression that we ran so much more ball than usual.

We had considered not changing our game for the final but came to the conclusion that the way to beat Australia was by running at them in the midfield, trying to win quick ball, hit again and then move it wide. Where the plan, ultimately, came unstuck was in our failure to tie in enough of their forwards to give us the space to exploit. In saying that, we made enough chances to win the game. Our problem, simply, was that we did not capitalise on them.

There was a feeling of tremendous pride in defeat, despite the overwhelming sense of disappointment. We played just about as well as we could have, in my view, but lost to the best side in the world that year. And make no mistake – they were a truly great side.

To go on and succeed in the Five Nations' Championship could never make up for losing the World Cup final, but it was nevertheless an extremely special campaign. I certainly had doubts – and I was not alone – about whether I would be able to get myself going 100 per cent for the Championship. To us it seemed a world away, even less than a month beforehand, because our minds were still going over and over the World Cup. Yet suddenly it was time to go again – and we not only performed, but showed that we had already digested the lessons of the World Cup by producing a dramatically improved level of performance. And that, for me, was what made the campaign so satisfying.

As we headed back to Murrayfield again for the Calcutta Cup opener, we were well aware that all Anglo-Scot contests, going back over the last three or four years, had been nip-and-tuck affairs. We felt we had never exactly played to our potential and this time we wanted to move the ball more against them, which we managed to do in the second half (won 25-7). Up front, before the break, some of the older internationals would say they did not play nearly as well as they could and, indeed, the Scots surprised us in the line-out and scrum. With hindsight, I think we got slightly over-complicated.

Ireland's visit to Twickenham (won 38-9) coincided with one of the best sustained performances we had put in for a while. The day was a great personal triumph for Jon Webb, who not only broke the national single-match scoring record with 22 points but included two tries in his haul. I remember playing with him in an England trial in 1987 and he was a brilliant attacking fullback then. We all knew he was capable of it and maybe it was circumstances or confidence that never brought it out. But against the Irish he was a revelation.

> ❝ *At international level you have to be incredibly disciplined. There is so much pressure placed on you, so much media attention and so much emotion involved – and you have to be able to control it all*❞

The crucial link in the Grand Slam chain, as in 1991, was the French connection (won 31-13). We again took control although I am bound to say I was surprised by events in the closing stages when they had two front-row forwards sent off. The French tend to get a bit excited when they are losing but, on this occasion, they really did lose their discipline badly. While you can understand frustration, you can never understand the reasoning behind the unsavoury scenes that occurred. It did nobody any good. Some blamed it on French club rugby, others on their attitude towards the game, and some even on referees. Now I have never played against France when the referee has struck me as having gone against them. No, you cannot lay any blame on the officials. At international level you have to be incredibly disciplined. There is so much pressure placed on you, so much media attention and so much emotion involved – and you have to be able to control it all.

In my team-talk prior to the game against Wales I stressed that they were a much better side than in the past two years and we had to be careful. I also stressed the need not to get too carried away with the occasion, and to maintain our primary objective of winning the game. People expected a show and a glamour performance but Wales, to their credit, managed to frustrate us in that we could never really find our rhythm. They managed to stop us winning quick ball which had the effect of stifling our ability to open them up. And we never really came to terms with that. But at the end of the day we beat Wales 24-0, a scoreline virtually unthinkable three years ago.

All in all, then, it was a brilliant Championship for us, highlighted by our standing on the balcony after the Welsh game and looking out over the jubilant crowd. I think that will be my abiding memory though it is tinged with sadness that I did not get the bench reserves up there as well. It was a mistake on my part because the Grand Slam was a squad achievement and they were as much a part of it as were we who played in each game.

That we have achieved successive Grand Slams and are now working towards an unprecedented hat-trick is a testimony to the structure which manager Geoff Cooke has set in place. The blend of personnel is right on the coaching and management side and, as such, there should be a continued period of great success for English rugby over the next few years.

Off the field the movement is also in the right direction as regards the thorny topic of amateurism. There remain a number of issues unresolved but we are lucky that a majority on the RFU Committee now realise that things have to change. I believe 75 per cent of them realise what sacrifices the players are making and the increased profile that we have given the game. Now it is down to defining exactly what players can and cannot do, and I am genuinely hopeful that a fair deal is just around the corner.

ENGLAND'S BACK-TO-BACK GRAND SLAMS

		P	W	D	L	F	(t, c, p, dg)	A	(t, c, p, dg)	Pts
1991 –	England	4	4	0	0	83	(5, 3, 18, 1)	44	(4, 2, 8, 0)	8
1992 –	England	4	4	0	0	118	(15, 11, 11, 1)	29	(4, 2, 3, 0)	8
TOTAL:	England	8	8	0	0	201	(20, 14, 29, 2)	73	(8, 4, 11, 0)	16

RESULTS: Wales 6, England 25 (Cardiff, 19.1.91); England 21, Scotland 12 (Twickenham, 16.2.91); Ireland 7, England 16 (Dublin, 2.3.91); England 21, France 19 (Twickenham, 16.3.91); Scotland 7, England 25 (Edinburgh, 18.1.92); England 38, Ireland 9 (Twickenham, 1.2.92); France 13, England 31 (Paris, 15.2.92); England 24, Wales 0 (Twickenham, 7.3.92)

SQUAD: P Ackford (Harlequins) **1991** – W, S, I, F; **R Andrew** (Wasps/Toulouse) **1991** – W, S, I, F, **1992** – S, I, F, W; **M Bayfield** (Northampton) **1992** – S, I, F, W; **W Carling** (capt, Harlequins) **1991** – W, S, I, F, **1992** – S, I, F, W; **W Dooley** (Preston Grasshoppers) **1991** – W, S, I, F, **1992** – S, I, F, W; **J Guscott** (Bath) **1991** – W, S, I, F, **1992** – S, I, F, W; **S Halliday** (Harlequins) **1991** – rS, rI, rF, **1992** – S, I, F, W; **R Hill** (Bath) **1991** – W, S, I, F, **1992** – rS, rI, rF, rW; **S Hodgkinson** (Nottingham) **1991** – W, S, I, F; **N Heslop** (Orrell) **1991** – W, S, I, F, **1992** – rS, rI, rF,

W(R73); **D Hopley** (Wasps) **1991** – rW; **M Hynes** (Orrell) **1992** – rS, rI, rF, rW; **J Leonard** (Harlequins) **1991** – W, S, I, F, **1992** – S, I, F, W; **B Moore** (Harlequins) **1991** – W, S, I, F, **1992** – S, I, F, W; **D Morris** (Orrell) **1991** – rW, rS, rI, rF, **1992** – S, I, F, W; **J Olver** (Northampton) **1991** – rW, rS, rI, rF, **1992** – rS, rI, rF, rW; **D Pears** (Harlequins) **1992** – rS, rI, F(R35), rW; **J Probyn** (Wasps) **1991** – W, S, I, F, **1992** – S, I, F, W; **P Rendall** (Wasps) **1991** – rW, rS, rI, rF; **D Richards** (Leicester) **1991** – W, S, I, F, **1992** – S(R63), rI, F, W; **T Rodber** (Northampton) **1992** – S, I, rF, rW; **M Skinner** (Harlequins) **1991** – rW, rS, rI, rF, **1992** – S, I, F, W; **M Teague** (Gloucester) **1991** – W, S, I, F; **R Underwood** (RAF & Leicester) **1991** – W, S, I, F, **1992** – S, I, F, W; **J Webb** (Bath) **1991** – rW, rS, rI, rF, **1992** – S, I, F, W; **P Winterbottom** (Harlequins) **1991** – W, S, I, F, **1992** – S, I, F, W.

(r = replacement not used)

SCORERS: 67 – Webb 3t, 11c, 11p. 60 – Hodgkinson 3c, 18p. 20 – Underwood 5t. 12 – Morris 3t. 8 – Teague 2t. 7 – Guscott 1t, 1dg. 4 – Carling 1t; Dooley 1t; Halliday 1t; Heslop 1t; Skinner 1t; penalty try. 3 – Andrew 1dg.

(t = try, c = conversion, p = penalty goal, dg = dropped goal)

ENGLAND'S INTERNATIONAL SEASON 1991/92

ENGLAND (P13 W10 D0 L3 F333 A142):

(A) v. Fiji (Suva, 20.7.91)	won	28-12
(A) v. Australia (Sydney, 27.7.91)	lost	15-40
(H) v. Soviet Union (Twickenham, 7.9.91)	won	53-0
		(non-cap)

World Cup

(H) v. New Zealand (Twickenham, 3.10.91)	lost	12-18
(H) v. Italy (Twickenham, 8.10.91)	won	36-6
(H) v. United States (Twickenham, 11.10.91)	won	37-9
(A) v. France (q/f: Paris, 19.10.91)	won	19-10
(A) v. Scotland (s/f: Edinburgh, 26.10.91)	won	9-6
(H) v. Australia (f: Twickenham, 2.11.91)	lost	6-12

Five Nations' Championship

(A) v. Scotland (Edinburgh, 18.1.92)	won	25-7
(H) v. Ireland (Twickenham, 1.2.92)	won	38-9
(A) v. France (Paris, 15.2.92)	won	31-13
(H) v. Wales (Twickenham, 7.3.92)	won	24-0

England B (P4, W4, D0, L0, F119, A46):

(A) v. Spain (Madrid, 19.1.92)	won	34-3
(H) v. Ireland B (Richmond, 31.1.92)	won	47-15
(A) v. France B (Paris, 15.2.92)	won	22-18
(A) v. Italy B (Rome, 7.3.92)	won	16-10

England U-21 (P4, W2, D1, L1, F173, A52):

(H) v. Belgium (Wolverhampton, 1.10.91)	won	94-0
(A) v. Ireland U-21 (Donnybrook, 23.10.91)	lost	10-19
(H) v. French Armed Forces (Twickenham, 2.5.92)	drew	21-21
(A) v. Netherlands (Leiden, 3.5.92)	won	48-12

England Students (P5, W3, D0, L2, F94, A101):

(–) v. England XV (Cambridge, 21.9.91)	lost	0-35
(A) v. Scotland (Edinburgh, 17.1.92)	won	32-9
(A) v. France (Toulouse, 14.2.92)	lost	9-22
(H) v. Wales (Newbury, 6.3.92)	won	25-16
(H) v. Ireland (Waterloo, 16.4.92)	won	28-19

English Universities (P3, W3, D0, L0, F72, A36):

(A) v. Scottish (Peffermill, 17.1.92)	won	15-7
(H) v. Irish (London Welsh, 31.1.92)	won	26-11
(H) v. Welsh (Bristol, 4.3.92)	won	31-18

England Colts (P4, W2, D1, L1, F82, A65):

(A) v. Italy (Padua, 14.3.92)	drew	15-15
(A) v. Wales (Brecon, 4.4.92)	won	29-18
(H) v. Scotland (Newcastle Gosforth, 18.4.92)	won	20-9
(H) v. France (Bournemouth, 25.4.92)	lost	18-23

England 18-Group (P4, W4, D0, L0, F73, A21):

(A) v. Scotland (Glasgow, 11.4.92)	won	28-0
(H) v. Ireland (Bedford, 15.4.92)	won	15-9
(A) v. France (Billancourt, 18.4.92)	won	12-9
(H) v. Wales (Doncaster, 25.4.92)	won	18-3

England 16-Group (P3, W2, D0, L1, F68, A32):

(H) v. Italy (Luton, 14.4.92)	won	32-3
(A) v. Spain (La Ville Joyosa, 18.4.92)	won	36-7
(A) v. Wales (Pontypridd, 25.4.92)	lost	0-22

COURAGE LEAGUES:

Division One:	P	W	D	L	F	A	Pts
Bath	12	10	1	1	277	126	20
Orrell	12	10	0	2	204	95	20
Northampton	12	9	1	2	209	136	19
Gloucester	12	7	1	4	193	168	15
Saracens	12	7	1	4	176	165	15
Leicester	12	6	1	5	262	216	13
Wasps	12	6	0	6	177	180	12
Harlequins	12	5	1	6	213	207	11
London Irish	12	3	3	6	147	237	9
Bristol	12	4	0	8	192	174	8
Rugby	12	2	3	7	124	252	7
Nottingham	12	2	1	9	133	204	5
Rosslyn Park	12	0	1	11	111	258	1

Division Two – Pro: London Scottish (c), West Hartlepool. **Rel:** Plymouth, Liverpool St H
Division Three – Pro: Richmond (c), Fylde. **Rel:** Nuneaton, Lydney
Division Four S – Pro: Havant (c). **Rel:** Sidcup, Ealing
Division Four N – Pro: Aspatria (c). **Rel:** Vale of Lune, Northern

Promoted: Berry Hill and Thurrock (to 4S) and Stoke-on-Trent and Rotherham (to 4N)

CUP FINALS:

Pilkington Cup
Bath 15, *Harlequins 12 aet (Twickenham, 2.5.92)

ADT County Championship
Lancashire 9, *Cornwall 6 (Twickenham, 18.4.92)

Provincial Insurance Cup
*Bradford Salem 12, Bicester 6 (Twickenham, 4.4.92)

Worthington National Sevens
London Scottish 38, Leicester 0 (Bath, 26.4.92)

Save & Prosper Middlesex Sevens
Western Samoa 30, *London Scottish 6 (Twickenham, 9.5.92)
(* holders)

IRELAND

Captains Phil Matthews
and Phil Danaher

Phil Matthews

IRISH rugby has to take a long, hard look at itself after the experiences of last season. All the excuses in the world cannot explain our diversity of performance. On the one hand we got closer than any nation in the world to beating Australia yet, either side of that unforgettable day in Dublin, we contrived to lose to Namibia, twice, and to Gloucester, and then to everyone during a humiliating Five Nations' whitewash.

Any amount of excuses can be made but, at the end of the day, my feeling was that it was the structure of the national game, rather

❛ *Ireland has to be more realistic about the demands of international rugby rather than being obsessed with remaining the last bastion of amateurism... The national structure, as it stands, does not present coach Ciaran Fitzgerald with players who are technically good enough and who know what is required at international level*❜

than the players directly involved, which was to blame. And now there is a lot of work required if we are to rescue the situation.

To get the structure of the game right from the very top we, first and foremost, have to be more realistic about the demands of international rugby rather than being obsessed with remaining the last bastion of amateurism. It is unfair to ask players to train 5 nights per week, 11 months of the year, and to compete on the same terms as other countries who are quite openly structuring the game differently. I am not talking about a professional attitude to line the players' pockets, but an attitude which will galvanise the game nationwide. I am talking about coaching standards throughout the country being raised.

Club coaches are not particularly strong in Ireland and if it means bringing in outsiders from New Zealand or Australia for a few years then so be it. The national structure, as it stands, does not present coach Ciaran Fitzgerald with players who are technically good enough and who know what is required at international level. Something urgently needs to be done at grass roots to raise the level of club rugby so that youngsters do not face such a huge jump when they graduate to the international arena.

If you want guys to compete at the top level you have to expose them to top-quality rugby. England have proved the point and they have now gone a stage further by sending B sides to New Zealand. We are so far away from that set-up. The IRFU say on the one hand they do not want to put pressure on players, yet, on the other, they are not prepared to do anything to alleviate that pressure.

So that was the backdrop to a season which began in Namibia in the summer of 1991. It is true to say that we were not familiar with the South African style of rugby they played. Even though we had watched videos of Wales' tour there the previous year and seen how difficult it was, you have to experience the game at first hand. We would certainly approach the tour in a very different way if we had that time again.

We went out there with the aim of finding a successor to Brian Smith in the No.10 jersey because we saw out-half as being a crucial position for us. Our failure to find a suitable candidate meant that we played the wrong game tactically and, position-wise, we did not have one of the key players we needed. It was a terrific blow losing Brian and I think it was only after he left that we really appreciated the depth of his contribution, defensively and in every way – even though

Ralph (Keyes) did so tremendously well in the World Cup and we were very lucky to have him.

Most people, in reviewing the Cup campaign, have looked back at only one game – Australia's visit to Dublin, but we also played very well for much of the Pool game against Scotland (lost 15-24). But from having them on the rack at 15-9 we let them go, which was so disappointing. We were able to dominate them up front in the set-pieces, but we were not able to use that possession to get the points on the board. In contrast, they were presented with a couple of half-chances and exploited them to win the game. Scotland have made very much better use of their resources over the years than we have, although I still believe that we possess a better squad of players than them.

In marked contrast, we were very pleased with our performance in the Australia game, though again glaring defensive errors ultimately cost us. Those deficiencies were a sign of things to come in the Five Nations' Championship. The loss of Brian Smith was keenly felt in defence, he was a key player in our rearguard– an excellent defensive out-half, both individually and in his ability to bring up his three-quarter line.

We had been on a hiding to nothing in the games against Zimbabwe (won 55-11) and Japan (won 32-16) where we were expected to win by high margins. For us the two wins were the main thing, to put us into the Scottish game on level-pegging. That was about the height of their significance although Brian Robinson will remember the Zimbabwe game because he scored four tries. It was a tremendous feat although I think he would be the first to concede that they had a very weak scrummage and a lot of credit should go to our front five.

We were very disappointed with ourselves for losing at Murrayfield after having had so much pressure and dominating for 60-70 per cent of the game. Obviously the second-half injury to fullback Jim Staples did change the complexion of the game but you have to hand it to the Scots for the way they capitalised, with Gary Armstrong playing the situation very, very well, putting up another garryowen from which they scored a try. Offered a half-chance they took full advantage.

To lose to Australia in the closing seconds was so demoralising. We showed a little bit of immaturity in the way we dealt with the kick-off after Gordon Hamilton's memorable try. Instead of putting it into the 100th row of the stand and slowing the game up, we missed touch, allowed them to get back into the game, and they, like Scotland before them, took their chances while we did not.

As a result of running the Aussies so close, I felt expectations were unrealistically high going into the Five Nations' Championship. That said, we the players had high expectations ourselves, at least of winning our two home games. We did not. Against the Welsh we just played badly. We should have won the game, having led 15-6 with only 30 minutes left against a side who had not won a Championship game since 1989, and I just do not know quite what went wrong. We scored a fine try just after halftime, through Richard Wallace, but it came out of nothing. We were not playing well up front, we were not scrummaging well, we were not getting any decent lineout ball and, when the backs pulled something out of the bag with that try, we failed to respond and ram that advantage home. Wales were there for the taking and yet we let them back in. I only hope that the side will learn from the experience. But I seem to have been hoping the same for years and years.

Defeat against Wales (15-16) put us under so much pressure in an England game which was always going to be tough. And, with the best will in the world, nobody would have beaten them on that performance. They were tremendous (won 38-9), they were a class side, and even had we won the Welsh game I am convinced that we would not have beaten England on that day. But the Press then started really to get on our case and the criticism intensified when again we played badly against Scotland (lost 10-18). I remain convinced that man-for-man we were the better side but we just played so badly leading to a total loss of confidence.

❛ Success breeds success in the world of sport and this side, unfortunately, has not yet learned how to win games ❜

What really upset us was the reaction of the Dublin crowd, slow handclapping and booing for the first time in memory. One of the positive aspects of the World Cup was that it increased the profile of the game. That meant that an awful lot of people who were not necessarily rugby enthusiasts were going along to matches and reading the type of rubbish that was being talked about Ireland going for Triple Crowns etc. That sent public expectation soaring unrealistically high and when we did so badly certain quarters gave us a fairly hard time – not that I think they were the real rugby supporters.

Success breeds success in the world of sport and this side, unfortunately, has not yet learned how to win games. We played a lot better in the 1991 Championship when we possessed a lot more naiive confidence, thanks to so many new players who did not know any different. The second year was always likely to be the real test for those individuals and we can only hope that they have learned from the experience.

Phil Danaher

I AGREE with Phil in that we have to plan for the future. In the past Ireland have tended to concentrate solely on the senior squad with the result that anyone outside that has been forgotten. Last season we paid the price for such short-sightedness. Two-thirds of the team that lost to Australia had gone by the time I took charge in Paris (lost 12-44). We were basically looking at a new Irish line-up, consisting of raw players not prepared for the task to which they had been assigned.

The only thing the French match could have proved was whether the guys were willing to take up the gauntlet and go for it or just fall down and let things happen. From the outside it might have appeared the latter was exactly what happened but I think we just totally lacked cohesion and organisation, as against the playing ability of each individual.

> ❜ We are at the bottom of the hill from where the only way is up. But we require proper organisation and monitoring... All too few players are fed into the system in readiness for the future❜

Indeed, the performances were probably of the same standards as previous ones and overall there was no great decline in the actual playing abilities of the 15 guys on the park. What there was a notable decline in, with so many new faces, was the organisation that goes with a team that has played together for a period.

We are at the bottom of the hill from where the only way is up. But we require proper organisation and monitoring. England lost Paul Ackford after the World Cup and brought in Dewi Morris, Tim Rodber and Martin Bayfield and yet, thanks to a strong national structure, their overall standard did not drop.

That structure is exactly what we seem to lack. When we lose players there are no ready-made ends replacements waiting in the wings and we immediately find ourselves in trouble. All too few players are fed into the system in readiness for the future. Therein lies the problem.

IRELAND'S INTERNATIONAL SEASON 1991/92

IRELAND (P10, W2, D0, L8, F187, A227):

(A) v. Namibia (Windhoek, 20.7.91)	lost	6-15
(A) v. Namibia (Windhoek, 27.7.91)	lost	15-26

World Cup

(H) v. Zimbabwe (Dublin, 6.10.91)	won	55-11
(H) v. Japan (Dublin, 9.10.91)	won	32-16
(A) v. Scotland (Edinburgh, 12.10.91)	lost	15-24
(H) v. Australia (q/f: Dublin, 20.10.91)	lost	18-19

Five Nations' Championship

(H) v. Wales (Dublin, 18.1.92)	lost	15-16
(A) v. England (Twickenham, 1.2.92)	lost	9-38
(H) v. Scotland (Dublin, 15.2.92)	lost	10-18

(A) v. France (Paris, 21.3.92)	lost	12-44

Ireland B (P2, W1, D0, L1, F44, A66):
(A) v. Scotland (Edinburgh, 28.12.91)	won	29-19
(A) v. England (Richmond, 31.1.92)	lost	15-47

Ireland U-21 (P2, W1, D0, L1, F34, A32):
(A) v. Wales (Newport, 16.10.91)	lost	15-22
(H) v. England (Dublin, 23.10.91)	won	19-10

Ireland Students (P2, W1, D0, L1, F40, A48):
(H) v. Scotland (Dublin, 14.2.92)	won	21-20
(A) v. England (Waterloo, 16.4.92)	lost	19-28

Irish Universities (P2, W1, D0, L1, F53, A32):
(H) v. Welsh (Dublin, 17.1.92)	won	42-6
(A) v. English (London, 31.1.92)	lost	11-26

Ireland Youth (P1, W0, D0, L1, F0, A4):
(H) v. Scotland (Galway, 11.4.92)	lost	0-4

Ireland Schools U-18 (P3, W2, D0, L1, F33, A30):
(H) v. Scotland (Galway, 4.4.92)	won	17-6
(H) v. Wales (Cork, 11.4.92)	lost	7-9
(A) v. England (Bedford, 15.4.92)	lost	9-15

INSURANCE CORPORATION LEAGUE

Division One:	P	W	D	L	F	A	Pts
Garryowen	8	7	0	1	162	91	14
Shannon	8	5	1	2	101	88	11
Ballymena	8	5	1	2	101	96	11
Old Wesley	8	4	0	4	83	91	8
Young Munster	8	3	1	4	71	72	7
St Mary's College	8	3	0	5	78	78	6
Cork Constitution	8	3	0	5	100	112	6
Lansdowne	8	2	1	5	93	92	5
Instonians	8	2	0	6	68	137	4

2 – Pro: Dungannon (c), Greystones. **Rel:** Sunday's Well, CIYMS
Promoted to 2: Old Crescent and Clontarf

CUP FINALS:

Connacht Cup
Ballinasloe 10, Sligo 6 (Galway, 25.4.92)

Leinster Cup
Blackrock College 12, Old Wesley 6 (Lansdowne Road, 25.4.92)

Munster Cup
Shannon 9, Young Munster 7 (Thomond Park, 25.4.92)

Ulster Cup
Malone 13, NIFC 3 (Ravenhill, 25.4.92)

SCOTLAND

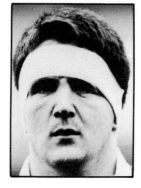

David Sole

IT was a season of transition for Scottish rugby – the end of the road for a number of familiar faces who had served Scotland through arguably the most successful period of her history, and the birth of a new generation. Yet through all the change we succeeded in reaching the semi-finals of the World Cup and in sharing second place in the Five Nations' Championship.

The most enduring memory for me was not of a single incident, nor even a specific match; rather the fanatical Murrayfield fans who inspired us through the month of October in our quest for the Webb Ellis Cup. The crowd grew its own identity as we progressed through the tournament and it was a fantastic atmosphere in which to be involved.

The entire nation's fervent support complemented the hard work we had put in over the summer to prepare ourselves for the tournament. Two tough games, against Romania (lost 12-18) in Bucharest, and a very strong Barbarians XV (drew 16-16) in Edinburgh, brought us perfectly to the boil in time for our World Cup opener against Japan, a point we underlined with a 47-9 win.

Japan showed themselves to be very dangerous when they had the ball, as we expected they would. So we set out to deny them possession. We also knew that they would view the game as their best opportunity of qualifying for the quarter-finals. Nothing, therefore, was left to chance. We competed well, maintained a high level of concentration, and were well rewarded.

We were, of course, fortunate in that we played all our Cup-ties at Murrayfield and so were able to base ourselves at the lavish Dalmahoy Hotel. It was there we spent the four days until Zimbabwe formed our next opposition in town. The occasion struck us as an ideal opportunity to give many of the senior players a rest, bearing in mind the very tough Pool-deciding match against Ireland to come three days later, and the fact that we had suffered in the 1987 tournament for not fully utilising our squad. A calculated risk then, resting eight of the team which had beaten Japan, and after about half an hour, when we were pegged back to 12-15, I was wondering whether we had done the right thing. But we belatedly came together, scoring three of our eight tries in the final ten minutes.

> ❛ It was a titanic forward battle – quite brutal up front. You never ask for too much against the Irish and you certainly don't get given a great deal ❜

So to the Irish, with their lovely way of trying to con you into believing they did not mind whether they won or lost because they would be quite happy to play a quarter-final at Lansdowne Road against Australia rather than travel to Murrayfield for a potentially less daunting tie against Western Samoa. Within two minutes of the kick-off their true intentions became clear. It was a titanic forward battle – quite brutal up front. You never ask for too much against the Irish, and you certainly don't get given a great deal. They started the better but, funnily enough, I felt even when we were 15-9 down that we were never really out of touch, that in fact our fitness was beginning to tell.

There was a lot written about the second-half incident in which Irish fullback Jim Staples was injured, but to me it seemed an innocuous enough challenge from Fin (Calder) which was blown out of all proportion. Looking at it on the video afterwards confirmed my belief. Fin did the damage with his shoulder, not with his fist. But Ireland were undoubtedly unsettled by it and we were quick to capitalise (won 24-15).

The management's view of our South Pacific quarter-final

❛ I'm not saying you win by foul means or fair but you must always look to exploit weaknesses. We would have expected Ireland to do the same if the roles had been reversed ❜

opponents was that they were very strong in the tackle but liking to line people up and tending to be fairly blinkered in so doing. We felt that if we could shift the target and change the angles, so they did not get the opportunity to put the big hits straight-on, we would profit. The ploy worked. Using Gavin (Hastings) as a makeshift halfback, to keep things tight playing into the breeze first half, we established a rock-solid foundation from which we built a healthy winning margin (28-6). We played our best rugby of the tournament that day.

There was an enormous amount of pressure leading into the semi-final against England, for all the obvious reasons. Murrayfield produced a fairly electric atmosphere. Unfortunately, England had learned their lessons from the 1990 Grand Slam decider. They knew exactly how they wanted to play against us, closing down the game, keeping it tight and, while it was far from inspirational rugby, it was undoubtedly effective and proved the right way to play against us.

The overriding emotion afterwards was one of bitter disappointment to have come so close to the final only to be denied by Rob Andrew's dropped goal, seven minutes from time. Consequently, it was very difficult to get excited about the third/fourth place play-off, just four days later in Cardiff, although the one saving grace was that it was against the All Blacks who I was eager to help Scotland beat for the first time.

We were really hanging on by our fingernails for the first half, a lot of first-time tackles being missed. Gary Armstrong turned in a really quite incredible game for the amount of covering and try-saving tackles he made. Largely due to him we trailed by only three points at half-time and were able to pull things round a wee bit in the second period when we started winning a bit of ball. The game could actually have gone either way in the later stages, right up to Walter Little's last-minute try (lost 6-13). My regret afterwards was that JJ (John Jeffrey) and Fin (Calder) had to bow out of the international arena on a losing note in a game which really did not have the same importance as the final or even a Five Nations' game.

It really was an incredibly taxing season. Just two and a half months after trooping off the Arms Park we were having to raise ourselves for the Calcutta Cup visit of England. Yet in that short period the appearance of the side had been transformed. In addition to the back row retirements we had lost the services of Gary (Armstrong), Graham Marshall and Chris Gray, all injured.

However, we felt no trepidation going into the game with four new caps, including scrum-half Andy Nicol, who was to prove the find of the season. The personnel brought into the back row (Dave McIvor and Ian Smith) were such different players from Fin and JJ, namely a genuine open-side and a genuine blind-side, that it meant we could play a different, more expansive style of rugby, which did wonders for rekindling enthusiasm.

> ❛ I felt we were at least nine points better than England in the first half, but unfortunately we could not turn that pressure into points ❜

I did not feel the 25-7 scoreline, in England's favour, fairly represented the way the game went. We had all the pressure in the first half, heaving the much-vaunted England pack over their own line for a memorable pushover try and, really, their two tries came about from our mistakes. Add to that the fact that Gavin did not have his kicking boots on and Jon Webb did. Such factors make all the difference in international rugby. I felt we were at least nine points better than them in the first half, but unfortunately we could not turn that pressure into points. To find ourselves with a losing margin instead made it very difficult to maintain effort and energy in the second half when England again closed down the game.

It was very important from the new team's point of view that we got the confidence of a win in our next outing against Ireland in Dublin (won 18-10). It is one thing to play well but another to play well and win. In a howling wind we stuck to our task well and, I think it is fair to say, produced a gritty rather than shining performance.

The French visit to Murrayfield (won 10-6) was another game played in atrocious conditions, and to complicate matters further we played 65 per cent of the game without the ball. Neil Edwards scored a try very early on, but we were then left to defend a slender lead. In many respects it was an outstanding performance from a defensive point of view and very encouraging in the way everybody tackled to frustrate the French. From a personal standpoint, as it was my last frustrate the French. From a personal standpoint, as it was my last Scotland appearance at Murrayfield, I felt satisfied to have gone out with a win, albeit not in the style we might have hoped. But experience soon teaches you that wins never come easily at international level – you have to take each one as you find it, and cherish it.

Which, unfortunately, was exactly what we did not 3' 3 do in our final game against Wales in Cardiff. Instead we produced our poorest performance of the year, and I just do not know why. The Welsh, though, to give them credit, played with a lot of fire and commitment, and nothing should be taken from the fact that they deserved to win on the day... even though there were a lot of curious refereeing decisions which went against us. Had we won, we would have finished second in the table, which I think would have been a pretty fair effort, all things considered.

Potentially, we have laid the foundations for some really great years ahead, with new stands at Murrayfield and a good bunch of players. A lot depends on how the newcomers react and whether the new coaches can not only maintain the standards set in the past but improve on them. If they can do that, then Scottish rugby will remain in good shape.

SCOTLAND'S INTERNATIONAL SEASON 1991/92

SCOTLAND (P12, W6, D1, L5, F237, A154):

(A) v. Romania (Bucharest, 31.8.91)	lost	12-18	
(H) v. Barbarians (Edinburgh, 7.9.91)	drew	16-16	
		(non-cap)	

World Cup

(H) v. Japan (Edinburgh, 5.10.91)	won	47-9	
(H) v. Zimbabwe (Edinburgh, 9.10.91)	won	51-12	
(H) v. Ireland (Edinburgh, 12.10.91)	won	24-15	
(H) v. Western Samoa (q/f: Edinburgh, 19.10.91)	won	28-6	
(H) v. England (s/f: Edinburgh, 26.10.91)	lost	6-9	
(A) v. New Zealand (3/4: Cardiff, 30.10.91)	lost	6-13	

Five Nations' Championship

(H) v. England (Edinburgh, 18.1.92)	lost	7-25	
(A) v. Ireland (Dublin, 15.2.92)	won	18-10	
(H) v. France (Paris, 7.3.92)	won	10-6	
(A) v. Wales (Cardiff, 21.3.92)	lost	12-15	

Scotland A (P1, W1, D0, L0, F36, A16):

(H) v. Spain (Edinburgh, 28.12.91)	won	36-16	

Scotland B (P2, W0, D0, L2, F37, A56):

(H) v. Ireland B (Edinburgh, 28.12.91)		lost	19-29
(A) v. France B (Albi, 2.2.92)		lost	18-27

Scotland U-21 (P2, W1, D0, L1, F38, A44):
(A) v. England Students U-21 (Newcastle, 5.4.92)	won	19-16
			(non-cap)
(H) v. Wales (Stirling, 18.4.92)		lost	19-28

Scotland Students (P4, W0, D0, L4, F47, A89):
(H) v. England (Myreside, 17.1.92)	lost	9-32
(A) v. Ireland (Monkstown, 14.2.92)	lost	20-21
(H) v. France (Boroughmuir, 4.3.92)	lost	9-22
(A) v. Wales (Llanelli, 20.3.92)	lost	9-14

Scotland Universities (P3, W0, D0, L3, F26, A55):
(H) v. England (Peffermill, 17.1.92)	lost	7-15
(A) v. Ireland Dev Squad (Dublin, 14.2.92)	lost	9-27
(H) v. Lyons Institute (Peffermill, 6.3.92)	lost	10-13

Scotland U-19 (P2, W0, D0, L2, F21, A36):
(A) v. England (Gosforth, 11.4.92)	lost	9-20
(H) v. Wales (Stirling, 18.4.92)	lost	12-16 3^ 3

Scotland U-18 (P2, W1, D0, L1, F16, A13):
(H) v. Spain (Burnbrae, 4.4.92)	lost	12-13
(A) v. Ireland (Galway, 11.4.92)	won	4-0

Scotland Schools (P4, W1, D0, L3, F31, A75):
(H) v. France (Edinburgh, 21.12.91)	won	10-6
(A) v. Wales (Neath, 4.1.92)	lost	15-24
(A) v. Ireland (Galway, 4.4.92)	lost	6-17
(H) v. England (Glasgow, 11.4.92)	lost	0-28

Scotland U-15 (P1, W0, D0, L1, F12, A28):
(H) v. Wales (Edinburgh, 5.4.92)	lost	12-28

McEWAN'S LEAGUES

Division One:	P	W	D	L	F	A	Pts
Melrose	13	11	1	1	263	142	23
Edinburgh Acads	13	10	1	2	266	130	21
Heriot's FP	13	7	1	5	198	218	15
Boroughmuir	12	6	1	5	210	179	13
Gala	13	6	0	7	237	202	12
Selkirk	12	6	0	6	228	210	12
Watsonians	13	5	2	6	202	185	12
Currie	13	6	0	7	231	227	12
Jedforest	13	6	0	7	174	173	12
Stirling Co.	13	6	0	7	145	207	12
Hawick	13	4	2	7	176	193	10
Glasgow H/K	13	4	2	7	206	245	10
Stewart's-Mel	13	5	0	8	164	261	10

3 – **Pro:** Grangemouth (c), Clarkston. **Rel:** Trinity Acads, Highland
4 – **Pro:** Morgan Acad (c), St Boswells. **Rel:** Penicuik, Madras FP
5 – **Pro:** Stewartry (c), Livingston. **Rel:** Greenock Wdrs, Dunbar
6 – **Pro:** Clydebank (c), Irvine. **Rel:** Walkerburn, Carnoustie
7 – **Pro:** Berwick (c), Duns. **Rel:** Aberdeen Univ, Rosyth, Cumnock
Promoted (to 7) from Highland Leagues: Hyndland, Holy Cross, Waid
Acad

CUP FINALS:

Alloa Brewery Cup:
Boroughmuir 37, Currie 9 (Meggatland, 25.4.92)

Castlemaine XXXX Trophy:
Duns 52, Royal High 11 (Meggatland, 25.4.92)

Sevens:
Gala: Hawick 34, North & Midlands 20
Hawick: Stewart's-Melville FP 26, Glasgow H/K 14
Jedforest: Jedforest 28, Hawick 16
Melrose: Bay of Plenty (NZ) 19, Kelso 12

WALES

Ieuan Evans

THE decision to appoint as Wales coach an outsider, someone not tarnished by the brush of previous seasons, and someone with no Welsh club loyalty, was critical to the revival of our fortunes last season. We lifted no trophies and did not qualify even for the quarter-final stage of the World Cup, yet by the season's end Alan Davies had helped us restore our self-respect.

Being an outsider was especially vital because there is so much Welsh inter-club rivalry, and sometimes that acrimony shows itself at national level. His neutrality undoubtedly helped him. That said, he had an awful lot of weight to burden on his shoulders – being touted as The Saviour of Welsh rugby.

It might have told in the final game of the season when rumours were rife that Alan and manager Bob Norster might lose their jobs if we lost to Scotland. It was a ridiculous notion, bearing in mind all the work they – not to mention the players – had put in. Fortunately we came up with the result, and all was well that ended well.

> *❛ Alan Davies' neutrality undoubtedly helped him. That said, he had an awful lot of weight to burden on his shoulders – being touted as The Saviour of Welsh rugby ❜*

It was never going to be an easy season, not after our demoralising tour to Australia. We returned home totally shellshocked, especially after going down 71-8 to a provincial side (New South Wales). In our defence, we had not been helped in our psychological preparation by those people who said the tour was a disaster waiting to happen. The last thing you want on your mind before a major international tour is that sort of vote of no-confidence.

The tour was compared with the 1988 trip to New Zealand but, in truth, there was no comparison. Those All Blacks were the best team I have ever seen; a superb unit, a machine. And we weren't bad either, having just won the Triple Crown. We went out there on the crest of a wave, confidence-wise, and just got taken to the cleaners. The difference in Australia was that we had been all but whitewashed in the 1991 Five Nations' Championship and so headed Down Under more in hope than expectation.

Everybody gave as much as they could – well hopefully they did, put it that way – but it was just not good enough... not nearly. And we came home to a certain amount of abuse, to say the least. But the Welsh nation as a whole are very thick-skinned – sportsmen more than most – and, with a lot of help from messrs Davies and Norster (I don't think we could have turned it around without them), we picked ourselves up.

When I was offered the captaincy in succession to Paul Thorburn, my feeling was one of overwhelming pride, mixed with disbelief. 'Who me?' I said, looking behind to see if they were talking to someone else. To captain your country is an honour which you should treasure for the rest of your life. And I immediately thought positively about the task ahead. I knew we had players who could perform a lot better, and it would be a question of instilling a measure of confidence in them.

Our first engagement of the season came with the visit of France to Cardiff to mark the inauguration of the new Arms Park floodlights (lost 9-22). It was an encouraging evening from our point of view and I think we surprised an awful lot of people, including ourselves; especially after the last international we played, two months earlier, when we lost 63-6 to Australia.

The danger, of course, to emerge from such a promising display was that the country expected too much in the World Cup. Even so, we let ourselves down in one or two games, especially against Western

Samoa (lost 13-16), a game we should have won, no question about it. They were a good side but not that good. We played very poorly.

As captain, I was delighted by the manner with which we accepted their try which never was; when Robert Jones won the race for the ball behind our posts but the referee saw differently. That reflected great credit not only on the players but also on the coaching and management regime. We carried ourselves better than we might have done in previous seasons. Pride and discipline certainly went hand in hand, and that spirit showed itself three days later when we got the better of Argentina (16-7). When you forget how to win, it becomes extremely difficult to remind yourselves, and this most welcome success represented the first step towards recapturing Welsh rugby's successful past.

It also left us requiring victory over Australia to deny Western Samoa the runners-up qualifying slot in the quarter-finals: always likely to be a tall order, with the disturbing memories of that Brisbane summer occasion still fresh in the mind. We did well to hold them to seven points in the first half, but defence can only take you so far and after defending for such a long period we tired and Australia ran out convincing 38-3 winners.

It would have been easy to feel downhearted, perhaps even dejected, at our failure to make the last eight but there was no time for self-pity; not with the Five Nations' Championship just around the corner. And anyway, we had shown Australia how, in the space of two months, we had made considerable strides in terms of defence and in the way we carried ourselves during the game.

Still, the bookies were not impressed, offering ridiculous and, frankly, insulting odds against our winning in Dublin against an Irish side who had come so close to beating Australia in their quarter-final. All of which made our 16-15 win the sweeter. Desperate to win for the public back home, our defensive concentration particularly impressed me, and in the second half there was only one team in it.

France then returned to Cardiff and this really was a game we should have won (lost 9-12). Indeed, I was bitterly disappointed at our failure to do so. Our problem was that we gave away too many early points and had to play catch-up, a fatal tactic at international level in any sport. While we succeeded in doing just that against Ireland, France were a different proposition. People have suggested that we lacked pace. The real problem was the lack of pace on the ball. Possession did not come back quickly enough and, consequently, we were not able to penetrate the French rearguard.

It is very difficult to score these days from set-pieces,   3 3 and we did not win sufficient decent set-piece ball or sufficient second-phase ball with which to attack. Players always look quicker when they play with second-phase ball because the gaps are there. With defences so well organised these days, first-phase possession is almost impossible to exploit.

Even England, without a shadow of a doubt a very well organised side, struggled to break us down. For an hour they failed to build on Will Carling's first-minute try. In the end they settled for knocking over a penalty from in front of the posts, with only a minute to go and leading 21-0. It was a great compliment to our team that England couldn't budge us, and we have got to expand on such positive factors this season.

> ❛ *We have not yet restored the pride in Welsh rugby, but it is nice to be a part of the turning point* ❜

England's frustration could not disguise the fact that they bore one distinct hallmark of a quality 15-man team, namely good intercommunication. All through the game I could hear them talking to each other. But it is impossible to compare them with the great Welsh sides from the past because the circumstances have altered so drastically, with levels of fitness, pace and power so very different nowadays. Nevertheless, they did the rugby world credit in the way they played the game.

The hype preceding our final game against Scotland concerned the futures of Davies and Norster. The players were angry at such talk. After the amount of work that had been put in by the management, for their respective futures to hang on this one game was crazy – especially to those of us who had been around in Australia last year and seen the difference made to the set-up.

As a result, when the whistle blew I felt relief before satisfaction. Satisfied with the win, of course – to win in front of our home support for the first time in the Championship since 1989 – but relieved that we had managed to secure not only Alan and Bob's future but also our own... at least, for the time being.

We scored a cracking try, Hugh Williams-Jones showing a remarkable turn of pace to create the opening for Richard Webster and, in so doing, illustrate the direction in which the modern game is going. Even props are now doing what used to be left to us boys outside the scrum.

There is much hard work still to do by Wales, but we go forward with a great deal more optimism than a year ago. We cannot afford to drop our guard with Australia on the way this autumn, and we must be under no illusions about the size of the task still facing us. We have not yet restored the pride in Welsh rugby, but it is nice to be a part of the turning point.

WALES' INTERNATIONAL SEASON 1991/92

WALES (P9, W3, D0, L6, F87, A209):
(A) v. Australia (Brisbane, 21.7.91)	lost	6-63
(H) v. France (Cardiff, 4.9.91)	lost	9-22

World Cup
(H) v. Western Samoa (Cardiff, 6.10.91)	lost	13-16
(H) v. Argentina (Cardiff, 9.10.91)	won	16-7
(H) v. Australia (Cardiff, 12.10.91)	lost	3-38

Five Nations' Championship
(A) v. Ireland (Dublin, 18.1.92)	won	16-15
(H) v. France (Cardiff, 1.2.92)	lost	9-12 3: 3
(A) v. England (Twickenham, 7.3.92)	lost	0-24
(H) v. Scotland (Cardiff, 21.3.92)	won	15-12

Wales U-21 (P2, W2, D0, L0, F50, A34):
(H) v. Ireland (Newport, 16.10.91)	won	22-15
(A) v. Scotland (Stirling, 18.4.92)	won	28-19

Wales Students (P4, W2, D0, L2, F51, A70):
(H) v. Welsh Exiles (Pontypridd, 15.1.92)	won	15-10
(H) v. France (Swansea, 31.1.92)	lost	6-26
(A) v. England (Newbury, 6.3.92)	lost	16-25
(H) v. Scotland (Llanelli, 21.3.92)	won	14-9

Welsh Districts (P3, W2, D0, L1, F78, A31):
(H) v. Germany (Cardiff, 15.12.91)	won	50-0
(H) v. Netherlands (Aberavon, 15.2.92)	lost	10-25
(A) v. Belgium (Brussels, 4.3.92)	won	18-6

Welsh Universities (P3, W0, D0, L3, F32, A86):
(A) v. English (Bristol, 5.3.92)	lost	13-30
(H) v. Scottish (Llanrumney, 21.3.92)	lost	13-14
(A) v. Irish (Dublin, 16.1.92)	lost	6-42

Wales Youth (P4, W2, D0, L2, F81, A81):
(H) v. Welsh Schools (Ystradgynlais, 12.2.92)	won	25-7
(H) v. Italy (Glamorgan Wdrs, 29.2.92)	won	29-22
(A) v. France (Dax, 14.3.92)	lost	9-23
(H) v. England (Brecon, 4.4.92)	lost	18-29

Wales U-19 (P1, W1, D0, L0, F16, A12):
(A) v. Scotland (Stirling, 18.4.92)	won	16-12

Welsh Schools U-18 (P2, W2, D0, L2, F39, A47):
(H) v. France (Maesteg, 22.4.92)	lost	3-7
(H) v. Scotland (Neath, 4.1.92)	won	24-15
(A) v. Ireland (Cork, 11.4.92)	won	9-7
(A) v. England (Doncaster, 25.4.92)	lost	3-18

Welsh Schools U-16 (P1, W1, D0, L0, F22, A0):
(H) v. England (Pontypridd, 25.4.92)	won	22-0

Welsh Schools U-15 (P1, W1, D0, L0, F28, A12):
(A) v. Scotland (Edinburgh, 6.4.92)	won	28-12

HEINEKEN LEAGUES

Division One:	P	W	D	L	F	A	Pts
Swansea	18	13	1	4	393	205	27
Llanelli	18	11	1	6	381	233	23
Pontypridd	18	11	0	7	289	245	22
Neath	18	9	2	7	309	236	20
Newbridge	18	10	0	8	259	271	20
Bridgend	18	10	0	8	246	270	20
Pontypool	18	7	4	7	282	275	18
Newport	18	7	2	9	240	237	16
Cardiff	18	5	1	12	240	306	11
Maesteg	18	1	1	16	169	530	3

2– Pro: SWP (c), Aberavon. **Rel**: None.

3– Pro: Tenby Utd (c), Llandovery, Blaina, Narbeth. **Rel**: None.

4– Pro: Tumble (c), Kenfig Hill, Abercynon, St Peter's, Blackwood, **Pontypool Utd. Rel**: None

Promoted (to 4) from feeder leagues: Garndiffaith, Cardiff Harlequins, Builth Wells, Tondu, Vardre, Carmarthen Quins, Cardigan, Colwyn Bay

Schweppes Challenge Cup final:
*Llanelli 16, Swansea 7 (Cardiff, 16.5.92)
(* holders)

THE 1991/92 INTERNATIONAL PLAYER'S PLAYER OF THE YEAR

TOP 20

1.	Will Carling (England)
	Dewi Morris (England)
3.	Andy Nicol (Scotland)
4.	David Campese (Australia)
5.	Jonathan Webb (England)
	Richard Webster (Wales)
7.	Peter Winterbottom (England)
8.	Emyr Lewis (Wales)
9.	Wade Dooley (England)
10.	Scott Gibbs (Wales)
	Tim Horan (Australia)
	David McIvor (Scotland)
	Jeff Probyn (England)
	Mickey Skinner (England)
	Doddie Weir (Scotland)
	Derek White (Scotland)
17.	Laurent Cabannes (France)
	Anthony Clement (Wales)
	Phil Danaher (Ireland)
	Rory Underwood (England)

ROLL OF HONOUR

1990/91 Serge Blanco (France)
1991/92 Will Carling/Dewi Morris (England)

THE PLAYERS A-Z

KEY TO INDIVIDUAL STATISTICS

Take Joe Blarney (below) as an example. Joe made his Ireland B debut in 1981 and last season won two B caps, scoring 4 points. He was first capped at senior Ireland level in 1982, won 4 caps last season (was replacement in one), and has 32 caps in all, with 58 points to his credit. He also played in the non-cap International against the Barbarians last season, landing a conversion. In 1992, Joe toured New Zealand with Ireland. He won selection to the 1983 British Lions tour to New Zealand but did not play in a Test. However, he played in the 1986 IRB Centenary match in Cardiff (Lions 7, The Rest 15) which has been included as a Lions cap. In 1989 he played one Test in the series against Australia. If an uncapped player is selected as bench replacement and does not play, the fact is recorded as 'Ireland (1991/92) 1 rep'. A new feature, each full international has his caps listed in order, plus a breakdown of his points tally, again in chronological order. For example, Joe marked his debut against France in 1982 with two tries and a penalty goal. If a nation is played more than once in the same year, the statistic is recorded in one of two ways. For a 3-match series against, say, Australia, the statistic reads: A(1, 2,3). If our player has previously turned out against the Ausies in the same year, that statistic reads: A(a), followed by A(b1, b2, b3). This makes identification possible when it comes to points scored. e.g. A(b3: 1t) means that our player scored a try against Australia in the third Test of the second series.

	apps	pts
Ireland B (1981)		
Last Season	2 caps	4
Ireland (1982)		
Last Season	4 caps	0
	1 rep	
v. Barbarians	1 app	2
1992	Tour to New Zealand	
Career	32 caps	58
Lions 1983		
1986		
1989	1 Test	0

Caps (32): **1982** F, E, S, W **1983** NZ(1, 2), E, F, W, S **1984** W, F, E, S, Fj **1987** S, E, W wc–T, W, A **1989** W, S, E, F, Arg (1, 2), Fj **1991** F, S, J, W

Points (58 – 9t, 5c, 3p, 1dg): **1982** F(2t, 1p) S(1t), W(1t) **1983** NZ(1:1dg), E(2t) **1989** Fj(2p) **1991** F(1t), W(2t)

---

* The qualification for entry in *The Rugby Union Who's Who* is involvement in one of the four Home Union squads (U-21 up to senior XV) during the 1991/92 season (September 1991–May 1992). Players' statistics DO **NOT** include summer tours.

Adams, G. E. England

Full Name: Gareth Edward Adams
1991/92 International category:
England U-21
Club: Bath
Position: Flanker
Height: 5'11" **Weight:** 14st 7lbs
Occupation: Chemistry student
(Bath Univ)
Born: Wakefield, 12.9.70
Family: Single
Family links with rugby: Brother
(Jonathan) and father (Jack) played
for Sandal
Former club: Sandal
International debut (U-21):
England 16, Ireland 22, 1990
Best moment in rugby: Winning
1991 National Sevens with Bath
Worst moment in rugby: Tearing
knee cartilage in first match of
England 18-Group's 1988 tour to
Australia
Most respected opponent: The
French

	apps	pts
England U-21 (1990)		
Last Season	3 caps	0
Career	6 caps	0

Biggest influence on career: Bath RFC and club coach Jack Rowell
Other sporting achievements: Cricket for Yorkshire Schools, Rugby League
for Yorkshire U-13s
Serious injuries: Torn knee cartilage
Best memory last season: Captaining England U-21s three times
Suggestions to improve rugby: *On-field* – Make referees take a
man-management course to stop them being so dictatorial. *Off-field* – Players
deserve better. Commitment outweighs the rewards in general and players are
not looked after in the way they should be
Notable landmarks in rugby career: Became England's U-21s'
longest-serving captain when he led the side on three occasions last season to
take his tally to five from a total six appearances. Yet he was unable to make
Bath's Pilkington Cup final-winning squad. Having captained the U-21s to a
20–18 win over the Netherlands ('s-Hertogenbosch, 18 May 1991) and in the
7–9 loss to the French Armed Forces (Dunkirk, 22 May 1991) during 1990/91,
he continued in charge last season in the 94–0 defeat of Belgium
(Wolverhampton, 1 Sep 1991), the 10–19 loss to Ireland U-21 (Donnybrook,
23 Oct 1991) and the 21–21 draw with the French Armed Forces

1

(Twickenham, 2 May 1992). Previously, he played two seasons at both England 16-Group and 18-Group level. Member of England Students' 1992 World Cup squad, having represented them in 0–35 loss to England's senior XV (21 Sep 1991)

Player to watch: Ben Clarke (Bath)
Player of the year: Peter Winterbottom (England)

Aherne, L. F. P.   Ireland

Full Name: Leslie Fergus Patrick Aherne
1991/92 International category: Ireland Full
Club: Lansdowne
Position: Scrum-half
Height: 5′9″ **Weight:** 12st 3lbs
Occupation: Civil engineer
Born: Cork, 16.3.63
Family: Elaine (wife)
Family links with rugby: Father (Gerald) played for Munster
Former clubs: Univ College Cork, Dolphin
International debut: Ireland 10, England 21, 1988
Five Nations' debut: Ireland 21, France 26, 1989
Best moment in rugby: Playing for Ireland against 1989 All Blacks
Most respected opponent: Robert Jones (Swansea & Wales)
Best memory last season: Re-establishing place in Ireland team
Suggestions to improve rugby: *On-field* – Differentiate more between penalty and try. *Off-field* – Remuneration for loss of earnings due to rugby – but guard against game going professional

Ireland (**1988**)	apps	pts
Last Season	3 caps	0
1992	Tour to New Zealand	
Career	15 caps	4

Caps (15): **1988** E(b), WS, It **1989** F, W, E, S, NZ **1990** E, S, F, W(R) **1992** E, S, F

Points (4 – 1t): **1988** It(1t)

Notable landmarks in rugby career: Played for UCC for four seasons, captaining them to 1984/85 Munster Senior League title. Made Provincial bow with Leinster, after breaking into Ireland team and returning with them from tour of France. Toured with Ireland to North America (1989) and captained Leinster in 1989/90 Irish Inter-Provincial Championship. Bench reserve for Ireland B in 27–12 win over Argentina in 1990/91 and toured Namibia (1991) without making the Test team (played against Namibia B and Namibia South Sub-Union). Included in 1991 World Cup squad, warming bench in all four matches, but returned to Test arena (first start for two years) for trip to Twickenham (1 Feb 1992) in 1992 Five Nations' Championship. After three Championship games, toured New Zealand with Ireland

Touchlines: Golf

Player to watch: Conor O'Shea (Lansdowne)

Allan, J. Scotland

Full Name: John Allan
1991/92 International category: Scotland Full
Club: Glenwood Old Boys (South Africa)
Position: Hooker
Height: 6′ **Weight:** 15st
Occupation: Computer consultant with ABS Computers (Durban, SA)
Born: Glasgow, 25.11.63
Family: Claire (wife)
Family links with rugby: Brothers both play – William in Italy and Richard for Empangeni in Durban, SA
Former clubs: Northern Transvaal Defence (SA), Edinburgh Academicals
International debut: New Zealand 31, Scotland 16, 1990
Five Nations' debut: Scotland 32, Wales 12, 1991
Best moment in rugby: Representing Scotland in 1991 World Cup
Worst moment in rugby: Snapping knee ligaments playing in club game (1988)
Most respected opponent: Springbok hooker Uli Schmidt – totally dedicated to the game

	apps	pts
Scotland A (**1990**)		
Career	1 cap	0
Scotland (**1990**)		
Last Season	6 caps	0
Career	9 caps	0

Caps (9): **1990** NZ(1) **1991** W, I, R wc-J, I, WS, E, NZ

Points Nil

3

Serious injuries: Snapped knee ligaments
Other sporting achievements: Softball for Scotland Schools
Best memories last season: South Africa's readmission into world sport. Playing against England in World Cup semi-final
Suggestions to improve rugby: *On-field* – Stop negative rugby by preventing players from spoiling the opposition's ball. Penalise offenders heavily, perhaps by automatic penalty in front of the posts. *Off-field* – Contented now that South Africa has been brought back into the international rugby fold. And delighted that they have been awarded the 1995 World Cup
Notable landmarks in rugby career: Returned to live in South Africa last summer with new wife Claire, having collected the last of his nine caps in the World Cup third/fourth place play-off against New Zealand at Cardiff (30 Oct 1991). Figured in five of Scotland's six Cup ties before being usurped by perennial rival Kenny Milne for the 1992 Five Nations' Championship. Warmed replacements' bench throughout the latter, as he had done in 1990/91 season, when also replacement for Scotland B against Ireland and France, before making full debut in first Test at Dunedin on summer tour of New Zealand (lost 16–31, 16 Jun 1990). Five Nations' debut came the following season against Wales (2 Feb 1991)
Touchlines: Reading
Player to watch: Derek Ross (Natal – ex-Edinburgh Acads)
Player of the year: David McIvor (Scotland)

Andrew, C. R. England

Full Name: Christopher **Robert** Andrew
1991/92 International category: England Full
Club: Toulouse
Position: Outside-half
Height: 5′9″ **Weight:** 12st 7lbs
Occupation: Chartered surveyor with Debenham Jean Thouard Zadelhoff (Toulouse, France)
Born: Richmond, Yorkshire, 18.2.63
Family: Sara (wife) and Emily (daughter)
Family links with rugby: Brothers (Richard and David) play for Headingley
Former clubs: Middlesbrough,

Cambridge Univ (Blues: 1982/83/84), Nottingham, Gordon (Sydney, Aus), Wasps

International debut: England 22, Romania 15, 1985

Five Nations' debut: England 9, France 9, 1985

Best moment in rugby: Beating France 21–19 at Twickenham to win 1991 Five Nations' Grand Slam – still my ultimate rugby thrill

Worst moment in rugby: Losing 1990 Grand Slam decider 13–7 to Scotland – losing the World Cup final was disappointing but in a different way

Most embarrassing moment: Missing 9 out of 10 kicks at goal for Nottingham at Beeston against London Welsh in fourth round of 1985 John Player Cup (lost 11–12)

Most respected opponent: Michael Lynagh (Australia)

Other sporting achievements: Played first-class cricket for Yorkshire 2nd XI and Cambridge Univ, 1984 and 1985 (as captain). Scored 101 n. o. for Univ against Notts at Trent Bridge (1984)

	apps	pts
England B (1988)		
Last Season	0 caps	0
England (1985)		
Last Season	12 caps	18
Career	48 caps	148
Lions		
1989	2 Tests	8

Caps (48): **1985** R, F, S, I, W **1986** W, S, I, F **1987** I, F, W wc-J(R), US **1988** S, I(1,2), A(a1, a2), Fj, A(b) **1989** S, I, F, W, R, Fj. Lions-A(2,3) **1990** I, F, W, S, Arg(b) **1991** W, S, I, F, Fj, A(a) wc-NZ, It, US, F, S, A(b) **1992** S, I, F, W

Points (148 – 1t,9c,28p,14dg): **1985** R(4p,2dg), F(2p,1dg), S(2p), I(2p), W(1c,2p,1dg) **1986** W(6p,1dg), S(2p), I(3c,1p) **1987** F(1dg) **1988** S(1dg), I(1:3c) **1989** S(2p), I(1c,2p), F(1p), W(2p,1dg), R(1dg), Fj(1c). Lions-A(2:1c,1p,1dg) **1991** F(1dg), Fj(1t,2dg) wc-NZ(1dg), S(1dg)

Best memory last season: England's performance in the World Cup final and the Five Nations' Championship. We always knew we had the ability to open up but it was nice to show it. As a squad we took a lot of pleasure from being organised and being able to play whichever style suited. Whereas in 1991 winning was everything and our style was down to earth, virtually the same set of players last season played a totally different game

Suggestions to improve rugby: *On-field* – Reduce number of offences for which kicks at goal are permitted. Be careful not to go too far with rule changes designed to speed up game and make it more entertaining. XV-a-side needs to maintain a distinct identity from Sevens. End season with Five Nations' (in March-April). Remove the ten-yard law for offside for players in front of ball (revert to old law). *Off-field* – Allow players to take advantage of commercial activities. RFU are moving in right direction. It's not about making fortunes out of the game – the sums are largely peanuts – it's the principle of being able to benefit from our massive commitment to rugby. The game is a multi-million pound industry and should be administered accordingly. I would still question the future of the International Board

Notable landmarks in rugby career: World's most-capped outside-half (47 of his 48 caps in the No.10 jersey). Appeared on BBC's *Wogan* after setting then England records for points scored in an international (21: 6p, 1dg) and penalties kicked in England's 21–18 win over Wales at Twickenham (17 Jan 1986). Replaced injured Paul Dean (13 Jun 1989) on triumphant Lions tour of Australia and played in last two Tests (1c, 1p, 1dg in Brisbane second Test). Either side of trip Down Under captained England to 58–3 win in Romania (13 May 1989) and British Lions XV to 29–27 success over France (4 Oct 1989) in French Revolution Bicentenary match. Most dropped goals by England international (14). Captained Wasps to 1989/90 Courage Championship and London to 1990 Divisional Championship (having represented North in 1985 and 1986). Non-cap England appearances at Twickenham against centenary Barbarians (29 Sep 1990) and Soviet Union (7 Sep 1991). Moved family, work and rugby to Toulouse after 1991 World Cup

Reasons for move to France: Leaving Wasps was a very big wrench and the move was only made after a year's consideration. Took the view that a move would give myself and my family an opportunity to taste a whole range of different experiences. I have long wanted to experience playing in south-west France, and it is a massive and exciting new challenge. The game is treated very differently here in France. For example, we train four times a week, including two lunchtimes (!), and play on Sundays

Touchlines: Learning French; gardening and DIY in new home

Player to watch: Michel Marfaing (Toulouse)

Player of the year: Jonathan Webb (England)

Australia captain Nick Farr-Jones leads by splendid example in the Wallabies' World Cup semi-final defeat of arch rivals New Zealand. The 16–6 Dublin epic provided the highlight of the tournament

Appleson, M. E.   Scotland

Full Name: Mark Edward Appleson
1991/92 International category:
Scotland B
Club: London Scottish
Position: Fullback
Height: 5'10" **Weight:** 13st 5lbs
Occupation: PE/games teacher at
City of London Freemans School
Born: Islington, North London,
26.2.68
Family: Single
Family links with rugby: Father
(Peter) played for Roundhay
Former club: Headingley (four
years playing wing)
International debut (B): Scotland
19, Ireland 29, 1991
Best moment in rugby: Winning
1991 Middlesex Sevens with
London Scottish
Most embarrassing moment:
Losing pair of shorts in tackle against
Bedford

	apps	pts
Scotland B (**1991**)		
Last Season	2 caps	7
Career	2 caps	7

Most respected opponent: Gavin
Hastings (Watsonians & Scotland)
Biggest influence on career: London Scottish fitness coaches Allan and
Margot Wells – transformed club
Serious injuries: Snapped medial ligaments in England U-18 Trial
Other sporting achievements: Placed third in long jump at 1985 English
Schools Athletics Championships. County cricket for Yorkshire U-16s
Best memories last season: Selection for Scotland B. Promotion with
London Scottish
Suggestions to improve rugby: *On-field* – Work to improve consistency of
refereeing
Notable landmarks in rugby career: Represented England Schools,
England Students and Combined Students before switching allegiance to
Scotland courtesy of Jedburgh-born father. Marked Scotland B debut last
season with conversion and penalty goal against Ireland B at Murrayfield (28
Dec 1991), and landed a conversion in the 18–27 loss to France B in Albi (3
Feb 1992). Having won 1991 Middlesex Sevens with London Scottish, helped
club reach 1992 final (lost to Western Samoa) and also to win London Floodlit

Sevens (beating Samoans en route to final win over London Irish) and Courage League division two
Touchlines: Watching films. Involved in theatre production – producing and backstage
Player to watch: Gregor Townsend (Gala)
Player of the year: Dewi Morris (England)

Armstrong, G. Scotland

Full Name: Gary Armstrong
1991/92 International category: Scotland Full
Club: Jedforest
Position: Scrum-half
Height: 5'8" **Weight:** 13st 7lbs
Occupation: Lorry driver with A & R Gold
Born: Edinburgh, 30.9.66
Family: Shona (wife) and Darren James (son)
Family links with rugby: Father (Lawrence) played for Jedforest. Brother (Kevin) plays for Jedforest and Scotland U-21s
Former club: Jed Thistle
International debut: Scotland 13, Australia 32, 1988
Five Nations' debut: Scotland 23, Wales 7, 1989
Best moment in rugby: Beating England to win 1990 Grand Slam
Worst moment in rugby: Knee injury suffered against Currie (11 Jan 1992) which put me out of the Five Nations' Championship
Most respected opponent: Pierre Berbizier (Agen & France)
Biggest influence on career: Family – mum, dad and wife
Serious injuries: Torn knee, ankle ligaments, damaged elbow, three-quarter tear of medial ligament

	apps	pts
Scotland B (1987)		
Career	2 caps	12
Scotland (1988)		
Last Season	6 caps	4
Career	24 caps	16
Lions 1989		

Caps (24): **1988** A **1989** W, E, I, F, Fj, R **1990** I, F, W, E, NZ(1,2), Arg **1991** F, W, E, I, R wc-J, I, WS, E, NZ

Points (16 – 4t): **1989** W(1t) **1990** Arg(1t) **1991** W(1t) wc-I(1t)

in left knee (v. Currie, Riverside Park, 11 Jan 1992)

Best memory last season: Representing Scotland in the World Cup

Suggestions to improve rugby: *On-field* – Give players more time to learn new rules before changing them. Far too many new rules introduced, though happy that try has been increased to five points. Should still increase conversion to three points to encourage even more open game. Scrap 90-degree wheel law. There needs to be a more unified interpretation of laws by referees. *Off-field* – Things moving slowly in right direction as regards player welfare. When I was injured last season the SRU helped me out financially, but you should not have to go asking for everything. The player should be approached. It was a little embarrassing

Notable landmarks in rugby career: Represented Scotland at U-18, Youth, U-21 and twice at B level in 1988, v. Italy (won 37–0) and France (won 18–12). Scored hat-trick of tries on B debut against Italians at Seafield, Aberdeen (1987). Selected to tour Australia with 1989 Lions, playing against Australia B (won 23–18), Queensland B (won 30–6), New South Wales B (won 39–19), Australian Capital Territory (won 41–25) and New South Wales Country (won 72–13), and accumulating five tries. But could not budge Wales' Robert Jones from the Test team. An integral part of Scotland's 1990 Five Nations' Grand Slam-winning side and was leading light in the Murrayfield World Cup run to the semi-finals. Injury sustained in club match the week before Calcutta Cup clash against England ruled him out for rest of the season

Player to watch: Gregor Townsend (Gala)

Player of the year: David Campese (Australia)

Jean-Baptiste Lafond leaves the Canadian defence in his wake as he races in for a try in France's 19–13 World Cup pool-deciding win at Agen

Arnold, P. Wales

Full Name: Paul Arnold
1991/92 International category:
Wales Full
Club: Swansea
Position: Lock
Height: 6'5" **Weight:** 16st 2lbs
Occupation: Management
representative for Phil Carling
Management Services
Born: Morriston, 28.4.68
Family: Single
International debut: Namibia 9,
Wales 18, 1990
Best moment in rugby: Going to
Namibia after injured Gareth
Llewellyn withdrew
Worst moment in rugby: Missing
out on selection for 1992 Five
Nations' squad
Most respected opponent: David
Waters (Newport & Wales)
Biggest influence on career:
Richard Moriarty (Swansea &
Wales)
Best memory last season: Scoring
World Cup try against Argentina in
Cardiff
Suggestions to improve rugby:
On-field – Permit non-powered
scrum if team loses prop. Abandon
new mauling rule – it is ridiculous.

	apps	pts
Wales U-21 (**1990**)		
Career	1 cap	0
Wales B (**1990**)		
Career	1 cap	0
Wales (**1990**)		
Last Season	3 caps	4
Career	10 caps	8

Caps (10): 1990 Na(1,2), Ba **1991** E,
S, I, F, A(a) wc-Arg, A(b)

Points (8 – 2t): **1991** I(1t) wc-Arg(1t)

Permit support for jumpers in lineout. *Off-field* – Consider introducing win
bonuses. Believe that game will go semi-professional by next World Cup.
Keep encouraging the kids

Notable landmarks in rugby career: In fifth season at Swansea, having
progressed through All Whites' youth set-up. Also gained experience playing
in New Zealand (summer 1989). Quickly progressed up representative ladder
after making Wales U-21 debut in 24–10 defeat of Scotland at Ayr (28 Apr
1990). Within five weeks had won a full cap, playing in the 18–9 first-Test
win over Namibia in Windhoek (2 Jun 1990). Added a B cap in Leiden when
helped down Netherlands 34–12 (2 Dec 1990). Made Five Nations' debut
the following season against Grand Slam 1991 England and scored first Test

try later in the Championship in the 21st minute of the 21–21 draw with Ireland in Cardiff (16 Feb 1991). Toured Australia in summer 1991 and played twice in World Cup, scoring the solitary Welsh try in a 16–7 win over Argentina (9 Oct 1991). Overlooked for 1992 Championship

Touchlines: Sunday soccer, indoor 5-a-side, indoor cricket, squash, swimming

Player to watch: Scott Quinnell (Llanelli)

Player of the year: Richard Webster (Wales)

Back, N. A. England

Full Name: Neil Antony Back

1991/92 International category: England B

Club: Leicester

Position: Openside flanker

Height: 5′10″ **Weight:** 13st 10lbs

Occupation: Assurance clerk with Equity & Law Life Assurance Society (Coventry)

Born: Coventry, 16.1.69

Family: Single

Former club: Nottingham

International debut (B): England B 12, Emerging Australians 12, 1990

Best moment in rugby: Playing for the Barbarians against England (Twickenham, 29 Sep 1990)

Worst moment in rugby: Still not had one

Most respected opponent: Peter Winterbottom (Harlequins & England)

Serious injuries: Broken arm (aged 16), 21 stitches in ear, trapped nerve (missed France B v. England B, Paris 15 Feb 1992)

	apps	pts
England U-21 (**1989**)		
Career	3 caps	12
England B (**1990**)		
Last Season	3 caps	8
Career	7 caps	8
England XV (**1990**)	1 app	4

Other sporting achievements: Cricket for Coventry and Warwickshire Schools

Best memory last season: Involvement in England B's 'Grand Slam' and summer tour

Suggestions to improve rugby: *On-field* – Agree wholeheartedly with notion of taking emphasis away from goal kicking. *Off-field* – Establish worldwide, uniform guidelines concerning amateurism

Notable landmarks in rugby career: Announced himself on international stage with three tries for inaugural England U-21 side against Romania U-21 (Bucharest, 13 May 1989), having previously represented England U-18s (1985–87) and England Colts (1987/88). In busy fortnight period wore England jersey three times – his second and third U-21 appearances against the Netherlands (won 24–3, Hilversum 29 Apr 1990) and French Armed Forces (won 23–16, Fontainebleu, 12 May 1990) sandwiching an outing for an England XV against Italy in Rovigo (won 33–15, 1 May 1990) during which he scored a try. Came on as a 49th-minute replacement in centenary 1990 Barbarians' 16–18 loss to England and was described by the *Daily Telegraph*'s John Mason as 'the pocket-sized Hercules among England back row forwards' for his 'masterly' performance. He has since picked up seven England B caps, including three (v. Sp, I, It) last season when he claimed two tries (v. Sp, I)

Touchlines: Training five days a week for rugby. Weight training, squash, badminton

Player to watch: Ian Hunter (Northampton)

Player of the year: Rory Underwood (Leicester)

Baldwin, G. P. S. England

Full Name: Gavin Paul Samuel Baldwin

1991/92 International category: England B

Club: Northampton

Position: Prop

Height: 6'1" **Weight:** 17st

Occupation: Senior health and fitness instructor at Dallington Health and Country Club

Born: Hereford, 6.12.68

Family: Single

Family links with rugby: Father (Mark) played for Gloucester

Former clubs: Worcester, Nottingham, Loughborough Students

International debut (B): Spain 3, England B 34, 1992

Best moment in rugby: Making

England B debut in Madrid (19 Jan 1992)

Worst moment in rugby: Northampton's 60–0 loss to Orrell in 1990/91

Most respected opponent: Bob Phillips (Gloucester)

Biggest influence on career: Gary Pearce (Northampton & England)

	apps	pts
England U-21 (**1990**)		
Career	2 caps	0
England B (**1991**)		
Last Season	4 caps	0
Career	4 caps	0
England	1995 Development squad	

Other sporting achievements: Squash for Dallington

Best memory last season: Scoring last-minute try against Leicester to win match

Suggestions to improve rugby: *On-field* – Play League games home and away; do away with 'Mickey Mouse' games. *Off-field* – Reimburse players and/or employers for time lost to rugby

Notable landmarks in rugby career: Ever present at loosehead prop for England B during 'Grand Slam' campaign last season, playing in all four wins (v. Sp, I, F and It). Toured New Zealand with England B (1992). Previously, represented Midlands at Schools and U-21 level, and England at Students, Universities and U-21 (twice in 1989/90: v. Netherlands and French Armed Forces) grades. Named in England's most recent development squad. Played in Northampton's 1991 Pilkington Cup final side

Touchlines: Weights, keep-fit, travel

Player to watch: Matt Dawson (Northampton)

Player of the year: Ian Hunter (England B)

Scotland skipper David Sole holds Stuart Davies at bay in Cardiff. The Swansea No. 8 had the last laugh as Wales won 15–12

13

Barnes, S.   England

Full Name: Stuart Barnes
1991/92 International category:
England B
Club: Bath
Position: Outside-half
Height: 5'6½" **Weight:** 13st 5lbs
Occupation: Marketing manager
with Robson Taylor, Accountants
Born: Grays, Essex, 22.11.62
International debut: England 3,
Australia 19, 1984
Five Nations' debut: Scotland 33,
England 6, 1986
Best memory last season:
Dropped goal with last kick of
extra-time to win Pilkington Cup
Final for Bath against Harlequins

**Notable landmarks in rugby
career:** Educated at Bassaleg, East
Wales, and Oxford Univ, where
played in three Varsity matches
(1981–82–83) and finished on losing
side each time. Strangely out of
keeping with a playing career in
which he has been closely associated
with success throughout. In 1989 he
made history by becoming the first
player to captain a side (Bath) to the
English League and Cup double. He
has appeared in seven Cup Finals at
Twickenham – two with Bristol
(1983–84), five with Bath
(1986–87–89–90–92) – and only
once (1984) played on the losing

	apps	pts
England B (**1983**)		
Last Season	4 caps	40
1992	Tour to New Zealand	
England (**1984**)		
Last Season	0 caps	0
Career	8 caps	34

Caps (8): **1984** A **1985** R (R),
NZ(1,2) **1986** S(R), F(R) **1987**
I(R) **1988** Fj

Points (34 – 5c,7p,1dg): **1984** A(1p)
1985 NZ(1:1c,1p),
NZ(2:2c,1dg) **1986** F(R:2p)
1988 Fj(2c,3p)

side. Ironically, on that occasion, Bath were the winners (10–9). A Bath career
which has also included the 1991/92 Courage League Championship title has
seen him contribute 1,492 points in 161 appearances. His last outing of the
1991/92 season produced a match-winning moment of classic Barnes. With
the last kick of extra-time in the Pilkington Cup Final at Twickenham, he
launched a 40-yard dropped goal attempt which ensured a 15–12 win. Spent
much of 1991/92 in the colours of England B whom he captained to a four-win
Grand Slam: scoring 7 points in 34–3 win over Spain (Madrid, 19 Jan 1992),

11 in 47–15 defeat of Ireland B (Richmond, 31 Jan 1992), 14 as France B were downed 22–18 (Paris, 15 Feb 1992) and 8 in a 16–10 close-call against Italy B (Rome, 7 Mar 1992). He then led the B squad on tour in New Zealand (1992). Also captained Barbarians in 16–16 draw with Scotland (Murrayfield, 7 Sep 1991), landing two conversions. Despite being named in England's 33-man 1992 Five Nations' squad, he was not required to add to his remarkably modest tally of eight caps, amassed since his debut against the Wallabies back in 1984 when he kicked a penalty goal – the first instalment of his 34-point career contribution to the national cause. For all his domestic success, he has yet to start a Five Nations' Championship match

Barry, N. Ireland

Full Name: Nick Barry
1991/92 International category:
Ireland B
Club: Garryowen
Positions: Wing, outside-half
Height: 5′11″ **Weight:** 12st 7lbs
Occupation: BSc student
Born: 5.1.69
Family: Single
Family links with rugby: All family, except females, play
International debut: Namibia 26, Ireland 15, 1991
Five Nations' debut: None
Best moments in rugby: Captaining Irish Schools. Touring France with Ireland aged 19. Making debut on 1991 Namibia tour

Worst moment in rugby: Losing Munster Senior Cup Final
Most embarrassing moment: Once playing a match with no boots
Most respected opponent: David Campese (Mediolanum Milan & Australia) – tremendous ability to attack from anywhere on field
Serious injuries: Broken hand
Other sporting achievements: All-Ireland sprint (athletics)
Best memory last season: Winning first cap in Windhoek
Suggestions to improve rugby: Move season to May and June to allow a faster game of rugby to be played
Notable landmarks in rugby career: Won first Ireland cap against Namibia, on 1991 tour, when entering fray as half-time replacement for Keith Crossan

in the 15–26 second Test defeat. Previously, toured Australia (with Irish Schools), Canada and France (with Ireland). Graduated to Ireland B team after two seasons with U-21s and won caps against Argentina (won 27–12, Limerick 20 Oct 1990) and England (won 24–10, Old Belvedere 1 Mar 1991). Landed one conversion and two penalty goals in the 27–12 defeat of the touring Pumas at Thomond Park. Contributed 14 points (two tries and three conversions) to Ireland U-25's 36–17

	apps	pts
Ireland U-21 (**1988**)		
Last Season	0 caps	0
Ireland U-25 (**1990**)		
Career	1 cap	14
Ireland B (**1990**)		
Last Season	0 caps	0
Career	2 caps	8
Ireland (**1991**)		
Last Season	1 cap	0
Career	1 cap	0

Caps (1): **1991** Na(2)
Points: Nil

win over Spain at Limerick (8 Sep 1990). During Namibian tour, also played in 35–4 win over Namibia South Sub-Union, landing a penalty and conversion
Touchlines: Greyhound racing

Bates, S. M. England

Full Name: Steven Michael Bates
1991/92 International category: England B
Club: Wasps
Position: Scrum-half
Height: 5'10" **Weight:** 13st
Occupation: Teacher at Radley College
Born: Merthyr Tydfil, 4.3.63
Family: Sarah (wife) and Lottie (daughter)
Former clubs: West London Institute, Welwyn
International debut: Romania 3, England 58, 1989
Best moment in rugby: Winning first cap in Bucharest
Worst moment in rugby:

Twickenham pitch invasion near end of Wasps' 1987 John Player Cup final defeat by Bath. Took dignity out of occasion: referee was forced to abandon game
Most respected opponent: Dave Loveridge (ex-New Zealand)
Biggest influence on career: Rob Andrew and Tony Jordan (Wasps coach)

Serious injuries: Broken jaw (1983/84) and arm (1986 JP Cup final), medial ligaments (1990)
Other sporting achievements: Soccer for Hertfordshire. Golf (handicap 14)
Best memory last season: England's unbeaten B campaign, especially scoring 40-plus points against Ireland

	apps	pts
England B (1989)		
Last Season	3 caps	0
Career	5 caps	0
England (1989)		
Last Season	0 caps	0
Career	1 cap	0
England XV (1989/90)	1 app	0

Caps (1): **1989** R
Points: Nil

Suggestions to improve rugby:
On-field – Careful not to make too many law changes because rugby will otherwise become a two-tier game with the top bearing no resemblance to the bottom. *Off-field* – Danger that certain people will become elitist in their views about 'professionalism'. Any new regulations must not apply just to the cream. If game is to become more pro, provisions must be made for all levels
Notable landmarks in rugby career: Joined Wasps (1981) and immediately represented Herts. English Colleges (1981–83). Toured Japan with England Students (1982). Played for London Division since 1986 and for England U-23s in 15–10 Twickenham defeat of Spain (9 Apr 1986). England B debut against USSR at Northampton (won 18–10, 23 Dec 1989). Helped Wasps win 1989/90 English League Championship. England replacement for first time against 1988 Wallabies and won first cap the following year in 58–3 win over Romania in Bucharest (13 May 1989). Flew out to Argentina to join 1990 England tour as a replacement, playing in the 15–12 win over Cordoba (31 Jul 1990). Missed bulk of 1990/91 through medial ligament injury, out for six months after operation (15 Sep 1990). Back in time to help England B defeat Italy B 12–9 at Waterloo (27 Mar 1991) and an England XV beat Italy 33–15 in Rovigo (1 May 1990). After touring Australia with London (1991) played in three of England B's four wins (v. I, F, W) last season
Touchlines: Photography – built own darkroom
Player to watch: Steve Pilgrim (Wasps)
Player of the year: Jonathan Webb (England)

Bayfield, M. C.   England

Full Name: Martin Christopher Bayfield

1991/92 International category: England Full

Club: Northampton

Position: Lock

Height: 6'10" **Weight:** 18st

Occupation: Police constable with the Bedfordshire Constabulary

Born: Bedford, 21.12.66

Family: Single

Former clubs: Metropolitan Police, Bedford

International debut: Fiji 12, England 28, 1991

Five Nations' debut: Scotland 7, England 25, 1992

Best moments in rugby: Twice representing England B during 1990/91 season

Worst moment in rugby: Bedford's relegation from Courage English League division one at end of season 1989/90

Most respected opponent: Paul Ackford (Harlequins & England)

Best memory last season: Winning Grand Slam with England

Suggestions to improve rugby: *On-field* – Lifting should be permitted at the line-out. It is a bit of an art and, anyway, everyone does it. *Off-field* – Put an end to confusion over amateurism. Personally I believe money spells bad news for rugby. But while there should be no financial reward for playing, there is no reason why players should not be reimbursed for loss of earnings and even given a free holiday with their family each year

Notable landmarks in rugby career: The tallest forward to play for England, he played three games for England 18-Group, represented Midlands Division and British Police for three seasons, toured with British Police to Italy (1989) and broke into England B set-up during 1990/91 season, playing against Emerging Australians (12–12, Wasps 4 Nov 1990) and Italy (12–9, Waterloo 27 Mar 1991). Progressed to England squad for 1991 tour to Fiji and Australia,

	apps	pts
England B (1991)		
Last Season	0 caps	0
Career	2 caps	0
1992	Tour to New Zealand	
England (1991)		
Last Season	6 caps	0
Career	6 caps	0

Caps (6): **1991** Fj, A **1992** S, I, F, W

Points: Nil

playing in both Tests after Wade Dooley sustained hand injury. Missed out on the World Cup squad but, following Paul Ackford's retirement, booked a permanent berth alongside Dooley in England's 1992 Grand Slam XV. Back on the road last summer, touring with England B to New Zealand
Touchlines: Weight training
Player to watch: Neil Back (Leicester)

Bidgood, R. A.   Wales

Full Name: Roger Anthony Bidgood
1991/92 International category:
Wales Full
Club: Newport
Position: Centre
Height: 6' **Weight:** 14st 4lbs
Occupation: Fireman at Whitchurch Fire Station
Born: Caerphilly, 15.9.65
Family: Deborah (wife)
Former clubs: Glamorgan Wanderers Youth, Pontypridd, Pontypool (two spells), Cardiff
International debut: Wales 15, Scotland 12, 1992
Five Nations' debut: As above
Best moment in rugby: Finally making Wales debut, five years after first selected

Worst moment in rugby: Missing potential debut (Wales 11, Ireland 15, Cardiff 1987) after match was postponed
Most embarrassing moment: Tackling a goal post and being taken to hospital with concussion
Most respected opponent: Tony Bond (Sale, Askeans & England)
Biggest influence on career: Tom Hudson (Newport coach)

	apps	pts
Wales B (**1986**)		
Last Season	0 caps	0
Career	2 caps	0
Wales (**1992**)		
Last Season	1 cap	0
Career	1 cap	0
Caps (1): 1992 S		
Points: Nil		

Serious injuries: Shoulder operation – tendon shortened (1988)
Best memory last season: Being told by Wales manager Robert Norster that I was in to play Scotland
Suggestions to improve rugby: *On-field* – Happy with five points for a try;

19

promises to make the game more exciting for players and spectators alike.
Off-field – As long as I keep my place in the Welsh team I am happy

Notable landmarks in rugby career: Thought his chances of a Wales cap had gone when freezing weather postponed Wales' 1987 Championship match against Ireland. Had been selected in place of the injured John Devereux but by the time the match was rearranged Devereux was fit. Won two Wales Youth caps (v. F, E) in 1984 while with Glamorgan Wanderers. During time at Pontypool, represented Wales B twice against France B – at Pontypridd in October 1986 (won 13–10) and at Bègles in October 1987 (lost 0–26). Helped Newport win 1990/91 Heineken League division one title in his first season with the club and belatedly received his first full cap against Scotland last season. Has also represented Monmouthshire Counties, Crawshays and the Barbarians

Touchlines: Snooker

Player to watch: Richard Brown (Newbridge)

Player of the year: Will Carling (England)

Blair, A. G. Ireland

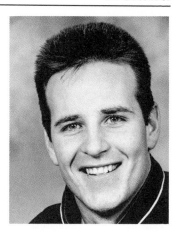

Full Name: Ashley Graham Blair

1991/92 International category: Ireland B

Club: Dungannon

Position: Scrum-half

Height: 6′ **Weight:** 12st 8lbs

Occupation: PE teacher

Born: Dungannon, 20.10.64

Family: Single

Family links with rugby: Uncle played for Dungannon

International debut (B): Scotland 19, Ireland 29, 1991

Best moment in rugby: Ulster debut against 1989 All Blacks

Worst moment in rugby: Being left out of Irish Schools team

Most embarrassing moment: Terribly miscuing a penalty from touch in front of large school crowd

Most respected opponent: Nigel Carr (Ards & Ireland)

Other sporting achievements: Irish League B Division football with Dungannon Swifts

Best memory last season: Breaking into Ireland B side for Murrayfield

Suggestions to improve rugby: Listen to players and recognize their commitment
Notable landmarks in rugby career: Top points scorer and club record holder with Dungannon – 237 (1986–89). Represented Ireland U-25s in 12–10 defeat of touring US

	apps	pts
Ireland U-25 (**1990**)		
Career	1 cap	0
Ireland B (**1991**)		
Last Season	1 cap	0
	1 rep	
Career	1 cap	0

Eagles (Limerick, 10 Mar 1990) and, last season, earned Ireland B recognition with No.9 jersey in 29–29 win over Scottish counterparts at Murrayfield (28 Dec 1991). Bench reserve in ensuing 15–47 loss to England B at Richmond
Touchlines: Travelling

Boobyer, N.   Wales

Full Name: Neil Boobyer
1991/92 International category: Wales U-21
Club: Llanelli
Position: Centre
Height: 5′10″ **Weight:** 12st 2lbs
Occupation: Student at Bridgend Technical College
Born: Bridgend, 11.6.72
Family: Single
Family links with rugby: Father (Brian) played for Tondu and Bridgend Sports
International debut (U-21): Scotland 19, Wales 28, 1992
Best moment in rugby: Selection to represent Wales U-21 against Scotland in Stirling
Worst moment in rugby: Missing out on selection for Wales Youth against Italy

	apps	pts
Wales U-21 (**1992**)		
Last Season	1 cap	0
Career	1 cap	0

Most respected opponent: Mike Hall (Cardiff & Wales)
Best memory last season: Scoring a 70-yard try against Cardiff
Suggestions to improve rugby: *On-field* – Reduce value of penalty goal to two points. *Off-field* – Keep players together after U-21, perhaps a Wales U-23 side

Notable landmarks in rugby career: Already a Llanelli first-teamer, he played a full and active role for Wales U-19s, turning out against Scotland and then touring Canada and playing against the host nation. There was also a Welsh youth cap (won against Japan) for the family sideboard before, last season, Neil was selected to represent Wales U-21s against Scotland U-21s (17 Apr 1992), a match in which the Welsh extended their monopoly in the fixture to six wins from six starts. That day, partnered Bristol's Justin Redrup in the centres
Touchlines: Golf, swimming, football
Player to watch: Andrew Gibbs (Newbridge)
Player of the year: Stuart Davies (Wales)

Boyle, L. S. England

Full Name: Laurence Stuart Boyle
1991/92 International category:
England U-21
Club: Moseley
Position: Centre
Height: 5'10" **Weight:** 13st 1lbs
Occupation: Student
Born: Warwick, 29.1.70
Family: Single
Family links with rugby: Brother
played for England U-16s
Former club: Leamington
International debut: French
Armed Forces 16, England U-21s
23, 1990
Best moment in rugby: Winning
first cap at England U-16 level
Worst moment in rugby: Losing to
Bath in semi-final of 1989/90
Pilkington Cup
Most respected opponent: Les
Cusworth (Leicester & England) –
leadership skills

	apps	pts
England U-21 (**1990**)		
Last Season	1 cap	4
Career	4 caps	4

Other sporting achievements:
Athletics all-rounder for
Warwickshire. Javelin at All-England Championships
Best memory last season: Scoring first points for England U-21s, against
Belgium

Suggestions to improve rugby: At representative level, tell people who have been dropped where they went wrong and how they can improve

Notable landmarks in rugby career: Represented England 16-Group against Italy, England 18-Group B against Japan, Warwickshire Colts against Sweden, Midland Colts against Italy and Midland U-21 against NZ U-21. Won second England U-21 cap in 16–22 loss to Ireland U-21 (The Reddings, 29 Oct 1990), third in 20–18 win over Netherlands ('s-Hertogenbosch, 18 May 1991) and fourth, last season, in 94–0 rout of Belgium (Wolverhampton, 1 Sep 1991), when weighed in with one of the 18 tries

---

Bradley, M. T.   Ireland

Full Name: Michael Timothy Bradley
1991/92 International category: Ireland tour squad
Club: Constitution
Position: Scrum-half
Height: 5′10″ **Weight:** 13st 2lbs
Occupation: Sales manager
Born: Cork, 17.11.62
Family: Gillian (wife)
Family links with rugby: Father played for Constitution
International debut: Ireland 9, Australia 16, 1984
Five Nations' debut: Scotland 15, Ireland 18, 1985
Best moment in rugby: Captaining Cork Con to 1990/91 All-Ireland League victory
Worst moment in rugby: Ireland losing 3–35 to England at Twickenham in 1988, having led 3–0 at half-time
Most respected opponent: Nick Farr-Jones (NSW & Australia)
Serious injuries: Torn ankle ligaments (1990)
Best memory last season: Returning to Ireland squad for New Zealand tour
Suggestions to improve rugby: *Off-field* – Players should receive bonus payments for international matches and reimbursement for loss of earnings
Notable landmarks in rugby career: Played four games for Irish Schools and captained them on 1980 tour of Australia. Captained Irish U-19s and U-21s. Completed journey up representative ladder with appearances for U-25s and B (1983 against Scotland). Chosen as replacement for Ireland in

23

1984 before having played provincial rugby for Munster. Played in Ireland's 1985 Triple Crown-winning side. Returned to Ireland's B team in 1990/91 and captained side to victories over Argentina (27–12, Limerick 20 Oct 1990) and England (24–10, Old Belvedere 1 Mar 1991). Scored try in defeat of touring Pumas. Unused replacement in Ireland's 20–18 win over Argentina (1990/91). Led Constitution to 1990/91 All-Ireland League title. Toured New Zealand with Ireland in 1992

	apps	pts
Ireland B (1983)		
Last Season	0 caps	0
Ireland (1984)		
Last Season	0 caps	0
1992	Tour to New Zealand	
Career	23 caps	16

Caps (23): **1984** A **1985** S, F, W, E **1986** F, W, E, S, R **1987** E, S, F, W(a) wc-W(b), C, T, A **1988** S, F, W, E(a) **1990** W

Points (16 – 4t): **1986** R(1t) **1987** F(1t) wc-C(1t) **1988** S(1t)

Touchlines: Golf, landscaping in Robert Kennedy's garden (summer house)
Player to watch: Paul McCarthy (Constitution)

Bridges, C. J.   Wales

Full Name: Christopher Jeffrey Bridges
1991/92 International category: Wales Full
Club: Neath
Position: Scrum-half
Height: 5′11″ **Weight:** 13st
Occupation: Labourer, Humes Pipe
Born: Pontypridd, 31.8.68
Family: Sarah (wife) and Daniel (son)
Former club: Beddau
International debut: Namibia 9, Wales 18, 1990
Best moment in rugby: Scoring try on full debut
Worst moment in rugby: Losing to Llanelli in 1988 Welsh Cup final
Most respected opponent: Former Wales scrum-half Jonathan Griffiths

Other sporting achievements: Cricket for Glamorgan U-15s. Won players' golf tournament in Namibia
Best memory last season: End-of-season form at Neath

Suggestions to improve rugby:
On-field – I cannot see the point of the new rules. It strikes me that they have just been brought in to suit the Southern Hemisphere nations. *Off-field* – Look after players better. We get nothing back for the massive commitment we put in. The game will have to end up semi-professional to generate interest for the youngsters to play the game

	apps	pts
Wales B (**1989**)		
Career	1 cap	0
Wales (**1990**)		
Last Season	1 cap	0
Career	7 caps	4

Caps (7): **1990** Na(1,2), Ba **1991** E(R), I, F(a), A(a)

Points (4 – 1t): **1990** Na(1:1t)

Notable landmarks in rugby career: Lost place in the Wales side to Robert Jones following the 63–6 defeat by Australia in Brisbane (21 Jul 1991), having turned out in three of the four 1991 Championship games in first Five Nations' season. Previously captained Wales Youth (1986/87), represented Wales U-21s, and toured New Zealand with U-19s (1987), Canada with Wales B (1989, playing in 31–29 'test' win, Edmonton 3 Jun 1989) and Namibia with Wales (1990), where picked up first cap (and first try) in 18–9 opening Test win in Windhoek (2 Jun 1990)

Touchlines: Golf (handicap 25/26)

Player to watch: Matthew McCarthy (Neath)

Player of the year: Richard Webster (Wales)

Buckton, J. R.   England

Full Name: John Richard Buckton
1991/92 International category: England B
Club: Saracens
Position: Centre
Height: 6′2″ **Weight:** 13st
Occupation: Manager with Owners Abroad Travel
Born: Hull, 22.12.61
Family: Carol (wife) and child
Family links with rugby: Brother (Peter) is player-coach at Waterloo; brother (Nick) plays for junior club in Liverpool
Former clubs: Hull and East Riding, Marist Old Boys
International debut: England 28, Australia 19, 1988

Best moment in rugby: Coming on as last-minute replacement for captain Will Carling to win first cap
Worst moment in rugby: Getting injured with England in Australia immediately prior to first Test (1988)
Most embarrassing moment: Missing Yorkshire-Lancashire County game while stuck on train from London to Manchester
Most respected opponent: Saracens' centre Lawrence Smith (in training)

	apps	pts
England B (1988)		
Last Season	4 caps	0
England (1988)		
Last Season	0 caps	0
Career	3 caps	0
England XV (1990)	1 app	4

Caps (3): **1988** A(R) **1990** Arg(1,2)
Points: Nil

Best memory last season: Saracens beating Harlequins and Wasps convincingly in Courage League division one to confirm us as London's premier club
Suggestions to improve rugby: *On-field* – More consistency among referees. Reduce value of penalty goals to two points. *Off-field* – Compensate players for time lost to rugby. Commercially, there are still great avenues for rugby to explore
Notable landmarks in rugby career: Earned first England cap the easy way when replacing concussed debut-captain Carling in 79th minute against 1988 touring Wallabies. Partnered Carling in England XV which beat Italy 33–15 in Rovigo (1 May 1990), scoring one of the four tries, and then toured Argentina with England, winning second and third caps in 1–1 drawn series in Buenos Aires (won 15–12, 28 Jul 1990; lost 13–15, 4 Aug 1990). Captained Saracens (for second season) in 1991/92 to fifth place in League division one. Previously, helped them win 1988/89 Courage League division two. Ever present for England B during unbeaten 1991/92 season (wins against Sp, I, F and It). Picked up 1987 County Championship winners' medal with Yorkshire
Touchlines: Stamp collecting, travel, golf, cricket, tennis
Player to watch: Justyn Cassell (Saracens)
Player of the year: Scott Gibbs (Wales)

Burnell, A. P.　　　　　Scotland

Full Name: Andrew Paul Burnell
1991/92 International category:
Scotland Full
Club: London Scottish
Position: Prop
Height: 6′ **Weight:** 16st 9lbs
Occupation: Sales rep with Lease
and Financing Services of Reading
Born: Edinburgh, 29.9.65
Family: Single
Former clubs: Marlow, Harlequins,
Leicester
International debut: England 12,
Scotland 12, 1989
Five Nations' debut: As above
Best moment in rugby: Beating
England to win 1990 Grand Slam
Worst moments in rugby:
Scotland losing 3–19 to France in
1989; London Scottish getting
relegated from English Second
Division (1988/89); missing 1992
tour to Australia due to torn knee
medial ligament sustained in 12–15
defeat by Wales in 1992 Five
Nations' Championship finale
Most respected opponent: David
Sole (Edinburgh Acads & Scotland)
– good scrummager, great ball
player, superb captain
Serious injuries: Ruptured disc in
back (1989, required surgery), acute
tear in knee medial ligament (1992)
Best memory last season:
Scotland's pushover try against
England

	apps	pts
Scotland B (**1988**)		
Career	1 cap	4
Scotland A (**1991**)		
Last Season	1 cap	0
Career	1 cap	0
Scotland (**1989**)		
Last Season	11 caps	0
Career	25 caps	0

Caps (25): 1989 E, I, F, Fj, R 1990 I,
F, W, E, Arg 1991 F, W, E, I, R
wc-J, Z, I, WS, E, NZ 1992 E,
I, F, W

Points: Nil

Suggestions to improve rugby: *On-field* – Clamp down on scrummage
collapsing with penalty awarded if shoulder dips below hip. Alter law of the
penalty. Side awarded penalty is given throw-in at line-out after ball is kicked
to touch. *Off-field* – Permit players to benefit from rugby-related activities.
More recognition from the Unions to the amount of time required away from
work to meet the standards required to play international rugby. Many clubs

are outdated in their administration. Until more people who care about the game are recruited to run clubs financially, rather than committee men who treat the club as their own private property, then I am afraid junior and senior rugby will suffer

Notable landmarks in rugby career: Scored on first team debut for Leicester and Scotland B debut in 26–3 win over Italy in L'Aquila (1989). Twice helped London Scottish win promotion, as 1989/90 Third Division and 1991/92 Second Division champions, and featured in their triumphant 1990/91 Middlesex Sevens side. Toured with Scotland to Zimbabwe (1988) and New Zealand (1990), having been ever present as tight-head in Grand Slam campaign, but missed tours to Japan (1989) and Australia (1992) through injury. Prior to injury against Wales had played in 24 of the previous 26 cap internationals, including all six World Cup games. Switched to loose-head for 51–12 win over Zimbabwe. Represented Scotland A in 36–16 win over Spain (28 Dec 1991)

Touchlines: Cinema-going

Players to watch: Neil Probyn, David Millard (both London Scottish)

Player of the year: Kenny Milne (Scotland)

Carling, W. D. C.   England

Full Name: William David Charles Carling

1991/92 International category: England Full

Club: Harlequins

Position: Centre

Height: 5'11" **Weight:** 14st 2lbs

Occupation: Runs own marketing/promotion (management training) company: 'Insight'

Born: Bradford-on-Avon, Wiltshire, 12.12.65

Family: Single

Family links with rugby: Father (Bill) played for Cardiff

Former club: Durham Univ

International debut: France 10, England 9, 1988

Five Nations' debut: As above

Best moments in rugby: England beating Australia 28–19 in my first game as captain, and leading side to back-to-back Grand Slams

Worst moment in rugby: Losing 1990 Grand Slam decider to Scotland

Most embarrassing moment: Not touching down try for Harlequins against Rosslyn Park at Twickenham after crossing line in 1990 Middlesex Sevens

Most respected opponent: Denis Charvet (Toulouse & France)

Serious injuries: Fracture of leg (1989)

Best memory last season: Wade Dooley's try against Wales on his 50th England appearance – rarely can there have been a more fitting score. Such a great England player and servant

	apps	pts
England B (**1987**)		
Last Season	0 caps	0
England (**1988**)		
Last Season	12 caps	12
Career	36 caps	24

Caps (36): **1988** F, W, S, I(1,2), A(a2), Fj, A(b) **1989** S, I, F, W, Fj **1990** I, F, W, S, Arg(a1, a2), Arg(b) **1991** W, S, I, F, Fj, A(a) wc-NZ, It, US, F, S, A(b) **1992** S, I, F, W

Points (24 – 6t): **1989** F(1t) **1990** F(1t), W(1t) **1991** wc-US(1t), F(1t) **1992** W(1t)

Suggestions to improve rugby:

On-field – Involve players in rule-changes. New rules should have an impact on the game by speeding it up. In turn, players will change to a more conformed 'flanker' body type. General level of coaching in English club rugby must be raised – still too stuck in our ways. We must learn from other countries.

Off-field – Players should be allowed to benefit from rugby-related activities because everything we do is naturally related to rugby. But we do not want to be paid to play. Confident that things will get better. More constructive appreciation of rugby from the media

Notable landmarks in rugby career: England's most-capped centre (36) and joint-holder (with NZ's Wilson Whineray) of world record for most international wins as captain (22 in 29 games). Began playing career with Terra Nova School U-11s as a six-year-old. First fifth-former (15-year-old) to play in Sedbergh's first XV (three years in team – experienced only two defeats), prior to captaining England 18 Group (1984) and moving on to Durham Univ on an Army scholarship (reading psychology) where switched to fullback. Northern Division selectors Geoff Cooke and Dave Robinson advised playing centre, where he has remained ever since. Rates a county performance for Durham against Lancashire as one of the most influential in shaping his future career. Bought himself out of Army (2nd Lt heading towards Royal Regiment of Wales) when told he would not be able to play representative rugby. Helped England B beat France B 22–9 (Bath, 20 Feb 1987). England's youngest captain for 57 years (since P. D. Howard of Old Millhillians, 1931) when handed reins aged 22 years and 11 months for England's 28–19 win over Australia (5 Nov. 1988). Captain in two Grand Slams and 1991 run to World Cup final. Confessed, on Radio 4's *Desert Island Discs* (May 1992) that, if cast away, he would want with him Tolkein's book *The Hobbit*, Louis Armstrong's record 'What a Wonderful World', and a flotation tank

Touchlines: Painting – sketching and inks, social golf

Cassell, J. P. S.   England

Full Name: Justyn Paul Sheldon Cassell

1991/92 International category: England B

Club: Saracens

Position: Openside flanker

Height: 6'3" **Weight:** 15st

Occupation: Accounts manager for P. I. A. (graphic design company)

Born: Reading, 25.5.67

Family: Melissa (wife)

Former club: Marlow (Bucks)

International debut (B): France 18, England 22, 1992

Best moment in rugby: Winning 1986 Buckinghamshire Cup final against High Wycombe

Worst moment in rugby: Being sent-off against Bath in final Courage League division one match of 1991/92 season – threatened my place on summer B tour to New Zealand

Most respected opponent: Peter Winterbottom (Harlequins & England)

	apps	pts
England B (**1992**)		
Last Season	1 cap	0
1992	Tour to New Zealand	
Career	1 cap	0

Biggest influences on career: Nigel Ashton (Marlow), Mark Evans (Saracens)

Other sporting achievements: Athletics for London Schools. Shot put at All-England Championships. Canoeing training instructor (teach up to two-star). Soccer for South England Public Schools whilst at Dulwich College

Best memory last season: Making B debut in Paris (15.2.92)

Suggestions to improve rugby: *On-field* – Revert to old ruck/maul laws. The new rule will encourage cheating in the game. *Off-field* – Look after players better. There were no loss-of-earnings payments for the England B boys in New Zealand last summer (just Communications allowance) which made life difficult. Allow players to benefit from rugby-related activities

Notable landmarks in rugby career: Joined Marlow in 1985 and won two

Bucks Cup winners' medals with the club (1986–88) before moving to Saracens, on the advice of Chalky White (South-South West U-21 coach) in 1988. Represented South England Schools at lock before switching to back row later in career. Last season represented Barbarians at the Hong Kong Sevens and on their Easter Tour of Wales. Also a bench reserve for London Division and played for South-South West U-21s. Lenient ban followed sending off at Bath in League, allowing him to tour New Zealand with England B
Touchlines: Waterskiing, spending time with Melissa
Player to watch: Richard Cockerill (Coventry)
Player of the year: Andy Nicol (Scotland)

Chalmers, C. M.   Scotland

Full Name: Craig Minto Chalmers
1991/92 International category: Scotland Full
Club: Melrose
Position: Outside-half
Height: 5'10" **Weight:** 13st 11lbs
Occupation: Marketing advisor with Scottish Power
Born: Galashiels, 15.10.68
Family: Single
Family links with rugby: Father (Brian) coaches at Melrose
International debut: Scotland 23, Wales 7, 1989
Five Nations' debut: As above
Best moments in rugby: Winning 1990 Grand Slam by beating England; winning 1989/90 and 1991/92 Scottish Championships with Melrose
Worst moment in rugby: Being dropped by 1989 Lions, after playing in first Test against Australia (lost 12–30)
Most respected opponents: Grant Fox (New Zealand), Michael Lynagh (Australia)
Biggest influences on career: Father, Ian McGeechan, Jim Telfer
Serious injuries: Torn knee cartilage, strained groin, dead leg
Best memory last season: Beating Glasgow High Kelvinside to clinch league title with Melrose
Suggestions to improve rugby: *On-field* – Play game without flankers (give

me more room to run). Reduce size of Scottish first division to 10 clubs. Make game more fluid, but not by decreasing value of penalty goals for that would increase the number of infringements committed. *Off-field –* Introduce trust funds for international players; something per match, to be collected at the end of their careers. I do not believe players should be directly paid to play, but why should we not be permitted to receive money for rugby-related activities – say, wearing a particular brand of boots? We are not doing anyone any harm

Notable landmarks in rugby career: Youngest player ever to represent Scotland B – as a 19-year-old in the 18–12 defeat of France B at Chalon-sur-Saône (20 Mar 1988) – having already turned out for Scottish Schools, U-18, U-19 and U-21. Scored a try and dropped goal on full debut against Wales (21 Jan 1989). Earned selection to 1989 Lions tour of Australia and kicked six points in first Test before being replaced by Rob Andrew for remainder of series. Scotland's Grand Slam No.10 in 1990. Scored 46 points in 1991 Five Nations' Championship (9 v. F, 12 v. W, 12 v. E, 13 v. I) including 'Grand Slam' against Wales (1t, 1c, 1p, 1dg). Toured with Scotland to New Zealand (1990), North America (1991) and Australia (1992)

Touchlines: Golf (handicap 12), ten-pin bowling

Player to watch: Gregor Townsend (Gala)

Player of the year: Will Carling (England)

	apps	pts
Scotland B (**1988**)		
Career	2 caps	14
Scotland (**1989**)		
Last Season	11 caps	19
Career	27 caps	109
Lions (**1989**)	1 Test	6

Caps (27): **1989** W, E, I, F, Fj **1990** I, F, W, E, NZ(1,2), Arg **1991** F, W, E, I, R wc-J, Z, I, WS, E, NZ **1992** E, I, F, W

Points (109 – 4t,6c,22p,5dg): **1989** W(1t,1dg) **1990** I(1c,1p), F(2c,2p), W(3p), E(3p), Arg(1t) **1991** F(2p,1dg), W(1t,1c,1p,1dg), E(4p), I(2c,3p), wc-J(1t,1p), I(1dg) **1992** W(1dg,2p)

Clarke, B. B.   England

Full Name: Benjamin Bevan Clarke
1991/92 International category:
England B
Club: Bath
Position: No.8
Height: 6′5″ **Weight:** 17st
Occupation: Farmer
Born: Bishop's Stortford, 15.4.68
Family: Single
Family links with rugby: Father
(Bevan) played for Bishop's
Stortford and is now club chairman
Former clubs: Bishop's Stortford,
Saracens
International debut (B): England
B 50, Spain 6, 1990
Best moment in rugby: Saracens
beating Bath in 1990/91 Courage
League division one
Worst moment in rugby:
Damaging shoulder and missing
England XV's game against an Italy
XV in Rovigo (1 May 1990)
Most respected opponent: Dean
Ryan (Wasps & England)
Biggest influence on career: Tony
Russ (ex-Saracens coach)

	apps	pts
England B (**1990**)		
Last Season	4 caps	8
Career	5 caps	8
England	1995 Development squad	

Serious injuries: Sprung shoulder joint, torn ligaments
Other sporting achievements: Swimming for Hertfordshire
Best memory last season: Stuart Barnes' last-gasp dropped goal that won
us (Bath) the Pilkington Cup final against Harlequins
Suggestions to improve rugby: *On-field* – Sceptical of new mauling rule.
No one I know at Colts level, where they have experience of it, is in favour.
Better policing of line-outs by referees. *Off-field* – Compensate players or
employers for time lost to rugby
Notable landmarks in rugby career: Represented Hertfordshire Colts, U-21
and full teams while with Stortford. On joining Saracens at start of 1990/91,
was selected for London Division, Public School Wanderers, Penguins,
England Students and England B. Toured Australia (1991) with London, and
New Zealand (1992) with England B. A member of the B Grand
Slam-winning side which last season accounted for Spain, Ireland B, France
B and Italy B (scored tries v. Sp, I). Included in England's 33-man Five

Nations' squad and new development squad last season. Represented Bath at No.8 in 1992 Pilkington Cup triumph
Touchlines: Golf, squash, hockey
Player to watch: John Mallett (Bath)
Player of the year: Jim Fallon (England B)

Clarke, J. D. Ireland

Full Name: Jack David Clarke
1991/92 International category: Ireland Full
Club: Dolphin
Positions: Wing, centre
Height: 6′ **Weight:** 13st 7lbs
Occupation: Pensions assistant with Standard Life (Dublin)
Born: Kisumu, Kenya, 2.9.68
Family: Single
Family links with rugby: Brother (Garoid) plays for Athlone and Irish Colleges
International debut: Wales 21, Ireland 21, 1991
Five Nations' debut: As above
Best moment in rugby: Running out onto Cardiff Arms Park for full debut
Worst moment in rugby: Losing to Australia at the death in 1991 World Cup quarter-final
Most embarrassing moment: Having to leave field after landing on boil on my backside when tackled
Serious injuries: Broken ankle (1984), torn hamstring
Other sporting achievements: Javelin for Irish Schools
Best memory last season: Inclusion in Ireland's squad for World Cup
Suggestions to improve rugby: *On-field* – Approve of the new regulations in principle, though it will

	apps	pts
Ireland U-21 (**1989**)		
Career	2 caps	0
Ireland U-25 (**1990**)		
Career	2 caps	4
Ireland B (**1990**)		
Career	3 caps	8
Ireland (**1991**)		
Last Season	4 caps	0
Career	5 caps	4

Caps (5): 1991 W, Na(1,2) wc-J, A
Points (4 – 1t): **1991** W(1t)

be interesting to see how some of them work in practice. *Off-field* – The game is heading in the right direction but there is still a long way to go

Notable landmarks in rugby career: Spent 12 years in Kenya before moving to Ireland and representing Irish Schools, Munster, Ireland U-21s (won 10–9 v. Italy, Treviso 30 Sep 1989; drew 13–13 v. New Zealand, Donnybrook 19 Nov 1989), Ireland U-25s (won 12–10 v. US Eagles, Limerick 10 Mar 1990; won 36–17 v. Spain, Limerick 8 Sep 1990) and Ireland B (won 27–12 v. Argentina, Limerick 20 Oct 1990; won 16–0 v. Scotland B, Ravenhill 22 Dec 1990; won 24–10 v. England B, Old Belvedere 1 Mar 1991). Scored try on full debut against Wales (16 Feb 1991) prior to touring Namibia, where played in both Tests, and making two appearances in World Cup. Toured New Zealand with Ireland (1992)

Touchlines: Squash, swimming

Player to watch: Keith Wood (Garryowen)

Player of the year: David Campese (Australia)

Clement, A.   Wales

Full Name: Anthony Clement
1991/92 International category: Wales Full
Club: Swansea
Positions: Outside-half, fullback
Height: 5'9" **Weight:** 13st 8lbs
Occupation: Car leasing executive with Days Contract Hire (subsidiary of CEM Day Group)
Born: Swansea, 8.2.67
Family: Debra (wife)
Family links with rugby: Father (Malcolm) played for Bonymaen; brother (Michael) plays for Bonymaen
Former club: Morriston Youth
International debut: Wales 46, US Eagles 0, 1987
Five Nations' debut: England 3, Wales 11, 1988

Best moments in rugby: Scoring two tries for Wales on debut. Helping Wales beat Australia 16–10 in quarter-finals of 1990 Hong Kong Sevens. Beating Scotland (21 Mar 1992) to end three-year winless run at Arms Park

Worst moment in rugby: Being dropped by Wales for second time (before 1988/89 Five Nations' Championship) when playing well

Most respected opponent: Mike Rayer (Cardiff & Wales)

Serious injuries: Hamstring strain

Best memories last season: Wales winning twice in Five Nations', and Swansea winning League

Suggestions to improve rugby:
On-field – Disagree with new maul ruling; encourages negative play. Reduce value of penalty goals (2), drop goals (2) and conversions (1).
Off-field – Don't put too much store in tradition because it is a stumbling-block to progress. There can be no hiding the fact that during the Five Nations' Championship the game is semi-professional for those involved. Financial assistance is required for the commitment both of players and companies

Notable landmarks in rugby career: After playing six games for Welsh Youth (1984), joined Swansea (1985) and captained Wales U-20s. Also represented Wales U-21s, B – twice against France (lost 0–26, Bègles 17 Oct 1987; lost 12–18, Brecon 29 Oct 1988) and also against the Netherlands (won 34–12, Leiden 2 Dec 1990) and the Barbarians. Toured South Africa with World XV (1989). Finally secured much-cherished Wales fullback slot last season, after returning from 1991 tour of Australia. Turned out against Western Samoa and Australia during World Cup and proved a major success in 1992 Five Nations' Championship. Equally impressive for Swansea who won 1991/92 Heineken Championship

Touchlines: Soccer, cricket

Player to watch: Simon Davies (Swansea)

Player of the year: Richard Webster (Wales)

	apps	pts
Wales B (1987)		
Career	3 caps	7
Wales (1987)		
Last Season	8 caps	0
Career	19 caps	11
Lions 1989		

Caps (19): **1987** US(R) **1988** E, NZ, WS(R), R **1989** NZ **1990** S(R), I(R), Na(1,2) **1991** S(R), A(a:R), F(b) wc-WS, A(b) **1992** I, F, E, S

Points (11 – 2t,1dg): **1987** US(R:2t) **1990** Na(2:1dg)

Collins, R. G.   Wales

Full Name: Richard (**Richie**)
Graham Collins
1991/92 International category:
Wales Full
Club: Cardiff
Position: Flanker
Height: 6'1" **Weight:** 14st 7lbs
Occupation: Policeman
(Caerphilly)
Born: Cardiff, 2.3.62
Family: Single
Former clubs: Pontypridd,
Newport, South Wales Police
International debut: Wales 19,
England 12, 1987
Five Nations' debut: As above
Best moment in rugby: Wales
winning 1988 Triple Crown in
Ireland
Worst moment in rugby: 1991
Wales tour of Australia
Most embarrassing moment:
Whole of above tour
Most respected opponent: Finlay
Calder (Stewart's-Melville &
Scotland)
Best memory last season: Scoring
try against France under the Arms
Park's new lights (4 Sep 1991)
Other sporting achievements:
Welsh basketball international;
playing for Caer in English National
League division two

	apps	pts
Wales B (**1986**)		
Career	3 caps	4
Wales (**1987**)		
Last Season	3 caps	4
Career	17 caps	4

Caps   (17): **1987** E(a), I(a:R), US
      wc-I(b), E(b), NZ **1988** E, S, I,
      F, R **1990** E, S, I **1991** A(a),
      F(b) wc-WS

Points (4 – 1t): **1991** F(b:1t)

Notable landmarks in rugby career: Played initially to sharpen reflexes and
bulk-up for basketball. Spent season playing Wellington club rugby in New
Zealand before returning to join Pontypridd, and Newport, with whom played
in 1986 Welsh Cup final. Scored try on Wales B debut in 24–12 win over
Italy (1986). Made full Wales debut as replacement at Cardiff in 1987.
Returned to national set-up for 1991 tour of Australia and played in 6–63 loss
to host nation before opening try account with only Welsh touchdown in 9–22
loss to France in September 1991. World Cup duty was restricted to a solitary
appearance, in the 16–13 defeat by Western Samoa

Copsey, A. H.   Wales

Full Name: Anthony Hugh Copsey
1991/92 International category:
Wales Full
Club: Llanelli
Position: Lock
Height: 6'7" **Weight:** 17st 2lbs
Occupation: Quality systems
development co-ordinator
Born: Romford, Essex, 25.1.65
Family: Amanda (wife)
Family links with rugby: Brother
(Peter) plays for Old Edwardians
Former clubs: Old Edwardians,
Cardiff Institute
International debut: Ireland 15,
Wales 16, 1992
Five Nations' debut: As above
Best moment in rugby: Winning
first cap in Dublin
Worst moments in rugby: Every
time I am on a losing side
Most embarrassing moment:
Press finding out about the tattoo on
my behind
Most respected opponent: Wade
Dooley (Preston Grasshoppers &
England)

	apps	pts
Wales (1992)		
Last Season	4 caps	0
Career	4 caps	0

Caps (4): **1992** I, F, E, S
Points: Nil

Biggest influences on career: Andy Sankey and Steve Drake (school
teachers)
Serious injuries: 48 stitches in all, dislocated collarbone, fractured ribs
Best memory last season: Reaching Schweppes Challenge Cup final for
second consecutive season
Suggestions to improve rugby: *On-field* – Help referees to get things right.
Invite a second opinion. Give more power to the touchjudges. *Off-field* – More
financial support for players and their employers from the Unions. As game
continues to change more commitment is expected from players so they must
at least be given freedom to earn from rugby-related activities
Notable landmarks in rugby career: Joined Llanelli (1989/90) via county

rugby for Essex Colts and Eastern Counties U-21s. Moved to work in Wales in 1986 and then enrolled at South Glamorgan Institute (Human Movements), allowing him to represent Welsh Colleges and England Students, with whom toured Namibia. Member of London Division squad. Selected for England Development squad before opting for Wales. Represented Barbarians last season against Scotland at Murrayfield (drew 16–16, 7 Sep 1991), Cork Constitution and Old Wesley. Ever present in Wales' 1992 Five Nations' campaign

Touchlines: Basketball, water-polo
Player to watch: Scott Quinnell (Llanelli)
Player of the year: Emyr Lewis (Wales)

Costello, V. C. P.   Ireland

Full Name: Victor Carton Patrick Costello
1991/92 International category: Ireland U-21
Club: Blackrock College
Positions: No.8, lock
Height: 6'5 1/2" **Weight:** 18st
Occupation: Business Studies student
Born: Dublin, 23.10.70
Family: Single
Family links with rugby: Father (Patrick) played for Ireland in 6–23 loss to France in 1960 Paris match while with Bective Rangers; cousin is Ireland B centre Martin Ridge
International debut (U-21): Italy 9, Ireland 10, 1989
Best moment in rugby: Scoring try against England U-21s on 21st birthday (23 Oct 1991)
Worst moment in rugby: Captaining beaten side in semi-final replay of 1988 Leinster Schools Cup
Most respected opponent: Donal Lenihan (Cork Constitution & Ireland)

	apps	pts
Ireland U-21 (**1989**)		
Last Season	1 cap	4
Career	3 caps	4

Other sporting achievements: Irish Olympic squad for shotput. Irish junior (U-21) record-holder with 16.67m. National champion since aged 16

39

Best memory last season: Regaining Ireland U-21 place two injury-hit seasons after debut in Treviso

Suggestions to improve rugby: *Off-field* – Older members of clubs must recognise the advances in rugby from 20 years ago. It is a lot more professional in its technical aspects and specific training methods. I feel older people tend not to appreciate this and knock it with their 'In my day...' attitude. The game can improve a lot more if it is allowed to

Notable landmarks in rugby career: Broke into Ireland U-21 side as a 19-year-old, playing twice against Italy, before sustaining a shoulder injury which ruled out 1990/91 season. Returned in time to play lead role in 19–10 Donnybrook win over England and score decisive try. Selected for Leinster squad, having previously represented Leinster Schools, Ireland Schools (1987–89) and Leinster U-20s (two seasons)

Touchlines: Athletics

Player to watch: Matthew Ridge (Blackrock College)

Player of the year: David Campese (Australia)

Cronin, D. F. Scotland

Full Name: Damian Francis Cronin
1991/92 International category: Scotland Full
Club: London Scottish
Position: Lock
Height: 6'6" **Weight:** 17st 10lbs
Occupation: Sales manager with Walcot Reclamation Ltd (Bath)
Born: Wegberg, West Germany, 17.4.63
Family: Annie (wife)
Family links with rugby: Father a past-president of Ilford Wanderers
Former clubs: Ilford Wanderers, Bath
International debut: Ireland 22, Scotland 18, 1988
Five Nations' debut: As above
Best moment in rugby: Winning 1990 Grand Slam with Scotland

Worst moment in rugby: Being dropped by Scotland during 1991 World Cup

Most respected opponent: Robert Norster (Cardiff & Wales)

Serious injuries: Ligament damage in both knees. Staple put in right knee

Best memory last season: London Scottish beating Sale to clinch promotion to Courage League division one

Other sporting achievements: Drove in celebrity race round Brands Hatch

Suggestions to improve rugby: *On-field* – Make people stay on their feet more and referees more aware of players, especially flankers, coming over the top. Do not change the line-out. It is a lottery which is half the fun. Those who survive are technicians who learn to survive.

	apps	pts
Scotland B (1987)		
Last Season	0 caps	0
Scotland A (1990)		
Last Season	1 cap	4
Scotland (1988)		
Last Season	4 caps	0
1992	Tour to Australia	
Career	23 caps	8

Caps (23): **1988** I, F, W, E, A **1989** W, E, I, F, Fj, R **1990** I, F, W, E, NZ(1,2) **1991** F, W, E, I, R wc-Z

Points (8 – 2t): **1989** I(1t) **1990** W(1t)

Better off working on keeping the game flowing more. *Off-field* – Look seriously at commercialisation of rugby in support of players. Some sort of trust fund for international players. The SRU needs to be more sympathetic and flexible towards the players

Notable landmarks in rugby career: Returned to rugby after fracturing base of spine aged 22. Built reputation in Scotland with performances for Anglo-Scots, having become eligible thanks to Lothian-based grandparents. Helped 1987 Anglo's beat French at Cupar and was included in Scottish XV which achieved a similar feat. Toured Zimbabwe with Scotland (1988) and captained against Mashonaland District. Ever present alongside Chris Gray in Scotland second row during 1991 Five Nations' Championship after missing early season win (49–3) over Argentina through injury but was kept out of 1992 campaign by Doddie Weir and Neil Edwards. Lust for the game returned on moving to London Scottish. Toured Australia with Scotland last summer

Touchlines: DIY (restoring the house)

Player to watch: Dave Millard (London Scottish)

Player of the year: Wade Dooley (England)

Crossan, K. D.　　　　　Ireland

Full Name: Keith Derek Crossan
1991/92 International category:
Ireland Full
Club: Instonians
Position: Wing
Height: 5'7" **Weight:** 11st 4lbs
Occupation: Banker
Born: Belfast, 29.12.59
Family: Joanna (wife), David (son)
and Victoria (daughter)
Family links with rugby: Uncle
(Derek Monteith) captained Ireland
(1947)
International debut: Ireland 21,
Scotland 12, 1982
Five Nations' debut: As above
Best moment in rugby: Being
selected to tour South Africa with
Ireland (1981)
Worst moment in rugby:
Withdrawing from Ireland's match
against Australia (1984) because of
illness
Most embarrassing moment:
Being sick on pitch (too much
alcohol previous night) after scoring
two tries for Instonians against
Trinity
Most respected opponent: Mike
Harrison (Wakefield & England) –
always scores against me, either for
Yorkshire or England
Serious injuries: Broke jaw in two
places (1985, out for three months),
broken leg (Nov 1990)

	apps	pts
Ireland (1982)		
Last Season	5 caps	0
Career	41 caps	48

Caps (41): **1982** S **1984** F, W, E, S
1985 S, F, W, E **1986** E, S, R
1987 E, S, F, W(a) wc-W(b), C,
T, A **1988** S, F, W, E(a), WS, It
1989 W, S, NZ **1990** E, S, F,
W, Arg **1991** E, S(a), Na(2)
wc-Z, J, S(b) **1992** W

Points (48 – 12t): **1985** W(1t) **1986**
R(3t) **1987** E(1t) wc-C(2t) **1988**
WS(2t), It(2t) **1991** S(1t)

Best memory last season: Playing in World Cup tournament
Suggestions to improve rugby: *On-field* – Change playing season so don't
have to play in depths of winter. Standardise refereeing interpretations.
Off-field – None. All-Ireland League has been a great success
Notable landmarks in rugby career: Ireland's most capped wing with 41
appearances – broke Trevor Ringland's record of 34 (1981–88) in 7–16 loss
to England (1991). Played over 70 times for Ulster but never for Irish Schools,

Ireland U-23s or B. First Irish player to score three tries in one international at Lansdowne Road (v. Romania, 1986). Ever present for Ireland in 1987 World Cup and played in three of four games in 1991 tournament. Toured with Ireland to North America (1989) and Namibia (1991). Total of 12 Irish tries is third on all-time list behind Brendan Mullin (16) and George Stevenson (14). Missed two-and-a-half months of 1990/91 after breaking fibula bone in leg in (Nov 1990)

Touchlines: Try to treat rugby as a 'sport' but this is becoming more difficult as more pressure is put on winning at all costs

Player to watch: Simon Geoghegan (London Irish)

Cunningham, V. J. G.   Ireland

Full Name: Vincent John Gerald Cunningham

1991/92 International category: Ireland Full

Club: St Mary's College

Position: Centre, outside-half

Height: 5'11" **Weight:** 13st

Occupation: Bank official

Born: Dublin, 14.3.67

Family: Single

Family links with rugby: Father played for (and coached and selected) St Mary's

International debut: Ireland 10, England 21, 1988

Five Nations' debut: None

Best moment in rugby: Winning first cap in Millennium match

Worst moment in rugby: Breaking hand in training to miss Ireland's tour to North America (1989)

Most respected opponent: Serge Blanco (Biarritz & France)

Serious injuries: Broken hand

Other sporting achievements: Cricket for Irish Schoolboys

Best memory last season: Selection for World Cup and New Zealand tour squads

Suggestions to improve rugby: *Off-field* – Broken time payments

Notable landmarks in rugby career: Outside-half in first Irish Schools team to beat Wales. Played in Irish touring side which beat France four seasons ago. Amassed seven caps since debut against England in 1988 Dublin Millennium match. Toured Namibia with Ireland (1991), playing in both

Tests (scoring try in second), and added a further couple of caps in World Cup. Scored Ireland U-25s' try in 12–10 defeat of US Eagles (Limerick, 10 Mar 1990) and landed conversion in 36–17 defeat of Spain (Limerick, 8 Sep 1990). Kicked penalty goal in Ireland B's 16–0 defeat of Scotland (Ravenhill, 22 Dec 1990). Toured to New Zealand (1992) with Ireland

Touchlines: Enjoy horse-racing at Leopardstown and Phoenix Park, cricket, golf

Player to watch: Aidan White (St Mary's Coll)

	apps	pts
Ireland U-25 (**1990**)		
Last Season	0 caps	0
Career	2 caps	6
Ireland B (**1990**)		
Last Season	0 caps	0
Career	1 cap	3
Ireland (**1988**)		
Last Season	4 caps	4
1992	Tour to New Zealand	
Career	7 caps	6

Caps　(7): **1988** E(b), It **1990** Arg(R) **1991** Na(1,2) wc-Z, J(R)

Points　(6 – 1t,1c): **1988** It(1c) **1991** Na(2:1t)

Curtis, D. M. Ireland

Full Name: David Michael Curtis
1991/92 International category: Ireland Full
Club: London Irish
Position: Centre
Height: 5'10" **Weight:** 13st
Occupation: Civil engineer
Born: Harare, Zimbabwe, 10.4.65
Family: Andrea (wife)
Family links with rugby: Father (Bryan) capped by Ireland against France, England and Scotland in 1950. He was also an Oxford Blue and represented Barbarians
Former clubs: Univ of Cape Town, Western Province U-20s, Oxford Univ
International debut: Wales 21, Ireland 21, 1991
Five Nations' debut: As above
Best moment in rugby: Being picked to play for Ireland
Worst moment in rugby: Being injured and having to revert from being a player to a spectator

Most respected opponent: Michel du Plessis (Western Province & South Africa)

Other sporting achievements: Oxford golf squad for 1990 Varsity match at Muirfield GC

Best memory last season: Scoring try against Zimbabwe in World Cup and pushing Australia so close

Suggestions to improve rugby: *On-field* – Greater effort to encourage rugby at schoolboy level. *Off-field* – Some Unions are outdated. Player should have freedom to earn money in non-rugby related activities (e.g. speaking, advertisements)

	apps	pts
Ireland B (1990)		
Last Season	0 caps	0
Career	1 cap	0
Ireland (1991)		
Last Season	10 caps	7
Career	13 caps	7

Caps (13): **1991** W, E, S, Na(1,2) wc-Z, J, S, A **1992** W, E, S(R), F

Points (7 – 1t,1dg): **1991** Na(2:1dg) wc-Z(1t)

Notable landmarks in rugby career: Educated at Falcon College, Esogodine, near Bulawayo and attended univ at Cape Town and Oxford, where he won a Blue in 1989. Grew up in Zimbabwe and represented Springbok age-group sides and Western Province U-20. Played for Connacht in Ireland's Inter-Provincial Championship. Made Ireland B debut in 16–0 defeat of Scotland in Belfast (Ravenhill, 22 Dec 1990) before graduating to full side for drawn match with Wales in Cardiff. Toured Namibia with Ireland (1991), dropping a goal in first Test loss. Ever present in 1991 World Cup (scoring try in 55–11 win over Zimbabwe) and Five Nations' Championship, although only played against Scotland as a 40th-minute replacement for Simon Geoghegan

Touchlines: Golf, cricket, fly fishing

Player to watch: Simon Geoghegan (Ireland)

A formidable trio: French front row Pascal Ondarts, Philippe Marocco and Gregoire Lascube prepare to pack down against England in the World Cup quarter-final at Parc des Princes

Danaher, P. P. A.   Ireland

Full Name: Philip Paul Anthony
Danaher
1991/92 International category:
Ireland Full
Club: Garryowen
Position: Fullback
Height: 5'11" **Weight:** 13st 10lbs
Occupation: Insurance consultant
with Norwich Union Life Insurance
(Limerick)
Born: Limerick, 5.10.65
Family: Single
Former clubs: Abbeyfeale,
Lansdowne
International debut: Ireland 22,
Scotland 18, 1988
Five Nations' debut: As above
Best moment in rugby: Winning
1991/92 All-Ireland League with
Garryowen
Worst moment in rugby: Being
dropped second time round after
31–12 Paris loss (3 Mar 1990)
Most embarrassing moment:
Touching ball down behind line and
conceding 5-metre scrum against
Wales (ref was wrong!)
Most respected opponent: Jeremy
Guscott (Bath & England)
Biggest influence on career: Don
Spring (Dublin Univ & Ireland No.8, 1978–81)

	apps	pts
Ireland B (1990/91)	1 rep	
Ireland (**1988**)		
Last Season	2 caps	0
1992	Tour to New Zealand	
Career	10 caps	6

Caps (10): **1988** S, F, W, WS, It **1989**
F, NZ(R) **1990** F **1992** S, F

Points (6 – 2p): **1988** It(2p)

Serious injuries: Broken both ankles, serious hamstring injuries
Other sporting achievements: Badminton at national level while at school.
Gaelic football for Limerick (helped them reach 1991 Munster Cup final
against Kerry)
Suggestions to improve rugby: *On-field* – Referees must be more universal
in their interpretations. Improve coaching of schools and age-group levels.
Off-field – More recognition from Unions for amount of time and commitment
involved in playing. Allow players to benefit financially from rugby-related
activities
Notable landmarks in rugby career: Succeeded Phil Matthews as Ireland
captain for final game of 1992 Five Nations' Championship, against France

46

in Paris (21 Mar 1992). Ireland lost 44–12 to complete whitewashed Wooden Spoon. Then led side to New Zealand for summer tour, having previously toured France and North America. Collected first international honours in 1982 when represented Ireland Schools (v. E, W). Left Garryowen for Lansdowne in 1984 but returned four years later. The 1987/88 season brought his Munster debut and first full cap (at fullback) against Scotland (16 Jan 1988). In and out of favour ever since – including missing out on appearance in 1991 World Cup – but came back in second half of last season's Five Nations' campaign

Touchlines: Social golf
Player to watch: Martin Ridge (Blackrock College)
Player of the year: Will Carling (England)

Davies, A. Wales

Full Name: Adrian Davies
1991/92 International category:
Wales Full
Clubs: Cardiff, Cambridge Univ
Position: Outside-half
Height: 5′10″ **Weight:** 12st 2lbs
Occupation: Land Economy
student
Born: Bridgend, 9.2.69
Family: Single
Family links with rugby: Brother
(Graham) plays for Bridgend;
brother (Lloyd) plays for Cambridge
Univ
Former clubs: Pencoed Youth,
Neath
International debut: Wales 24,
Barbarians 31, 1990

Best moment in rugby: Helping
Neath beat the mighty Pontypool side in the 1986/87 Schweppes Welsh Cup
semi-finals
Worst moment in rugby: 1990 Varsity match
Most respected opponent: Aled Williams (Bridgend)
Biggest influence on career: Ron Waldron (coach at Wales U-19s & Neath)
Serious injuries: Neck problem for one and a half years
Other sporting achievements: Football Blue at Cambridge (offered trials
with Leeds United and Sheffield Wednesday aged 16), having played for
Wales U-15s

Best memory last season:
Captaining Cambridge to victory in Varsity match

Suggestions to improve rugby:
On-field – Legalise lifting in line-out if it will make the set-piece less of a mess. Abandon idea of quick throw-ins at line-outs. Preserve kicking in rugby – it is an art. *Off-field* – For us to compete with Southern Hemisphere nations we must sort ourselves out off the field. Players do not necessarily have to gain but they must certainly not lose out by playing top-level rugby. It is a joke when nations tour short-handed because certain players cannot afford time off work. Unions have accepted some kind of responsibility that people cannot train four or five times per week and then play purely for enjoyment. The players must not be ignored

Notable landmarks in rugby career: Captained Wales at U-18, U-19 and U-21 levels. Kicked four penalty goals for Wales B in 15–28 loss to France B at La Teste (12 Nov 1989). Made full debut for Wales when coming on as 47th minute replacement for Mark Ring during 24–31 loss to Barbarians (6 Oct 1991) and dropped a goal against Australia in Wales' humiliating 6–63 reversal in Brisbane (21 Jul 1991). Included in Welsh World Cup squad but was not utilised. Switched from Neath to Cardiff seeing 'a perfect opportunity, with their great back-division, to be in a position to take hold of a game and run the show'. Captained Cambridge to 17–11 win over Oxford in 110th Varsity Match (10 Dec 1992), kicking nine points. Played also in 1990 and 1991 Varsity matches

Touchlines: Cricket, piano, trumpet

Player to watch: Simon Holmes (Cambridge Univ)

Player of the year: Will Carling (England)

	apps	pts
Wales B (1989)		
Last Season	0 caps	0
Career	1 cap	12
Wales (1990)		
Last Season	1 cap	3
Career	2 caps	3

Caps (2): **1991** Ba(R), A

Points (3 – 1dg): **1991** A(1dg)

Davies, P. T.   Wales

Full Name: Philip Thomas Davies
1991/92 International category:
Wales Full
Club: Llanelli
Positions: No.8, lock, flanker
Height: 6'3" **Weight:** 18st
Occupation: Director with Quasar
Chemicals, Neath
Born: Seven Sisters, 19.10.63
Family: Caroline (wife), Rebecca
and Danikka (daughters)
Family links with rugby: Wife,
Caroline, is Jonathan Davies' sister
Former clubs: Sevens Sisters,
South Wales Police
International debut: Wales 24,
England 15, 1985
Five Nations' debut: As above
Best moments in rugby:
Captaining Llanelli to three
Schweppes Challenge Cup triumphs
(1988, 1991 and 1992) against
Neath, Pontypool and Llanelli
respectively
Worst moment in rugby: Wales'
1990 whitewash
Most embarrassing moment:
Having ball knocked from grasp by
Kenfig Hill centre while touching
down in Cup last season
Most respected opponent:
Laurent Rodriguez (Dax & France)
Biggest influence on career:
Gareth Jenkins (Lanelli coach)
Serious injuries: Broken
cheekbone, misplaced disc in neck,
dislocated elbow

	apps	pts
Wales B (1987)		
Last Season	0 caps	0
Career	1 cap	0
Wales (1985)		
Last Season	5 caps	0
Career	32 caps	16

Caps (32): **1985** E, Fj **1986** E, S, I, F,
Fj, T, WS **1987** F, E(a), I wc-T,
C, NZ **1988** WS, R **1989** S, I,
F, E, NZ **1990** F, E, S **1991** I,
F(a), A(a), F(b) wc-WS, Arg,
A(b)

Points (16 – 4t): **1985** Fj(2t) **1986** I(1t)
1990 E(1t)

Other sporting achievements: Swam for West Wales Schools
Best memory last season: Leading Llanelli to Welsh Cup final win over
League champions Swansea (16 May 1992)
Suggestions to improve rugby: *On-field* – Allow handling in rucks when it

improves continuity of game. Improve general organisation from national viewpoint. *Off-field* – Remuneration for time spent away from work

Notable landmarks in rugby career: First played for Wales at 16-Group. Former policeman. Broke into full Welsh squad in 1984. Marked second cap with two tries in 40–3 win over Fiji at the National Stadium (9 Nov 1985). Had jaw broken by punch in controversial Five Nations' clash with England (Twickenham, 7 Mar 1987). Dropped after playing in 1987 World Cup and became Wales B captain. Returned against Western Samoa in 1988 but missed that year's Championship. Retired from international arena when left out of team to play the centenary Barbarians (6 Oct 1990) but returned during 1991 Five Nations' and held place through 1992 Australia tour and World Cup before being replaced by Swansea's Stuart Davies for 1992 Championship campaign. Llanelli's most-capped international (32 at lock, blindside flanker and No.8), has also represented Crawshays and the Barbarians. Stepped down as Scarlets' captain last summer after 5 years in the job (four Cup Finals, three wins, match against 1989 All Blacks

Touchlines: Golf
Player to watch: Ian Jones (Llanelli)
Player of the year: Richard Webster (Wales)

Davies, S.   Wales

Full Name: Stuart Davies
1991/92 International category:
Wales Full
Club: Swansea
Position: No.8
Height: 6'3" **Weight:** 16st 7lbs
Occupation: Environmental Health Officer with Swansea City Council
Born: Swansea, 2.9.65
Family: Lorna (wife)
Family links with rugby: Father (Elwyn) played at centre for Swansea
Former club: South Glamorgan Institute
International debut: Ireland 15, Wales 16, 1992
Five Nations' debut: As above
Best moment in rugby: Whole debut weekend in Ireland

Worst moment in rugby: Losing two successive Schweppes Challenge Cup semi-finals (1989/90 to Neath, 16–24; 1990/91 to Pontypool, 10–28)

Most embarrassing moment: Falling over when running out onto pitch for Swansea against All Blacks (21 Oct 1989, lost 22–37)

Most respected opponent: Wayne Shelford (Northampton & New Zealand)

Biggest influence on career: My father

	apps	pts
Wales (1992)		
Last Season	4 caps	4
Career	4 caps	4

Caps (4): **1992** I, F, E, S
Points (4 – 1t): **1992** I(1t)

Serious injuries: Cartilage operation on each knee, torn medial ligaments in left knee

Best memory last season: Scoring try on full debut

Suggestions to improve rugby: *On-field* – More discussion between players and referees. Increase feedback from both sides can only improve on-field understandings. *Off-field* – Greater rewards for efforts put in by players

Notable landmarks in rugby career: Represented Wales at U-15, U-16 and U-18 levels and was U-21 squad member (1987). Attended South Glamorgan Institute, where represented Welsh Colleges, Students and Academicals. Selected for Wales B squad in 1989 but the match against France coincided with his wedding. Called into Wales squad post–1991 World Cup and played full 1992 Championship season at No.8. As vice-captain of Swansea, was particularly proud to collect 1992 Heineken Championship winners' medal, though missed out on Cup winners' medal when Llanelli triumphed at the National Stadium (16 May 1992)

Touchlines: Golf (handicap 22), seeing my wife

Player to watch: Robin McBryde (Swansea)

Player of the year: Richard Webster (Wales)

Scotland No. 8 Derek White eyes open ground, supported by Scott Hastings, during the World Cup quarter-final loss to England at Murrayfield

51

Davis, M. E.   Wales

Full Name: Mark Edwin Davis
1991/92 International category:
Wales Full
Club: Newport
Position: Loosehead prop
Height: 5'9 1/2" **Weight:** 16st
Occupation: Student (Cheltenham CHE)
Born: Newport, 18.9.70
Family: Single
Former club: Pontypool
International debut: Australia 63, Wales 6, 1991
Best moment in rugby: Taking field as 20-year-old for Wales debut against Australia (21 Jul 1991)
Worst moment in rugby: Coming off field after Wales debut against Australia
Most embarrassing moment: Getting beaten 71–8 by New South Wales in Sydney (14 Jul 1991)
Most respected opponent: Ewen McKenzie (Randwick & Australia)
Serious injuries: Torn ankle ligaments
Best memory last season: Beating Cup winners Llanelli at Newport in Heineken League (30 Nov 1991)

	apps	pts
Wales U-21 (1991)		
Last Season	1 cap	0
Career	2 caps	0
Wales (1991)		
Last Season	1 cap	0
Career	1 cap	0

Caps (1): **1991** A(a)
Points: Nil

Suggestions to improve rugby:
On-field – Better and more sensitive refereeing of scrum. Different points system. *Off-field* – Better organisational structure (U-21 onwards to B level)
Notable landmarks in rugby career: Helped Newport win 1990/91 Heineken League division one and, in same season, twice represented Wales U-21s in winning causes (v. New Zealand Youth XV and Scotland U-21s). Made third U-21 appearance last season in 28–19 defeat of Scottish counterparts at Stirling. Previously, represented Gwent Schools, Welsh Tertiary Colleges, British Colleges, Pontypool (one game v. Maesteg) and Wales at U-18 (1989 v. S, I, E, F) and senior level, touring Australia (1991) and playing against ACT (won 7–3, Canberra 10 Jul 1991), NSW and Australia. Although earned selection to Wales' 1991 World Cup squad was not required for duty by coach Alan Davies

Touchlines: Reading, weight training
Player to watch: Robert Howley (Bridgend)
Player of the year: Dewi Morris (England)

Dawe, R. G. R. England

Full Name: Richard **Graham** Reed Dawe
1991/92 International category: England B
Club: Bath
Position: Hooker
Height: 5'11" **Weight:** 13st 10lbs
Occupation: Farmer
Born: Plymouth, 4.9.59
Family: Liz (wife)
Former club: Launceston
International debut: Ireland 17, England 0, 1987
Five Nations' debut: As above
Best moment in rugby: Winning 1986 John Player Cup final with Bath (25–17 over Wasps, 26 Apr 1986)
Worst moment in rugby: Being told that I had been banned by England after 1987 Wales match
Most respected opponents: Alan Simmons (Wasps), Neil Hitchen (Orrell)
Biggest influence on career: Don Palmer (coach at Launceston)
Best memory last season: Beating Italy B to achieve four-game winning 'slam' with England B
Suggestions to improve rugby:
On-field – Anything to speed up the game. Abolish law that demands use of same ball that went out of play at line-out. Diminish value of conversion or get rid of it (takes up too much time). *Off-field* – Somehow reduce my travelling. Arrange individual rates of compensation for players or employers for time committed to rugby. When I toured NZ with England B last summer I left my farm for five weeks. The IRB minimum could never cover the expense I incurred

	apps	pts
England B (1990)		
Last Season	4 caps	0
1992	Tour to New Zealand	
Career	8 caps	0
England (1987)		
Last Season	0 caps	0
Career	4 caps	0

Caps (4): 1987 I,F,W,WC–US
Points: Nil

53

Notable landmarks in rugby career: Played four times for England in 1987 (v. I, F, W in Five Nations', and USA in World Cup). But suspension after Wales match (Twickenham, 7 Mar 1987) seemed to put paid to long-term senior future. Nevertheless, has become vital member of successful England B side over the past two seasons, turning out on eight occasions (1990/91: v. Em. A, Sp, I, F. 1991/92: Sp, I, F, It). At county level helped Cornwall win 1990/91 ADT County Championship (29–20 v. Yorks, 20 Apr 1991) and reach 1991/92 final; while at club level helped Bath retain Courage League Championship last season and complete League and Cup double, with extra-time win over Harlequins in Pilkington final (2 May 1992) presenting Cup winners' medal number five

Touchlines: Bell ringing, cycling, sheep shearing

Player to watch: John Mallett (Bath)

Player of the year: Ben Clarke (England B)

De Glanville, P. R.   England

Full Name: Philip Ranulph de Glanville

1991/92 International category: England B

Clubs: Bath

Position: Centre

Height: 6′ **Weight:** 13st

Occupation: Marketing executive

Born: Loughborough, 1.10.68

Family: Single

Family links with rugby: Father played for Loughborough and Rosslyn Park. Now MD of Rhino scrum machines

Former clubs: Durham Univ, Oxford Univ

International debut (B): Italy 0, England 44, 1989

Best moment in rugby: Coming on as England B replacement for Barry Evans as 20-year-old in win over Italy B (19 Mar 1989)

Worst moment in rugby: English Students losing 16–6 to Welsh in Cardiff (1989)

Most embarrassing moment: Losing match for Durham Univ on Canadian tour when dropped a goalbound penalty effort beneath posts, and Univ of Victoria scored try from resultant scrum

54

Most respected opponent: Fran Clough (Wasps & England)
Best memories last season: Scoring try for Bath in Pilkington Cup final, and seeing Stuart Barnes' last-second dropped goal clear Harlequins' bar to give us victory
Serious injuries: Broken arm, dislocated collarbone

	apps	pts
England U-21 (**1989**)		
Career	2 caps	8
England B (**1989**)		
Last Season	4 caps	0
Career	7 caps	0
England	1995 Development squad	

Suggestions to improve rugby: Retain County Championship as a meaningful entity
Notable landmarks in rugby career: Formed a successful partnership with Saracens' John Buckton in England B midfield last season, playing alongside him in all four wins (v. Sp, I, F, It), to take his B tally to seven caps and seven wins. Two caps at U-21 level included two tries in the inaugural match against Romania U-21s (won 54–13, Bucharest 13 May 1989) on debut. Following B debut in Piacenza, turned out in wins against Namibia and Spain in 1990/91. Helped underdogs Oxford Univ to win 1990 Varsity match (21–12, 11 Dec 1990) and favourites Bath to win 1991/92 Pilkington Cup (2 May 1992). Included in the latest national development squad prior to touring New Zealand with England B last summer
Touchlines: Windsurfing

Delaney, L.   Wales

Full Name: Laurance Delaney
1991/92 International category: Wales Full
Club: Llanelli
Position: Prop
Height: 5'11" **Weight:** 16st 10lbs
Occupation: Welder with British Steel Corporation
Born: Llanelli, 8.5.56
Family: Lynne (wife), Simon (son) and Vicky (daughter)
Family links with rugby: Grandfather (Charlie) captained New Dock Stars and represented West Wales
Former club: New Dock Stars
International debut: Wales 13, Ireland 19, 1989

Five Nations' debut: As above
Best moment in rugby: Winning first cap
Worst moment in rugby: Being dropped by Wales after 6–34 defeat by England (17 Feb 1990)
Most respected opponent: Ian Stephens (Bridgend & Wales)
Serious injuries: Muscular spasms in back (1986), torn retina in eye (out for four months)

	apps	pts
Wales B (1985)		
Career	3 caps	0
Wales (1989)		
Last Season	7 caps	0
Career	11 caps	0

Caps (11): **1989** I, F, E **1990** E **1991** F(b) wc-WS, Arg, A(b) **1992** I, F, E

Points: Nil

Other sporting achievements: Bowls for New Dock BC
Best memory last season: Representing Wales in World Cup
Suggestions to improve rugby: *On-field* – Reduce value of penalty from three to two points to make rugby even more open. *Off-field* – Broken time payments for players. Game is bound to turn semi-professional in the end
Notable landmarks in rugby career: Capped by Wales Youth (1974/75), under the captaincy of a certain Terry Holmes, and three times by Wales B (from 1983). Joined Llanelli in 1977 from New Dock Stars and finally won full cap in 1989, as a 33-year-old, following knee-ligament injury to incumbent David Young. Also turned out in colours of Barbarians (1987) and Crawshays. Experienced club campaigner, with nearly 500 Llanelli appearances and four Cup winners' medals from a possible five to his credit. Wales coach Alan Davies brought him back into his side for the 1991 World Cup. Retained tighthead berth until replaced by Hugh Williams-Jones against Scotland in final round of 1992 Five Nations' Championship
Touchlines: Sea fishing (best: 31lb tope)
Player to watch: Emyr Lewis (Llanelli)
Player of the year: Will Carling (England)

Dods, P. W.   Scotland

Full Name: Peter William Dods
1991/92 International category:
Scotland Full
Club: Gala
Positions: Fullback, centre
Height: 5'9" **Weight:** 12st 8lbs
Occupation: Self-employed joiner
Born: Galashiels, 6.1.58
Family: Hazel (wife), Lindsay and
Lucy (daughters)
Family links with rugby: Brother
(Michael) plays for Gala
Former club: Gala Wanderers
International debut: Scotland 13,
Ireland 15, 1983
Five Nations' debut: As above
Best moment in rugby: Scotland's
1984 Grand Slam
Worst moment in rugby:
Relegation to McEwan's League
division two with Gala (1986/87)
Most embarrassing moment:
Going into the bakers with a black
eye on the Monday after helping
Scotland win 1984 Grand Slam and
being asked: 'Son, did you get that
fighting?' Who said the Borders are a
is a rugby hot-bed?!
Most respected opponent: Serge
Blanco (Biarritz & France)
Serious injuries: Broken bones in
back, cheekbone
Best memory last season:
Captaining Scotland for the first time
against Zimbabwe in World Cup and
kicking 16 points
Suggestions to improve rugby:
On-field – Open play up by banning
kicking between the 22s. But allow
players to go back into their 22s to
kick. Disagree with new maul
regulation. A fundamental principle

	apps	pts
Scotland B (1979)		
Last Season	0 caps	0
Career	4 caps	
Scotland A (1990)		
Last Season	1 cap	20
Career	2 caps	31
Scotland (1983)		
Last Season	3 caps	24
1992	Tour to Australia	
Career	23 caps	210
Lions 1989		

Caps (23): **1983** I, F, W, E, NZ **1984**
W, E, I, F, R, A **1985** I, F, W, E
1989 W, E, I, F **1991** I(R), R
wc-Z, NZ(R)

Points (210 – 2t, 26c, 50p): **1983**
I(2p), F(1c,1p), W(1c,3p),
E(1c,3p), NZ(5p) **1984**
W(2c,1p), E(2c,2p), I(1t,3c,2p),
F(1c,5p), R(1t,1c,3p), A(4p)
1985 I(4p), F(1p), W(2c,1p),
E(1p) **1989** W(1c,2p), E(1c,2p),
I(4c,3p), F(1p) **1991** R(1c,2p)
wc-Z(5c,2p)

57

of rugby is that the team going forward gets the put-in. *Off-field* – None, now that touring allowance has risen to £40 per day. When I toured New Zealand in 1981 it was only £6

Notable landmakrs in rugby career: Scotland's 1984 Grand Slam fullback who has scored in every international started (21). Only blanks came in 1991 when replacement against Ireland, in Five Nations' Championship, and New Zealand, in World Cup third place play-off. After five years in International wilderness, returned in 1989 when Gavin Hastings was injured and scored 36 points in Five Nations' campaign to earn place on Lions tour. Represented Scotland in France, New Zealand, Romania, United States, Spain and Australia, where toured last summer before slipping into international retirement. Once scored 43 points in a game (4t, 12c, 1p in 79–0 win v. Alberta, 22 May 1985) – 19 more than next best but non-counter because Scottish record as not a major tour. Scored 20 points (2t, 3c, 2p) in Scotland A's 36–16 Murrayfield defeat of Spain last season (28 Dec 1991)

Player to watch: Gregor Townsend (Gala)

Player of the year: Andy Nicol (Scotland)

Dooley, W. A.   England

Full Name: Wade Anthony Dooley
1991/92 International category: England Full
Club: Preston Grasshoppers
Position: Lock
Height: 6′8″ **Weight:** 18st
Occupation: Police constable with Lancashire Constabulary
Born: Warrington, 2.10.57
Family: Sharon (wife), Sophie Helen and Sara Eleanor (daughters)
Family links with rugby: Father (Geoff) played Rugby League. Brother (Paul) also plays for Grasshoppers
Former club: Fylde
International debut: England 22, Romania 15, 1985
Five Nations' debut: England 9, France 9, 1985

Best moments in rugby: Achieving double Grand Slam (1991–92) with England; 1991 World Cup final

Worst moment in rugby: England losing Grand Slam match to Scotland (1989)

Most embarrassing moment: Being banned for one match for part in Wales-England fracas at Twickenham (lost 12–19, 7 Mar 1987)

Most respected opponents: Steve Cutler (Australia), Bob Norster (Wales), Gary Whetton (NZ)

Biggest influence on career: Dick Greenwood (ex-Grasshoppers & England coach)

Serious injuries: Torn medial ligament (right knee)

Other sporting achievements: Blackpool police division volleyball champions

	apps	pts
England (1985)		
Last Season	9 caps	4
Career	50 caps	12
Lions 1986		
1989	2 Tests	0

Caps (50): **1985** R, F, S, I, W, NZ(2R) **1986** W, S, I, F **1987** F, W wc-A, US, W **1988** F, W, S, I(1,2), A(a1, a2), Fj, A(b) **1989** S, I, F, W, R, Fj. Lions-A(2,3) **1990** I, F, W, S, Arg(a1, a2), Arg(b) **1991** W, S, I, F wc-NZ, US, F, S, A **1992** S, I, F, W

Points (12 – 3t): **1986** F(1t) **1987** wc-US(1t) **1992** W(1t)

Best memories last season: Scoring try on 50th England appearance against Wales at Twickenham (won 24–0, 7 Mar 1992)

Suggestions to improve rugby: *On-field* – Repeal 90-degree scrummaging law at international level. *Off-field* – Trust funds for international players. Relax regulations on players' earning money from promoting goods, sponsors for players, etc. Clarification of what players can and cannot do. RFU must get act together

Notable landmarks in rugby career: Only the third Englishman to surpass 50-cap milestone (Rob Andrew and Peter Winterbottom being the others). Celebrated feat with 77th minute try against Welsh last season. A Rugby League man at school, he has since met with considerable success in Union, becoming England's most-capped lock (overtaking Bill Beaumont's previous best on the Argentina tour in July 1990) and helping the British Lions win the 1989 Test series 2–1 in Australia. Featured in both World Cup tournaments (1987 and 1991), and has been at the epicentre of all England's best work since his debut in 1985

Touchlines: All types of music except jazz. Watching old black and white movies. Fell walking. Eating out. Passion for gardening

Player to watch: Paul Grayson (Preston Grasshoppers)

Player of the year: Will Carling (England)

Douglas, S. M.   England

Full Name: Stephen Mark Douglas
1991/92 International category:
England B
Club: Newcastle Gosforth
Position: Scrum-half
Height: 6′ **Weight:** 13st
Occupation: Accountancy student
Born: Newcastle-upon-Tyne, 21.4.71
Family: Single
International debut (B): Spain 3,
England B 34, 1991
Best moment in rugby: Scoring try
on B debut against Spain
Worst moment in rugby: Broken
ankle last season which kept me out
of England Students match against
full England side
Most respected opponents:
England's Richard Hill (Bath) and
Dewi Morris (Orrell)
Biggest influence on career:
Father (George)
Serious injuries: Broken left ankle
(out for three months), broken
collarbone
Best memory last season:
Selection to England B squad
Suggestions to improve rugby:

	apps	pts
England U-21 (**1991**)		
Last Season	2 caps	12
Career	2 caps	12
England B (**1991**)		
Last Season	1 cap	4
Career	1 cap	4
England	1995 Development squad	

On-field – Fewer rule changes but six
points for a try and less (one) for a penalty goal. *Off-field* – More sympathy
and understanding towards different problems players encounter in getting
time off work
Notable landmarks in rugby career: Played for England Colts (1989/90),
Students (1990/91 v. France) and U-21s, twice (won 94–0 v. Belgium,
Wolverhampton, 1 Sep 1991; lost 10–19 v. Ireland U-21, Donnybrook 23
Oct 1991), before graduating to England B against Spain in Madrid (also
bench v. Ireland B, Richmond 31 Jan 1992). Weighed in with three tries for
England U-21s in comprehensive defeat of Belgium. Finals examinations
prevented touring New Zealand with England B last summer
Touchlines: Social golf
Player to watch: Ben Clarke (Bath)
Player of the year: Peter Winterbottom (England)

Edwards, N. G. B.　　　　Scotland

Full Name: Neil George Barry
Edwards
1991/92 International category:
Scotland Full
Club: Harlequins
Position: Lock
Height: 6'4" **Weight:** 18st
Occupation: Chartered surveyor
with Furnitureland of Catford
Born: Carshalton, Surrey, 20.8.64
Family: Single
Family links with rugby: Father
(Barry) played for Army and
Richmond
Former club: Rosslyn Park
International debut: Scotland 7,
England 25, 1992
Five Nations' debut: As above
Best moments in rugby:
Scotland's pushover try against
England on my debut. Reaching
semi-finals with Barbarians at 1989
Hong Kong Sevens
Worst moment in rugby:
Captaining Harlequins to a 20–42
loss at the hands of Cambridge Univ
the day before the 1991 World Cup
final
Most embarrassing moment:
Singing Flower of Scotland prior to

	apps	pts
Scotland B (**1991**)		
Last Season	1 cap	0
Career	1 cap	0
Scotland (**1992**)		
Last Season	4 caps	4
1992	Tour to Australia	
Career	4 caps	4

Caps (4): **1992** E, I, F, W
Points (4 – 1t): **1992** F(1t)

Scottish debut I was smiling at
someone in the crowd, totally lost my concentration, and visibly sang the
wrong line
Most respected opponent: John Morrison (Bristol & England B)
Biggest influences on career: Father and Dick Best (Harlequins coach)
Serious injuries: Compressed vertebrae of neck (Nov 1990)
Other sporting achievements: Soccer trial for Crystal Palace FC, as a
goalkeeper, when aged 18
Best memory last season: Scoring try against France at Murrayfield and
seeing my family and friends, who had taken the 40–1 odds against my scoring
the first try, clean out the bookies to the tune of £1,500. Apparently that
bookie has me 4–1-on favourite for the next game!

Suggestions to improve rugby: *On-field* – Eliminate the wearing of long Australian Rugby League studs, which are long, thin and much sharper, like stiletto heels. Easily able to severely damage someone's back at the bottom of a ruck. People forget that there are no rucks in Rugby League and we have to go to work on Monday. *Off-field* – Greater involvement of wives and girlfriends by Unions. Easier to get blessing for periods away from them if they are made to feel special

Notable landmarks in rugby career: Spent five years with Rosslyn Park on leaving school aged 17. Made debut against Newport aged 19 when Paul Ackford left to join Harlequins. Represented England Students and British Polys while studying at Oxford Polytechnic before attending England's 1989 training camp in Portugal. The previous year he had helped Harlequins win the John Player Special Cup at Twickenham. Quins' coach Dick Best selected him for the London XV which beat the touring Wallabies, but with messrs Ackford and Dooley firmly ensconsed in the England set-up, Neil turned to his Scottish qualification (Dundonian grandparents). Impressed playing for the Anglo-Scots, Scotland B and the Junior Reds in the national trial and was consequently one of four newcomers to be blooded in the Calcutta Cup clash

Touchlines: Skiing, cricket

Player to watch: Mark Russell (Harlequins)

Player of the year: Will Carling (England)

Emyr, A.   Wales

Full Name: Arthur Emyr (**Jones**)
1991/92 International category: Wales Full
Club: Cardiff
Position: Wing
Height: 6'2" **Weight:** 14st 10lbs
Occupation: Bilingual TV presenter for HTV and Nant Films
Born: Bangor, 27.7.62
Family: Ana (wife)
Family links with rugby: Brother (Garmon) plays for Cardiff Harlequins
Former club: Swansea
International debut: Wales 12, England 9, 1989
Five Nations' debut: As above
Best moment in rugby: Scoring

first try for Wales against Scotland (3 Mar 1990)

Worst moment in rugby: Knee injury, suffered against Maesteg (1987), which required two operations

Most respected opponents: John Kirwan (New Zealand), David Campese (Australia)

Biggest influence on career: The late Gwyn Evans during my time at Aberystwyth Univ

Serious injuries: Damaged knee, calves and ankle ligaments, sprung shoulder joint and rib cartilage

	apps	pts
Wales B (1985)		
Last Season	0 caps	0
Career	4 caps	24
Wales (1989)		
Last Season	4 caps	4
Career	13 caps	16

Caps (13): **1989** E, NZ **1990** F, E, S, I, Na(1,2) **1991** F(a), F(b) wc-WS, Arg, A(b)

Points (16 – 4t): **1990** S(1t), Na(2:2t) **1991** wc-WS(1t)

Other sporting achievements: Welsh International 4 x 100m relay athlete

Best memory last season: Being a part of the encouraging Welsh performance against France in coach Alan Davies' first match in charge (4 Sep 1991)

Suggestions to improve rugby: *On-field* – Delighted that they have awarded five points for a try. More freedom to play ball on floor to keep game moving, not kill it. *Off-field* – More consideration for players and their employers. Current amateur regulations are a farce. So far people are just toying with new ideas. More and more administrators are appearing at clubs on large salaries. Players will soon be looking for the same. The game is being kicked and cajoled in the right direction but there is still too much hypocrisy: it is clearly not an amateur game for all concerned – certain players are making substantial money. Rugby has not yet worked out how to handle the issue of money. It is very much a cloak-and-dagger situation. We must encourage honesty and responsibility in dealing with this issue which taints our game. All credit to the England players who have done much to unsettle the status quo

Notable landmarks in rugby career: Career disrupted by serious knee injury (1987) which sidelined him for fourteen months. In and out of Welsh squad since 1983 but finally won first cap in Wales' against-all-odds 1989 defeat of England. Also represented Welsh Universities, Welsh Students, Barbarians, Wales B (scoring five tries in 80–9 win over Spain in 1985). At Sevens, represented Wales, and Barbarians in Hong Kong. Missed two-thirds of 1990/91 due to shoulder and ankle injuries but returned to national side for final Five Nations' match in Paris (lost 3–36). Took cap-tally to 13 with four appearances last season, including being ever present in the No.11 jersey during the World Cup. Scored fourth international try in defeat against Western Samoa

Touchlines: Cinema-going, soccer, golf

Player to watch: Simon Davies (Swansea)

Player of the year: David Campese (Australia)

Evans, D. W.   Wales

Full Name: David Wyn Evans
1991/92 International category:
Wales Full
Club: Cardiff
Positions: Outside-half, centre
Height: 5'9" **Weight:** 11st 8lbs
Occupation: Development officer
for Sports Council of Wales
Born: Wootton Bassett, Wiltshire,
1.11.65
Family: Roberta (wife)
Family links with rugby: Father
(Gareth) captained Carnegie
College; brother (Geraint) plays for
Caldicott
Former clubs: Swansea and Oxford
Universities, Aberaman Youth
International debut: France 31,
Wales 12, 1989
Five Nations' debut: As above
Best moment in rugby: Wales
defying odds to beat England 12–9 at
Cardiff (1989)
Worst moment in rugby: Wales
losing 6–34 to England at
Twickenham (1990)
Most respected opponent:
Philippe Sella (Agen & France)
Biggest influence on career:
Father and ex-Cardiff coach Gary
Samuel

	apps	pts
Wales B (1989)		
Last Season	0 caps	0
Career	1 cap	0
Wales (1989)		
Last Season	3 caps	0
Career	11 caps	6

Caps (11): **1989** F, E, NZ **1990** F, E, S, I, Ba **1991** A(a:R), F(b:R) wc-A(b:R)

Points (6 – 2dg): **1990** F(1dg), Ba(1dg)

Serious injuries: Dislocated and fractured shoulder, concussion, tendon reattached to kneecap (out most of 1991/92 season)
Best memory last season: The end, because of above injury
Suggestions to improve rugby: *On-field* – Reduce number of games played by top players. More consistent refereeing. I approve of law preventing players taking possession back inside 22 to then kick to touch, but maul rule is confusing. Improve coaching structure. *Off-field* – Leagues in Wales are not a good development. Enjoyment has gone out of the game and I don't think standards have improved as a result. The rules are trying to encourage a more open game but the need to win at all costs is counter-productive

Notable landmarks in rugby career: Partnered Robert Jones at half-back three times for 1984 Welsh Schools, scoring 16 points in 20–0 defeat of France. Also represented Welsh Students, Welsh Universities, Swansea Univ (1988 UAU final) and Oxford Univ (1988 Blue). Toured Fiji, Australia, New Zealand and USA with Oxbridge, Japan with Oxford, and Canada with Wales B (where made B debut). Dropped goal for Wales in 24–31 early-season loss to Barbarians (1990/91) before fracturing left shoulder for second time. Last three Wales appearances have produced a total of just 13 minutes' action: coming on in the 79th minute of Australia's 63–6 win in Brisbane (21 Jul 1991), the 73rd minute of France's floodlit visit to Cardiff (4 Sep 1991), and the 75th minute of Wales' World Cup loss to Australia (12 Oct 1991)

Touchlines: Learning to speak Welsh and to play Spanish guitar

Player to watch: Jason Hewlett (Cardiff)

Player of the year: Mark Edwards (Cardiff)

Evans, I. C.   Wales

Full Name: Ieuan Cenydd Evans
1991/92 International category:
Wales Full
Club: Llanelli
Position: Wing
Height: 5'10½" **Weight:** 13st 2lbs
Occupation: Leasing executive with Autopia Contract Hire (Cardiff)
Born: Pontardulais, 21.3.64
Family: Single
Family links with rugby: Father (John) played for Aberavon
Former club: Carmarthen Quins
International debut: France 16, Wales 9, 1987
Five Nations' debut: As above
Best moment in rugby: Scoring try that clinched Test series for 1989 Lions in Australia
Worst moment in rugby: New South Wales 71, Wales 8, 1991
Most respected opponent: David Campese (Mediolanum Milan & Australia) – can never let him out of your sight
Serious injuries: Recurring dislocated shoulder, broken leg
Best memory last season: Two international wins in Championship, and winning Schweppes Challenge Cup with Llanelli for second consecutive season

Suggestions to improve rugby: *Off-field* – Reimburse employers for employees' time spent away from work playing rugby. Credit WRU for moving in right direction

Notable landmarks in rugby career: Named Wales' 103rd captain when appointed under the management of Robert Norster and Alan Davies prior to 1991 World Cup. Playing career severely hampered by injury – five dislocations and two operations. Played all three Tests in 1989 Lions series win (2–1) in Australia, scoring series-clinching try in final Test in Sydney (won 19–18, 15 Jul 1989). On return was forced to miss whole of 1989/90 season through injury. Played in five matches in 1987 World Cup, scoring four tries in 40–9 defeat of Canada, and contributed one (against Western Samoa) to Wales' 1991 Cup challenge. Scored six tries for Wales B in 1985 defeat of Spain (80–9) at Bridgend

Touchlines: Tennis, cricket, squash, golf

Player to watch: Rupert Moon (Llanelli)

Player of the year: Dewi Morris (England)

	apps	pts
Wales B (1985)		
Last Season	0 caps	0
Career	3 caps	28
Wales (1987)		
Last Season	9 caps	4
Career	31 caps	32
Lions 1989	3 Tests	4

Caps (31): **1987** F, E(a), S, I(a) wc-I(b), C, E(b), NZ, A **1988** E, S, I, F, NZ(1,2) **1989** I, F, E. Lions-A(1,2,3) **1991** E, S, I, F(a), A(a), F(b) wc-WS, Arg, A(b) **1992** I, F, E, S

Points (32 – 8t): **1987** I(a:1t) wc-C(4t) **1988** S(1t), F(1t) **1989** Lions-A(3:1t) **1991** wc-WS(1t)

Eric Champ is contained by England's Richard Hill (left) and Will Carling (right) during the World Cup quarter-final tie in Paris, which England won 19–10

Evans, I. L.   Wales

Full Name: Iwan Luc Evans
1991/92 International category:
Wales Full
Club: Bridgend
Positions: Fullback, centre
Height: 5′8″ **Weight:** 12st
Occupation: Student at Cardiff
Dental School
Born: Treherbert, 13.6.71
Family: Single
Family links with rugby: Father
(Gwyn) played for Swansea
Former clubs: Treherbert,
Treorchy, Llanelli
International debut: Wales 9,
France 22, 1991
Best moment in rugby: Learning
of selection to tour with Wales to
Australia (1991)
Worst moments in rugby:
Breaking leg (January 1991), and
Australia tour (major
disappointment)
Most embarrassing moment:
Having to run across field to catch
kick while changing shorts, playing
for Bridgend against Gloucester
Most respected opponent: Allan
Bateman (ex-Neath & Wales)

	apps	pts
Wales U-21 (**1990**)		
Last Season	1 cap	4
Career	3 caps	11
Wales (**1991**)		
Last Season	1 cap	0
Career	1 cap	0

Caps (1): 1991 F(b:R)
Points: Nil

Biggest influences on career:
Father, schoolmasters Arwel Owen (Rhydfelen) and Robin Barlow
(Llandovery College)
Other sporting achievements: Welsh Schools 400m hurdler
Best memories last season: Winning first senior cap; helping Bridgend beat
champions-to-be Swansea in the League
Suggestions to improve rugby: *On-field* – Reduce the number of matches
at the top end and, therefore, the number of teams in the top division.
Ridiculous in Wales that we are being advised to play less and yet the size of
divisions is being increased. This season (1992/93) I reckon that 32 out of
the 35 Saturdays will play host to big games for me
Notable landmarks in rugby career: Represented Wales Schools (U-18) in
1989 and Wales U-21 team for last three seasons, since the age of 18; twice

against Scotland (1990–91), and once against Ireland last season when scored try (won 22–15, Newport 16 Oct 1991). Scored two tries for WRU President's (U-21) XV in 34–13 win over New Zealand Youth XV at Pontypridd (8 Nov 1990). Included on Wales B bench for 34–12 defeat of Netherlands (2 Dec 1990), and toured Australia with senior squad (1991: playing in 35–7 win over Queensland Country, Rockhampton 17 Jul 1991) before making senior bow as a 78th-minute replacement for captain Ieuan Evans in non-Championship international against France under the Arms Park floodlights (4 Sep 1991). Included in Wales' preliminary World Cup squad but discarded when coach Alan Davies trimmed to 26 names. Helped Bridgend beat Wales in 1990/91. Returned to Bridgend in January 1991 after brief spell at Llanelli

Player to watch: Robert Howley (Bridgend)
Player of the year: Mickey Skinner (England)

Fitzgerald, D. C.   Ireland

Full Name: Desmond Christopher Fitzgerald
1991/92 International category: Ireland Full
Club: De La Salle Palmerston
Position: Prop
Height: 6'1" **Weight:** 16st 10lbs
Occupation: Sales engineer with Digital International
Born: Dublin, 20.12.57
Family: Luke (son), Rachel and Rebecca (daughters)
Former clubs: Dublin Univ, Lansdowne
International debut: England 12, Ireland 9, 1984
Five Nations' debut: As above
Best moment in rugby: Playing for 1986 Lions in Cardiff
Worst moment in rugby: Being dropped by Ireland for first time after 1984 season (missed 1985 Triple Crown)
Most respected opponent: Jeff Whitefoot (ex-Cardiff & Wales)
Serious injuries: Dislocated both shoulders, broke ribs, torn hamstrings
Other sporting achievements: 1980/81 British and Irish Universities heavyweight boxing champion. Ex-competitive wrestler

Suggestions to improve rugby:
Off-field – Address pro-am dilemma. With levels of expectation constantly increasing, administrators must decide how to reward players of the future

Notable landmarks in rugby career: Injuries postponed Ireland B debut for three years, finally arriving in 1983 against Scotland B (lost 13–22, Melrose). Had toured with Ireland to South Africa two years previously (1981), as well as Romania with Leinster in 1980. Two full caps in 1984 preceded two seasons out of the limelight, before he returned for the 1986 Five Nations' championship, and also played for the Lions at Cardiff against the Rest of the World (lost 7–15, 16 Apr 1986) in a match to celebrate the centenary of the International Board. An almost permanent fixture in the Irish XV between 1986–88 (including the 1987 World Cup). Has represented Ireland at loose and tight-head. In 1990/91 was selected for Ireland while playing for Lansdowne second XV. Toured Namibia (1991) and played four of Ireland's five 1991 World Cup matches

Touchlines: Golf (handicap 18), shooting

Player to watch: Jim Staples (London Irish)

	apps	pts
Ireland B (**1983**)		
Last Season	0 caps	0
Ireland (**1984**)		
Last Season	7 caps	0
Career	34 caps	0
Lions 1986		

Caps (34): **1984** E, S **1986** W, E, S, Ro **1987** E, S, F, W(a) wc-W(b), C, A **1988** S, F, W, E(a) **1989** NZ(R) **1990** E, S, F, W, Arg **1991** F, W, E, S(a), Na(1,2) wc-Z, S(b), A **1992** W, S(R)

Points: Nil

George 'Doddie' Weir drives into trouble against Ireland. Scotland teammate Neil Edwards (left) is on hand to offer his assistance

69

Fitzgerald, J. J. Ireland

Full Name: John Joseph Fitzgerald
1991/92 International category:
Ireland Full
Club: Young Munster
Position: Loosehead prop
Height: 5′11″ **Weight:** 16st 4lbs
Occupation: Business development
executive with Lombard and Ulster
Banking
Born: London, 31.8.61
Family: Caroline (wife), Nicole
(daughter) and Killian (son)
Family links with rugby: Younger
brother (Mick) plays for Shannon
Former club: Waikato, Tokoroa (NZ)
International debut: Ireland 22,
Scotland 18, 1988
Five Nations' debut: As above
Best moment in rugby: Scoring try
against Scotland in 1990 Five
Nations' Championship
Worst moment in rugby: Being
trounced 25–6 by France in Paris in
1988
Most respected opponent: Pascal
Ondarts (Biarritz & France)
Biggest influence on career: Tony
Graint (Young Munster coach)
Other sporting achievements:
Played Hurling and Gaelic
Best memory last season: Beating

	apps	pts
Ireland B (**1990**)		
Last Season	1 cap	0
Career	2 caps	0
Ireland (**1988**)		
Last Season	1 cap	0
Career	10 caps	4

Caps (10): **1988** S, F **1990** S, F, W
    1991 F, W, E, S(a) wc-J
Points (4 – 1t): **1990** S(1t)

Cork Constitution to retain status in All-Ireland League division one
Suggestions to improve rugby: *On-field* – Concentrate on general levels of
fitness. *Off-field* – Work on attitude and approach to big-day games. Reimburse
players for time lost to rugby commitments
Notable landmarks in rugby career: Started playing rugby aged 16, did not
represent Ireland at age-group level. Spent a season playing in New Zealand
with Tokoroa. Enjoyed living out there for four months during summer 1989
– way of life and manner in which they approach rugby was very interesting.
Won 1990/91 Munster Senior Cup with Young Munster. Included in Irish
World Cup squad as deputy to first-choice loosehead to Nick Popplewell,

playing in 32–16 over Japan. Captained Ireland B last season in 47–15 defeat by England B (Richmond, 31 Jan 1992)
Touchlines: Weight lifting, jogging
Player to watch: Richard Wallace (Garryowen)
Player of the year: Philip Danaher (Ireland)

Fitzgibbon, M. J.   Ireland

Full Name: Michael Joseph Fitzgibbon
1991/92 International category: Ireland Full
Club: Shannon
Position: Openside flanker
Height: 6'1½" **Weight:** 14st 7lbs
Occupation: Maintenance engineer with Waterford Glass
Born: Askeaton, County Limerick, 2.4.66
Family: Single
Family links with rugby: Uncle (Basil) played for Munster
Former club: Trinity
International debut: Ireland 15, Wales 16, 1992
Five Nations' debut: As above
Notable landmarks in rugby career: Won six caps in two seasons of representing Irish Schools. Also played for Irish Universities, whilst at Dublin Univ, before getting Ireland B call-up for 24–10 win over England (Old Belvedere, 1 Mar 1991). Second B cap (Edinburgh 28 Dec 1991) yielded a Fitzgibbon try, in the 29–19 win over Scotland B. Won a Munster Senior Cup medal with Shannon in 1986. Included in 44-man preliminary Ireland squad for 1991 World Cup but was omitted from final selection. Broke into full side in 1992 Five Nations' Championship when was an ever present at openside flanker, and then went on summer tour to New Zealand

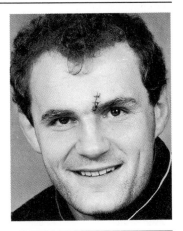

	apps	pts
Ireland U-25 (**1988**)		
Last Season	0 caps	0
Ireland B (**1991**)		
Last Season	1 cap	4
Career	2 caps	4
Ireland (**1992**)		
Last Season	4 caps	0
1992	Tour to New Zealand	
Career	4 caps	0

Caps (4): **1992** W, E, S, F
Points: Nil

Ford, S. P. Wales

Full Name: Stephen Paul Ford
1991/92 International category:
Wales Full
Club: Cardiff
Position: Right wing
Height: 6' **Weight:** 12st 7lbs
Occupation: Carpet fitter
Born: Cardiff, 15.8.65
Family: Single with son
Family links with rugby: Phil
(brother) plays Rugby League for
Leeds and Great Britain
Former clubs: Glamorgan
Wanderers, Rumney
International debut: Ireland 14,
Wales 8, 1990
Five Nations' debut: As above
Best moment in rugby: Scoring try
in first International
Worst moment in rugby: Being
banned for two and a half years after
having Rugby League trial with
Leeds
Most respected opponent: John
Kirwan (Auckland & New Zealand)
Serious injuries: Damaged Achilles
tendon
Suggestions to improve rugby:
Bring money into game

	apps	pts
Wales B (**1989**)		
Last Season	0 caps	0
Career	2 caps	12
Wales (**1990**)		
Last Season	1 cap	0
Career	8 caps	8

Caps (8): 1990 I, Na(1,2), Ba **1991** E, S, I, A

Points (8 – 2t): **1990** I(1t) **1991** S(1t)

Notable landmarks in rugby career: Set Welsh try-scoring record by scoring seven for Wales B in 47–0 win over Saskatchewan on 1989 Canadian tour. Played both 'tests' in Namibia on 1990 summer tour and held his place on Wales wing through three-quarters of the 1991 Five Nations' Championship (scoring one of only three Wales tries during the campaign, in the 12–32 loss to Scotland at Murrayfield), before losing out when Arthur Emyr returned for the final game against France. Toured Australia with Wales in 1991 and wore the No.11 jersey during the 6–63 Test defeat. Did not feature thereafter, despite being included in the World Cup squad and warming the bench for the Argentina game in Cardiff

Fox, D. C.   Wales

Full Name: David Clifford Fox
1991/92 International category:
Wales Full (bench)
Club: Llanelli
Position: Hooker
Height: 5'9" **Weight:** 13st 7lbs
Occupation: Fireman at Llanelli
Fire Station
Born: Swansea, 4.12.59
Family: Sian (wife), Lynsey
(daughter) and Matthew (son)
Family links with rugby: Anthony
(brother) plays for Gorseinon
Former club: Bonymaen
Best moment in rugby: Beating
Swansea last season to win
Schweppes Challenge Cup for
fourth time
Worst moment in rugby: Losing to
Swansea last season in Heineken
League decider at St Helens
Most respected opponent: Ian
Watkins (Cardiff & Wales)

	apps	pts
Wales (1991/92)	4 reps	

Biggest influence on career: Coaching set-up at Llanelli RFC
Serious injuries: Broken ankle (1987), damaged shoulder (missed 1989/90
season after operation)
Best memory last season: Being involved with Welsh squad in Five Nations'
Championship
Suggestions to improve rugby: *On-field* – Referees must officiate scrum-half
put-ins more firmly. There are far too many crooked feeds. Overall refereeing
standards need improving. *Off-field* – Players' employers must be treated
better. The game is so much more professional nowadays and the Unions
must realise that players cannot meet the increased demands on them without
sympathetic employers. Hence, the need to keep them sweet. It is a nonsense
that employers should be required to subsidise their rugby-playing employees
when the Unions are bringing in so much money from international gate
receipts etc
Notable landmarks in rugby career: Bench reserve for Wales 16-Group
against England. Joined Llanelli from Bonymaen in 1983 and has since played
in four Cup-winning sides (1985, 1988, 1991 and 1992). Selected for Wales
B against France four years ago but had to withdraw with cracked bone in
ankle. First selected for senior squad in 1988 but did not feature, and missed

virtually all of the following season through injury. Included in Wales' 1991 World Cup squad and on bench throughout 1992 Five Nations' Championship, but is still looking for his first cap. A member of the team which won the Fire Brigade World Sevens titles in Canada and Memphis. Represented Barbarians against Leicester (Dec 1990)

Touchlines: Keep-fit, volleyball
Player to watch: Andrew Lamerton (Llanelli)
Player of the year: Richard Webster (Wales)

Francis, N. P. Ireland

Full Name: Neil Patrick Francis
1991/92 International category:
Ireland Full
Club: Blackrock College
Position: Lock
Height: 6'6" **Weight:** 17st 3lbs
Occupation: Banker with
Gatehouse Leasing
Born: Dublin, 17.3.64
Family: Single
Former clubs: London Irish, Manly
(Aus)
International debut: Ireland 32,
Tonga 9, 1987 (World Cup)
Five Nations' debut: Scotland 37,
Ireland 21, 1989
Best moment in rugby: Winning
1981 Schools Cup final with
Blackrock
Worst moment in rugby: Being
dropped by Ireland on 1989 North
American tour
Most respected opponent:
Laurent Rodriguez (Dax & France)
Serious injuries: Broken vertebrae
(out for two years)
Other sporting achievements:
Javelin for Ireland (national junior
and senior champion)
Best memory last season: Coming
so close to beating Australia in the
World Cup

	apps	pts
Ireland U-25 (**1986**)		
Last Season	0 caps	0
Ireland (**1987**)		
Last Season	9 caps	0
Career	19 caps	4

Caps (19): 1987 wc-T, A 1988 WS, It 1989 S 1990 E, F, W 1991 E, S(a), Na(1,2) wc-Z, J, S(b), A 1992 W, E, S

Points (4 – 1t): 1988 WS(1t)

Notable landmarks in rugby career: Represented Irish Schools five times (1981–82), but back injury meant no representative rugby for four years from the age of 19, by which time he had already won Leinster Senior Cup medal with Blackrock. Did not represent Leinster until 1986. Rejoined Blackrock from London Irish in 1989. Made full Ireland debut in 1987 World Cup but not called upon again until October 1988 when scored only international try to date against touring Western Samoans. Sole Irish representative in Home Unions team which played Rest of Europe at Twickenham in 1990 Romania Appeal match. Ever present last season, including each 1991 World Cup-tie, until final Five Nations' match in Paris when Brian Rigney returned against France. Toured Namibia (1991) with Ireland but missed trip to New Zealand (1992)

Galwey, M. J. Ireland

Full Name: Michael Joseph Galwey
1991/92 International category:
Ireland Full
Club: Shannon
Position: Lock
Height: 6′4″ **Weight:** 17st
Occupation: Sales representative with Hibernian Business Equipment
Born: County Kerry, 8.10.66
Family: Single
Former club: Castle Island
International debut: Ireland 13, France 21, 1991
Five Nations' debut: As above
Best moment in rugby: Winning first cap against French in Dublin (2 Feb 1991)
Worst moment in rugby: Losing 1988/89 Munster Cup final to Constitution
Most respected opponent: Donal Lenihan (Cork Constitution & Ireland)
Serious injuries: Damaged Achilles tendon
Other sporting achievements: Winner of All-Ireland Gaelic Football medal with Kerry in 1986
Notable landmarks in rugby career: Selected to play with Munster U-20 whilst a member of Castle Island, he took possession of a Munster Senior Cup medal in three successive seasons, and was awarded a Shannon RFC cap for the achievement. Played for Ireland U-25s in wins over US Eagles (12–10,

Limerick 10 Mar 1990) and Spain (36–17, Limerick 8 Sep 1990). First called into Irish squad for 1988 tour of France but did not break into the senior team until the 1991 Five Nations' Championship, playing against France and Wales having warmed bench in season-opener against Argentina. Made B debut in 1989 against Scotland at Murrayfield (drew 22–22, 9 Dec 1989) and added caps against Argentina (scoring try), Scotland and England in 1990/91. Toured with Ireland to Namibia (1991) and New Zealand (1992)

Touchlines: Fishing the Kerry Lakes

	apps	pts
Ireland U-25 (**1990**)		
Last Season	0 caps	0
Career	2 caps	0
Ireland B (**1989**)		
Last Season	0 caps	0
Career	4 caps	4
Ireland (**1991**)		
Last Season	5 caps	0
1992	Tour to New Zealand	
Career	7 caps	0

Caps (7): **1991** F, W, Na(2R) wc-J
1992 E, S, F

Points: Nil

Geoghegan, S. P. Ireland

Full Name: Simon Patrick Geoghegan
1991/92 International category: Ireland Full
Club: London Irish
Position: Wing
Height: 6′ **Weight:** 13st
Occupation: Articles clerk with Rosling King
Born: Barnet, Herts, 1.9.68
Family: Single
Former club: Wasps (Colts)
International debut: Ireland 13, France 21, 1991
Five Nations' debut: As above
Best moment in rugby: Scoring try on second full international appearance for Ireland in 21–21 draw with Wales (16 Feb 1991)

Worst moment in rugby: Seeing Australia's Michael Lynagh score last-gasp try to deny us victory in 1991 World Cup quarter-final
Most respected opponent: Eddie Saunders (Rugby)

Best memory last season: London Irish retaining Courage League division one status

Suggestions to improve rugby: *On-field* – Alter amount of points awarded for penalty goals as this tends to devalue the worth of a try which, after all, is the essence of rugby union. *Off-field* – Players should be properly remunerated for time spent training at international squad sessions etc

Notable landmarks in rugby career: Represented Ireland at U-25, Students, B and Full level. Quickly

	apps	pts
Ireland U-25 (**1990**)		
Last Season	0 caps	0
Career	1 cap	4
Ireland B (**1990**)		
Last Season	0 caps	0
Career	1 cap	4
Ireland (**1991**)		
Last Season	7 caps	4
Career	11 caps	16

Caps (11): **1991** F, W, E, S(a), Na(1) wc-Z, S(b), A **1992** E, S, F

Points (16 – 4t): **1991** W(1t), E(1t), S(a:1t) wc-Z(1t)

rose to prominence, with try-scoring debuts for Ireland U-25 (36–17 v. Spain, Limerick 8 Sep 1990) and Ireland B (27–12 v. Argentina, Limerick 20 Oct 1990). Quality Inter-Provincial performances for Connacht sped his progress into the senior national XV, for whom he opposed the Bayonne Express, Patrice Lagisquet, on his debut against France at Lansdowne Road (2 Feb 1991). Scored tries in next three internationals, against Wales, Ireland and Scotland. Toured Namibia (1991), playing in first Test, and claimed fourth Ireland try in 55–11 World Cup defeat of Zimbabwe

Touchlines: Cinema, reading, swimming, tennis, cricket

Player to watch: Richard Wallace (Garryowen)

Wade Dooley celebrates scoring against Wales on his 50th appearance for England. Mickey Skinner shares in the moment

Gibbs, I. S.   Wales

Full Name: Ian Scott Gibbs
1991/92 International category:
Wales Full
Club: Swansea
Position: Centre
Height: 5'10" **Weight:** 13st 4lbs
Occupation: TV researcher at
Rugby Vision Ltd
Born: Bridgend, 23.1.71
Family: Single
Family links with rugby: None.
Father (Graham) is a former pole
vaulter and international gymnast
Former clubs: Pencoed, Bridgend,
Neath
International debut: Wales 6,
England 25, 1991
Five Nations' debut: As above
Best moment in rugby: Welsh
victories over Ireland and Scotland
last season
Worst moment in rugby: Losing to
Western Samoa in the 1991 World
Cup after improved second half
performance
Most respected opponent:
Philippe Sella (Agen & France)
Biggest influence on career:
Father – kept me on the right track
without ever pressuring me

	apps	pts
Wales B (1990)		
Last Season	0 caps	0
Career	1 cap	4
Wales (1991)		
Last Season	9 caps	0
Career	13 caps	0

Caps (13): 1991 E, S, I, F(a), A(a), F(b) wc-WS, Arg, A(b) 1992 I, F, E, S

Points: Nil

Serious injuries: General wear and
tear from playing 18 matches for Wales and 30-odd league games in 12-month
period
Other sporting achievements: Play tennis for club in Bridgend
Best memory last season: Scoring hat-trick of tries on Swansea debut at
Cardiff (joined club in order to play a more open and clinical 15-man game)
Suggestions to improve rugby: *Off-field* – In order to attain a better standard,
players need a lot more time to train. Therefore, either players/employers need
to be subsidised. I train as much as I can (all aspects) yet I still do not feel
up to the standards of the Southern Hemisphere nations or even England
Notable landmarks in rugby career: Made full debut against England aged
19: first pupil of Ysgol Gyfun Llanharry to be capped by Wales. Switched to

Swansea in January 1992 in time to share in Championship win, having previously played with Neath, Bridgend (toured USA with Brewery Field club in 1990) and Pencoed, with whom won seven Welsh Youth caps (over two seasons) and captained side in 1989/90. Quickly progressed up the representative ladder on joining Neath, marking Wales B debut in Holland with try in 34–12 win (Leiden, 2 Dec 1990) before being called into the full side for the 1991 Five Nations' Championship. Voted youngest-ever Welsh Player of Year (1990/91). Toured Australia with Wales (1991), appearing in five of the six matches, and played throughout 1991 World Cup and 1992 Five Nations' campaign. Rejected massive Rugby League bid in May 1992 for second consecutive season

Touchlines: Boxing, music, golf, tennis
Player to watch: Scott Quinnell (Llanelli)
Player of the year: Will Carling (England)

Gray, C. A. Scotland

Full Name: Christopher Anthony Gray
1991/92 International category: Scotland Full
Club: Nottingham
Position: Lock
Height: 6'5" **Weight:** 16st 12lbs
Occupation: Dental surgeon
Born: Haddington, 11.7.60
Family: Judith (wife) and Jamie (son)
Family links with rugby: Older brother (Laurence) played and introduced me to game
Former club: Edinburgh Academicals
International debut: Scotland 23, Wales 7, 1989
Five Nations' debut: As above
Best moment in rugby: Winning 1990 Five Nations' Grand Slam
Worst moment in rugby: Scotland's 6–9 1991 World Cup semi-final defeat by England
Most embarrassing moment: Destroying half-way marker post when running out at Kingsholm
Most respected opponents: Paul Ackford (Harlequins & England) and Gary Whetton (Auckland & New Zealand)

Biggest influences on career: Coaches Ian McGeechan, Jim Telfer (both Scotland) and Alan Davies (Nottingham)

Serious injuries: Broken collarbone (1980), Achilles tendonitis, torn calf muscle

Other sporting achievements: Golf (handicap 6)

Best memory last season: Beating Western Samoa 28–6 in 1991 World Cup quarter-finals

Suggestions to improve rugby: *On-field* – Referees should keep in touch (verbally) with captains.

	apps	pts
Scotland B (**1986**)		
Last Season	0 caps	0
Career	4 caps	0
Scotland (**1989**)		
Last Season	5 caps	0
1992	Tour to Australia	
Career	22 caps	12

Caps (22): **1989** W, E, I, F, Fj, Ro **1990** I, F, W, E, NZ(1,2), Arg **1991** F, W, E(a), I(a) wc-J, I(b), WS, E(b), NZ

Points (12 – 3t): **1989** Fj(1t) **1990** NZ(1:1t), Arg(1t)

Organise pre-season get-togethers between referees, coaches and administrators. Officials still too inconsistent in their interpretations. *Off-field* – Better communications between top administrators and players. Get amateur laws properly sorted out. What can we do? Surely everything is rugby-related

Notable landmarks in rugby career: Debut for Edinburgh Academicals aged 18. County debut for Notts/Lincs/Derby in 1985 English County Championship final. Captained Anglo-Scots in 1987 and 1990 Scottish Inter-District Championship. Won four caps for Scotland B. Captained Scotland XV against Goshawks on 1988 tour of Zimbabwe (played four of five games, scoring try in each of first three games). Captained Nottingham (1989–91). Scored first tries for Scotland during 1989/90 season against Fiji and New Zealand (first Test) and added a third in 49–3 win over Argentina at Murrayfield (1990/91). Member of Scotland's 1990 Grand Slam side. Injury after 1991 World Cup kept him out of 1992 Five Nations' Championship but returned in time for summer tour to Australia

Touchlines: Golf, tennis, relaxing hard

Player to watch: Martin Pepper (Nottingham)

Player of the year: David Campese (Australia)

Griffiths, M.   Wales

Full Name: Michael Griffiths
1991/92 International category:
Wales Full
Club: Cardiff
Position: Loosehead prop
Height: 6′ **Weight:** 16st 7lbs
Occupation: Self-employed builder
with G D Griffiths, Rhondda (will go
anywhere!)
Born: Tonypandy, 18.3.62
Family: Anne (wife), Joel Michael
and Luc Rhys (sons)
Family links with rugby: Brother
plays for Ystrad Rhondda
Former clubs: Ystrad Rhondda,
Bridgend
International debut: Wales 24,
Western Samoa 6, 1988
Five Nations' debut: Scotland 23,
Wales 7, 1989
Best moment in rugby: Winning
first Welsh cap against touring
Samoans (12 Nov 1988)
Worst moment in rugby: Wales
losing 6–34 to England at
Twickenham (18 Feb 1990)
Most embarrassing moment:
Twice having to change shorts
against France last season in front of
the Princess of Wales
Most respected opponents: Jeff
Probyn (Wasps & England: for his
technique) and Iain Milne (Heriot's
FP & Scotland: for his size and
strength)

	apps	pts
Wales B (**1988**)		
Last Season	0 caps	0
Career	1 cap	0
Wales (**1988**)		
Last Season	8 caps	0
Career	22 caps	0
Lions 1989		

Caps (22): 1988 WS, Ro 1989 S, I, F,
E, NZ 1990 F, E, Na(1,2), Ba
1991 I, F(a), F(b) wc-WS, Arg,
A(b) 1992 I, F, E, S

Points: Nil

Biggest influence on career: Ian Stephens and Merideth James (Bridgend)
Serious injuries: Broken ribs, fractured arm, twisted shoulder muscles,
damaged ankle and knee ligaments
Other sporting achievements: Accomplished soccer player (centre-back)
Suggestions to improve rugby: *On-field* – Abandon new ruck and mauling
law. Good mauling is an art. *Off-field* – Look after players better. They are
the people who draw the crowds

Notable landmarks in rugby career: Started career in back-row but moved to front of scrum shortly before joining Bridgend. Moved to Cardiff for new challenges and found them: playing for Crawshays, Wales B (in 12–18 loss to France B, Brecon 29 Oct 1988), Wales and 1989 Lions. Despite failing to oust David Sole in Test side, he played in six of the Lions' 12 games, including the final game (as a replacement) against the ANZAC XV. Played at tighthead against Barbarians (6 Oct 1990). Only Welsh representative in Home Unions' team which played Rest of Europe at Twickenham on behalf of Romania Appeal (won 43–18, 22 Apr 1990). Missed the 1991 tour to Australia but was quickly recalled for the duration of the World Cup and 1992 Five Nations' Championship
Touchlines: Mountain biking
Player to watch: Scott Quinnell (Llanelli)
Player of the year: Emyr Lewis (Wales)

Guscott, J. C. England

Full Name: Jeremy Clayton Guscott
1991/92 International category:
England Full
Club: Bath
Position: Centre
Height: 6'1" **Weight:** 13st 5lbs
Occupation: Marketing
co-ordinator with British Gas
Born: Bath, 7.7.65
Family: Jayne (wife)
International debut: Romania 3,
England 58, 1989
Five Nations' debut: England 23,
Ireland 0, 1990
Best moment in rugby: Try scored
for 1989 Lions v. Australia in second
Test

Worst moment in rugby: Being
dropped by Bath for semi-finals of
1989/90 Pilkington Cup
Most embarrassing moment: Any time I miss a tackle
Most respected opponent: All of them
Biggest influence on career: S J Halliday (Harlequins & England)
Best memory last season: Watching Stuart Barnes' winning dropped goal in the final seconds (of extra time) of the Pilkington Cup final
Suggestions to improve rugby: *On-field* – Reduce the amount of offences

in the lineout. There must be 100-odd, when there should be no more than five or six, and it is such an annoying part of the game. Scrap 90-degree scrum wheel law. *Off-field* – Allow players to earn money through off-field activities. The situation is improving but there remains no overall consensus: each Union applies the rules as they see fit. The International Board should insist the same applies worldwide, but they seem to back away from confrontation

Notable landmarks in rugby career: Started career with Bath's mini-section as a wing, aged seven. Meteoric rise in 1989 brought two caps for England B, three tries on full England debut in Bucharest, and one invitation from the British Lions (before capped by England). Scored crucial try in Brisbane (second Test: won 19–12, 8 Jul 1989) to bring Lions back into the series which they went on to win 2–1. Ever present throughout England's back-to-back Grand Slams (1991–92) and wore No.12 jersey in 1991 World Cup final, having previously toured Australia (1991). Toured New Zealand with World XV (Apr 1992), playing in first two Tests, including famous 28–14 first Test defeat of All Blacks. Collected fourth Pilkington Cup winners' medal last season (1987–89–90–92)

Touchlines: Golf (handicap 15)

Player to watch: Ben Clarke (Bath)

Player of the year: Jeff Probyn (England)

	apps	pts
England B (**1988**)		
Last Season	0 caps	0
Career	2 caps	0
England (**1989**)		
Last Season	11 caps	19
Career	22 caps	55
Lions 1989	2 Tests	4

Caps (22): **1989** Ro, Fj. Lions-A(2,3) **1990** I, F, W, S, Arg(b) **1991** W, S(a), I, F(a), Fj, A(a) wc-NZ, It, F(b), S(b), A(b) **1992** S, I, F, W

Points (55 – 13t,1dg): **1989** Ro(3t), Fj(1t). Lions-A(2:1t) **1990** I(1t), F(1t), S(1t), Arg(b:2t) **1991** A(a:1t) wc-It(2t) **1992** S(1dg), I(1t)

Haag, M.   England

Full Name: Martin Haag
1991/92 International category:
England B
Club: Bath
Position: Lock
Height: 6'5½" **Weight:** 16st 7lbs
Occupation: Financial advisor with
Abbey National Financial Services
(Bristol)
Born: Chelmsford, 28.7.68
Family: Single
Former club: St Ives
International debut: Spain 3,
England B 34, 1992
Five Nations' debut: None
Best moment in rugby: Winning
1991/92 League and Cup double
with Bath
Most respected opponent: There
is no-one I really respect, but I idolise
Gary Whetton (Auckland & New
Zealand)
Biggest influence on career: Jack
Rowell (Bath & England B coach)
Best memory last season: Breaking
into England B set-up

	apps	pts
England B **(1992)**		
Last Season	2 caps	4
1992	Tour to New Zealand	
Career	2 caps	4

Suggestions to improve rugby: *On-field* – Disagree with new ruck/maul law. Will encourage negative tactics, with some sides intentionally preventing the ball from coming out. *Off-field* – Game should be profiled better; take a leaf out of Australian Rugby League who, with Tina Turner, produced a magnificent promotional video. Missed a great opportunity during 1991 World Cup to really sell the game

Notable landmarks in rugby career: Represented Cornwall at the tender age of 18. Two years after turning out for England Schools (1984/85) he switched allegiances from St Ives to Bath and credits the move as the turning point in his career. Voted Bath's most promising player in 1990/91 (first full season with club), he further enhanced his reputation last season in the colours of England B, playing against Spain (Madrid, 19 Jan 1992) and Ireland B (won 47–15, Richmond 31 Jan 1992), scoring a try against the Irish. Played 25 times for Bath last season, including Pilkington Cup final win against Harlequins

Touchlines: Sun, sea and surfing

Hall, M. R.   Wales

Full Name: Michael Robert Hall
1991/92 International category:
Wales Full
Club: Cardiff
Positions: Centre, wing
Height: 6'1" **Weight:** 14st 10lbs
Occupation: Surveyor with Cooke
and Arkwright (Cardiff)
Born: Bridgend, 13.10.65
Family: Single
Former clubs: Bridgend, Maesteg,
Cambridge Univ
International debut: New Zealand
52, Wales 3, 1988
Five Nations' debut: Scotland 23,
Wales 7, 1989
Best moments in rugby: Selection
for 1989 British Lions. 1990 Hong
Kong Sevens with Barbarians
Worst moment in rugby: Every
time I go to Twickenham!
Most embarrassing moment:
England 34, Wales 6 (17 Feb 1990,
record defeat at Twickenham)
Most respected opponent:
Philippe Sella (Agen & France)
Biggest influence on career: Brian
Nicholas (coach at Bridgend)
Serious injuries: Hamstring tears
Other sporting achievements:
Schoolboy honours at county level in
soccer, basketball and cricket
Best memory last season:
Returning to winning ways with

	apps	pts
Wales B (1987)		
Last Season	0 caps	0
Career	1 cap	0
Wales (1988)		
Last Season	9 caps	0
Career	21 caps	8
Lions 1989	1 Test	0

Caps (21): **1988** NZ(R1,2), WS, Ro
     1989 S, I, F, E, NZ. Lions-A(1)
     1990 F, E, S **1991** A(a), F(b)
     wc-WS, Arg, A(b) **1992** I, F, E,
     S

Points (8 – 2t): **1989** S(1t), E(1t)

Wales. In particular, beating Scotland at Cardiff Arms Park because there was
more hinging on the result (the future of coach Alan Davies) than just beating
the Scots
Suggestions to improve rugby: *On-field* – Too many of the new rules are

half-measures. The mauling rule will encourage players to kill the ball. I cannot see that one lasting! The line-out shambles still needs addressing. *Off-field* – Market game properly. Clear up ambiguities in laws on amateurism. WRU are doing well (appointing marketing manager etc), but I would still like to see players better looked after, with more sympathy from the unions with regard to employers etc.

Notable landmarks in rugby career: Past captain of British Universities, Welsh Students and Wales U-21s. Two Blues at Cambridge (1987,88). Wales B against France in 1987 (lost 0–26). 1989 Lions against Australia in first Test (lost 12–30). Toured to New Zealand (1988) and Australia (1991) with Wales, and to South Africa (1989) with World XV. Scored winning try against England (Cardiff, 18.3.89, won 12–9) to deny them 1989 Five Nations' Championship. Tore hamstring on first appearance in 1990/91 season and having recovered, promptly did it again. Returned to international duty Down Under 1991 and was ever present thereafter, moving from centre to wing for 1992 Five Nations' campaign

Touchlines: Golf (handicap 18)

Player to watch: Stuart Davies (Swansea)

Player of the Year: Dewi Morris (England)

Halpin, G. F. Ireland

Full Name: Garrett Francis Halpin
1991/92 International category:
Ireland Full
Club: London Irish
Position: Tight-head prop
Height: 5'11" **Weight:** 17st 4lbs
Occupation: Post Graduate student
Born: Dublin, 14.2.66
Family: Carol (wife)
Former clubs: Rockwell College,
Wanderers
International debut: England 23,
Ireland 0, 1990
Five Nations' debut: As above
Best moment in rugby: Winning
first full cap, at Twickenham
Worst moment in rugby: Losing
place after above match
Most respected opponent: Tom
Clancy (London Irish & Ireland)
Other sporting achievements:

Irish International hammer thrower – American Indoor Collegiate champion. Represented Ireland in 1987 World Athletics Championships (Rome)

Best memory last season: Establishing regular spot at tighthead in 1992 Five Nations' Championship

Suggestions to improve rugby: *On-field* – Scrap 90-degree scrummage wheel law as it slows game down and inspires dubious tactics

	apps	pts
Ireland B (**1990**)		
Last Season	0 caps	0
Career	1 cap	0
Ireland (**1990**)		
Last Season	4 caps	0
Career	5 caps	0

Caps (5): **1990** E **1991** wc-J **1992** E, S, F

Points: Nil

Notable landmarks in rugby career: Joining Wanderers on return from a sports scholarship with Univ of Manhattan in New York. Played four times for Ireland Schools (1983–84). Toured North America with Ireland (1989), scoring try in defeat of Mid West in Chicago. Won 1989/90 Leinster League and Cup double with Wanderers. Lost his place after debut against England at Twickenham (lost 0–23, 20 Jan 1990) and had to be content turning out in Ireland U-25s' 36–17 win over Spain (Limerick, 8 Sep 1990) and Ireland B's 27–12 win over Argentina (Limerick, 20 Oct 1990). Ever present on Irish replacements' bench during 1991 Five Nations' Championship and failed to make Test team on summer tour to Namibia. Cap number two finally arrived against Japan in 1991 World Cup, before taking over from flu victim Des Fitzgerald to make three Championship appearances

Player to watch: Simon Geoghegan (London Irish)

A rare moment of joy for Ireland in the 1992 Five Nations' Championship as Ralph Keyes rounds Jason Leonard to score at Twickenham. England won 38–9

Hamilton, G. F.   Ireland

Full Name: Gordon Fredric Hamilton
1991/92 International category: Ireland Full
Club: Ballymena
Position: Flanker
Height: 6′ **Weight:** 14st 9lbs
Occupation: Shipping executive with Hamilton Shipping & Travel (Belfast)
Born: Belfast, 13.5.64
Family: Single
Family links with rugby: Father (Jimmy) played for NIFC
Former clubs: Blackheath, North of Ireland (NIFC)
International debut: Ireland 13, France 21, 1991
Five Nations' debut: As above
Best moment in rugby: Scoring my first try for Ireland
Worst moment in rugby: Losing to Australia in quarter-finals of 1991 World Cup
Most embarrassing moment: Fell over when running out for team photo prior to full debut. Cut thumb badly and needed stitches
Most respected opponent: John Jeffrey (Kelso & Scotland)
Biggest influence on career: My father

	apps	pts
Ireland B (**1990**)		
Last Season	0 caps	0
Career	1 cap	0
Ireland (**1991**)		
Last Season	5 caps	4
Career	9 caps	4

Caps (9): **1991** F, W, E, S(a), Na(2) wc-Z, J, S(b), A

Points (4 – 1t): **1991** wc-A(1t)

Serious injuries: Prolapsed disc (ruled me out of 1992 New Zealand tour)
Best memory last season: Lansdowne Road crowd's reaction to my try against Australia
Suggestions to improve rugby: *On-field* – None, game is in good shape. *Off-field* – Compensation for time lost from work to rugby. Clarify what players can and cannot do. No-one knows where they stand
Notable landmarks in rugby career: Prop at school and had final Ulster Schools trial. But was wrong shape for a prop. Played three seasons for Scottish Universities while at Dundee Univ. Also played for Blackheath (1986/87) and Kent before returning to join NIFC to become their first capped player for

ten years when he was capped against France (2 Feb 1991). Also represented Ulster (two years) and Ireland B, in 16–0 defeat of Scotland B (22 Dec 1990) at Ravenhill (having withdrawn injured from team to play Argentina on 20 Oct 1990). Ever present throughout 1991 Five Nations' Championship, he then toured Namibia before returning to play in all four of Ireland's World Cup fixtures. Prolapsed disc injury playing for Ulster against Munster ruled him out of 1992 Championship and summer tour to New Zealand

Touchlines: Sailing (half-tonners), golf
Player to watch: Dean McCartney (Ballymena)
Player of the year: Steve Smith (Ireland)

Harries, P. T. Wales

Full Name: Peter Timothy Harries
1991/92 International category: Wales U-21
Club: Pontypridd
Positions: Fullback, wing
Height: 6′2″ **Weight:** 13st
Occupation: Student at Cardiff Institute
Born: Harold Hill, 10.9.70
Family: Single
Family links with rugby: Father (Gwynne) and brother (David) played for London Welsh
Former clubs: Brentwood (Essex), South Glamorgan Institute
International debut (U-21): Wales 22, Ireland 15, 1991
Best moment in rugby: Getting picked to play for Wales U–21 last season
Worst moment in rugby: Losing to Swansea at St Helens in 1991/92 Heineken League match
Most respected opponent: Scott Gibbs (Swansea & Wales)
Other sporting achievements: English Schools Golf Final. 1990 Welsh Colleges 100m and 200m champion
Best memory last season: Scoring two tries against Maesteg and one against Scotland U-21

	apps	pts
Wales U-21 (1991)		
Last Season	2 caps	4
Career	2 caps	4

Suggestions to improve rugby: *On-field* – Reduce worth of penalties. Pleased that value of try has been increased

Notable landmarks in rugby career: Represented England at 18-Group (1989), Welsh Colleges (1990), British Colleges and Welsh Students (1991), and Wales U-21s (1991/92) against Ireland and in 28–19 win over Scotland at Stirling (18 Apr 92), scoring a try in the latter

Touchlines: Golf, all sports

Player to watch: Paul Jones (Neath)

Player of the year: David Campese (Australia)

Harrold, F. R.   Scotland

Full Name: Fraser Harrold

1991/92 International category: Scotland B

Club: London Scottish

Position: Centre

Height: 6′ **Weight:** 12st 7lbs

Occupation: Product manager with Campden Instruments

Born: Leicester, 11.8.66

Family: Single

Former clubs: Bournemouth, WLIHE

International debut (B): Scotland 19, Ireland 29, 1991

Best moment in rugby: Gaining promotion with 1991/92 Courage League division two champions London Scottish

Worst moment in rugby: Failing to gain promotion in 1990/91

Most respected opponent: Derek White (London Scottish & Scotland)

Serious injuries: Fractured cheekbone

	apps	pts
Scotland B (**1991**)		
Last Season	1 cap	0
Career	1 cap	0

Best memory last season: Clinching promotion against Sale

Other sporting achievements: Cricket for Bournemouth

Suggestions to improve rugby: *On-field* – Get kids more involved in game. *Off-field* – More professional administration, but stay clear of professionalism. Reimburse players/employers for time lost to rugby commitments

Notable landmarks in rugby career: Brought up in Bournemouth after ten years in Johannesburg, South Africa. Represented Middlesex whilst a student at West London Institute of Higher Education and declared Scottish allegiance (mother and father from Edinburgh) when joined Exiles in 1987. Helped London Scottish win 1991 Middlesex Sevens and, last season, represented Anglo-Scots against Edinburgh and a pre-World Cup Scotland XV, prior to Scotland B debut at Murrayfield against Ireland (28 Dec 1991). Unused replacement in Scotland B's 18–27 loss to France in Albi (3 Feb 1992)

Touchlines: Cricket

Players to watch: Graham Shiel (Melrose), Andy Nicol (Dundee HSFP)

Player of the year: Will Carling (England)

Hastings, A. G. Scotland

Full Name: Andrew Gavin Hastings

1991/92 International category: Scotland Full

Club: Watsonians

Position: Fullback

Height: 6′2″ **Weight:** 14st 9lbs

Occupation: Sports marketing executive with the Carnegie Partnership

Born: Edinburgh, 3.1.62

Family: Single

Family links with rugby: Clifford (father) played No.8 for Edinburgh XV and Watsonians; Scott (brother) plays for Watsonians, Scotland and British Lions; Graeme (brother) plays centre for Melbourne RFC and Victoria State (Australia); Ewan (brother) plays on wing for Watsonians

Former clubs: Cambridge Univ, London Scottish

International debut: Scotland 18, France 17, 1986

Five Nations' debut: As above

Best moments in rugby: Winning 1990 Grand Slam; 1989 British Lions' 2–1 series win in Australia; taking part in the 1992 New Zealand Rugby Football Union Centenary celebrations

Worst moment in rugby: Missing kick in front of posts against England in 1991 World Cup semi-final at Murrayfield (26 Oct 1991)

Most embarrassing moment: Missing plane home from Ireland after B international

Most respected opponent: The All Blacks, because of their record – I've only beaten them once in nine attempts (first Test: NZ 14, World XV 28, 1992)

Biggest influence on career: Parents (Clifford and Isobel)

Other sporting achievements: Appearing on TV in *Trail Blazers* (1988) and *Pro-Celebrity Golf* (1990)

Best memory last season: Flattening All Black prop Richard Loe during World Cup third/fourth place play-off at Cardiff

Suggestions to improve rugby: *On-field* – Pretty satisfied now that IRB have banned the scrum-half dummy pass and banned players from charging fullback immediately he has caught high ball; both of which I suggested in last year's edition. Get fit and stay fit. Practise your weaknesses. *Off-field* – Players should be looked after adequately – certainly not allowed to be disadvantaged for loss of earnings. You cannot differentiate between rugby related and non-related activities. There are more opportunities in these post-World Cup days. The SRU are good to players in Scotland, however there is a myth about the 1991 *Timberland* episode. England's players were banned from appearing in a match programme advertising the product, yet myself, brother Scott and David Sole were allowed to 'fill their boots' in the Scottish programme. However, all we received in return, along with every member of the team, was a pair of the company's boots – the England boys received **exactly** the same, despite the fact that their advertisement was aborted

Notable landmarks in rugby career: Won two Blues at Cambridge Univ (1984–85) and five caps for Scotland B before establishing Scottish record with six penalty goals on full debut (17 Jan 1986). Holds Scottish points-scoring record with 384 in 40 internationals, and Scottish record for most points scored in a Five Nations' season (52 in 1986). Toured with Scotland to North America (1985), the 1987 World Cup (where scored 62 points in four games), and New Zealand (1990). Scored go-ahead try in

	apps	pts
Scotland B (1983)		
Last Season	0 caps	0
Career	5 caps	
Scotland (1986)		
Last Season	9 caps	83
1992	Tour to Australia	
Career	40 caps	384
Lions 1986		
1989	3 Tests	28

Caps (40): **1986** F, W, E, I, Ro **1987** I, F, W, E wc-F, Z, R, NZ **1988** I, F, W, E, A **1989** Fj, Ro. Lions-A(1,2,3) **1990** I, F, W, E, NZ(1,2), Arg **1991** F, W, E(a), I(a) wc-J, I(b), WS, E(b), NZ **1992** E, I, F, W

Points (384 – 10t,58c,76p): **1986** F(6p), W(1t,1p), E(3c,5p), I(2p), Ro(3c,5p) **1987** I(1c), F(1c,4p), W(2c,2p), E(1c,2p) wc-F(4p), Z(1t,8c), Ro(2t,8c,1p), NZ(1p) **1988** I(2c,2p), F(1t,4p), W(4p), E(2p), A(1t,1c,1p) **1989** Fj(1t,4c,2p), Ro(3c,2p). Lions-A(1:2p), A(2:1t,1p), A(3:5p) **1990** F(1p), NZ(1:2c), NZ(2:2c,2p), Arg(1t,5c,1p) **1991** W(1c,2p), I(a:1t,1p) wc-J(1t,5c,2p), I(b:2c,3p), WS(2c,4p), E(b:2p), NZ(2p) **1992** E(1p), I(2c,2p), F(2p), W(1p)

second Test for 1989 Lions and 15 points in victorious decider. Kicked penalty for 1986 British Lions in 7–15 defeat by The Rest at Cardiff in match to celebrate centenary of IRFB. Played in '1989 Home Unions' 29–27 win over France (scored 22 points) and for '1989 Barbarians' against All Blacks. Led London Scottish to 1989/90 Courage League division three title, and Watsonians to promotion (1990/91) to McEwan's League division one. Represented World XV in three-Test series against All Blacks (NZRFU centenary celebrations), kicking penalty in 28–14 first Test win and scoring try in second. Captained Barbarians at 1991 Hong Kong Sevens

Touchlines: Playing golf with Sam Torrance against Ronan Rafferty and Peter Alliss – most nervous I've ever been in my life, including winning first cap at Murrayfield

Player to watch: Fraser Harold (London Scottish)

Player of the year: Andy Nicol (Scotland)

Hastings, S.   Scotland

Full Name: Scott Hastings
1991/92 International category: Scotland Full
Club: Watsonians
Positions: Centre, wing, full-back
Height: 6'1" **Weight:** 14st 4lbs
Occupation: Advertising account manager with Barker's, Scotland
Born: Edinburgh, 4.12.64
Family: Jenny (wife)
Family links with rugby: Clifford (father) played No.8 for Edinburgh XV and Watsonians; Gavin (brother) plays for Watsonians, Scotland and British Lions; Graeme (brother) plays centre for Melbourne RFC and Victoria State (Australia); Ewan (brother) plays on wing for Watsonians
Former club: Newcastle Northern
International debut: Scotland 19, France 18, 1986
Five Nations' debut: As above
Best moment in rugby: British Lions Test series win; winning 1990 Grand Slam with Scotland; playing in Hong Kong Sevens
Worst moment in rugby: Sustaining hamstring injury on first appearance in 1987 World Cup (55–28 win v. Romania)

93

Most embarrassing moments: My 1987 World Cup injury and discovering I did not have any Y-fronts to change into after a match

Most respected opponent: Ireland centre Brendan Mullin – have played opposite him since we captained our respective countries in a Schools international

Biggest influence on career: Family's involvement in rugby

Serious injuries: Torn hamstring, cartilage operation (1985), broken cheekbone (1987 v. Wales)

Best memory last season: Murrayfield crowd during the 1991 World Cup

Suggestions to improve rugby: *On-field* – Take all conversions in front of the posts. Put posts on dead-ball line so penalties cannot be kicked from the halfway line and teams will be more inclined to run the ball. Increase try-worth to six points. *Off-field* – Allow players to undertake any commercial activity. Why can we not wear and promote a certain brand of boots? It would not hurt anyone. Relax amateurism rules totally as IRB have no apparent jurisdiction

Notable landmarks in rugby career: Captained Watsonians in 1989/90. With Gavin became the first Scottish brothers to play together in a Lions' Test. Shares with Sean Lineen the world record for an international centre partnership of 26 games prior to the 1992 Australia tour. Helped Edinburgh to three Inter-District Championship 'grand slams' between 1986–88. Former captain of Scottish Schools. Played three times for Scotland U-21s and once for Scotland B (at fullback in 9–0 win over Italy B, Glasgow 7 Dec 1985). Also played at outside-half, for Anglo-Scots, during time at Newcastle Polytechnic. Key cog in Scotland's 1990 Grand Slam machine, making famous try-saving tackle on England's Rory Underwood in Grand Slam decider

Touchlines: Underwater hockey refereeing; bandit golfer (handicap 18), watching films, viticulture

Player to watch: Gregor Townsend (Gala)

Player of the year: David Campese (Australia)

	apps	pts
Scotland B (**1985**)		
Last Season	0 caps	0
Career	1 cap	0
Scotland (**1986**)		
Last Season	10 caps	8
1992	Tour to Australia	
Career	40 caps	28
Lions 1989	2 Tests	0

Caps (40): **1986** F, W, E, I, Ro **1987** I, F, W wc-Ro **1988** I, F, W, A **1989** W, E, I, F, Fj, Ro. Lions-A(2,3) **1990** I, F, W, E, NZ(1,2), Arg **1991** F, W, E(a), I(a) wc-J, Z, I(b), WS, E(b), NZ **1992** E, I, F, W

Points (28 – 7t): **1986** E(1t), Ro(1t) **1987** F(1t) **1988** I(1t) **1991** I(1t) wc-J(1t), Z(1t)

Heslop, N. J.   England

Full Name: Nigel John Heslop
1991/92 International category:
England Full
Club: Orrell
Position: Wing
Height: 5'10" **Weight:** 12st 7lbs
Occupation: Police officer
(Merseyside)
Born: Hartlepool, 4.12.63
Family: Denise (wife)
Family links with rugby: Brother
(Simon) played Rugby League for
Leeds Poly
Former clubs: Waterloo, Liverpool
International debut: Argentina 12,
England 25, 1990
Best moment in rugby: Scoring
only try of match in England's 21–12
defeat of Scotland (1991)
Worst moment in rugby: Letting
Wasps' Chris Oti in for winning try
in 1990/91 League match against
Orrell
Most embarrassing moment:
Tackled by stray dog while playing
for Liverpool
Most respected opponent:
England wing Rory Underwood
Biggest influences on career: Mike
Slemen, Des Seabrook
Serious injuries: Dislocated elbow
(1986)
Other sporting achievements:
Sprinted in Police Championships

	apps	pts
England B (1989)		
Last Season	0 caps	0
Career	2 caps	0
England (1990)		
Last Season	3 caps	4
Career	10 caps	12

Caps (10): **1990** Arg(a1, a2), Arg(b)
1991 W, S, I, F(a) wc-US, F(b)
1992 W(R)

Points (12 – 3t): **1990** Arg(a2:1t) **1991**
S(1t) wc-US(1t)

Best memory last season: Marking return to England team with try against
United States in 1991 World Cup
Suggestions to improve rugby: *On-field* – Anything to make game flow
more; too many stoppages. *Off-field* – Quite happy personally but players
should be able to benefit from off-field activities. A little more could be done
– not direct payment but reimbursement for working time given up to rugby
Notable landmarks in rugby career: Represented England Colts (1980)
but then waited nine years for B cap, on summer tour to Spain. Helped

Lancashire win 1989/90 County Championship and reach 1991/92 final (had to miss final win over Cornwall because Orrell commitment took preference). Played for England XV's 33–15 defeat of Italy XV in Rovigo (May 1990). Toured with England to Argentina (1990), where he made full debut (and scoring try in 13–15 second Test loss), and Australia (1991). Ever present in England's 1991 Grand Slam-winning side, scoring decisive try in England's 21–12 win over Scotland. Lost place to Simon Halliday in 1991/92, but still turned out in the World Cup against USA and France, and as a 73rd minute replacement for Will Carling against Wales in 1992 Grand Slam decider

Player to watch: Michael Fielden (Orrell)
Player of the year: Dewi Morris (England)

Hill, R. J.   England

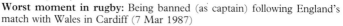

Full Name: Richard John Hill
1991/92 International category:
England Full
Club: Bath
Position: Scrum-half
Height: 5'7" **Weight:** 12st 11lbs
Occupation: Financial consultant
with Noble Lowndes, financial
consultants and actuaries
Born: Birmingham, 4.5.61
Family: Karen (wife), Joshua (son)
and Natalie (daughter)
Former clubs: Exeter Univ,
Salisbury
International debut: South Africa
33, England 15, 1984
Five Nations' debut: Ireland 13,
England 10, 1985
Best moment in rugby: Scoring
first try for England, in 34–6 defeat
of Wales (1990)
Worst moment in rugby: Being banned (as captain) following England's match with Wales in Cardiff (7 Mar 1987)
Most embarrassing moment: Having pass intercepted by Philippe Sella, who ran in to score from 65 yards, during England's 15–19 Twickenham defeat by France (21 Feb 1987)
Most respected opponent: David Bishop (ex-Pontypool & Wales) – could win matches on his own

Biggest influences on career: Steve Ralph-Bowman (School PE teacher) and Stuart Barnes (Bath)

Serious injuries: Knee operation (summer 1990)

Best memory last season: Final whistle of World Cup quarter-final in Paris (France 10, England 19)

Suggestions to improve rugby: *On-field* – Consult players and referees before making and implementing new laws. The new ruck/maul regulation is appalling. *Off-field* – Establish an Anglo-Welsh championship to strengthen fixture lists. Home and away system in League. Financial compensation has to be made to help players and employers cope with the staggering commitment that is expected of us. Since 1988 we have knackered ourselves for work by becoming the fittest England side to ever take the field. If we are to compete in the 1995 World Cup in South Africa we will have to train even harder. That will just not be possible if provisions are not made for players/employers

Notable landmarks in rugby career: Kept out of England Colts by Nigel Melville but represented England Students whilst at Exeter Univ. Joined Bath and played England final Trial (1983) and won first full cap following season. Shares, with Gareth Chilcott, the distinction of having played in all seven of Bath's Cup final-winning teams (1984–85–86–87–89–90–92), captaining club to 1987 win over Wasps (19–12) and scoring try in 1986 win over Wasps (25–17). Not yet dropped by Bath, which is pleasing. Captained England four times (1986–87). Represented England in 1987 World Cup (v. USA). England tours include South Africa (1984), New Zealand (1985), Australasia (1987 World Cup), Argentina (1990) and Australia (1991). Ever present in 1991 Five Nations' Grand Slam-winning side and played in 1991 World Cup final. Dropped by England after 20 consecutive games because 'I was getting too predictable. I will go back to the drawing board and come back a better player'

Player of the year: Jon Webb (England)

	apps	pts
England B (**1986**)		
Last Season	0 caps	0
England (**1984**)		
Last Season	8 caps	0
Career	29 caps	8
Lions 1986		

Caps (29): **1984** SA(1,2) **1985** I(R), NZ(2R) **1986** F(R) **1987** I, F, W(a) wc-US **1989** Fj **1990** I, F, W, S, Arg(a1, a2), Arg(b) **1991** W, S(a), I, F(a), Fj, A(a) wc-NZ, It, US, F(b), S(b), A(b)

Points (8 – 2t): **1990** W(1t), Arg(b:1t)

Hodgkinson, S. D.　　　England

Full Name: Simon David Hodgkinson
1991/92 International category: England Full
Club: Nottingham
Position: Fullback
Height: 5′10″ **Weight:** 12st 4lbs
Occupation: Regional sales manager with HFS Loans (Macclesfield)
Born: Bristol, 15.12.62
Family: Fiona (wife)
Family links with rugby: Father played for Thornbury (Bristol) and Scarborough
International debut: Romania 3, England 58, 1989
Five Nations' debut: England 23, Ireland 0, 1990
Best moment in rugby: Winning 1991 Grand Slam with England
Worst moment in rugby: Performance for England XV in 7–13 defeat by England B XV (1988) – England final trial
Most embarrassing moment: Failing to turn up for a Sevens quarter-final
Most respected opponent: French centre Philippe Sella
Serious injuries: Two out of three ankle ligaments badly sprained (v. USSR, 7 Sep 1991), vertebrae nipping on disc, must have pulled every muscle in body by now
Other sporting achievements: Midlands U-15 cricket

	apps	pts
England B (**1988**)		
Last Season	0 caps	0
England (**1989**)		
Last Season	1 cap	17
Career	14 caps	203

Caps (14): **1989** Ro, Fj **1990** I, F, W, S, Arg(a1, a2), Arg(b) **1991** W, S(a), I, F(a) wc-US

Points (203 – 1t,35c,43p): **1989** Ro(8c,1p), Fj(5c,2p) **1990** I(2c,1p), F(1c,4p), W(3c,4p), S(1p), Arg(a1:1c,5p), Arg(a2:1t,1c, 1p), Arg(b:7c,3p) **1991** W(7p), S(1c,5p), I(1c,2p), F(1c,4p) wc-US(4c,3p)

Best memory last season: Nottingham beating Northampton in Courage League division one
Suggestions to improve rugby: *On-field* – Scrap many of the new rules, just because there are too many changes. Do not reduce value of penalty goal – it is up to players to make sure they do not offend. But it is good that they

have reduced less offensive infringements from penalty to free-kick. *Off-field* – Resolve payment to players position. Allow sponsorship payments to players. Unions are getting closer to a solution but there is still nothing like a parity among nations. Authorities appear so blinkered as to what is going on elsewhere

Notable landmarks in rugby career: Established Five . Nations' Championship points scoring record in 1991 with 60 (3c,18p) in England's Grand Slam, but only lasted until last season when Jon Webb (67) surpassed mark. Took tally to 83 for season with 23 (then a national record) in England's 51–0 rout of Argentina (3 Nov 1990). Was also leading scorer in the 1989/90 Five Nations' Championship with 42 points (6c,10p). Member of select gathering to have scored more than 40 points in Championship season. Holds English record for conversions in an international (8 v. Romania, 13 May 1989), and for penalty goals in a Championship season (18 in 4 games, 1991). Toured with England to Argentina (1990) and Australia/Fiji (1991). Scored 14 points for England XV against both Italy (1990, won 33–15) and Barbarians (1990, won 18–16). Last season, damaged ankle ligaments in pre-World Cup game against Soviet Union and played just one international all season thereafter: scoring 17 points in 37–9 World Cup win over United States (11 Oct 1991)

Touchlines: Golf

Player to watch: Matt Greenwood (Nottingham)

Player of the year: Dewi Morris (England)

A rare moment of joy for Ireland in the 1992 Five Nations' Championship as Ralph Keyes rounds Jason Leonard to score at Twickenham. England won 38–9

Hogan, N. A.   Ireland

Full Name: Niall Andrew Hogan
1991/92 International category:
Ireland U-21
Club: Terenure College
Position: Scrum-half
Height: 5'8" **Weight:** 11st
Occupation: Medical student (in
third year of six)
Born: Dublin, 20.4.71
Family: Single
Family links with rugby: Brother
(Kevin) captained UC Dublin last
season
International debut: Netherlands
21, Ireland U-21 7, 1990
Best moment in rugby: Helping
Irish Schools beat England Schools
against all odds in 1989
Worst moment in rugby: Losing in
first round of Schools Cup to St
Andrews College
Most respected opponents: Colin
Stephens (Llanelli & Wales),
Adedayo Adebayo (Bath & England
B)

Ireland U-21 (**1990**)	apps	pts
Last Season	2 caps	0
Career	3 caps	0

Serious injuries: Broken ankle (chipped bone)
Best memory last season: Captaining Ireland U-21 to victory over England
U-21s (23 Oct 1991)
Suggestions to improve rugby: *On-field* – Develop a greater continuity in
the game by adjusting legislation to prevent so many potential breakdowns
Notable landmarks in rugby career: Captained Leinster at Schools, U-19
and U-20 levels. Replacement in senior provincial squad three times last
season. Represented Irish Colleges and Irish Students. Broke into Ireland U-21
team in 1990/91 on tour to Netherlands and was appointed captain last season
for the games against Wales (lost 15–22) and England (won 19–10)
Touchlines: Golf
Player to watch: Martin Ridge (Blackrock College)
Player of the year: David Campese (Australia)

Hogan, P. J.   Ireland

Full Name: Paul John Hogan
1991/92 International category:
Ireland Full
Club: Garryowen
Positions: Flanker, No.8
Height: 6′3″ **Weight:** 16st
Occupation: Sales representative
with Frank Hogan Ltd
Born: Limerick, 25.6.68
Family: Single
Family links with rugby: Father
(Frank) captained Garryowen and
played for Munster
International debut: France 44,
Ireland 12, 1992
Five Nations' debut: As above
Best moment in rugby: Selection
for first cap. Winning 1991/92
All-Ireland League title with
Garryowen

Worst moment in rugby: Losing
1990/91 All-Ireland League decider
to Cork Constitution
Most respected opponent: All of
them
Serious injuries: Detached eye
retina, damaged ankle and knee
ligaments, dislocated shoulder
Best memory last season: Running
out onto Parc des Princes for first cap

	apps	pts
Ireland U-21 (1988)		
Career	1 cap	0
Ireland (1992)		
Last Season	1 cap	0
Career	1 cap	0

Caps (1): 1992 F
Points: Nil

Suggestions to improve rugby: *On-field* – Rid rugby of dirty play. *Off-field* – Players should not lose out financially from playing rugby
Notable landmarks in rugby career: represented first ever Ireland U-21 team on 24 Sep 1988 when Italy U-21 formed the opposition at Lansdowne Road and were beaten 22–13. Next representation for Ireland came in final round of 1992 Five Nations' Championship when he was selected to wear the No.6 jersey ahead of captain Phil Matthews against France in Paris. Also represented Irish Wolfhounds and Munster at Schools, U-21 and senior grades. Helped Garryowen win 1991/92 All-Ireland League Championship
Touchlines: Golf
Player to watch: Richard Wallace (Garryowen)
Player of the year: Jeremy Guscott (England)

Howley, R.   Wales

Full Name: Robert Howley
1991/92 International category:
Wales U-21
Clubs: Bridgend/Swansea Univ
Position: Scrum-half
Height: 5'10½" **Weight:** 12st 5lbs
Occupation: Student
Born: Bridgend, 13.10.70
Family: Single
Best moments in rugby: Scoring
winning try in 13–7 win over
Scotland U-18; selection for Wales B
bench for 1990 match v. Holland in
Leiden
Worst moment in rugby: Tearing
knee cartilage playing for Swansea
Univ against Cardiff Univ in 1991
UAU final at Twickenham (20 Mar
1991, lost 3–14) – out for rest of
season
Most embarrassing moment:
Slicing clearance over my own
winger's head for opposition to score
during Bridgend-Pontypool game
Other sporting achievements:
Cricket for Welsh Schools (U-15,
U-16 and U-17)

	apps	pts
Wales U-21 (**1991**)		
Last Season	2 caps	4
Career	2 caps	4
Wales B (1990/91)	1 rep	

Most respected opponent: Robert Jones (Swansea & Wales)
Serious injuries: Three cartilage tears, plus one ligament tear (all on left knee)
Best memory last season: Bridgend's 22–15 win over champions-to-be Swansea in Heineken League
Suggestions to improve rugby: *On-field* – Less kicking and more running. Reduce value of penalty goal to two points. Get rid of 'mark' in 22. *Off-field* – Ensure a solid structure to the national game, particularly to bridge gap between U-21 and senior. Bright future for Welsh rugby with some fine young players coming through
Notable landmarks in rugby career: Welsh Schools U-18 captain (1989), playing against Scotland, Ireland, England and France. Called into Wales U-21 squad two seasons before making cap-debut against Ireland last season. Marked the occasion with a try. Added second cap in 28–19 defeat of Scotland U-21 at Bridgehaugh, Stirling, as Wales maintained their record of never

having lost an U-21 match to the Scots. An unused Wales B replacement in Holland (2 Dec 1990), he was able to improve on that last season because there were no B games
Touchlines: Cricket, golf
Player to watch: Neil Boobyer (Llanelli)
Player of the year: Richard Webster (Wales)

Hunter, I. England

Full Name: Ian Hunter
1991/92 International category: England B
Club: Northampton
Positions: Fullback, wing, centre
Height: 6′2″ **Weight:** 14st 7lbs
Occupation: Student at Leicester Polytechnic
Born: Harrow, London 15.2.69
Family: Single
Family links with rugby: Father played in New Zealand
Former clubs: Windermere, Carlisle, Nottingham
Best moment in rugby: Playing in Hong Kong Sevens
Worst moments in rugby: Losing to Harlequins in extra-time in 1990/91 Pilkington Cup final
Most embarrassing moment: Falling over for no reason in front of capacity crowd at Northampton just before kick-off
Most respected opponent: Steve Pilgrim (Wasps & England B)
Best memory last season: England B's Grand Slam

	apps	pts
England B (**1990**)		
Last Season	4 caps	19
1992	Tour to New Zealand	
Career	9 caps	27
England	1995 Development squad	

Suggestions to improve rugby: *On-field* – Play league games on a home and away basis. *Off-field* – RFU to sort out their amateur regulations, like every other nation has
Notable landmarks in rugby career: Took tally of B caps to nine last season when wore the No.15 jersey throughout the four-match winning sequence. Only failed to score against France B (won 22–18, Paris 15 Feb 1992). Scored two tries and dropped a goal in the 34–3 win over Spain (Madrid 19 Jan

1992), one try in the 47–15 defeat of Ireland B (Richmond 31 Jan 1992) and another try in the 16–10 clincher against Italy B (Rome 7 Mar 1992). Played five B games the previous season against the Emerging Australians, Spain (try), Italy B, Ireland B (try) and France B. Included in England's latest development squad for 1995 World Cup. Helped Northampton win promotion to first division (1989/90) and into 1990/91 Pilkington Cup final against Harlequins. Represented centenary Barbarians (1990/91) and toured Australia with England (1991) and New Zealand with England B (1992)

Touchlines: Working for my degree

Players to watch: Tony Underwood and Neil Back (both Leicester & England B), Rupert Moon (Llanelli & Wales)

Hynes, M. P.   England

Full Name: Martin Peter Hynes
1991/92 International category: England Full (bench)
Club: Orrell
Position: Prop
Height: 5′9″ **Weight:** 15st 4lbs
Occupation: Electrician for James Scotts (Amex Group)
Born: Wigan, Lancs, 23.8.68
Family: Single
Family links with rugby: Father (Michael) played Rugby League for Wigan Colts
Former club: Durban Crusaders (SA)
International debut (U-21): Romania 13, England 54, 1989
Best moment in rugby: Making England debut in Bucharest – the start of my representative career
Worst moment in rugby: Orrell losing to Wasps to last-gasp dropped goal by Huw Davies to effectively blow the 1991/92 Championship
Most embarrassing moment: Being sent off for punching against Bedford
Most respected opponent: Jeff

	apps	pts
England U-21 (**1989**)		
Last Season	0 caps	0
Career	1 cap	0
England B (1990/91)	2 reps	
1992	Tour to New Zealand	
England (1991/92)	4 reps	
1995	Development squad	

104

Probyn (Wasps & England) – gave me a hard time last season

Biggest influence on career: Sammy Southern (Orrell & England B) and Des Seabrook (Orrell & Lancashire coach) – both very strong characters who pushed me in right direction

Serious injuries: Broken coccyx, aggravated back

Other sporting achievements: Swam butterfly for Wigan Wasps in National Championships

Best memory last season: Orrell beating Gloucester

Suggestions to improve rugby: *On-field* – Abolish 90-degree wheel law. Cannot think why they brought in the rule in first place. Whenever you try to work a skilful back row move, the opposition just negatively wheel. *Off-field* – reimbursement of wages lost through playing rugby

Notable landmarks in rugby career: Played for Lancashire Colts and was reserve for Northumberland Colts. Played for Lancashire and North of England U-21s and, after Lancashire's 1989/90 County Championship success, toured with county to Zimbabwe (1990). Since making England U-21 debut in Bucharest there has been a slightly wooden feel to representative career: warming 1990/91 England B bench against France B and Italy B and 1991/92 senior bench throughout 1992 Five Nations' Championship (against Scotland, Ireland, France and Wales). Included in England's latest 1995 Development squad. Helped Lancashire to 1991/92 County Championship final but was then required, along with the rest of the Orrell contingent, to miss final, which Lancashire won. Toured New Zealand with England B (1992)

Touchlines: Karate, swimming, rugby

Player to watch: Harvey Thorneycroft (Northampton)

Player of the year: Sammy Southern (Orrell)

Jardine, I. C.   Scotland

Full Name: Ian Carrick Jardine
1991/92 International category:
Scotland B
Club: Stirling County
Position: Centre
Height: 6'1" **Weight:** 13st 7lbs
Occupation: Teacher training
(mathematics) at Jordanhill College
Born: Dunfermline, 20.10.64
Family: Ann (wife)
Family links with rugby: Four
brothers (Stephen, Neil, Colin and
Aitken) play at Stirling
International debut (B): Scotland
22, Ireland 22, 1990
Best moments in rugby: Winning
promotion from Scottish Second to
First Division (1988/89). Winning
Inter-District Championship with
Glasgow (1989/90). Gaining
selection for Scotland's summer tour
to North America
Worst moment in rugby: Not
being selected to tour Australia with
Scotland (1992)

	apps	pts
Scotland B (**1989**)		
Last Season	2 caps	4
Career	3 caps	4

Most respected opponent: John Wright (Young Munster)
Best memory last season: Scottish Trial
Suggestions to improve rugby: *On-field* – Refereeing consistency must be improved so players know exactly where they stand. Get all referees together and work things out. *Off-field* – Players compensated for earnings lost due to rugby. Allow us to advertise rugby-related items – main potential earnings source
Notable landmarks in rugby career: Replacement for Scotland U-21s (1986) and Scotland B in Italy (1988/89). Made B debut in 22–22 draw with Ireland B (9 Dec 1989) and, after being only bench reserve in 0–16 loss to Ireland B (22 Dec 1990), made the No.12 jersey his own last season, turning out against Ireland B at Murrayfield (lost 19–29, 28 Dec 1991) and in Albi against France B (3 Feb 1992) where scored try in 18–27 defeat. Toured Canada and the United States with Scotland (1991), appearing against Alberta (won 76–7) and Ontario (won 43–3)
Touchlines: Hill walking, cycling
Player to watch: Gregor Townsend (Gala)
Player of the year: Tim Horan (Australia)

Jenkins, G. R.   Wales

Full Name: Garin Richard Jenkins
1991/92 International category:
Wales Full
Club: Swansea
Position: Hooker
Height: 5'10" **Weight:** 15st 2lbs
Occupation: Builder
Born: Ynysybwl, 18.8.67
Family: Single
Family links with rugby: Father's
uncle played for Wales. Mother's
cousin propped for Wales and Lions
Former clubs: Ynysybwl,
Pontypridd, King Country (NZ),
Pontypool
Best moment in rugby: Breaking
into Wales full team last season
Worst moment in rugby: Being
dropped as replacement when Ian
Watkins returned from suspension
(1990/91)
Most respected opponent: All of
them
Best memory last season: Wales'
wins against Ireland and Scotland
**Notable landmarks in rugby
career:** Represented Boys Clubs of
Wales U-18s and Glamorgan U-23s.

	apps	pts
Wales (1991)		
Last Season	8 caps	0
Career	8 caps	0

Caps (8): 1991 F(b) wc-WS(R), Arg,
A(b) 1992 I, F, E, S

Points: Nil

Toured Kenya with Pontypool (1990), having started his career with
Ynysybwl, the birthplace of national coach Alan Davies. Broke into Wales
team at the start of 1991/92 season when Davies was appointed coach
following the 1991 Australia tour, and played in all eight games spanning the
French 'floodlit' game, the 1991 World Cup and 1992 Five Nations'
Championship. Completed great season by securing Heineken League premier
division honours with Swansea
Touchlines: Soccer, cricket, weightlifting

Jenkins, N. R.   Wales

Full Name: Neil Roger Jenkins
1991/92 International category:
Wales Full
Club: Pontypridd
Position: Outside-half
Height: 5′10″ **Weight:** 13st
Occupation: PR consultant for Just
Rentals (Pontypridd)
Born: Church Village, Pontypridd,
8.7.71
Family: Single
International debut: Wales 6,
England 25, 1991
Five Nations' debut: As above
Best moment in rugby: Full debut
for Wales at Cardiff
Worst moment in rugby: Being
sent-off in 39th minute of 6–27
Schweppes Cup semi-final against
Llanelli at Arms Park
Most respected opponents: Didier
Camberabero (Beziers & France)
and Philippe Sella (Agen & France)
Biggest influences on career:
Parents and two uncles
Best memory last season: Beating
Ireland and Scotland in
Championship (first wins with
Wales)
Suggestions to improve rugby:
On-field – Award less points for
goals. *Off-field* – Unions should pay
players wages when rugby takes
them away from work, rather than
expecting goodwill from employers

	apps	pts
Wales U-21 (**1991**)		
Last Season	1 cap	10
Career	2 caps	25
Wales B (**1990**)		
Last Season	0 caps	0
Career	1 cap	18
Wales (**1991**)		
Last Season	4 caps	18
Career	8 caps	28

Caps (8): 1991 E, S, I, F 1992 I, F, E, W

Points (28 – 1t,7p,1dg): **1991** E(1p), I(1t,1dg) **1992** I(3p), F(3p)

Notable landmarks in rugby career: Played for East Wales U-11s v. West Wales, East Glamorgan and Wales Youth (1989/90). Having broken into Wales U-21s into 1990/91 – playing against New Zealand U-21 XV (14pts:4c,2p) and Scotland U-21 (15pts: 1t,1c,3p) – added a second cap and ten points in 22–15 win over Ireland U-21 last season (2c,2p). An eventful 1990/91 also saw him graduate to Wales B where he scored 18 points in 34–12 win over Netherlands (1t,4c,2p) in Leiden. Next onto senior status where

played throughout 1991 and 1992 Five Nations' Championships but missed out on World Cup
Touchlines: Golf
Player to watch: Scott Quinnell (Llanelli)
Player of the year: Will Carling (England)

Johns, P. S.   Ireland

Full Name: Patrick Stephen Johns
1991/92 International category:
Ireland B
Club: Dungannon
Positions: Lock, No.8
Height: 6'6" **Weight:** 16st
Occupation: Dental student
Born: Portadown, 19.2.68
Family: Single
Former clubs: Newcastle Univ,
Gosforth, Dublin Univ
International debut: Ireland 20,
Argentina 18, 1990
Five Nations' debut: None
Best moment in rugby: First match
for Ireland (Schools v. Australia,
1988)
Most embarrassing moment:
Getting my shorts ripped off aged 13
Most respected opponent: Alan
Whetton (Auckland & New
Zealand) – the best about
Serious injuries: Neck injury,
broken wrist
Best memory last season:
Selection for New Zealand tour
Suggestions to improve rugby:
On-field – Less emphasis on set-play.
Encourage more open rugby
**Notable landmarks in rugby
career:** Represented Ulster against
1989 All Blacks (lost 3–21, Ravenhill

	apps	pts
Ireland U-21 (**1988**)		
Career	1 cap	0
Ireland U-25 (**1990**)		
Last Season	0 caps	0
Career	2 caps	0
Ireland B (**1989**)		
Last Season	1 cap	0
Career	3 caps	4
Ireland (**1990**)		
Last Season	0 caps	0
Career	1 cap	0

21 Nov 1989) and helped them win record sixth Irish Inter-Provincial Championship. Toured Canada with Dungannon (1989). Played for Ireland at Schools, U-21 (Ireland 22, Italy 13, Dublin 24 Sep 1988) and U-25 level.

Represented Ireland B in 22–22 draw with Scotland B at Murrayfield (9 Dec 1989), in 24–10 win over England B at Old Belvedere (scoring try, 1 Mar 1991) and again, last season, against England B (No.8 in 15–47 loss, Richmond 31 Jan 1992). Capped by Ireland against touring Argentina Pumas (27 Oct 1990)
Touchlines: Cycling

Johnson, M. O.   England

Full Name: Martin Osborne Johnson
1991/92 International category: England U-21/B
Club: Leicester
Position: Lock
Height: 6'7" **Weight:** 17st 7lbs
Occupation: Bank officer with Midland Bank (Market Harborough)
Born: Solihull, 9.3.70
Family: Single
Former clubs: Wigston, College Old Boys (NZ)
International debut (B): France 18, England 22, 1992
Best moment in rugby: Making B debut in Paris last season (15 Feb 1992)
Worst moment in rugby: Leicester's semi-final defeat by Harlequins in last season's Pilkington Cup
Most respected opponent: Paul Ackford (Ex-Harlequins & England)
Serious injuries: Dislocated left shoulder (Apr 1991) playing for Midlands U-21s v. London U-21s. Required operation and out for four months

	apps	pts
England U-21 (**1991**)		
Last Season	1 cap	0
Career	1 cap	0
England B (**1992**)		
Last Season	2 caps	0
1992	Tour to New Zealand	
Career	2 caps	0

Best memory last season: Representing Leicester against the Barbarians in the Christmas fixture
Suggestions to improve rugby: *On-field* – Beware not to alter too much of the game. If we try to make too many changes, in an attempt to pamper for

110

television etc, we stand the chance of changing the face of the game, and that would be disastrous. *Off-field* – Use commonsense to resolve the amateurism question. Do what is fair

Notable landmarks in rugby career: Spent 18 months playing out in New Zealand for College Old Boys (1990–91), during which time played for New Zealand U-21 against Australia counterparts on two-week tour. Had previously represented England Schools (1987–88), England Colts (1988/89) and both England U-21 and B last season. Partnered Gloucester's David Sims in England U-21 side which routed Belgium 94–0 (Wolverhampton, 1 Sep 1991), before turning out, again alongside Sims, in England B's wins against France B (Paris, 15 Feb 1992) and Italy B (Rome, 7 Mar 1992). Toured to New Zealand with England B (1992)

Jones, I. W.   Wales

Full Name: Ian Wynn Jones
1991/92 International category:
Wales U-21
Club: Llanelli
Position: Fullback, wing
Height: 5'10" **Weight:** 12st 7lbs
Occupation: Optics student at Cardiff Univ
Born: Carmarthen, 12.5.71
Family: Single
Family links with rugby: Wales captain Ieuan Evans is third cousin
Best moment in rugby: Scoring try in Llanelli's 1990/91 Schweppes Cup final win (24–9) over Pontypool
Worst moment in rugby: Tearing hamstring on Welsh Students debut against Scotland last season
Most embarrassing moment: Tearing shorts on one occasion last season (against Pontypool) that I was jockstrap-less
Most respected opponent: Simon Halliday (Harlequins & England)
Biggest influence on career: Randall Jones (coach at Llandovery College, 1989/90)

	apps	pts
Wales U-21 (**1992**)		
Last Season	1 cap	0
Career	1 cap	0
Wales 1991	Tour to Australia	

Serious injuries: Torn hamstring, ankle ligaments; concussion
Other sporting achievements: Cricket for 1988/89 Welsh Independent Schools; 1987 Welsh Junior javelin champion
Best memory last season: Being selected for 1992 Student World Cup
Suggestions to improve rugby: *On-field* – Harsher penalties for killing the ball. Award penalty kick in front of posts irrespective of where crime is committed. *Off-field* – Ease up on amateur regulations. Game has to go semi-professional to keep in step with other nations
Notable landmarks in rugby career: Represented Welsh Schools (five caps) in 1987/88. Played for WRU President's (U-21) XV in 34–13 win over New Zealand Rugby News Youth XV (Pontypridd, 8 Nov 1990) but tonsyllitis put paid to debut against Scotland until 1991/92 season when turned out in 28–19 win at Stirling. Scored one of Wales' five tries against Pontypool in 1990/91 Cup final and also played in 1991/92 final win over Swansea. Toured Australia with Wales (1991), playing against Western Australia and Australian Capital Territory, and was included in preliminary World Cup squad
Touchlines: Playing violin, piano, golf and surfing
Player to watch: David Morgan (Swansea/Cardiff Univ)
Player of the year: Tony Clement (Wales)

Jones, P. M.   Scotland

Full Name: Peter Martin Jones
1991/92 International category: Scotland Full
Club: Gloucester
Position: Prop
Height: 5'11" **Weight:** 15st 8lbs
Occupation: Engineer with Severn Trent Water Authority
Born: Arbroath, 28.12.64
Family: Sarah (wife)
Former club: Longlevens
International debut: Wales 15, Scotland 12, 1992
Five Nations' debut: As above
Best moment in rugby: Coming on as replacement at Cardiff to win first full cap
Worst moment in rugby: Losing to Bath in extra-time in 1991/92 Pilkington Cup semi-finals at Kingsholm

Most respected opponent: Phil Blakeway (ex-Gloucester & England)

Biggest influence on career: Derek Cook (coach at Longlevens)

Best memory last season: Receiving call-up for Scotland A team on my birthday

Suggestions to improve rugby: *On-field* – More consistency in refereeing. The new ruck/maul law promises to remove a lot of skill from forward play. *Off-field* – If there is too much cash floating about people will start playing for the wrong reasons. But, we should be compensated for loss of wages

	apps	pts
Scotland B (**1990**)		
Last Season	1 cap	0
Career	2 caps	0
Scotland A (**1991**)		
Last Season	1 cap	0
Career	1 cap	0
Scotland (**1992**)		
Last Season	1 cap	0
1992	Tour to Australia	
Career	1 cap	0

Caps (1): **1992** W(R)

Points: 0

Notable landmarks in rugby career: Left Scotland at the age of eight when family moved to Gloucester, but 19 years later earned full Scotland cap as a 53rd minute replacement for Paul Burnell at the Arms Park (21 Mar 1992). Had previously been selected for England B bench against Emerging Australians at Wasps (4 Nov 1990). Chose to play for Scotland because 'they seemed more genuine'. Made Scotland B debut the following month in 0–16 loss to Ireland B (Ravenhill, 22 Dec 1990), and added second B cap against France in Albi (lost 18–27, 3 Feb 1992). Represented Scotland A (28 Dec 1991) in 36–16 defeat of Spain at Murrayfield. Toured Australia (1992) with Scotland. Started out as a wing, before switching to prop to represent Gloucester Schools. First senior game for Gloucester came in 1982 and four years ago broke into Anglo-Scots side

Touchlines: Hill walking with dog

Player to watch: John Hawker (Gloucester)

Player of the year: Andy Nicol (Scotland)

Jones, R. N.   Wales

Full Name: Robert Nicholas Jones
1991/92 International category:
Wales Full
Club: Swansea
Position: Scrum-half
Height: 5'7" **Weight:** 11st 10lbs
Occupation: Business development
executive with Swansea Building
Society
Born: Trebanos, 10.11.65
Family: Megan (wife)
Family links with rugby:
Father-in-law (Clive Rowlands)
played for Wales and Lions. Brother
has played for Llanelli and Aberavon
International debut: England 21,
Wales 18, 1986
Five Nations' debut: As above
Best moments in rugby:
Captaining Wales. 1989 Lions
winning decisive third Test against
Australia
Worst moments in rugby:
Captaining Wales in 1990 whitewash
– very, very despondent. Defeat by
New Zealand in 1987 World Cup
Most embarrassing moment:
Attempted dropped goal for Wales
against Ireland, hit ground before
ball and sent it 3 yards. Paul Dean
collected and initiated move which
led to Irish try
Most respected opponents: Pierre
Berbizier (ex-Agen & France) and
Gary Armstrong (Jedforest &
Scotland)
Biggest influence on career:
Father (Cliff)

	apps	pts
Wales B (1985)		
Last Season	0 caps	0
Career	1 cap	0
Wales (1986)		
Last Season	8 caps	0
Career	42 caps	4
Lions 1989	3 Tests	0

Caps (42): **1986** E, S, I, F, Fj, T, WS **1987** F, E(a), S, I(a), US wc-I(b), T, E(b), NZ, A **1988** E, S, I, F, NZ(1), WS, Ro **1989** I, F, E, NZ, Lions-A(1,2,3), 1990 F, E, S, I 1991 E, S, F(b) wc-WS, Arg, A(b) 1992 I, F, E, S

Points (4 – 1t): **1987** wc-E(1t)

Other sporting achievements: Cricket for Wales at three age-groups
Best memory last season: Beating Ireland after poor World Cup. We stuck
to pattern, knew exactly what we wanted to do. We are getting our organisation
and communication back but there is still a long way to go

114

Suggestions to improve rugby: *On-field* – England winning 1991 Grand Slam with hardly any tries made a mockery of old scoring system. However, increasing try value will only serve to make for a greater disparity between the major and the developing nations, discouraging the latter. Better to have reduced penalty value for technical offences. I am not happy with that. Take Wales' 63–6 loss to Australia. Under the new system that score would have been 75–7. *Off-field* – Greater depth of consideration for players. Reconsider amateur issue so that players can benefit away from play. Look after players' employers with tickets etc. WRU trying to be more forward looking than other Unions but they are governed by IRB. Moves still have to be made to improve situation because there are still very few player-benefits considering time put in. Commitments and time involved ever-increasing. Yet athletes are able to benefit from their amateur sport

Notable landmarks in rugby career: Most-capped Swansea player and former captain of the St Helens club as well as of Wales. First represented All Whites while still at Cwmtawe School, having already played for West Wales U-11s and Wales 12-Group. Represented Welsh Schools for two seasons before graduating, by way of Wales B in 1985, to senior XV for 1986 Five Nations' Championship. Enjoyed outstanding World Cup (1987) and equally magnificent tour, to Australia, with 1989 Lions. Partnered Jonathan Davies in 22 internationals before he switched codes. Missed Welsh tour of Namibia last summer through injury but did go to Fiji, Tonga and Western Samoa (1986), New Zealand (1988) and Australia (1991). Scored only Wales try in 1987 World Cup quarter-final win over England

Touchlines: Golf (handicap 24)

Player to watch: Scott Gibbs (Swansea)

Player of the year: Will Carling (England)

Keyes, R. P. Ireland

Full Name: Ralph Patrick Keyes
1991/92 International category:
Ireland Full
Club: Cork Constitution
Position: Outside-half
Height: 5'9" **Weight:** 12st 7lbs
Occupation: Inspector with
Norwich Union Life Insurance
Born: Cork, 1.8.61
Family: Married with son and
daughter
Family links with rugby: Father
played for Cork and Munster
International debut: England 25,
Ireland 20, 1986
Five Nations' debut: As above
Best moment in rugby: Finishing
leading scorer in 1991 World Cup
(68 points)
Worst moment in rugby:
Sustaining injury in club game seven
days after Ireland debut, which
forced me out of next game against
Scotland
Most respected opponent: Paul
Dean (St Mary's College & Ireland)
Serious injuries: Ripped hamstring
Best memory last season: World
Cup
Suggestions to improve rugby:
On-field – Reduce impact of penalty
kicks. *Off-field* – Re-structure present
archaic amateur laws

	apps	pts
Ireland B (**1984**)		
Last Season	0 caps	0
Ireland (**1986**)		
Last Season	7 caps	94
Career	8 caps	94

Caps (8): **1986** E **1991** wc-Z, J, S, A
1992 W, E, S

Points (94 – 1t,9c,22p,2dg): **1991**
wc-Z(4c,5p), J(2c,4p),
S(4p,1dg), A(1c,3p,1dg) **1992**
W(1c,3p), E(1t,1c,1p), S(2p)

Notable landmarks in rugby career: Member of 1983 and 1985 Munster
Cup-winning Cork teams. Represented Munster against 1989 All Blacks (lost
9–31, Musgrave Park 11 Nov 1989). Captained Cork Constitution in 1989/90
season. Made Ireland B debut in 23–20 defeat of Scotland at Galway in 1984.
Bench reserve for Ireland in 1985 and toured Japan that same year. Replaced
Paul Dean at half-time of second Test in Tokyo (won 38–15) and again
replaced unfortunate Dean when winning first full cap (1986). Injured in club
game seven days later that put paid to international career for next five years,
although remained a regular on Irish replacements' bench, until earning recall

for 1991 World Cup after Brian Smith's move to Rugby League. Responded by becoming tournament's leading scorer, including an Irish scoring record of 23 points in his first game back: the 55–11 win over Zimbabwe (Dublin, 6 Oct 1991). World Cup points breakdown – Zimbabwe 23, Japan 16, Scotland 15, Australia 14. Added further 26 points in 1992 Five Nations' Championship before being dropped after Scotland game and left out of New Zealand tour squad

Touchlines: Golf
Player to watch: Simon Geoghegan (London Irish)

Kingston, T. J.   Ireland

Full Name: Terence John Kingston
1991/92 International category:
Ireland Full
Club: Dolphin
Position: Hooker
Height: 5′10″ **Weight:** 14st 9lbs
Occupation: Computer consultant
with Arkle Computers
Born: Cork, 19.9.63
Family: Single
Former club: Lansdowne
International debut: Ireland 6,
Wales 13, 1987 (World Cup)
Five Nations' debut: Ireland 22,
Scotland 18, 1988
Best moment in rugby: Selection
for 1987 World Cup and gaining
first cap against Wales during the
tournament
Worst moment in rugby: Being
dropped from Irish team and
Dolphin's failure to qualify for
National League in 1989/90 play-off
match
Most respected opponent: All of
them
Best memory last season:
Captaining Ireland against Japan
during World Cup
Suggestions to improve rugby:
On-field – An extra five metres

	apps	pts
Ireland B (**1990**)		
Last Season	0 caps	0
Career	1 cap	0
Ireland (**1987**)		
Last Season	1 cap	0
Career	10 caps	8

Caps (10): **1987** wc-W, T, A **1988** S, F, W, E(a) **1990** F, W **1991** wc-J

Points (8 – 2t): **1988** W(1t) **1990** W(1t)

should be added to all penalties as an increased deterrent and to encourage team benefiting to take fast, running ball while opposition is retreating

Notable landmarks in rugby career: Added only one cap to tally last season but he was accorded the honour of captaining the side to a 32–16 win over Japan (Dublin, 9 Oct 1991). That apart watched Ireland's seven other matches (World Cup and 1992 Five Nations' Championship) from bench, as Steve Smith monopolised the No.2 jersey. In all, has represented Irish Schools (1982), Ireland U-21s (1984), Ireland U-25s (1987, three caps), Ireland B (beat Argentina 27–12, Limerick 20 Oct 1990) and, on ten occasions since debut in 1987 World Cup (in place of injured Harry Harbison), Ireland Full. Toured Namibia (1991) and New Zealand (1992)

Touchlines: Golf (handicap 18)

Player to watch: Jack Clarke (Dolphin)

Knight, P.   Wales

Full Name: Paul Knight
1991/92 International category: Wales Full (tour squad)
Club: Pontypridd
Position: Prop
Height: 6' **Weight:** 16st 8lbs
Occupation: Production controller
Born: Tonypandy, 30.4.61
Family: Jennifer (wife) and Nadia Kylie (daughter)
Family links with rugby: Brother (Tony) plays for Treorchy
Former clubs: Treorchy, Aberavon
International debut: Namibia 9, Wales 18, 1990
Five Nations' debut: Wales 25, England 6, 1990
Serious injuries: Torn knee cartilage
Best moment in rugby: Winning first full cap in first Test at Windhoek (2 Jun 1990)
Best memory last season: Reaching Welsh Cup semi-finals with Pontypridd
Suggestions to improve rugby:

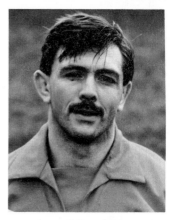

	apps	pts
Wales (**1990**)		
Last Season	0 caps	0
Career	5 caps	0

Caps (5): **1990** Na(1,2), Ba(R) **1991** E, S

Points: Nil

On-field – Needs no improving. *Off-field* – Become more professional in administration

Notable landmarks in rugby career: Attended Welsh Youth trials. Represented Mid-District, West Wales, Crawshays and 1990/91 centenary Barbarians against Argentina (Cardiff, 17 Nov 1990). Bench reserve for Wales B in early 1980s. Selected for Wales tour of Namibia (1990) and played in both Tests. Came on as 14th minute minute replacement for Brian Williams in Wales' 24–31 loss to Barbarians (Cardiff, 6 Oct 1990), and started 1991 Five Nations' matches against England (lost 6–25, Cardiff 19 Jan 1991) and Scotland (lost 12–32, Edinburgh 2 Feb 1991)

Touchlines: Gardening, DIY

Player to watch: Neil Jenkins (Pontypridd)

Lavin, G. J.   Ireland

Full Name: Gary John Lavin

1991/92 International category: Ireland U-21

Club: St Mary's College

Position: Centre

Height: 6'1½" **Weight:** 13st 7lbs

Occupation: Business and Computers student

Born: Dublin, 10.4.71

Family: Single

Former club: Queensland Univ (Aus)

International debut (U-21): Wales 22, Ireland 15, 1991

Best moment in rugby: Playing alongside Michael Lynagh for Queensland Univ (1991)

Most respected opponents: Jason Little (Australia), Michael Cosgrove (Wanderers)

Serious injuries: Broken left ankle (missed much of 1989 season – operation to insert pin)

Other sporting achievements: Fly helicopters (qualified for full commercial licence in Australia)

Best memory last season: Helping Ireland U-21s beat England at Donnybrook (23 Oct 1991)

	apps	pts
Ireland U-21 (**1991**)		
Last Season	1 cap	0
1991	Tour to Netherlands	
Career	1 cap	0

Suggestions to improve rugby: *On-field* – Referees keep whistles out of their mouths rather more. That is the main problem with the game at the moment. A more sympathetic approach to the game is required

Notable landmarks in rugby career: Spent six months (April–September 1991) at Queensland Univ, where played rugby with Michael Lynagh, Peter Slattery and Greg Martin. Represented Leinster at Schools (touring to Zimbabwe), U-19 and U-20, and Irish Schools in 1987/88 and 1988/89. Graduated to Ireland U-21 last season, wearing the No.12 jersey in the 15–22 defeat by Wales U-21 at Rodney Parade, Newport. Also played against Netherlands B (won 11–6, Leiden 18 Sep 1990)

Touchlines: Flying, waterskiing

Player to watch: Johnny Kenny (Bective Rangers)

Player of the year: Tim Horan (Australia)

Lawlor, P. J. Ireland

Full Name: Philip John Lawlor
1991/92 International category: Ireland Full (bench)
Club: Bective Rangers
Position: No.8
Height: 6'5" **Weight:** 16st 3lbs
Occupation: Farmer
Born: Kildare, 2.7.65
Family: Single
Former club: Naas
International debut: Ireland 20, Argentina 18, 1990
Best moment in rugby: Getting capped against touring Pumas
Worst moment in rugby: Breaking ankle playing for Leinster against South West Division (Sep 1989)

Other sporting achievements: Gaelic football for Naas

Most respected opponent: Wayne Shelford (Northampton & New Zealand)

Best memory last season: Being selected for Five Nations' squad and captaining club

Notable landmarks in rugby career: Played international rugby at three levels in 1990/91: for Ireland U-25s against Spain (won 36–17, Limerick 8 Sep 1990), for Ireland B against Argentina (won 27–12, Limerick 20 Oct 1990) and England (won 24–10, Old Belvedere 1 Mar 1991), and for Ireland against Argentina (Dublin, 27 Oct 1990). Last season was rather more static, being called upon only to fulfil bench reserve duties in the 1992 Five Nations' matches against England, Scotland and France. Made Leinster debut against Llanelli (1989/90), scoring two tries. Broke ankle on second provincial appearance and missed remainder of season. Captained Bective last season and would have played against England B but for an injury to Noel Mannion which led to his promotion to the senior bench

	apps	pts
Ireland U-25 (**1990**)		
Last Season	0 caps	0
Career	1 cap	0
Ireland B (**1990**)		
Last Season	0 caps	0
Career	2 caps	0
Ireland (**1990**)		
Last Season	0 caps	0
Career	1 cap	0

Caps (1): 1990 Arg
Points: Nil

Touchlines: Gaelic football, horse racing, golf
Player to watch: Mark Coddihy (Naas)

Leahy, K. T. Ireland

Full Name: Kelvin Tremaine Leahy
1991/92 International category: Ireland B
Club: Wanderers
Position: Flanker, No.8
Height: 6'2½" **Weight:** 16st
Occupation: Building Society manager
Born: Cork, 1.9.65
Family: Deidre (wife)
Family links with rugby: Father (Mick) played at lock (replacing Willie-John McBride) for Ireland in 6–15 loss to Wales in 1964
International debut: Ireland B 27, Argentina 12, 1990
Best moment in rugby: Captaining Ireland B to 16–0 win over Scotland B (1990/91)
Most respected opponent: Wanderers' flanker Philip Matthews
Best memory last season: Being selected to tour New Zealand with Ireland
Serious injuries: Shoulder dislocation (required operation)
Suggestions to improve rugby: *On-field* – Happy now try is worth five points. *Off-field* – Reimburse employers for lost working hours due to rugby
Notable landmarks in rugby career: Represented 1984 Irish Schools.

Replacement for Ireland U-25s v. US Eagles (1989/90). Captained Leinster and Ireland U-25s (against Spain) last season, scoring try for latter in 36–17 win (Limerick, 8 Sep 1990). Captained Ireland B to 16–0 defeat of Scotland (Ravenhill, 22 Dec 1990), having previously made debut in 27–12 win against touring Pumas (20 Oct 1990). Won third B cap last

	apps	pts
Ireland U-25 (**1990**)		
Last Season	0 cap	0
Career	1 cap	4
Ireland B (**1990**)		
Last Season	1 cap	0
Career	3 caps	0
Ireland		
1992	Tour to New Zealand	

season in 15–47 loss to England B (Richmond, 31 Jan 1992) prior to touring New Zealand with Ireland
Touchlines: Swimming, fishing (fly/spinning)
Player to watch: Richard Wallace (Garryowen)

Legge, S. Wales

Full Name: Sean Legge
1991/92 International category: Wales Full (bench)
Club: South Wales Police
Position: No.8
Height: 6'5" **Weight:** 16st 10lbs
Occupation: Police beat officer at Cardiff Central
Born: Cardiff, 21.8.68
Family: Claire (wife)
Family links with rugby: Brother (Darren) played for Royal Marines
Former clubs: Clandaff North Youth, Glamorgan Wanderers
International debut: Western Australia 6, Wales 22, 1991
Best moment in rugby: Scoring try for Wales in 7–3 win over Australian Capital Territory (Canberra, 10 Jul 1991)

	apps	pts
Wales (1991/92)	1 rep	

Worst moment in rugby: Being sent-off against Newbridge in 1989 and missing U-21 cap
Most embarrassing moment: Calling 'mark' in opposition half – crowd enjoyed it
Most respected opponent: Stuart Davies (Swansea & Wales)

Biggest influence on career: Steve Williams (ex-Glamorgan Wanderers coach)
Serious injuries: Stressed fractures of both legs; severed artery in arm (industrial accident)
Best memory last season: Being called onto Welsh replacements' bench for England game at Twickenham
Suggestions to improve rugby: *On-field* – Legalise lifting in lineout. It will make the set-piece more honest. Use two referees
Notable landmarks in rugby career: Not capped at any level, yet a member of every squad. Played centre in Youth rugby and called into Wales Youth in that position because there was no other recognised centre. However, broke leg a month before international. Represented Cardiff and District Youth and Glamorgan County. Gave up rugby between 14 and 18. Called into Wales squad last season after Martyn Morris moved up to replace food poisoned Emyr Lewis, thus vacating bench berth, for 24–0 defeat by England (7 Mar 1992)
Touchlines: Snooker
Player to watch: Scott Quinnell (Llanelli)
Player of the year: Emyr Lewis (Wales)

Leonard, J. England

Full Name: Jason Leonard
1991/92 International category: England Full
Club: Harlequins
Position: Loosehead prop
Height: 5'10" **Weight:** 17st 2lbs
Occupation: Self-employed builder
Born: Barking, London, 14.8.68
Family: Single
Former clubs: Barking, Saracens
International debut: England 12, Fiji 20, 1989
Five Nations' debut: Wales 6, England 25, 1991
Best moment in rugby: Winning two Grand Slams and helping Harlequins win 1991 Pilkington Cup final
Worst moment in rugby: Losing World Cup final with England

Most embarrassing moment: Ball landing on my head during B match in France (1989/90)

Most respected opponent: Jeff Probyn (Wasps & England) – technique and physical abilities

Serious injuries: Ruptured disc in back (1991/92)

Best memory last season: Adding second Grand Slam

Suggestions to improve rugby: *On-field* – Change ruck maul law. I fear it will be a big problem. Build more of an understanding with referees over interpretations. *Off-field* – If player loses out on pay because of rugby then reimburse him. It is an amateur game and players do not want to be paid but, equally, they do not want to lose out financially

Notable landmarks in rugby career: Only England forward to play all 12 games last season: both Tests on summer tour to Fiji and Australia, all six World Cup games (including final), and four games comprising 1992 Grand Slam. Stopped playing after Championship to have back sorted out; felt it start going against Scotland (18 Jan 1992) and finally rupture against Wales (7 Mar 1992). Replaced ruptured disc with piece of bone. Then waited for it to bond with existing vertebra. Off work for three months, taking it very slowly. Started career at Barking, helping them win Essex Colts Cup before tasting success at Twickenham with Eastern Counties winning U-21 County Championship. Won 1989/90 Courage League division two title with Saracens and sat on England U-21 bench in Romania (1989). Broke into England B ranks in 1989/90, winning caps against Fiji and France and warming bench against USSR before promoted to senior status on 1990 tour of Argentina

Player to watch: Justyn Cassell (Saracens)

Player of the year: Jon Webb (England)

	apps	pts
England B (1989)		
Last Season	0 caps	0
Career	2 caps	0
England (1990)		
Last Season	12 caps	0
Career	19 caps	0

Caps (19): 1990 Arg(a1, a2), Arg(b)
1991 W, S(a), I, F(a), Fj, A(a)
wc-NZ, It, US, F(b), S(b), A(b)
1992 S, I, F, W

Points: Nil

Lewis, E. W.   Wales

Full Name: Emyr Wyn Lewis
1991/92 International category:
Wales Full
Club: Llanelli
Positions: Flanker, No.8
Height: 6'4" **Weight:** 16st 9lbs
Occupation: Police beat officer
(Carmarthen)
Born: Carmarthen, 29.8.68
Family: Single
Former club: Carmarthen Athletic
International debut: Wales 21,
Ireland 21, 1991
Five Nations' debut: As above
Best moment in rugby: Selection
for first cap
Worst moment in rugby: Missing
England game last season due to
food poisoning on eve of game. I had
wanted to play in an England game
since I was a little boy
Most embarrassing moment:
Running down sidelines in support
of attack, playing against
Northampton (1990/91) and falling
over, twisting ankle in process
Most respected opponent:
Laurent Cabannes (Racing Club &
France)
Biggest influences on career: Peter
Herbert (fitness coach) and Gareth
Jenkins (Llanelli coach)

	apps	pts
Wales B (**1990**)		
Last Season	0 caps	0
Career	1 cap	0
Wales (**1991**)		
Last Season	8 caps	0
Career	10 caps	0

Caps   (10): **1991** I, F(a), A(a), F(b)
           wc-WS, Arg, A(b) **1992** I, F, S

Points: Nil

Best memories last season: Beating Ireland and Scotland in Five Nations'
Championship
Suggestions to improve rugby: *On-field* – Any rule to speed game up is all
right by me. *Off-field* – Reduce number of games being played. I reckon 35
Saturdays will be taken up with League, Cup or international matches this
season. Market the game better
Notable landmarks in rugby career: Missed playing for Welsh Schools
because too old by two days. Could not play for Wales Youth because still at
school, but on leaving represented Wales at U-20, U-21 and B (for two
minutes as replacement in 34–12 defeat of the Netherlands at Leiden, 2 Dec

1990) before graduating to senior level. Emerged from disastrous 1991 (tour to Australia and World Cup) with reputation enhanced. Having played for less than a minute of Llanelli's 1989 Schweppes Cup final loss to Neath (after coming on as a replacement), he was a Cup winner with the Scarlets in each of the past two seasons (1990/91 and 1991/92), scoring a try in 1990/91 defeat of Pontypool. Played in eight of Wales' nine matches last season

Touchlines: Fishing (river spinning), shooting
Player to watch: Neil Boobyer (Llanelli)
Player of the year: Peter Winterbottom (England)

Lewis, S. L. Wales

Full Name: Steele Lloyd Lewis
1991/92 International category:
Wales Full (tour squad)
Club: Pontypridd
Position: Centre
Height: 5'10" **Weight:** 13st 4lbs
Occupation: Roof tiler
Born: Rinteln, Germany, 29.10.64
Family: Alison (wife), Natasha (daughter)
Former clubs: Gilfach Goch, Tonyrefail
International debut (B): France 28, Wales 15, 1989
Best moment in rugby: Selection by Wales for 1991 tour to Australia
Most respected opponent: Ceri Jones (Pontypridd)
Best memory last season: Captaining Pontypridd to semi-finals of Schweppes Challenge Cup

Notable landmarks in rugby career: Toured Australia with Wales in 1991, playing against Australian Capital Territory (won 7–3,

	apps	pts
Wales B (**1989**)		
Last Season	0 caps	0
Career	2 caps	0
Wales 1991	Tour to Australia	

Canberra 10 Jul 1991) and Queensland Country (won 35–7, Rockhampton 17 Jul 1991). Was not required for 1991 World Cup, despite being a member of the preliminary squad. Made Wales B debut at La Teste (12 Nov 1989) when coming on as a 58th minute replacement for Colin Stephens during

15–28 loss to France B. Has also represented Mid-District and Glamorgan County
Touchlines: Swimming
Player to watch: Jason Lewis (Pontypridd)

Lineen, S. R. P.   Scotland

Full Name: Sean Raymond Patrick Lineen
1991/92 International category: Scotland Full
Club: Boroughmuir
Position: Centre
Height: 6'1½" **Weight:** 13st 5lbs
Occupation: Sales and Marketing manager with ScotRun Publications
Born: Auckland, New Zealand, 25.12.61
Family: Lynne (wife)
Family links with rugby: Terry (father) played twelve times for New Zealand (1957–60); Troy (brother) represented Auckland at junior level
Former clubs: Pakuranga, Papakura, Counties (all NZ), Bombay, Pontypool
International debut: Scotland 23, Wales 7, 1989
Five Nations' debut: As above
Best moment in rugby: First Scotland cap against Wales and winning 1990 Grand Slam
Worst moment in rugby: Losing to England in semi-finals of 1991 World Cup
Most embarrassing moment: Over-indulging on beverages at Gatwick on trip to join Boroughmuir after arriving early from New Zealand on 28-hour flight. When collected and taken straight to training with new team mates I brought everything up. So much for Muir's great New Zealand hope!
Most respected opponent: Philippe Sella (Agen & France)

	apps	pts
Scotland (**1989**)		
Last Season	10 caps	0
1992	Tour to Australia	
Career	27 caps	4

Caps (27): **1989** W, E, I, F, Fj, Ro **1990** I, F, W, E, NZ(1,2), Arg **1991** F, W, E, I, Ro wc-J, Z, I, E, NZ **1992** E, I, F, W

Points (4 – 1t): **1990** NZ(1:1t)

Biggest influence on career: My father

Serious injuries: Knee-cap popped off (required operation)

Other sporting achievements: Auckland junior badminton

Best memory last season: Beating Melrose in League and seeing my Kiwi mate Craig Segars cross for a try; having Scott Hastings as Best Man at my wedding

Suggestions to improve rugby: *On-field* – Standards of refereeing have improved but still nowhere near as good as the Southern Hemisphere officials. Problem is that nowadays we all have to go to university for four years just to understand the rules. *Off-field* – Clear cut definition of what players can and cannot do regarding rugby-related activities away from the field. At present 90% of earning opportunities for rugby union players have been taken away. Our responsibility is to leave the game, on and off the field, in a ship-shape condition for the next generation

Notable landmarks in rugby career: Share, with Scott Hastings, the distinction of being one half of the world's most-capped centre partnership (26 appearances prior to Australia tour). Boroughmuir's most-capped player. Helped Counties win first New Zealand National Sevens in 1985; first two performances for Boroughmuir – pleased with my start. Qualified for Scotland through grandfather who came from the Hebrides. Returned to New Zealand on tour with Scotland (1990) and also toured Japan (1989) and Australia (1992). Ever present throughout Scotland's last four Championship campaigns, having missed only one international (World Cup quarter-final v. Western Samoa – injured) since debut against Welsh in 1989. Helped Boroughmuir win first McEwan's League Championship in 1990/91

Touchlines: Racket sports, especially squash

Player to watch: Craig Joiner (Merchiston Castle)

Player of the year: Dewi Morris (England)

Llewellyn, G. D.   Wales

Full Name: Glyn David Llewellyn
1991/92 International category:
Wales Full
Club: Neath
Position: Lock
Height: 6'6" **Weight:** 17st 10lbs
Occupation: Sales executive with
Terotech (Dorking)
Born: Bradford on Avon, Wilts,
9.8.65
Family: Single
Family links with rugby: Brother
(Gareth) plays for Neath and Wales.
Father (David), who was in Army
with Will Carling's dad, is a qualified
WRU coach
Former clubs: Llanharan,
Bridgend, London Welsh, Llanelli
International debut: Namibia 9,
Wales 18, 1990
Five Nations' debut: Wales 6,
England 25, 1991
Best moment in rugby: Playing
with brother in Wales team for first
time, v. England at Cardiff (1990/91)
Worst moment in rugby: Getting
humiliated 63–6 by Australia in
Brisbane (21 Jul 1991)

	apps	pts
Wales **(1990)**		
Last Season	2 caps	0
Career	9 caps	0

Caps (9): 1990 Na(1,2), Ba **1991** E,
S, I, F(a), A(a), F(b)

Points: Nil

Most embarrassing moment: Having shorts ripped off when jockstrap-less
Most respected opponent: Phil May (Llanelli & Wales)
Biggest influence on career: The honesty of Neath RFC
Serious injuries: Torn knee ligaments (1987), broken thumb (1991)
Other sporting achievements: Welsh Schools basketball International
Best memory last season: Seeing the younger players in Neath squad
developing
Suggestions to improve rugby: *On-field* – More consistency in refereeing.
Eliminate line-out barging by preventing anyone from moving until ball has
been touched. Once penalty has been awarded move ball on 15 yards from
where offence occurred to discourage foul play while also encourage sides to
go for tries. I reckon the new lineout 'gap' rule will last three months before
the authorities find themselves back at square one. Too many petty new laws.
Off-field – Unification of laws. Present interpretations differ widely between

northern and southern hemispheres. WRU has slowly got its act together vis à vis the amateurism question, but the business management side of the operation still seems very naive

Notable landmarks in rugby career: Spent five years with London Welsh before returning to Wales on obtaining a post in Barry. Won six secondary caps. Ever present for Wales throughout five-game schedule in 1990/91 but lost place prior to 1991 World Cup after breaking thumb in a practice match against Wales U-21s. Toured Australia (1991), playing in 6–63 Test loss, and turned out under the Arms Park lights against France (4 Sep 1991). Partnered brother Gareth in second row on Five Nations' debut against England (19 Jan 1991). Missed 1991 World Cup after breaking thumb playing against the Welsh U-21s

Touchlines: Windsurfing, cricket, basketball and weights

Player to watch: Paul Jones (Neath)

Player of the year: Richard Webster (Wales)

Llewellyn, G. O.   Wales

Full Name: Gareth Owen Llewellyn
1991/92 International category: Wales Full
Club: Neath
Position: Lock
Height: 6'6" **Weight:** 17st 7lbs
Occupation: Fitter and turner with British Steel (Port Talbot)
Born: Cardiff, 27.2.69
Family: Single
Family links with rugby: Brother (Glyn) plays for Neath and Wales; father (David), who was in Army with Will Carling's dad, is a qualified WRU coach
Former club: Llanharan
International debut: Wales 9, New Zealand 34, 1989
Five Nations' debut: England 34, Wales 6, 1990

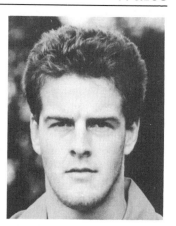

Best moment in rugby: Winning first Wales cap
Worst moment in rugby: Twice being dropped by Wales
Most embarrassing moment: Almost tripping over when running out at Cardiff for first cap
Most respected opponent: Ex-Cardiff & Wales lock Bob Norster

Biggest influence on career: Llanharan RFC as a whole
Serious injuries: Dislocated collarbone, damaged pelvis
Best memory last season: At last winning first game in a Welsh jersey, against Ireland
Suggestions to improve rugby: *On-field* – Greater consistency in refereeing interpretations. Ridiculous discrepancies exist at present. *Off-field* – Take better care of players

	apps	pts
Wales B (1989)		
Last Season	0 caps	0
Career	1 cap	0
Wales (1989)		
Last Season	5 caps	0
Career	11 caps	4

Caps (11): 1989 NZ 1990 E, S, I 1991 E, S, A(a:R) 1992 I, F, E, S

Points (4 – 1t): 1990 I(1t)

Notable landmarks in rugby career: Capped three times by Wales Youth. Toured New Zealand with Welsh U-19 team (1987), playing at No. 8. Also played for Crawshays and Barbarians. Represented Wales against England and Scotland in 1990/91 before losing place to Paul Arnold. Have partnered brother Glyn in second row both for Neath and Wales. Toured Australia with Wales in 1991, coming on as a 20th minute replacement for Phil Davies in 6–63 Test defeat to Wallabies. Omitted from Wales' World Cup squad. Recalled for 1992 Five Nations' Championship, as lock partner for Llanelli's Tony Copsey
Touchlines: Golf, squash, weights
Player to watch: Matthew McCarthy (Neath)
Player of the year: Peter Winterbottom (England)

David McIvor is the focus of attention at this gathering of the Gaelic clans during Scotland's 18–10 defeat of Ireland in Dublin. The visiting flanker is brought to earth by Nick Popplewell and Fergus Aherne

McAleese, D. R.   Ireland

Full Name: Derek Raymond
McAleese
1991/92 International category:
Ireland Full
Club: Ballymena
Position: Outside-half
Height: 6'2" **Weight:** 13st 10lbs
Occupation: Estate agent with
Halifax Property Services
Born: Limavady, 14.9.64
Family: Sharon (wife)
Former club: Limavady
International debut: France 44,
Ireland 12, 1992
Five Nations' debut: As above
Best moment in rugby: Running
out onto Parc des Princes for first
cap (21 Mar 1992)

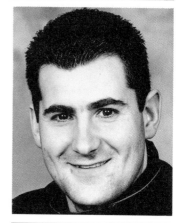

Worst moment in rugby: Breaking
jaw and cheekbone (1990) and being
out for four months
Most embarrassing moment:
Paris scoreline on debut
Most respected opponent:
Boroughmuir's Graham Drummond
Biggest influence on career: Davie
Smith (ex-Ballymena coach)
Serious injuries: Broken
jaw/cheekbone, recurring back
problem (chipped bone in spine)
Best memory last season: Landing

	apps	pts
Ireland B (**1990**)		
Last Season	1 cap	13
Career	2 caps	21
Ireland (**1992**)		
Last Season	1 cap	12
1992	Tour to New Zealand	
Career	1 cap	12

Caps (1): **1992** F
Points (12 – 4p): **1992** F(4p)

four penalty goals out of four on full debut against France
Suggestions to improve rugby: *On-field* – Legalise lifting in line-out. All
conversions to be taken in front of posts. More sympathetic and consistent
refereeing. We watch internationals on TV but when we try to emulate what
we see, at club level (i.e. rucking), we get penalised. Interpretations must be
unified between two hemispheres because rucking is a dead duck in the
northern hemisphere. *Off-field* – Full compensation for time lost to rugby and
travelling expenses for top players. New laws are going to demand extra fitness,
therefore increased commitment. Companies must be reimbursed when their
employees are away playing representative rugby. It is no longer a social game

although, in saying that, I do not need money. I would walk to Dublin to play for Ireland

Notable landmarks in rugby career: Represented Civil Service for three years. Joined Ballymena in 1987. Kicked two penalties and a conversion in Ireland B's 16–0 defeat of Scotland at Ravenhill (22 Dec 1990). Also represented Ulster U-20s and senior Ulster XV, winning first provincial cap against Bath (Sep 1990). Played key role in Ulster retaining Inter-Provincial Championship (1991/92). Helped Ballymena to hat-trick of Ulster Cup wins. After winning second B cap against Scotland B (Edinburgh, 28 Dec 1991) and scoring 13 points (2c,3p) in 29–19 win, he was promoted to senior side for final game of 1992 Five Nations' Championship and responded with 100 per cent success rate on goal kicks. Toured New Zealand with Ireland (1992)

Touchlines: Golf (handicap 9), summer soccer

Player to watch: Dean McCartney (Ballymena)

Player of the year: Will Carling (England)

McBride, W. D.   Ireland

Full Name: William **Denis** McBride

1991/92 International category:
Ireland Full (tour squad)

Club: Malone

Position: Flanker

Height: 5′11″ **Weight:** 14st

Occupation: Mechanical engineer

Born: Belfast, 9.9.64

Family: Catrina (wife)

Family links with rugby: Brother also plays

Former club: Queen's Univ Belfast

International debut: Ireland 9, Wales 12, 1988

Five Nations' debut: As above

Best moment in rugby: Ireland XV beating France XV 19–18 at Auch (1988) in non-cap tour match

Worst moment in rugby: Second half of Ireland's 3–35 defeat by England in 1988 when we conceded 35 points without reply

Most embarrassing moment: Ireland v. England (1988)

Most respected opponents: Wayne Shelford (Northampton & New Zealand) and Laurent Rodriguez (Dax & France)

Other sporting achievements:
Completed the 1982 Belfast City
Marathon
Best memory last season: Gaining
selection for Ireland's tour to New
Zealand
Suggestions to improve rugby:
On-field – Reduce value of penalty
goal. Scrap 90-degree scrummage
wheel law. *Off-field* – Better
marketing of the sport. All countries
should send teams to Hong Kong
Sevens. Permit players to benefit from off-field activities

	apps	pts
Ireland B (**1990**)		
Last Season	0 cap	0
Ireland (**1988**)		
Last Season	0 caps	0
1991	Tour to New Zealand	
Career	8 caps	8

Caps (8): **1988** W,E(a),WS,It **1989** S **1990** F,W,Arg

Points (8–2t): **1988** WS (It) **1990** W(It)

Notable landmarks in rugby career: Represented Ulster in 3–21 loss to
1989 All Blacks (Ravenhill, 21 Nov 1989). Attended 1989 Hong Kong Sevens
with Irish Wolfhounds. Represented Ireland B in 27–12 win over Argentina
B last season before winning eighth cap in 20–18 defeat of touring Pumas at
Lansdowne Road. Failed to add to his tally thereafter, but was recalled for
1992 tour to New Zealand, only to return early following a freak training
accident when he caught a stud in Kelvin Leahy and broke a toe
Touchlines: Athletics (400 metres)
Player to watch: Richard Wallace (Garryowen)

McCarthy, P. D.   Ireland

Full Name: Paul David McCarthy
1991/92 International category:
Ireland Full (bench)
Club: Cork Constitution
Position: Tighthead prop
Height: 6′ **Weight:** 18st
Occupation: Service engineer
Born: Cork, 27.8.63
Former club: Dolphin
International debut (B): Ireland
16, Scotland 0, 1990
Best moments in rugby: Helping
Ireland B beat England B 24–10
(1991), and Cork Con winning
inaugural All-Ireland League
(1990/91)
Worst moment in rugby: Getting
injured

Most respected opponent: Staff
Jones (ex-Pontypool & Wales)
Best memory last season: Being
called up onto Ireland bench for
England match at Twickenham
Suggestions to improve rugby:
On-field – Improve refereeing of
scrum

	apps	pts
Ireland B (**1990**)		
Last Season	1 cap	4
Career	3 caps	4
Ireland (**1991/92**)	1 rep	
1992	Tour to New Zealand	

Notable landmarks in rugby career: Selected to tour New Zealand (1992)
with Ireland's senior squad after season which featured bench reserve duty at
Twickenham in the 1992 Five Nations' Championship. Previously, had won
Schools Junior and Senior Cup medals. Represented Munster in Irish
Inter-Provincial Championships and Ireland B against Scotland B (won 16–0,
Ravenhill 22 Dec 1990), England B (won 24–10, Old Belvedere 1 Mar 1991)
and Scotland B (won 29–19, Edinburgh 28 Dec 1991), scoring a try in the
latter
Touchlines: Shooting, fishing
Player to watch: Philip Soden (Constitution)

Macdonald, A. E. D.   Scotland

Full Name: Andrew Edward
Douglas Macdonald
1991/92 International category:
Scotland B
Clubs: Heriot's FP
Positions: No.8, lock
Height: 6'8" **Weight:** 17st 10lbs
Occupation: Surveyor with Ryden
Chartered Surveyors (Edinburgh)
Born: Nairn, 17.1.66
Family: Single
Former clubs: Loughborough
Univ, London Scottish, Cambridge
Univ
International debut (B): Scotland
22, Ireland 22, 1989
Best moment in rugby: Winning
1989 Varsity match
Worst moment in rugby: Missing
out on selection for Scotland tour to Australia (1992)
Most embarrassing moment: Being sent-off and breaking hand

simultaneously in UAU semi-final, then being headlined as a 'villain' in *Times* report

Most respected opponent: Robert Norster (ex-Cardiff & Wales) – constantly outjumps taller opponents

Biggest influence on career: Ian Barnes' rucking scarf

	apps	pts
Scotland U-21 (**1991**)		
Last Season	0 caps	0
Career	1 cap	0
Scotland B (**1991**)		
Last Season	2 caps	0
Career	2 caps	0

Serious injuries: Broken hand, ankle ligaments, prolapsed disc (out for three months)

Other sporting achievements: Bowling Steve James (future cricket star with Glamorgan) in net practice

Best memory last season: Turning out at Murrayfield for Barbarians against Scotland

Suggestions to improve rugby: *On-field* – New mauling rule is going to cause problems for referees. Improve consistency of referees' decisions. Eliminate 90-degree wheel law. Get coaches more involved in selection. *Off-field* – Relax amateur laws to help growth of game

Notable landmarks in rugby career: Capped by Scotland at U-21 and B level and made four appearances on Scotland's six-match 1991 tour to North America, including both non-cap 'tests' against US Eagles (won 41–12 and scored try) and Canada (lost 19–24). Played against Scotland for Barbarians at Murrayfield (7 Sep 1991) and then went on Barbarians' Irish tour, opposing Old Wesley and Cork Constitution. Very close to full Scotland cap last year but Neil Edwards earned nod instead after a better Trial. Represented Scotland B in four losing causes – twice against Ireland B (0–16, Ravenhill 22 Dec 1990) and France B three times (9–31, Oyonnax 21 Jan 1990; 10–31, Hughenden 2 Mar 1991; 18–27, Albi 3 Feb 1992) – and in one draw (22–22 v. Ireland B, Murrayfield, 9 Dec 1989). Marked Scotland A debut (Murrayfield, 28 Dec 1991) with try in 36–16 win over Spain

Touchlines: Keen ukelele player, golf (handicap 14)

Players to watch: Alan Buzza (Wasps), Duncan Macrae (Boroughmuir)

Player of the year: Andy Nicol (Scotland)

McIntosh, D. L. M.   Scotland

Full Name: Dale Lynsay Manawa McIntosh
1991/92 International category: Scotland B
Club: Pontypridd
Positions: Flanker, No.8
Height: 6'3" **Weight:** 16st
Occupation: Labourer with Monk Construction, Cardiff
Born: Turangi, New Zealand, 23.11.69
Family: Single
Family links with rugby: Brother (Shane) plays for West of Scotland
Former clubs: King Country (NZ), Counties (NZ), Hawkes Bay (NZ), Taupo United (NZ)
International debut (B): Scotland 19, Ireland 29, 1991
Best moment in rugby: Being nominated for the 1992 Scottish Trial
Most respected opponent: Wayne Shelford (Northampton & New Zealand)
Biggest influence on career: Colin Meads (president at Kings Country)
Serious injuries: Dislocated both shoulders in past two seasons

	apps	pts
Scotland B (1989)		
Last Season	1 cap	0
Career	5 caps	0
Scotland A (1991)		
Last Season	1 cap	4
Career	1 cap	4

Best memory last season: Going to Cardiff Arms Park with Pontypridd for the Schweppes Challenge Cup semi-final against Llanelli
Suggestions to improve rugby: *On-field* – Standardise refereeing world-wide. Allow players to get on with game – too many needless stoppages. *Off-field* – All aspects could be improved
Notable landmarks in rugby career: Played two games for New Zealand U-18s before coming to Wales to play for Pontypridd (1990/91). Eligible for Scotland through Edinburgh-born grandfather and turned out for Scottish U-21s in 15–23 loss to Wales counterparts (Llanelli, 20 Apr 1991). Graduated to Scotland B in 1991/92 season, turning out at No.8 in both games, against Ireland (lost 19–29, Edinburgh 28 Dec 1991) and France (lost 18–27, Albi 3 Feb 1992)
Touchlines: Tennis, weightlifting

Players to watch: Paul John (Pontypridd), Shane McIntosh (West of Scotland)
Player of the year: Emyr Lewis (Llanelli & Wales)

McIvor, D. J. Scotland

Full Name: David John McIvor
1991/92 International category:
Scotland Full
Club: Edinburgh Academicals
Positions: No.8, flanker
Height: 6'1" **Weight:** 16st 8lbs
Occupation: Communications
technician for Fife Region
Born: Kirkcaldy, 29.6.64
Family: Pauline (wife), Jamie and
David (sons)
Former clubs: Dunfermline,
Glenrothes
International debut: Scotland 7,
England 25, 1992
Five Nations'' debut: As above
Best moment in rugby: Winning
first cap in 1992 Calcutta Cup match
Worst moment in rugby: Losing
above match to England
Most embarrassing moment:
Getting called 'Grandad' by the
opposition (because of my grey hair)
Most respected opponent: John
Jeffrey (Kelso & ex-Scotland)
Biggest influence on career:
Self-motivation
Best memory last season: Being
presented with my Scotland jersey
prior to first cap

	apps	pts
Scotland B (**1991**)		
Last Season	1 cap	0
Career	2 caps	0
Scotland (**1992**)		
Last Season	4 caps	0
1992	Tour to Australia	
Career	4 caps	0

Caps (4): **1992** E, I, F, W
Points: Nil

Suggestions to improve rugby:
On-field – Reduce value of penalty goal to two points. Pleased try's value has been increased – game was so boring before. *Off-field* – More financial assistance for international players. Compensation for time given to rugby over work
Notable landmarks in rugby career: Broke into Scotland side in time for 1992 Five Nations' Championship. One of four new caps fielded against

England. Played all four Championship games and then spent summer touring with senior party in Australia. Previously, played first District game for North and Midlands in 1986, having represented North/Mids U-18s in 1982 and U-21s in 1985. Helped North/Mids beat Anglo-Scots at Oxford (15 Dec 1990) for first win in McEwan's Scottish Inter-District Championship since 1984. Made Scotland B debut against France in 10–31 defeat at Hughenden (2 Mar 1991) and added second cap in 19–29 loss to Ireland B (Murrayfield, 28 Dec 1991)

Touchlines: Golf (handicap 14), table-tennis
Player to watch: Gregor Townsend (Gala)
Player of the year: Will Carling (England)

Malone, N. G.   Ireland

Full Name: Niall Gareth Malone
1991/92 International category:
Ireland U-21
Club: Loughborough Students
Position: Outside-half
Height: 5'11" **Weight:** 13st
Occupation: PE student
Born: Leeds, 30.4.71
Family: Single
Former club: Collegians (Belfast)
International debut: Netherlands 21, Ireland U-21 7, 1990
Best moment in rugby: Winning 1989 Schools Cup with Methodists (Belfast) against Wallace HS
Most embarrassing moment: Missing kick in front of posts in above match
Most respected opponent: Tony Underwood (Leicester, Cambridge Univ & England B)
Serious injuries: Dislocated elbow
Other sporting achievements: Soccer for Belfast Primary Schools
Best memory last season: Beating England U-21s for second successive season

	apps	pts
Ireland U-21 (**1990**)		
Last Season	2 caps	3
Career	4 caps	24

Suggestions to improve rugby: More feedback from selectors. They should be obliged to tell a player why he has been dropped
Notable landmarks in rugby career: Represented Ulster Schools, Ulster

U-19s, Ulster U-20s, 1989 Irish Schools, Irish Exiles U-21s, Irish Exiles, Ireland U-21s, England Universities. Last season, represented an International Select XV against the Irish President's XV (one of Ireland's World Cup build-up matches) and kicked dropped goal in 18–10 win over England U-21s. Previously, landed penalty goal on U-21 debut against Netherlands and kicked five penalty goals and a dropped goal against England in 1990/91 season
Player to watch: Diccon Edwards (Loughborough)

Mannion, N. P. S.   Ireland

Full Name: Noel Patrick Stephen Mannion
1991/92 International category: Ireland Full
Club: Lansdowne
Positions: No.8, flanker
Height: 6'5" **Weight:** 17st
Occupation: Sales representative with Dubarry Shoes/Pony sportswear
Born: Ballinasloe, 12.1.63
Family: Single
Family links with rugby: Brother (Jack) played for Galwegians and Connacht
Former clubs: Ballinasloe, Drumoyne (Aus), Corinthians
International debut: Ireland 49, Western Samoa 22, 1988
Five Nations' debut: Ireland 21, France 26, 1989
Best moment in rugby: Intercepting Welsh kick on own 22 and running ball back for Ireland try in 19–13 win (Cardiff, 4 Feb 1989)
Worst moment in rugby: Running a quick penalty for Connacht against Ulster, tripping for no apparent reason, and knocking ball forwards
Most embarrassing moment: As above
Most respected opponent: Wayne Shelford (Northampton & New Zealand)
Biggest influence on career: Oliver Burke (Connacht U-20 coach) – way ahead of his time

	apps	pts
Ireland (1988)		
Last Season	3 caps	8
Career	15 caps	12

Caps (15): **1988** WS, It **1989** F, W, E, S, NZ **1990** E, S, F, W, Arg **1991** Na(1R,2) wc-J

Points (12 – 3t): **1989** W(1t) **1991** wc-J(2t)

Serious injuries: Broken collarbone, wrist. Twisted knee
Other sporting achievements: Played one season of Gaelic football for Galway. Came on as replacement during 1987 All-Ireland semi-final replay defeat by Cork
Best memory last season: Scoring two tries against Japan in World Cup
Suggestions to improve rugby: *On-field –* Standardise refereeing in southern and northern hemispheres. Presently too many different interpretations. Conformity is desperately needed. *Off-field –* Clarify laws regarding amateurism. What, exactly, are we entitled to do? No-one is clear. If problem is not sorted, the other sports will start attracting the best players in Ireland
Notable landmarks in rugby career: Represented Connacht at Schools and U-20 level before making senior Provincial debut in 1985. Played for Ireland U-25s against Canada following season. First Corinthians player to be capped by Ireland. Scored famous try in second full appearance. Toured with Ireland to Canada (1989) and was an ever present. Made Barbarians bow against Newport in 1989/90. Switched clubs from Corinthians to Lansdowne at start of 1990/91, having won Connacht Senior Cup medal with former in 1988. Lost place in Ireland side after 20–18 defeat of Argentina. Nine times a replacement of Ireland, including on four occasions last season. Toured with Ireland to Namibia (1991) and New Zealand (1992)
Touchlines: Music, reading
Player to watch: Niall Hogan (Terenure College)
Player of the year: Nick Farr-Jones (Australia)

Dewi Morris wears a terrified expression as Scotland's forwards pile into a ruck at Murrayfield, during the Championship opener which England won 25–7

Marshall, G. R.   Scotland

Full Name: Graham Robert Marshall
1991/92 International category: Scotland Full
Club: Selkirk
Position: Flanker
Height: 6'3" **Weight:** 15st 7lbs
Occupation: PE teacher at Selkirk HS
Born: Glasgow, 23.5.60
Family: Anne (wife), Callum (son) and Kirsty (daughter)
Former clubs: Jordanhill, Wakefield
International debut: Scotland 13, Australia 32, 1988
Best moment in rugby: Coming on as replacement for Derek White against Wallabies to win first cap
Worst moment in rugby: Rupturing medial and cruciate ligaments in right knee (against Watsonians) the week prior to 1992 Calcutta Cup match
Most respected opponent: Whoever playing against next
Serious injuries: Ruptured medial/cruciate ligaments (right knee)
Other sporting achievements: Professional footballer with Dundee United reserves (1979) for a year. I did not think I was good enough and I was given a free transfer at the end of the year

	apps	pts
Scotland B (**1987**)		
Last Season	0 caps	0
Career	2 caps	0
Scotland A (**1990**)		
Last Season	1 cap	0
Career	2 caps	0
Scotland (**1988**)		
Last Season	1 cap	0
Career	4 caps	0
Scotland VII (**1991**)	Hong Kong Sevens	

Caps (4): **1988** A(R) **1989** Fj **1990** Arg **1991** wc-Z

Points: Nil

Most respected opponent: Peter Winterbottom (Harlequins & England)
Biggest influence in career: Richie Dixon (Scotland assistant coach) – Teacher at Currie HS who lured me from soccer to rugby
Best memory last season: The World Cup – wonderful experience and chance of a lifetime
Suggestions to improve rugby: *On-field* – Tidy up line-out which is such a mess at present. Perhaps revert to double-banking. Schools have played the new mauling rule with some success but I think it might be different at senior

level. *Off-field* – Clarify amateur situation. We are lagging behind other nations. Look after injured players. I got excellent medical treatment, with SRU covering my physiotherapy expenses, and my job (I was off for ten weeks) made sure that I did not lose out financially. But I wonder how non-international players would cope

Notable landmarks in rugby career: Toured with Scotland to Japan (1989), New Zealand (1990) and North America (1991). Played in 38–17 win v. Fiji (Oct 1989). Played one season for Scottish Schools (1978). Twice represented Scottish XVs and twice Scotland B (1988). Sat on U-21 bench. Won third full cap when Touring Pumas visited Murrayfield last season. Bench reserve throughout 1991 Five Nations' Championship. Played in first official Scotland VII at 1991 Hong Kong Sevens. Injury in January (11 Jan 1991) last season forced me out of game for an estimated 12 months. Previously, won fourth cap in World Cup-tie against Zimbabwe, turned out for Scotland XV in 16–16 draw with Barbarians (7 Sep 1991), and helped Scotland A beat Spain (for second consecutive season) 36–16 at Murrayfield (28 Dec 1991)

Player to watch: Stuart Reid (Boroughmuir)

Player of the year: Doddie Weir (Scotland)

. . . STOP PRESS . . . STOP PRESS . . . STOP PRESS . . .

SCOTLAND TO AUSTRALIA
May–June 1992 – Record: P8, W2, D2, L4, F150, A177.

Results: (1) Northern Territory Select, lost 16-17; (2) Queensland, drew 15-15; (3) Emerging Wallabies, drew 24-24; (4) New South Wales, lost 15-35; (5) New South Wales Country, won 26-10; (6) first Test: Australia, lost 12-27; (7) Queensland Country, won 29-12; (8) second Test: Australia, won 13-37.

1st Test: G Hastings (Watsonians); A Stanger (Hawick), S Hastings (Watsonians), S Lineen (Boroughmuir), I Tukalo (Selkirk); C Chalmers (Melrose), A Nicol (Dundee HSFP); D Sole (Edin Acads, capt), K Milne (Heriot's FP), P Wright (Boroughmuir), C Hogg (Melrose), N Edwards (Harlequins), G Weir (Melrose), I Smith (Gloucester), R Wainwright (Edin Acads). **Repl**: I Corcoran (Gala) for Milne, 10 mins.

Scorers – Try: Wainwright. **Conversion:** G Hasings. **Penalty goals:** G Hastings 2.

2nd Test: K Logan (Stirling Co); Stanger, S Hastings, Lineen, Tukalo; Chalmers, Nicol; Sole (capt), M Scott (Dunfermline), Wright, Hogg, D Cronin (London Scottish), Weir, Smith, Wainwright.

Scorers – Tries: Lineen, Sole. **Conversion:** Chalmers. **Penalty goal:** Chalmers.

Matthews, N. J.   England

Full Name: Neil John Matthews
1991/92 International category:
England U-21/B (NZ tour)
Club: Gloucester
Position: Outside-half
Height: 5'10" **Weight:** 12st 7lbs
Occupation: Director of Matthews
Leisure (fete equipment)
Born: Gloucester, 11.4.70
Family: Single
Family links with rugby: Father
(Tom) played for Longlevens.
Brother (Wayne) plays No.8 for
Gordon League
Former clubs: Longlevens,
Cheltenham Colts
International debut (U-21):
England 16, Ireland 22, 1990
Best moment in rugby: Touring
New Zealand with England B (1992)
Worst moment in rugby:
Gloucester losing 1991/92
Pilkington Cup semi-final to Bath in
extra-time
Most respected opponent: Stuart
Barnes (Bath & England B)

	apps	pts
England U-21 (**1990**)		
Last Season	1 cap	8
Career	4 caps	12
England B		
1992	Tour to New Zealand	

Best memory last season: Selection for England B tour to New Zealand
Serious injuries: Broken thumb
Suggestions to improve rugby: *On-field* – More points for a try. Less points for a penalty
Notable landmarks in rugby career: Made debut for England U-21s at outside-half against Ireland, retaining place throughout 1990/91 season, against Netherlands and French Armed Forces. Scored game's only try in 7–9 loss to French. Added two further tries to tally in England U-21s' 94–0 defeat of Belgium (Wolverhampton, 1 Sep 1991). Started out with Longlevens (until aged 17). Played for Cheltenham, Gloucestershire and England Colts (breaking thumb in first half of first Colts international against Italy). Invited to tour Portugal with Gloucester (aged 18). Invited to tour with England B to New Zealand (1992)
Touchlines: Pool, golf
Player to watch: Tony Windo (Gloucester)
Player of the year: Dewi Morris (England)

144

Matthews, P. M.   Ireland

Full Name: Philip Michael Matthews

1991/92 International category: Ireland Full

Club: Wanderers

Position: Flanker

Height: 6'3" **Weight:** 16st

Occupation: Marketing manager with Pitman-Moore (Dublin)

Born: Gloucester, 24.1.60

Family: Lisa (wife) and Hannah (daughter)

Family links with rugby: Father-in-law (Kevin Flynn) won 22 caps for Ireland (1959–73)

Former clubs: Queen's Univ Belfast, Ards

International debut: Ireland 9, Australia 16, 1984

Five Nations' debut: Scotland 18, Ireland 15, 1985

Best moment in rugby: Scoring for Barbarians against 1989 All Blacks at Twickenham

Worst moment in rugby: Missing out on selection for 1989 Lions

Most respected opponent: None in particular

Serious injuries: Dislocated elbow

Best memory last season: Coming so close to beating Australia in World Cup quarter-final

	apps	pts
Ireland (**1984**)		
Last Season	7 caps	0
Career	38 caps	16

Caps (38): **1984** A **1985** S, F, W, E, Ro **1987** E, S, F, W(a) wc-W(b), T, A **1988** S, F, W, E(a, b), WS, It **1989** F, W, E, S, NZ **1990** E, S **1991** F, W, E, S, Na (1) wc-Z, S, A **1992** W, E, S

Points (16 – 4t): **1987** E(1t) **1988** WS(1t), It(2t)

Suggestions to improve rugby: *On-field* – More points for a try and reduce value of penalty goal. All conversions to be taken under posts. *Off-field* – Pay players and coaches (you have to take extreme line to get any change). Remove shackles of amateurism and take realistic long-term view of what is happening in other sports. Bring younger retired players on to the committees

Notable landmarks in rugby career: The Bull & Bear in Hong Kong. Won five Schools caps (1977–78), captaining team three times. Became Ards' first International when capped in 1984. Missed 1985/86 season due to injury. Irish rugby writers' choice as 'Player of Year' in 1988. Captained Ireland six times between 1988 and the start of 1989/90 (v. WS, It, F, W, E, S), when

Willie Anderson took over. Represented Barbarians and Home Unions (against France) in 1989/90. Ever present for Ireland in 1991 Five Nations' Championship campaign and was given captaincy for second time, in succession to Rob Saunders for 1991 tour to Namibia, World Cup and three-quarters of 1992 Five Nations' Championship. Lost place in Irish team, after a career total of 13 matches as captain, for France game (21 Mar 1992)

Touchlines: Golf

Player to watch: Nick Popplewell (Greystones) – outstanding player. We really do not see the half of his ability in Irish rugby

Player of the year: Dewi Morris (England)

Ireland scrum-half Rob Saunders sees his life flash before him while being hugged by Wales hooker Garin Jenkins, during the Principality's first Championship win for three seasons, 16–15 in Dublin

May, P. S. Wales

Full Name: Philip Stephen May
1991/92 International category:
Wales Full
Club: Llanelli
Position: Lock
Height: 6′6″ **Weight:** 17st 7lbs
Occupation: General manager of
Llanelli RFC
Born: Llanelli, 1.7.56
Family: Ann (wife), Owen and
David (sons)
Former club: New Dock Stars
International debut: England 3,
Wales 11, 1988
Five Nations' debut: As above
Best moment in rugby: Making
Welsh debut at Twickenham
Worst moment in rugby:
Dislocating shoulder in 1991 World
Cup (required operation)
Most respected opponent: Paul
Ackford (ex-Harlequins & England)
– the best player I've ever seen
Serious injuries: Broken everything
Best memory last season: Playing
three or four games and being carried
off in most of those
Suggestions to improve rugby:

	apps	pts
Wales B (1986)		
Career	1 cap	0
Wales (1988)		
Last Season	1 cap	0
Career	7 caps	0

Caps (7): **1988** E, S, I, F, NZ(1,2)
1991 wc-WS

Points: Nil

On-field – Law makers should spend
a lot more time looking at the lineout.
Bring back double-banking and player assistance. *Off-field* – Heineken Leagues
and Alan Davies have made all the difference to Welsh rugby. Both have
improved standards enormously
Notable landmarks in rugby career: Returned to Wales line-up in 18th
first-class season with Llanelli, when selected ('a total surprise') by coach Alan
Davies for 1991 World Cup squad. It proved a fleeting return as he was helped
off after 30 minutes of the first game against Western Samoa (Cardiff, 6 Oct
1991). Previous six caps had come in 1988 season when he played throughout
Triple Crown campaign in Five Nations' Championship and then toured New
Zealand. Solitary Wales B cap came partnering Kevin Moseley at lock in
13–10 win over France B at Pontypridd in October 1986. Llanelli club captain

for five seasons, having first played for Scarlets in October 1974 as an 18-year old
Touchlines: National Hunt horse racing
Player to watch: Andrew Lamerton (Llanelli)
Player of the year: Mickey Skinner (England)

Milne, D. F.   Scotland

Full Name: David Ferguson Milne
1991/92 International category: Scotland Full
Club: Heriot's FP
Position: Prop
Height: 5'11½" **Weight:** 15st 8lbs
Occupation: Sales manager with Servier Laboratories
Born: Edinburgh, 7.12.58
Family: Julia (wife) and Rory (son)
Family links with rugby: Brothers Kenny and Iain play for Heriot's and Scotland
Former clubs: Bordeaux Students (France, 1981–82), Worcester, Stourbridge
International debut: Scotland 47, Japan 9, 1991 (World Cup)
Best moment in rugby: Helping comprise all-Milne front row for Barbarians against East Midlands in 1989 Mobbs Memorial match
Worst moment in rugby: Heriot's throwing away chance of 1990/91 McEwan's Scottish League Championship with diabolical team performance in defeat at hands of champions-to-be Boroughmuir
Most embarrassing moment: Missing the Zimbabwe match in the 1991 World Cup as a result of a pulled groin muscle sustained when slipping while in the act of leaving the Murrayfield stand to come on as a replacement for debut against Japan
Most respected opponent: Pascal Ondarts (Biarritz & France)
Biggest influence on career: Brothers and coach Randall Phillip

	apps	pts
Scotland B (**1986**)		
Last Season	1 cap	0
Career	6 caps	0
Scotland A (1991/92)	1 rep	
Scotland (**1991**)		
Last Season	1 cap	0
Career	1 cap	0

Caps (1): **1991** wc-J(R)
Points: Nil

Serious injuries: Ruptured cruciate ligaments in both knees. Prior to 1990/91 season surgeon advised me to stop playing. Undergone eight knee operations in all. Dislocated shoulder

Best memory last season: Winning first cap

Suggestions to improve rugby: *On-field* – Differential penalty to judge between technical and physical violation (worth one and three points respectively). Far too easy to score/concede points through technical infringements at present. Take all conversions in front of posts. *Off-field* – Relax demands on players at top level to have to play at various representative levels. Recognise the amount of time given by players to rugby. Compensate employers. If selected for a side one should be trusted more to devise one's own fitness programme etc. Too many squad sessions – more consideration for players' families. Reconstruct Scottish season, concluding leagues by December and playing a Cup competition up until the New Year. Leave January and February free for internationals so those involved do not have to play any club rugby. We should not have that dilemna

Notable landmarks in rugby career: Played for Edinburgh Schools and later, in Scottish Inter-District Championship, for Anglo-Scots and Edinburgh. First Scotland appearance was for U-21s against British Post Office! Scotland replacement in each of 1991 Five Nations' matches before finally winning first cap, at the age of 32 (5 Oct 1991), as a 75th minute replacement for David Sole. Made Scotland B debut five years previously in 12–10 defeat of France B at Villefranche-sur-Saône and won sixth and most recent B cap in 10–31 loss to France B at Hughenden (2 Mar 1991). Toured to North America with Scotland (1991)

Touchlines: Weightlifting, keeping fit

Player to watch: John Robertson (Heriot's FP)

Player of the year: Andy Nicol (Scotland)

Milne, I. G.   Scotland

Full Name: Iain Gordon Milne
1991/92 International category:
Scotland Full (bench)
Club: Heriot's FP
Position: Tighthead prop
Height: 6' **Weight:** 17st 9lbs
Occupation: Sales manager with
Sun Chemical Inks (UK) Ltd
Born: Edinburgh, 17.6.58
Family: Marian (wife) and Ross
Gordon (son)
Family links with rugby: Kenny
(brother) plays for Heriot's and
Scotland. David (brother) plays for
Heriot's and Scotland
Former club: Harlequins
International debut: Scotland 11,
Ireland 11, 1979
Five Nations' debut: As above
Best moments in rugby: Winning
1979 Scottish Championship with
Heriot's and 1984 Grand Slam with
Scotland
Worst moment in rugby:
Damaging bones in a foot against
Wales in 1989 and missing game
against England
Most embarrassing moment:
Putting on too much Deep Heat
before first match as Heriot's FP
captain and having to leave for a
shower midway through my first
pre-match team talk
Most respected opponent: Any
French front row forward

	apps	pts
Scotland (**1979**)		
Last Season	1 rep	
Career	44 caps	0
Lions 1983		
1986		

Caps (44): **1979** I, F, NZ, **1980** I, F
1981 NZ(1,2), Ro, A **1982** E, I,
F, W, A(1,2) **1983** I, F, W, E,
NZ **1984** W, E, I, F, A **1985** F,
W, E **1986** F, W, E, I, Ro **1987**
I, F, W, E wc-F, Z, NZ **1988** A
1989 W **1990** NZ(1,2)
Points: Nil

Biggest influences on career: Andy Irvine (Heriot's) and Jim Telfer
(Scotland)
Best memory last season: Selection for World Cup squad, prior to having
to pull out with neck injury
Suggestions to improve rugby: *On-field* – Do away with up-and-unders: far
too easy way of gaining 40 metres; takes away from handling skills. Play
Internationals later in season. 90-degree wheels: put-in should go to team

going forwards. Penalise heavily those players trying to be negative and destructive in pile-up situations. *Off-field* – Too many idiosyncracies between nations over amateurism. Should be unified and carved in tablets of stone. Open up the whole subject

Notable landmarks in career: First called into national squad as 20-year-old in 1978. Toured New Zealand with 1983 British Lions. With Scotland, toured New Zealand (1981 and 1990), Australia (1982) and North America (1985), and played in 1987 World Cup. Bench reserve for Scotland's 49–3 defeat of Argentina (Edinburgh, 10 Nov 1990) and, last season, for Scotland's 12–18 defeat to Romania in Bucharest (31 Aug 1991). Selected for World Cup squad but neck injury forced withdrawal

Touchlines: Keen angler (salmon and trout)

Player to watch: Andy Nicol (Dundee HSFP)

Player of the year: Andy Nicol (Scotland)

Milne, K. S.   Scotland

Full Name: Kenneth Stuart Milne
1991/92 International category:
Scotland Full
Club: Heriot's FP
Position: Hooker
Height: 6′ **Weight:** 15st 7lbs
Occupation: Sales representative
with P. E. C. Barr, Printers of Leith
Born: Edinburgh, 1.12.61
Family: Eleanor (wife), Stuart (son)
and Jenny (daughter)
Family links with rugby: Iain
(brother) plays for Heriot's,
Scotland and British Lions. David
(brother) plays for Heriot's and
Scotland

International debut: Scotland 23,
Wales 7, 1989
Five Nations' debut: As above
Best moment in rugby: 1990 Grand Slam
Worst moment in rugby: Being dropped at any level
Most embarrassing moment: Accidentally flooring the referee when the front rows of Heriot's and Jed-Forest squared up. He let me off
Most respected opponents: Gary Callender (Kelso & Scotland) and Brian Moore (Harlequins & England)
Biggest influence on career: Brothers Iain and David

Best memory last season: Being re-selected for World Cup

Suggestions to improve rugby: *On-field* – Stop changing the rules. Scottish Inter-District Championship should be broadened to include likes of Bath and Leicester. A British League of sorts, with stronger opposition, must be the way forward. *Off-field* – Clarification of amateurism issue desperately needed. More could be done for the players. Rewards are very minimal, espacially in Scotland

	apps	pts
Scotland B (1986)		
Last Season	0 caps	0
Career	6 caps	
Scotland (1989)		
Last Season	5 caps	0
Career	20 caps	12

Caps (20): **1989** W, E, I, F, Fj, Ro **1990** I, F, W, E, NZ(2), Arg **1991** F, W, E wc-Z **1992** E, I, F, W

Points (12 – 3t): **1989** Fj(1t) **1990** Arg(2t)

Notable landmarks in rugby career: Won back hooker's berth in Scotland team from John Allan last season, playing throughout 1992 Championship after making just the one appearance in World Cup. Scored first international try against Fiji (Oct 1989). First Scotland hooker to score two tries in International (in 49–3 defeat of Argentina, Edinburgh 10 Nov 1990). Toured with Scotland to North America (1985 & 1991) and New Zealand (1990). Lost out to John Allan in non-cap 'test' matches v. US Eagles and Canada during 1991 tour. Youngest of the three-capped Milne brothers

Touchlines: Fly fishing (salmon & trout)

Player to watch: John Robertson (Heriot's FP)

Player of the year: Doddie Weir (Scotland)

England replacement David Pears, covered in French hands, slips a pass to Peter Winterbottom during the 31–13 win in Paris

Moncrieff, M.   Scotland

Full Name: Mark Moncrieff
1991/92 International category:
Scotland B
Club: Gala
Position: Wing
Height: 5'10" **Weight:** 11st 10lbs
Occupation: Sales representative
with McQueen Ltd
Born: Edinburgh, 19.12.68
Family: Single
Former club: Hutt Old Boys
(Wellington, NZ)
International debut: Spain 7,
Scotland A 39, 1990
Best moment in rugby: Selection
to 1991 Scotland World Cup squad
Worst moment in rugby: Torn
hamstring, sustained in training after
World Cup, which put me out of
game for four months
Most embarrassing moment:
Missing eight weeks rugby after
injuring an ankle whilst trying to
rescue a neighbour's cat
Most respected opponent: Ian
Williams (NSW & Australia)
Biggest influence on career: Rob
Moffat (Gala Academy & Scottish
Schools coach)
Serious injuries: Torn hamstring

	apps	pts
Scotland U-21 (1989/90)	1 rep	
Scotland B (**1991**)		
Last Season	2 caps	0
Career	3 caps	0
Scotland A (**1990**)		
Last Season	0 caps	0
Career	1 cap	0

Best memory last season: Build-up to World Cup; Scotland beating Ireland
to reach quarter-finals
Suggestions to improve rugby: *On-field* – Reduce value of dropped goal
and penalty to two points. *Off-field* – Ensure that any future player-benefits
are spread equally throughout XV and not hogged by minority
Notable landmarks in rugby career: Won four caps for Scottish Schools
(U-18s) and one for U-19s (against Italy). Scored only try that Australian
Schools conceded during tour, for Scotland Schools (U-18s) at Murrayfield.
Played for triumphant South in last season's Scottish Inter-District
Championship, having previously turned out for South U-21s. Spent summer
of 1990 playing in New Zealand. Went to Hong Kong for XVs event prior
to Sevens (1991). Made Scotland B debut in 10–31 loss to France B

153

(Hughenden, 1991). Late call-up to Scotland's summer tour of North America and played in non-cap 'test' side against US Eagles and Canada. Scored hat-trick of tries in 76–7 win over Alberta. Only player in Scotland's World Cup squad not to get a game, but just being involved was 'a great experience'. Played both 1991/92 B games, against Ireland (lost 19–29, Murrayfield, 28 Dec 1991) and France (lost 18–27, Albi 3 Feb 1992)

Touchlines: Hill walking, holidays, golf (handicap 22), mountain-biking
Player to watch: Gregor Townsend (Gala)
Player of the year: Andy Nicol (Scotland)

Moon, R. H. St J. B.   Wales

Full Name: Rupert Henry St. John Barker Moon
1991/92 International category: Wales Full (squad)
Club: Llanelli
Position: Scrum-half
Height: 6′ **Weight:** 13st
Occupation: Student
Born: Birmingham, 1.2.68
Family: Single
Family links with rugby: Brother (Richard) plays scrum-half for Rosslyn Park. Sister (Estelle) plays scrum-half/back row for Wasps Ladies. All three of us have got winners' medals in national competitions. Is this a record?
Former clubs: Walsall, Abertillery, Neath
International debut (England): England B 12, Emerging Australians 12, 1990
International debut (Wales): None
Best moments in rugby: Kicking conversion from each touchline playing for Barbarians at 1991 Hong Kong Sevens; captaining Barbarians against Cork Constitution on centenary tour; selection to Wales squad

	apps	pts
England U-21 (**1989**)		
Career	1 cap	4
England B (**1990**)		
Last Season	0 caps	0
Career	4 caps	8
Wales (1991/92)	4 reps	

Worst moment in rugby: Head-high tackle by Gloucester's Dave Sims which dislocated my shoulder

Most embarrassing moments: Saying my full name on national television; losing kicking competition to Llanelli club mates Phil Davies and Gary Jones

Most respected opponents: David Bishop (ex-Pontypool & Wales) and brother Richard (Rosslyn Park & England B)

Biggest influence on career: Alfie 'the fruitbat' Brickell (Abertillery coach) – inspired to me go further at age of 18

Serious injuries: Popped rib cartilage, shoulder dislocation

Other sporting achievements: Cricket for Walsall. Soccer for Midlands Schools

Best memory last season: Winning man-of-the-match award in Schweppes Challenge Cup final win over Swansea; kicking dropped goal in final after telling team mates I would in training

Suggestions to improve rugby: *On-field* – Scrap farcical 90-degree scrum wheel law. Only allow kicking inside 22. Clarify interpretation of tackle law. Can you pass ball on ground or not? *Off-field* – Give all student rugby players free food vouchers (but never money). Organise cheap nose jobs for people with big noses, when finished playing career

Notable landmarks in rugby career: Llanelli captain. Declared allegiance to Wales last season having sat on bench for England Schools and stood on pitch for England Colts, U-21s (scored try in inaugural match: Romania 13, England 54, Bucharest 13 May 1989), Students (as captain) and B. Represented England in 1988 Student World Cup. Included in Neath's squad for Schweppes Cup final defeat of Bridgend. Joined Llanelli at start of 1990/91 season and was promptly selected for four England B games against Emerging Australians (drew 12–12, Wasps 4 Nov 1990), Ireland B (lost 10–24, Old Belvedere 1 Mar 1991), France B (lost 6–10, Bristol 15 Mar 1991) and Spain (won 50 –6, Gloucester 20 Jan 1991). Scored two tries in Kingsholm defeat of Spain. Picked up man-of-the-match awards in both 1990/91 and 1991/92 Schweppes Challenge Cup finals when Llanelli beat Pontypool and Swansea (scoring 1t,1dg) respectively. Captained England Students against pre-World Cup England XV. Selected to England's development squad but then switched to Wales, saying: 'After six years of living in Wales I have found myself being deeply affected by the passion for, and commitment to the game as shown by the whole community.' Bench reserve for Wales throughout 1992 Five Nations' Championship. Also represented Saltires, Public School Wanderers, Crawshays and Barbarians

Touchlines: Watching educational videos, eating out, ballet, theatre

Player to watch: Malcolm Walker (Nottingham)

Player of the year: Colin Stephens (Wales)

Moore, A.   Scotland

Full Name: Alexander Moore
1991/92 International category:
Scotland A
Club: Edinburgh Academicals
Position: Wing
Height: 5'9" **Weight:** 13st
Born: Queensland, Australia,
19.8.63
Family: Gareth and Christopher
(sons)
Former clubs: Livingston, Gala
International debut: New Zealand
21, Scotland 18, 1990
Five Nations' debut: France 15,
Scotland 9, 1991
Best moment in rugby: Scoring try
on debut in second Test at Auckland
(23 Jun 1990)
Worst moments in rugby: Being
left out of Edinburgh side to play
1988 Australians. Missing Irish
game (1991) with groin/pelvic injury
Most embarrassing moment:
Attempted to kick ball during
Scotland training game at St
Andrews, stubbed toe and went head
over heels
Most respected opponent: David
Wilson (Currie)
Serious injuries: Dislocated collar
bone (1982), groin/pelvic strain
(1991), trapped nerve in back
Best memory last season: Beating
Cougars at Melrose Sevens

	apps	pts
Scotland B (**1986**)		
Last Season	0 caps	0
Career	3 caps	4
Scotland A (**1991**)		
Last Season	1 cap	4
Career	1 cap	4
Scotland (**1990**)		
Last Season	0 caps	0
Career	5 caps	8

Caps (5): 1990 NZ(2), Arg 1991 F, W, E

Points (8 – 2t): 1990 NZ(2:1t), Arg(1t)

Suggestions to improve rugby: *On-field* – Differentiate between technical and physical violations. Make one point available for 'technical' penalty goals (minor misdemeanour) and three for 'physical'. Referees should allow more vigorous rucking, as long as players are going for the ball. Depends totally on skill of referee in knowing what's what. *Off-field* – Carry on with good work. New image rugby and Youth development officers are taking game in right direction but there is still so much work to be done in that area
Notable landmarks in rugby career: Won three Scotland 'B' caps (against

Italy, Ireland and France). Toured with Scotland to Zimbabwe in 1988. Helped Edinburgh win 1922 Scottish Inter-District Championship. Selected to tour North America (1991) but forced to withdraw with pelvic strain. Scored tries in each of first two Scotland senior appearances, against New Zealand and Argentina (won 49–3, Edinburgh 10 Nov 1990). Unavailable for 1991 Scotland tour to North America because of pelvic injury which put him onto sidelines after 1991 England game. Spent summer of 1992 playing in South Africa, having first scored try in Scotland A's 36–16 defeat of Spain (Edinburgh, 28 Dec 1991)

Touchlines: High jump, power weight-lifting, golf, budding saxophonist, golf (handicap 20)

Player to watch: Gregor Townsend (Gala)

Player of the year: Andy Nicol (Scotland)

Moore, B. C.   England

Full Name: Brian Christopher Moore

1991/92 International category: England Full

Club: Harlequins

Position: Hooker

Height: 5′9″ **Weight:** 14st 2lbs

Occupation: Civil litigations solicitor with Edward Lewis & Co.

Born: Birmingham, 11.1.62

Family: Dr Penny Sowden (wife)

Former clubs: Old Crossleyans, Nottingham

International debut: England 21, Scotland 12, 1987

Five Nations' debut: As above

Best moment in rugby: 1991 Grand Slam decider against France

Worst moment in rugby: Wales 16, England 3, (1987 World Cup quarter-final)

Most embarrassing moment: Being forced to watch pre-match team talks on video

Most respected opponent: England lock Wade Dooley's wallet – I have never managed to open it!

Biggest influence on career: Alan Davies (Nottingham coach)

Serious injuries: Fractured ego v. Scotland, Murrayfield 17 Mar 1990

Other sporting achievements: Intermediate swimming certificate

Best memory last season: Beating Wales to clinch back-to-back Grand Slams

Suggestions to improve rugby: *On-field* – Scrap nonsensical scrum-wheel law. Scrap new maul law asap; it is a disaster. If you reward people who kill the ball, more will do it. Refereeing must be more consistent. One set of laws for World Cup (which were good), then thrown out of window afterwards. I understand that referees are given all sorts of games at all sorts of levels. They should be considered at one level and then, if good enough,

	apps	pts
England B (1985)		
Last Season	0 caps	0
England (1987)		
Last Season	11 caps	0
Career	40 caps	4
Lions 1989	3 Tests	0

Caps (40): 1987 S wc-A, J, W(b) 1988 F, W, S, I(1,2), A(a1, a2), Fj, A(b) 1989 S, I, F, W, Ro, Fj. Lions-A(1,2,3) 1990 I, F, W, S, Arg(a1, a2) 1991 W, S(a), I, F(a), Fj, A(a) wc-NZ, It, F(b), S(b), A(b) 1992 S, I, F, W

Points (4 – 1t): 1989 I(1t)

moved up. Referees should consult players pre-season to discuss rule changes and interpretations. *Off-field* – No uniform interpretation of off-field activities. Why not? We should all be treated the same, irrespective of which hemisphere we are located. Automatic retirement from RFU Committee at 55. Major revision of amateurism laws, along with those concerning foul play, line-outs and kickable penalties. Player representation on all major decision and law-making committees. The latest rule changes were not made in any co-ordinated fashion, rather picked out of a hat! Administrators must learn to consult those who matter before making decisions. Until we step onto the field we do not which rules will work. Proper lines of communication are absolutely vital to the future of the game. After all, you cannot run a successful company without consulting people

Notable landmarks in rugby career: A beneficiary of Mark Bailey's understating and self-deprecating wit, has missed only three of England's last 43 internationals. Former captain of Nottingham and England B (on first appearance) who represented England Students in 1982 and toured Romania and Spain with England U-23s. First played for Nottingham in 1981 and left them for Quins prior to 1990/91 season. Voted 1990/91 Whitbread/*Rugby World* 'Player of Year'. Ever present in 1989 Lions' 2–1 series win over Australia. Toured with England to Australia/Fiji (1988), Argentina (1990) and Fiji/Australia (1991)

Touchlines: Opera, theatre, cooking, training, tennis, golf

Player to watch: Mark Russell (Harlequins)

Player of the year: Wade Dooley (England)

Morris, C. D.   England

Full Name: Colin **Dewi** Morris
1991/92 International category:
England Full
Club: Orrell
Position: Scrum-half
Height: 6′ **Weight:** 13st 7lbs
Occupation: Financial advisor with
HFS Loans
Born: Crickhowell, Wales, 9.2.64
Family: Single
Former clubs: Brecon, Crewe &
Alsager College, Winnington Park,
Liverpool St Helens
International debut: England 28,
Australia 19, 1988
Five Nations' debut: England 12,
Scotland 12, 1989
Best moments in rugby: Scoring
try on England debut and winning.
Scoring winning try for North in
15–9 defeat of Australia (Oct 1988)
Worst moment in rugby: Losing
9–12 to Wales at Cardiff (March
1989) and being dropped thereafter
Most embarrassing moment:
Being dropped by North for match
v. US Eagles after five consecutive
international caps and five
consecutive divisional caps
Most respected opponent:
Richard Hill (Bath & England)

	apps	pts
England B (**1988**)		
Last Season	0 caps	0
England (**1988**)		
Last Season	4 caps	12
Career	9 caps	16

Caps (9): **1988** A **1989:** S, I, F, W
1992 S, I, F, W

Points (16 – 4t): **1988** A(1t) **1992**
S(1t), I(1t), F(1t)

Serious injuries: Broken nose (three times), serious ligament damage to left
shoulder, both knees and right ankle
Other sporting achievements: Gwent Schools U-19 County cricket finalists
Best memories last season: Returning to England team for Five Nations'
Championship and scoring tries in first three games back
Suggestions to improve rugby: *On-field* – More consistency among referees.
Immediate action for serious offences. Refereeing must get better as discipline
becomes an ever-greater factor. Reduce points value of penalties to two points.
Scrap 90-degree scrummaging law
Notable landmarks in rugby career: Stormed back into international picture
in 1991/92, despite sitting out World Cup on bench. Replaced Richard Hill

for Five Nations' Championship and was big hit: scoring tries in first three games, against Scotland, Ireland and France. Disappeared as quickly as he rose when dropped by England after 1989 Five Nations' loss in Wales. Previously, had graduated from junior rugby to international level in six months, via Winnington Park, Liverpool St Helens, Lancashire, the North and England B (whom he first represented against 1988 touring Wallabies). Scored three tries to inspire Lancashire to 32–9 victory over Middlesex in 1990 County Championship final. Toured with England to Argentina (1990) and Australia (1991)

Touchlines: Motocross, lazy holidays spent on beaches
Player to watch: Martin Hynes (Orrell)
Player of the year: Jonathan Webb (England)

Morris, M. S. Wales

Full Name: Martyn Stuart Morris
1991/92 International category: Wales Full
Club: Neath
Position: Flanker
Height: 6'3" **Weight:** 14st
Occupation: Police officer in Swansea
Born: Neath, 23.8.62
Family: Rhian (wife) and Emily (daughter)
Former clubs: Neath Athletic, South Wales Police
International debut: Scotland 21, Wales 25, 1985
Five Nations' debut: As above
Best moment in rugby: Being recalled to Welsh team against Ireland in 1990/91 after five years in international wilderness

Worst moment in rugby: Experiencing losing sequence with Neath last season
Most respected opponent: 1989 All Blacks
Biggest influence on career: Ron Waldron (Neath & ex-Wales coach)
Serious injuries: Broken nose, sprung rib cartilage
Other sporting achievements: Cricket for Neath
Best memory last season: Playing for Wales against England at Twickenham
Suggestions to improve rugby: *On-field* – New mauling rule should not be

implemented. Better standard of refereeing in Wales required. *Off-field* – Improved treatment of players. Compensation for working (and family) time lost to rugby is vital

Notable landmarks in rugby career: Former captain of Wales Youth (played No.8 in same team as Mark Ring) and also represented Wales B before making full debut in 1985 against Scotland at Murrayfield. Scored try for Wales B in 23–11 win over France B in

	apps	pts
Wales B (1983)		
Last Season	0 caps	0
Career	2 caps	8
Wales (1985)		
Last Season	2 caps	0
Career	11 caps	0

Caps (11): 1985 S, I, F 1990 I, Na(1,2), Ba 1991 I, F(a) wc-WS(R) 1992 E

Points: Nil

Bourg-en-Bresse (1983) and another in corresponding fixture the following season (won 29–20 at Newport). After winning first three caps in 1985 had to wait five years for the fourth, by which time he had rejoined Neath (1989/90) from South Wales Police. Toured with Wales to Namibia (1990) and Australia (1991), in the latter missing out on the 63–6 Test loss. Alotted one World Cup match – the defeat by Western Samoa – and one outing in the 1992 Five Nations' Championship – against England, at Twickenham (7 Mar 1992), after Emyr Lewis went down with food poisoning on the eve of the match

Touchlines: Road running for training, cricket, crosswords

Player to watch: Matthew McCarthy (Neath) – like a young Jonathan Davies

Player of the year: Richard Webster (Wales)

France flanker Jean Francois Tordo is stopped in his tracks by Wade Dooley (downstairs) and Peter Winterbottom (upstairs) during England's 31–13 Championship win in Paris

Moseley, K.   Wales

Full Name: Kevin Moseley
1991/92 International category:
Wales Full
Club: Newport
Position: Lock
Height: 6′7″ **Weight:** 18st 7lbs
Occupation: Printer with Severn
Valley Press (Caerphilly) Ltd
Born: Blackwood, 2 Jul 1963
Former clubs: Blackwood, Bay of
Plenty (NZ), Pontypool
International debut: New Zealand
54, Wales 9, 1988
Five Nations' debut: Scotland 23,
Wales 7, 1989
Best moment in rugby: Winning
first cap for Wales
Worst moment in rugby: Being
sent off while playing for Wales
against France at Cardiff (20 Jan
1990, lost 19–29)
Most embarrassing moment: As
above
Best memory last season:
Returning to the Wales team and
proving those people wrong who said
my international career was over after
my 1990 dismissal against France
Worst memory last season: Being
punched by fan when returning to
Pontypool Park with Newport.
Disappointed in the reaction from
Pontypool RFC and from the Press
who attributed remarks to me which I did not make

	apps	pts
Wales B (1984)		
Last Season	0 caps	0
Career	6 caps	0
Wales (1988)		
Last Season	4 caps	0
Career	9 caps	0

Caps (9): **1988** NZ(2), Ro **1989** S, I **1990** F **1991** F(b) wc-WS, Arg, A(b)

Points: Nil

Biggest influence on career: Ray Prosser (Pontypool coach)
Serious injuries: Damaged foot (1988)
Suggestions to improve rugby: *On-field* – Pleased that the try value has been increased, though Newport will probably now have to change as we've been quite happy to kick in the past! *Off-field* – Clubs should treat players' families better
Notable landmarks in rugby career: A footballer until aged 17. Began rugby career with home-club Blackwood, before moving to Pontypool in 1984. Spent

season playing with Bay of Plenty in New Zealand's Inter-Provincial Championship (14 appearances). Played for Wales B and toured New Zealand (1988) with Wales. Was unavailable for 1991 tour to Australia but returned to team for first time since French dismissal in pre-World Cup match with France (lost 9–22). Ever present through Wales' World Cup campaign before losing place for 1992 Five Nations' Championship

Touchlines: DIY, walking dogs (cocker and springer spaniels)
Player to watch: Andrew Peacock (Newport)
Player of the year: Glen George (Wales)

Mullins, A. R. England

Full Name: Andrew Richard Mullins
1991/92 International category: England B
Club: Harlequins
Position: Tighthead prop
Height: 5'11" **Weight:** 16st 1lbs
Occupation: Accountant with Coopers & Lybrand, Deloitte
Born: Eltham, London, 12.12.64
Family: Married
Former clubs: Old Alleynians, Durham Univ
International debut: England 58, Fiji 23, 1989
Best moment in rugby: Running out at Twickenham against Fiji on full debut
Worst moment in rugby: Not making London team immediately after Fiji game. Knew that would determine England selection as Jeff Probyn got nod instead
Most disappointing moment: Grounding ball inches short of try-line against Fijians
Biggest problem in rugby: Jeff Probyn (Wasps & England)
Most respected opponent: Paul 'Judge' Rendall (Wasps & England) – good all-rounder in bar

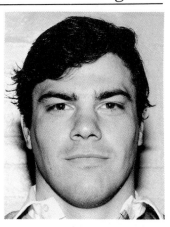

	apps	pts
England B (**1988**)		
Last Season	4 caps	0
England (**1989**)		
Last Season	0 caps	0
	1995 Development squad	
Career	1 cap	0

Caps (1): **1989** Fj
Points: Nil

Serious injuries: Broken nose, broken bone in foot

Other sporting achievements: London Schools breaststroke swimming champion

Suggestions to improve rugby: *Off-field* – Adopt a more professional (but realistic) approach over training. RFU sent out training timetables which are not practical because of time involved. More helpful if they arranged memberships of local gyms and health clubs for players

Notable landmarks in rugby career: Switched from flanker to prop aged 16 and immediately won selection to England Schools. Spent year in Army between school and Durham Univ. Represented England U-23s (1986) and joined Harlequins (1987/88). Share birthdate with fellow Quin Will Carling, who played in same Univ and England 18-Group team. Represented England in 1988 Student World Cup and, the same year, made B debut against Australia. Represented England B against Italy (won 12–9, Waterloo 27 Mar 1991) in 1990/91 and was an ever present in the 1991/92 'Grand Slam' side: wearing the No.3 jersey in the defeats of Spain (19 Jan 1992), Ireland B (31 Jan 1992), France B (15 Feb 1992) and Italy B (7 Mar 1992). Was also included in England's 33-man squad for the 1992 Five Nations' Championship

Touchlines: Enjoy black and white films, especially 'The Thirty Nine Steps'

Murphy, K. J.   Ireland

Full Name: Kenneth John Murphy
1991/92 International category:
Ireland Full
Club: Cork Constitution
Position: Fullback
Height: 6′ **Weight:** 12st 7lbs
Occupation: Family garage business
Born: Cork, 31.7.66
Family: Single
Family links with rugby:
Grandfather (Noel: 11 caps between 1930–33) and father (Noel Jnr: 41 caps between 1958–69) both played for Ireland
International debut: England 23, Ireland 0, 1990
Five Nations' debut: As above
Best moment in rugby: Winning 1990/91 All-Ireland League with Cork Con

Worst moment in rugby: Missing penalty which cost Christian Brothers College Junior Schools Cup
Most respected opponents: Gavin Hastings (Watsonians & Scotland) and Serge Blanco (ex-Biarritz & France)
Best memory last season: Recall to Ireland side for last two rounds of Five Nations' Championship
Notable landmarks in rugby career: Unique family record –

	apps	pts
Ireland B (**1989**)		
Last Season	0 caps	0
Ireland (**1990**)		
Last Season	2 caps	0
1992	Tour to New Zealand	
Career	10 caps	0

Caps (10): **1990** E, S, F, W, Arg **1991** F, W(R), S(R) **1992** S, F

Points: Nil

father and grandfather also having played for Ireland. Played Irish Schools against Junior All Blacks (1985). Represented Combined Provinces on internal tour and was a replacement for Ireland U-25s against Italy (1989). Toured France with Irish squad (1988) and, in December 1989, won first Ireland B cap against Scotland (drew 22–22, Murrayfield 9 Dec 1989). Two months later was promoted to senior side for 1990 Five Nations' Championship, and played in each of the four games. Lost No.15 jersey to Jim Staples for bulk of 1991 Five Nations' Championship, but still made three appearances, twice replacing the unfortunate Staples. A non-playing member of the Irish World Cup squad, he was recalled for duty in 1992 Championship against Scotland and France. Helped Cork Constitution win 1990/91 All-Ireland League title. Toured with Ireland to New Zealand (1992)
Player to watch: Philip Soden (Constitution)

Rory Underwood in characteristic pose: this time rounding Wales captain Ieuan Evans during England's Grand Slam clinching 24–0 win at Twickenham

Nicol, A. D. — Scotland

Full Name: Andrew Douglas Nicol
1991/92 International category: Scotland Full
Club: Dundee High School FP
Position: Scrum-half
Height: 5'11½" **Weight:** 12st 7lbs
Occupation: Business Studies student at Dundee Institute of Technology
Born: Dundee, 12.3.71
Family: Single
Family links with rugby: Alastair (brother) plays for Scotland U-18s, Army, and Dundee HSFP. George Ritchie (grandfather) played for Scotland against England at Twickenham (1932)
Former club: Heriot's FP
International debut: Scotland 7, England 25, 1992
Five Nations' debut: As above
Best moment in rugby: Winning first cap against England; scoring try against Ireland
Worst moment in rugby: Dislocating collarbone in Scotland B's 19–29 loss to Ireland B (28 Dec 1991) and thus missing the 1992 Scotland Trial
Most embarrassing moment: Ripping shorts open in a club game against Perthshire. Trying to change them and the ball came back to me
Most respected opponents: Gary Armstrong (Jedforest & Scotland, Nick Farr-Jones (NSW & Australia)
Biggest influence on career: Sandy Hutchison (Dundee High School PE teacher and coach)
Serious injuries: Sprung collarbone (five weeks out), medial ligament, dislocated elbow, concussion
Other sporting achievements: Cricket for Dundee High School CC
Best memories last season: Representing World XV in New Zealand; promotion to McEwan's League division one with Dundee HSFP
Suggestions to improve rugby: *On-field* – Should be able to alter new laws

	apps	pts
Scotland B (**1991**)		
Last Season	1 cap	4
Career	2 caps	8
Scotland (**1992**)		
Last Season	4 caps	4
1992	Tour to Australia	
Career	4 caps	4

Caps (4): **1992** E, I, F, W
Points (4 – 1t): I(1t)

immediately should they be seen not to work, rather than having to wait a year. More consistency in appreciation of laws from referees. *Off-field* – Allow players to benefit from rugby-related activities. IRB must clarify what players can and cannot do

Notable landmarks in rugby career: Played three seasons for Scotland Schools. Captained Schools and Scotland U-19s (great honour). One game for Scotland U-21s (concussed against Combined Services) before earning Scotland B call-up in 1990/91 for 10–31 loss to France B at Hughenden (2 Mar 1991). Scored solitary Scottish try in that game. Toured North America with Scotland (1991), scoring a try on each of three appearances (v. Alberta, Rugby East and Ontario). Not included in World Cup squad but good performances for Scottish Students (against Oxford Univ) and Scotland B (against Ireland B: another try) prompted selection for 1992 Five Nations' Championship in place of knee-ligament victim Gary Armstrong. Scored try against Ireland on second outing. Concluded amazing season (also helped Dundee HSFP gain promotion) with selection to World XV for Test series in New Zealand to celebrate centenary of NZRFU. Also represented Barbarians in 1992 Hong Kong Sevens and toured Australia (1992) with Scotland

Touchlines: Golf, cricket

Player to watch: Stewart Campbell (Dundee HSFP)

Player of the year: Peter Winterbottom (England)

O'Hara, P. T. Ireland

Full Name: Patrick Thomas O'Hara
1991/92 International category:
Ireland Full
Club: Cork Constitution
Position: Flanker
Height: 6′2″ **Weight:** 15st
Occupation: Sales director with Architectural and Metal Systems (Cork)
Born: Essex, England, 4.8.61
Family: Maire (wife), Darren and Grian (sons)
Former club: Sunday's Well
International debut: Ireland 49, Western Samoa 22, 1988
Five Nations' debut: Ireland 21, France 26, 1989

Best moment in rugby: First full cap against France

Worst moment in rugby: Getting concussed against England 1989 (lost 3–16)

Most embarrassing moment: Playing in front of provincial selectors in 1984/85, ended up in centre and attempted long pass to wing that was intercepted for try

Most respected opponent: Finlay Calder (Stewart's-Melville & Scotland) – great reader of game, very street wise, and always willing to advise

Biggest influence on career: Father (Tom)

Serious injuries: Two years of foot and shoulder ligament damage. Torn groin muscle

Other sporting achievements: Won a number of cross-country races when in Essex

Best memory last season: Seeing the back of Gordon Hamilton as he raced away to score try against Australia in World Cup quarter-final

Suggestions to improve rugby: *On-field* – Stopping messing about with the rules. Leave game alone. Allow playing ball on ground, within reason. *Off-field* – Greater financial support for tourists. Not looking to make money, just do not want to lose out

Notable landmarks in rugby career: Made Sunday's Well debut in 1979, aged 18, and the following year helped them win Cork Charity Cup. Won first Munster provincial cap in 1983 and went on to represent them against 1984 Wallabies and 1989 All Blacks. Toured with Ireland to France (1988), North America (1989) and Namibia (1991). Had to wait until 15 minutes from end of 1988 game against Western Samoa to replace Phil Matthews and win first cap. Voted 1989/90 Irish Player of Year. Given Ireland B debut at Old Belvedere (1 Mar 1991) when England B were beaten 24–10. Solitary appearance last season came in the 32–16 World Cup-tie against Japan in Dublin (9 Oct 1991), an occasion he marked with his first international try

Touchlines: Built garden shed all by myself

Player to watch: David Corkery (Cork Constitution)

Player of the year: Dewi Morris (England)

	apps	pts
Ireland B (**1991**)		
Last Season	0 caps	0
Career	1 cap	0
Ireland (**1988**)		
Last Season	1 caps	4
Career	11 caps	4

Caps (11): **1988** WS(R) **1989** F, W, E, NZ **1990** E, S, F, W **1991** Na(1) wc-J

Points (4 – 1t): **1991** wc-J(1t)

Oliver, G. H.   Scotland

Full Name: Greig Hunter Oliver
1991/92 International category:
Scotland Full
Club: Hawick
Position: Scrum-half
Height: 5'8½" **Weight:** 12st 8lbs
Occupation: Sports sub-editor with
The Southern Reporter
Born: Hawick, 12.9.64
Family: Single
Family links with rugby: Derek
(brother) plays for Hawick Linden,
as did father
Former clubs: Hawick PSA,
Hawick Trades
International debut: Scotland 60,
Zimbabwe 21, 1987 (World Cup)
Best moment in rugby: Winning
first cap

Worst moment in rugby: Any time
I lose
Most embarrassing moment: Not
being able to walk for a week because
of a skin burn on my behind
Most respected opponent: Roy
Laidlaw (Jedforest & Scotland) – for
his dedication to the game and
assistance to younger players
Biggest influence on career:
Family and coaches

	apps	pts
Scotland B (**1986**)		
Last Season	0 caps	0
Scotland A (**1990**)		
Last Season	1 cap	0
Career	2 caps	4
Scotland (**1987**)		
Last Season	1 cap	0
Career	3 caps	4

Caps (3): 1987 wc-Z 1990 NZ(2R)
1991 wc-Z

Points (4 – 1t): **1987** wc-Z(1t)

Other sporting achievements:
Won the 1986 St Ronan's Sprint.
Broke 100 at Minto Golf Club
Best memory last season: Winning Gala Sevens with Hawick
Suggestions to improve rugby: *On-field* – Make the scrum a way of starting
the game, and not a means of spoiling it. When scrum comes down, if ball is
in back row let play continue. Anything to speed up game is okay by me.
Off-field – Give more regard to players
Notable landmarks in rugby career: Made Hawick debut aged 18 in 1982.
Zimbabwe have played quite a role in his international career with two of his
three caps coming against them, in the 1987 and 1991 World Cup
tournaments, and also the southern African nation hosting him and a Scotland

169

squad in 1988. Scored try on debut against Zimbabwe (Wellington, 30 May 1987). Also toured with Scotland to Japan (1989) and New Zealand (1990), coming on as a 69th minute replacement for Gary Armstrong in second Test at Auckland. Scored one of six tries in Scotland A's 39–7 defeat of Spain in 1990/91 and turned out in same fixture (Murrayfield, 28 Dec 1991) last season. Permanent feature on Scotland bench last season. Toured North America (1991), partnering Craig Chalmers at half-back in non-cap internationals against US Eagles and Canada (played in total of five non-cap internationals on all tours, scoring three tries in first 'Test' against Zimbabwe in 1988). Overlooked for 1992 tour to Australia

Touchlines: Tennis and golf
Player to watch: Gregor Townsend (Gala)
Player of the year: Dewi Morris (England)

Olver, C. J. — England

Full Name: Christopher **John** Olver
1991/92 International category:
England Full
Club: Northampton
Position: Hooker
Height: 5'9" **Weight:** 13st 8lbs
Occupation: Teacher at
Northampton GS
Born: Manchester, 23.4.62
Family: Sue (wife) and Lisa
(daughter)
Former clubs: Sandbach,
Harlequins
International debut: England 51,
Argentina 0, 1990
Five Nations' debut: None
Best moments in rugby: Lifting
John Player Cup after captaining
Harlequins to 28–22 win over Bristol
in 1988 final. Winning first England
cap against Argentina (3 Nov 1990)

Worst moment in rugby: Losing two JP Cup semi-finals with Quins
Most embarrassing moment: Every time I lose a strike against head
Most respected opponents: Phil Keith-Roach and Peter Wheeler
Biggest influence on career: Bev Risman (ex-Loughborough College & England) – My lecturer at Borough Road College who advised me to switch from flanker to hooker

Serious injuries: Achilles tendon (operation). Dislocated shoulder (twice)

Other sporting achievements: Hit Australian cricket captain Allan Border for three consecutive sixes. 7-handicap golfer

Best memory last season: Contributing to England's 1991 World Cup final campaign

Suggestions to improve rugby:

	apps	pts
England B (**1988**)		
Last Season	1 cap	0
England (**1990**)		
Last Season	1 cap	0
	9 reps	
Career	2 caps	0
	27 reps	

Caps (2): **1990** Arg(b) **1991** wc-US
Points: Nil

On-field – Recruit referees who have actually played in front row. All referees seem to be backs who have no idea what is going on in the scrum. Structure season so that all League rugby is conducted on consecutive Saturdays (Sept-Nov). Then play divisionals (Dec) and then, after Christmas, Internationals. This would remove present ludicrous dilemma of players having to play major league games seven days before Internationals. *Off-field* – Compensate employers for loss of employees to rugby

Notable landmarks in rugby career: Hold England record for most matches watched from the bench – 27. Toured with England to Argentina (1990) and Australia (1991), winning long-awaited first full cap in between, in defeat of touring Pumas (3 Nov 1990). Won second cap in 37–9 World Cup win over the United States at Twickenham (11 Oct 1991). Also represented England XV in 33–15 win over Italy XV (1 May 1990) and in 18–16 win over centenary Barbarians (29 Sep 1990). Captained England B in 12–9 win over Italy (Waterloo, 27 Mar 1991) but did not add to his tally last season as was nine times a bench reserve for the senior XV

Touchlines: Fly fishing and shooting

Player to watch: Matthew Dawson (Northampton)

Player of the year: Jeff Probyn (England)

O'Mahony, B. G.   Ireland

Full Name: Barry Gerard O'Mahony
1991/92 International category: Ireland B
Club: Univ College Cork
Position: No.8
Height: 6'5" **Weight:** 15st
Occupation: Student
Born: Cork, 18.9.69
Family: Single
International debut (B): Scotland 19, Ireland 29, 1991
Best moment in rugby: Helping Ireland B beat Scots at Murrayfield (28 Dec 1991)
Worst moment in rugby: Missing a penalty under posts in a school U-16 final
Most embarrassing moment: Having to make a speech
Most respected opponent: The next one
Best memory last season: Selection for Ireland B
Suggestions to improve rugby: *On-field* – Delighted that the law-makers have increased value of try to five points. Shorten playing season. *Off-field* – Unions not moving as quickly as are clubs. Situation must change rapidly if Unions are not to lose power totally

	apps	pts
Ireland U-21 (**1990**)		
Last Season	0 cap	0
Career	2 caps	0
Ireland B (**1991**)		
Last Season	1 cap	0
Career	1 cap	0

Notable landmarks in rugby career: Won Munster Junior and Senior School Cups with PBC. Called into Ireland U-21 squad at start of 1990/91 season and toured Netherlands in September 1990, sitting out match against Netherlands B, but occupying No.8 jersey in 7–21 loss to the Dutch senior national XV (Leiden, 21 Sep 1990). Added a second cap when turned out against England U-21s at Moseley (29 Oct 1990) and beat them 22–16. Promoted to Ireland B in 1991/92 season, playing in the side that beat Scotland B 29–19 at Murrayfield
Touchlines: Cycling, travel, golf
Player to watch: Conor O'Shea (Lansdowne)

Orrell, T.   Wales

Full Name: Tony Orrell
1991/92 International category:
Wales U-21
Club: South Wales Police
Position: Loose-head prop
Height: 6'1" **Weight:** 18st 8lbs
Born: Church Village, 17.12.70
Family: Single
Family links with rugby: Keith
(brother) plays for Newport, Greg
(brother) plays for Llantwit Fardre
Former Club: Cardiff
International debut (U-21):
Scotland 10, Wales 24, 1990
Best moment in rugby: Cardiff
beating Neath at the Gnoll in
1990/91 season in Heineken League
– I had waited four years to win down
there
Worst moment in rugby: Being
dropped for 1989/90 semi-final tie
against Neath
Most embarrassing moment:
Having shorts ripped open after ten
minutes, playing against Neath, and
waiting 30 minutes for new pair to be brought on

	apps	pts
Wales U-21 (**1990**)		
Last Season	1 cap	0
Career	2 caps	0

Most respected opponent: Laurance Delaney (Llanelli & Wales)
Best memory last season: Wearing No.3 jersey in Wales U-21's win over
Ireland
Suggestions to improve rugby: *On-field* – No rule changes but encourage
a change of attitude in teams to adopt a more expansive approach. *Off-field*
– Allow game to go open and let players go wherever they want. Clubs asking
too much of players at present
Notable landmarks in rugby career: Represented Welsh Senior Schools
(two seasons) and Wales Youth prior to selection for Wales U-21s (28 Apr
1990) against Scotland. Only replacement the following season when Wales
again triumphed over the Scots, but won his place back last season in 28–19
win at Bridgehaugh, Stirling
Touchlines: Weight training
Player to watch: Mark Davis (Newport)
Player of the year: Scott Gibbs (Wales)

O'Shea, C. M. P.   Ireland

Full Name: Conor Michael Patrick O'Shea
1991/92 International category: Ireland U-21
Club: Lansdowne
Positions: Fullback, outside-half
Height: 6'2" **Weight:** 14st
Occupation: Commerce student
Born: Limerick, 21.10.70
Family: Single
Family links with rugby: Brothers (Donal and Diarmid) play for Terenure College
International debut: Netherlands 21, Ireland U-21 7, 1990
Best moment in rugby: Lansdowne beating Terenure to win 1990/91 Senior Cup
Worst moment in rugby: Lansdowne having to settle for third place in 1990/91 All-Ireland League after making slow start
Most respected opponent: Kenny Murphy (Cork Constitution & Ireland)

	apps	pts
Ireland U-21 (**1990**)		
Last Season	2 caps	4
Career	4 caps	4

Best memory last season: Scoring try in 19–10 win over England in Dublin
Suggestions to improve rugby: *On-field* – Satisfied now they have awarded more points for a try. *Off-field* – Nothing. Game is running very well
Notable landmarks in rugby career: Represented Leinster U-19s (two years) and U-20s (two years). Played both cap-games for Ireland U-21s (v. Netherlands and England) in 1990/91 season, in addition to 11–6 win over Netherlands B, and took his U-21 cap-tally to four last season with appearances against Wales (lost 15–22, Newport 16 Oct 1991) and England (won 19–10, Dublin 23 Oct 1991), scoring a try against the latter
Touchlines: Golf, tennis
Player to watch: Philip Soden (Constitution)

O'Shea, W. J.   Ireland

Full Name: William 'Billy' Joseph O'Shea
1991/92 International category: Ireland U-21
Club: Shannon
Position: Wing
Height: 6' **Weight:** 12st
Occupation: Sales representative with office furniture company
Born: Limerick, 24.9.70
Family: Single
Former club: Lansdowne
International debut (U-21): Ireland 19, England 10, 1991
Best moment in rugby: Winning 1990/91 Munster Senior Cup against Young Munster
Worst moment in rugby: Missing penalty kick at goal that would have given Shannon a draw with Garryowen in 1990/91 All-Ireland League
Most embarrassing moment: As above

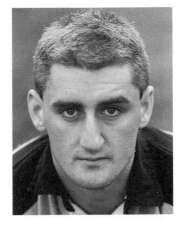

	apps	pts
Ireland U-21 (**1991**)		
Last Season	1 cap	0
Career	1 cap	0

Most respected opponent: Keith Crossan (Instonians & Ireland)
Serious injuries: Damaging shoulder ligaments against England U-21
Best memory last season: Making U-21 debut against England
Notable landmarks in rugby career: Joined Shannon after one season spent with Lansdowne. Represented Munster Schools, Munster U-20s and Munster (against London). Given debut against England in Dublin (23 Oct 1991) but was last game for a month as damaged shoulder ligaments therein
Player to watch: Niall Woods (Blackrock College)
Player of the year: Jeremy Guscott (England)

Oti, C.   England

Full Name: Christopher Oti
1991/92 International category:
England Full
Club: Wasps
Position: Wing
Height: 5'11" **Weight:** 14st
Occupation: Chartered surveyor
with Debenham, Tewson and
Chinnocks
Born: London, 16.6.65
Family: Single
Family links with rugby: Brothers
(Emmanuel and Stephen) play for
Mill Hill and London Nigerians
Former clubs: Nottingham,
Cambridge Univ
International debut: Scotland 6,
England 9, 1988
Five Nations' debut: As above
Best moment in rugby: Three tries
on England home debut in 35–3
defeat of Ireland (March 1988)
Worst moment in rugby:
Returning home early due to injury
from 1989 Lions' tour to Australia
Most embarrassing moment: Not
scoring hat-trick in every subsequent
International after Ireland 1988
Most respected opponent: Finlay
Calder (Stewart's-Melville &
Scotland) – superb captain and
leader

	apps	pts
England B (**1987**)		
Last Season	0 caps	0
England (**1988**)		
Last Season	4 caps	0
Career	13 caps	32
Lions 1989		

Caps (13): **1988** S, I(1) **1989** S, I, F,
W, Ro **1990** Arg(1,2) **1991** Fj,
A(a) wc-NZ, It

Points (32 – 8t): **1988** I(1:3t) **1989**
R(4t) **1990** Arg(1:1t)

Serious injuries: Knee ligament damage (operated on successfully in 1989),
snapped left Achilles tendon (1990/91)
Other sporting achievements: Hold Millfield School 100m sprint record –
10.8sec, achieved aged 17
Best memory last season: Scoring three second half tries against Bristol
Suggestions to improve rugby: *Off-field* – Allow players to market their own
skills – advertising, speeches etc. Compensate players for time and stress given
to rugby
Notable landmarks in rugby career: Announced himself to international
rugby with three tries on home debut against Ireland (19.3.88), followed by

four tries the following season against Romania in Bucharest (won 58–3, 13 May 1989). Little surprise then that he weighed in with four tries on his Barbarians debut in 1988. Earned selection to 1989 British Lions but returned prematurely (29 Jun 1989) after severely damaging knee ligaments. Cambridge Blue in 1986 (scoring only try of 15–10 Light Blue win) and 1987 (scoring two of Cambridge's three tries in 15–10 win). Scored try in England XV's 33–15 defeat of Italy in 1990 to confirm return to fitness. Toured Argentina with England in 1990 – adding eighth international try in 25–12 first Test win (Buenos Aires, 28 Jul 1990). Again injured on return to Blighty, out for five months before heading off again with England, this time to Australia/Fiji (1991). Played in both Tests and took cap-tally to 13 with two appearances in 1991 World Cup

Player of the year: The entire England team

Pearce, G. S. England

Full Name: Gary Stephen Pearce
1991/92 International category:
England Full
Club: Northampton
Position: Tighthead prop
Height: 6′ **Weight:** 15st 10lbs
Occupation: Quantity surveyor
with Q. M. P. Management and
Design
Born: Dinton, Bucks, 2.3.56
Family: Susan (wife), Daniel and
Matthew (sons)
Former club: Aylesbury
International debut: England 7,
Scotland 7, 1979
Five Nations' debut: As above
Best moment in rugby: Clinching
1989/90 Courage League division
two title with Northampton

Worst moment in rugby: Playing
at loosehead
Most embarrassing moment: Watching Northampton lose 0–60 to Orrell (1990/91)
Most respected opponent: Pierre Dospital (ex-Bayonne & France)
Biggest influence in career: Playing for Buckinghamshire in a squad practice against England at Bisham Abbey (1978). Joined Northampton soon after and made England debut the following year

Serious injuries: Tendon damage to left Achilles heel

Best memory last season: Northampton finishing third in Courage League division one

Suggestions to improve rugby: *On-field* – Rugby is going to become a faster, more interesting game for spectators. It will do away with the cross-section of physiques and now everyone will be flanker-shaped. The scrum will be de-powered. Referees need a better knowledge of scrummage laws. *Off-field* – Compensate players for time lost to rugby. There is enough money in rugby generated by the players to prevent their finishing out of pocket. Only right that the success should be reflected in the odd bit of money. It would be peanuts anyway. After all it is the players who put bottoms on seats

Notable landmarks in rugby career: England Schools U-16 trialist. Played for Aylesbury Colts before moving to Northampton in Easter 1978. Selected for England in first full season with Saints. England's most capped prop with 36 caps to his credit between 1979–91. Captained England B on four occasions during 1990/91 season (v. Emerging Australians, Sp, I and F). Only points for England came when representing B team against France in 1988. Captained Northampton in 1991 Pilkington Cup final (lost to Harlequins). Toured Australia/Fiji in summer of 1991, playing against Queensland, Fiji B and Emerging Australians. Selected for World Cup, collecting 36th cap (first since 1988) in 37–9 defeat of United States (11 Oct 1991)

Player to watch: Ian Hunter (Northampton)

Player of the year: Dewi Morris (England)

	apps	pts
England B (**1988**)		
Last Season	0 caps	0
Career	7 caps	4
England (**1979**)		
Last Season	1 cap	0
Career	36 caps	0

Caps (36): **1979** S, I, F, W **1981** Arg(1,2) **1982** A, S **1983** F, W, S, I, NZ **1984** S, SA(2), A **1985** R, F, S, I, W, NZ(1,2) **1986** W, S, I, F **1987** I, F, W (a), S wc-A, US, W(b) **1988** Fj **1991** wc-US

Points: Nil:

Pears, D.   England

Full Name: David Pears
1991/92 International category:
England Full
Club: Harlequins
Position: Outside-half
Height: 5'10" **Weight:** 12st 5lbs
Occupation: Trainee project
manager
Born: Workington, 6.12.67
Family: Single
Family links with rugby: Father
(Reg) played Rugby League for
Cumbria
Former clubs: Aspatria, Sale
International debut: Argentina 12,
England 25, 1990
Five Nations' debut: France 13,
England 31, 1992
Best moment in rugby: Winning
first full England cap in Buenos Aires
Worst moments in rugby: Missing
penalty kick which would have
earned Sale promotion from 1988/89
Courage League division two;
watching Bath's Stuart Barnes land
winning dropped goal with last kick
of extra-time in 1992 Pilkington Cup
final
Most embarrassing moment:
Asking Gary Pearce (England's most
capped prop, with 36 to his credit),
on England B trip to Italy in 1989,
whether it was his first International
Most respected opponent: Ian
Hunter (Northampton & England B)
Biggest influence on career: My father

	apps	pts
England U-21 (**1989**)		
Career	1 cap	2
England B (**1988**)		
Last Season	0 caps	0
Career	6 caps	45
England (**1990**)		
Last Season	1 cap	0
	9 reps	
	1995 Development squad	
Career	3 caps	0

Caps (3): 1990 Arg(1,2) 1992 F(R)
Points: Nil

Serious injuries: Torn knee ligaments (out for 12 weeks), broken nose
(against Wasps last season)
Other sporting achievements: Cumbria Schools soccer captain
Best memory last season: Coming on as a replacement against France in
Five Nations' Championship
Suggestions to improve rugby: *On-field* – Greater uniformity in refereeing

interpretations. Concerned that new rule changes will spoil game, with much confusion between players and referees. It will take three to four years to get a full understanding of them, by which time you can bet they will have changed them again. Leave alone. *Off-field* – Make game professional to raise standards even higher

Notable landmarks in rugby career: Frustrated for over 17 months since winning first England cap in Argentina (28 Jul 1990). Bench reserve on 11 occasions in all, including throughout 1991 World Cup and three-quarters of 1992 Five Nations' Championship. Big moment came in 35th minute of Paris match (15 Feb 1992) when replaced injured Rob Andrew at outside-half (favoured position). Toured Argentina with England in summer 1990 (wearing No.10 jersey in both Tests) and Australia/Fiji in 1991 (playing against Victoria Select, Fiji B and Emerging Australians). Made England B debut in 9–37 loss to 1988 Wallabies and in all has been capped six times by England B. Kicked all 12 points (4p) for England B in draw with Emerging Australians (Wasps, 4 Nov 1990), contributed a conversion to 50–6 defeat of Spain (Gloucester, 20 Jan 1991), and two penalty goals in 6–10 loss to France B (Bristol, 15 Mar 1991). Member of original England U-21 XV (kicked conversion in 54–13 defeat of Romania U-21, Bucharest 13 May 1989), he represented Harlequins in 1991 and 1992 Pilkington Cup final, emerging a winner in first (against Northampton, 4 May 1991)

Touchlines: Golf, tennis, swimming

Player to watch: Phil de Glanville (Bath)

Player of the year: Peter Winterbottom (England)

Will Carling is tagged by the Irish midfield at Twickenham, with David Curtis (right) circling on the look-out for scraps

Phillips, K. H.   Wales

Full Name: Kevin Huw Phillips
1991/92 International category:
Wales Full
Club: Neath
Position: Hooker
Height: 5'11" **Weight:** 14st 7lbs
Occupation: Farmer
Born: Hebron, 15.6.61
Family: Married
Former club: Cardigan
International debut: France 16,
Wales 9, 1987
Five Nations' debut: As above
Best moment in rugby: Winning
1988 Schweppes Challenge Cup
with Neath
Worst moment in rugby:
Dislocating shoulder against
Swansea at The Gnoll (1987/88)
and being out for three months
Most embarrassing moment:
Whenever I lose strike against head
Most respected opponent: Brian
Moore (Harlequins & England)
Biggest influences on career: Ron
Waldron (Neath & Wales coach),
Tudor Harris (Cardigan)
Serious injuries: Dislocated
shoulder, prolapsed disc in back (out
five months last season)

	apps	pts
Wales **(1987)**		
Last Season	1 cap	0
Career	20 caps	0

Caps (20): **1987** F, US wc-I, T, NZ **1988** E, NZ(1) **1989** NZ **1990** F, E, S, I, Na(1,2), Ba **1991** E, S, I, F, A(a)

Points: Nil

Other sporting achievements: Tug-of-war at international level
Best memory last season: Beating high-flying Bridgend in Heineken League
Suggestions to improve rugby: *On-field* – Concerned about collapsed
scrummages, especially after my back injury. We should be concerned with
safety rather than speed. Improve education of younger players to ensure
future of game; send players into schools. *Off-field* – Cut down on rugby
commitments for young players. Too many 19/20-year-olds are playing too
much and are risking burn-out
Notable landmarks in rugby career: First represented Wales in national
Seven at New South Wales tournament in Australia (1986). Following year
was selected to senior XV. Played in 1987 World Cup and toured with Wales
to New Zealand (1988), to Namibia, as captain (1990), and to Australia

(1991), where won last of 20 caps in 63–6 loss to hosts. Given pack leader duties when Paul Thorburn took over as captain in 1990/91 season. Captained Neath to inaugural Heineken League premier division title (1990/91) and to 1989 and 1990 Schweppes Challenge Cup wins. In 1990 led Neath to merit table-championship-cup treble. Only played four games last season due to back injury

Touchlines: Swimming, pool, keep-fit
Player to watch: Matthew McCarthy (Neath) – something special
Player of the year: Richard Webster (Wales)

Popplewell, N. J.   Ireland

Full Name: Nicholas James Popplewell
1991/92 International category: Ireland Full
Club: Greystones
Position: Loosehead prop
Height: 5'10" **Weight:** 16st 7lbs
Occupation: Warehouse manager with Argus Furniture
Born: Dublin, 6.4.64
Family: Single
Former club: Gorey
International debut: Ireland 6, New Zealand 23, 1989
Five Nations' debut: Ireland 15, Wales 16, 1992
Best moment in rugby: Winning first cap against 1989 All Blacks
Worst moment in rugby: Only lasting 20 minutes in above match before cracking a rib
Most respected opponent: Des Fitzgerald (DLSP & Ireland)
Serious injuries: Broken ribs (twice)
Other sporting achievements: Hockey for Irish Schools (three caps)
Best memories last season: Scoring two tries against Zimbabwe in World Cup; making Five Nations' debut three years after breaking into Ireland team
Suggestions to improve rugby: *On-field* – Decrease value of penalty goal to two points. Scrap 90-degree scrum wheel law. *Off-field* – Compensate players for time lost away from work – not payments, just reduced hassle in claiming legitimate expenses
Notable landmarks in rugby career: Took over the Irish No.1 jersey last season following 1991 tour to Namibia where he played in both both Tests.

Made great start to 1991 World Cup when scoring two tries in 55–11 curtain-raising win over Zimbabweans in Dublin (6 Oct 1991). With exception of Japan game, when John Fitzgerald took his turn, he retained his slot for remainder of tournament and then throughout 1992 Five Nations' Championship, before touring with Ireland to New Zealand. Previously, was a member of Irish party which toured France (May 1988) and North America (1989: playing in 24–21 defeat of Canada). Retired injured after 20 minutes of full debut against 1989 All Blacks and lost place for 1990 Championship. Redundant thereafter, except for 1990 Argentina (won 20–18) game, before heading off to Namibia. Helped train Presentation Juniors Bray U-15s to two Leinster Junior Cups in three years. Represented Ireland U-25s v. US Eagles (1990). Scored one of Ireland B's four tries in 24–10 win over England B (Old Belvedere, 1 Mar 1991)
Touchlines: Golf, tennis, squash

	apps	pts
Ireland B **(1991)**		
Last Season	0 caps	0
Career	1 cap	4
Ireland **(1989)**		
Last Season	9 caps	8
Career	11 caps	8

Caps (11): **1989** NZ **1990** Arg **1991** Na(1,2) wc-Z, S, A **1992** W, E, S, F

Points (8 – 2t): **1991** wc-Z(2t)

Probyn, J. A.   England

Full Name: Jeffrey Alan Probyn
1991/92 International category: England Full
Club: Wasps
Position: Tighthead prop
Height: 5'10" **Weight:** 15st 7lbs
Occupation: Furniture manufacturer with Probros Ltd
Born: London, 27.4.56
Family: Jennifer (wife), Jeffrey Paul, Steven James (sons) and Rebecca (daughter)
Family links with rugby: Brother (Chris) plays for Redbridge (ex-Surrey and London Counties)
Former clubs: Old Albanians, Ilford Wanderers, Streatham/Croydon, Richmond, Askeans

International debut: France 10, England 9, 1988
Five Nations' debut: As above
Best moment in rugby: Winning second Grand Slam with England
Worst moment in rugby: Leaving field concussed in Ireland (1989)
Most embarrassing moment: Getting lifted by Welsh prop Staff Jones for trying to be clever (Twickenham, 1988)
Most respected opponents: Paul Rendall (Wasps & England: technically still the best), Jason Leonard (Harlequins & England)
Biggest influence on career: Dennis Bedford (hooker/coach at Streatham/Croydon) – convinced me my future was at tighthead
Serious injuries: Damaged ligaments in left knee. Ear stitches
Best memory last season: World Cup quarter-final against France in Paris – most difficult game I have ever played in. Such mental pressure on us and the overall intensity of the game was awesome. The Five Nations' game against them was tough but we had control
Suggestions to improve rugby: *On-field* – Refereeing is still a major problem which the authorities have got to recognise. There are only five referees capable of refereeing internationals to a proper standard. Never mind the players, the professionalising of rugby must start with the referees. Hold seminars for officials to sort out common strategy. Get touch judges more involved in running of game. As for the rule changes, far too much tinkering goes on by people who do not understand what is going on in the scrum. Unions should get player representatives involved in lawmaking and not pretend they are administering for the whole game rather than for a select few. The need to be 100 per cent fitter to accommodate the new rule changes is taking away from the average player. That is not what I went into the game for and I have played at every level. I am sad to see the way things have changed. For example, none of the young players knew the words to our rugby songs on the Barbarians tour. Endemic of the problem – we have lost the social aspect. *Off-field* – I would like to think players could progress hand-in-hand with RFU into modern era. Allow players to benefit from off-field activities; after all, RFU market themselves on fame of players
Notable landmarks in rugby career: First England cap (Jan 1988) came at the age of 31. An occasional centre in junior rugby before moving to Wasps. Outside club rugby, has represented Hertfordshire and Surrey county clubs, Hertfordshire, Surrey, Middlesex, London Counties, London (only player to have featured in every divisional game prior to World Cup), Barbarians, Public

	apps	pts
England B (1986)		
Last Season	0 caps	0
Career	4 caps	0
England (1988)		
Last Season	11 caps	0
Career	33 caps	12

Caps (33): **1988** F, W, S, I(1,2), A(a1, a2), A(b) **1989** S, I, R(R) **1990** I, F, W, S, Arg(a1, a2), Arg(b) **1991** W, S, I, F, Fj, A(a) wc-NZ, It, F, S, A(b) **1992** S, I, F, W

Points (12 – 3t): **1989** R(1t) **1990** I(1t) **1991** Fj(1t)

School Wanderers, England B (four games), World XV (1989 against South Africa), and Home Unions (1989 v. France). Scored tries in England's wins over Romania (1989), Ireland (1990), Fiji (1991) and Queensland on 1988 tour of Australia. Returned Down Under on tour with England (1991) having attended Argentina the previous summer. Ever present throughout England's back-to-back Grand Slams and played in 1991 World Cup final
Touchlines: Sailing, shooting, fishing, watching children grow up and play sport
Player to watch: Damian Hopley (Wasps)
Player of the year: Peter Winterbottom (England)

Proctor, W. T.　　　　　　　Wales

Full Name: Wayne Thomas Proctor
1991/92 International category:
Wales U-21
Club: Llanelli
Positions: Wing, fullback
Height: 6′ **Weight:** 12st 6lbs
Occupation: Student
Born: Bridgend, 12.6.72
Family: Single
Former club: Cardigan Youth
International debut (U-21):
Scotland 19, Wales 28, 1992
Best moment in rugby:
Representing Wales for first time at Stirling
Worst moment in rugby: Missing out on a Welsh Schools cap
Most embarrassing moment:
Being interviewed by the BBC for the first time
Most respected opponent: Tony Underwood (Leicester, Cambridge Univ & England B)
Other sporting achievements:
Represented Wales 11 times at athletics; third in 1988 British Schools 400m hurdles

	apps	pts
Wales U-21 (1992)		
Last Season	1 cap	0
Career	1 cap	0

Best memory last season: Making Llanelli first team and playing in Schweppes Challenge Cup final win over Swansea; winning U-21 cap
Suggestions to improve rugby: *On-field* – Introduce alternative for the scrum

to help quicken up the game. *Off-field* – Sell the game better. Televise more live games at different levels

Notable landmarks in rugby career: A member of Llanelli's 1991/92 Schweppes Cup-winning side (beat Swansea 16–7, Cardiff 16 May 1992). Won first Wales U-21 cap in 28–19 win over Scotland (Stirling, 18 Apr 1992), having previously won four Welsh Youth caps and three Wales U-19 caps. Toured with U-19s to Canada. Final trial for Welsh Schoolboys U-18s but did not make the side

Touchlines: Athletics, tennis, badminton

Player to watch: Andrew Gibbs (Newbridge)

Player of the year: Emyr Lewis (Wales)

Quinnell, L. S. Wales

Full Name: Leon 'Scott' Quinnell

1991/92 International category: Wales U-21

Club: Llanelli

Position: No.8

Height: 6′4″ **Weight:** 16st 9lbs

Occupation: Sales representative with Chemtreat Ltd (Llanelli)

Born: Llanelli, 20.8.72

Family: Single

Family links with rugby: Father (Derek) played for Wales and Lions; uncles Barry John, Alan John and Clive John all played a bit too!

International debut (U-21): Scotland 19, Wales 28, 1992

Best moment in rugby: Scoring four tries for Wales Youth against England Colts

Worst moment in rugby: Ankle ligament injury (five months out)

Most respected opponent: Mickey Skinner (Harlequins & England)

Best memory last season: Getting established in Llanelli side and helping to beat Swansea in Schweppes Challenge Cup final

Biggest influence on career: My parents

	apps	pts
Wales U-21 (1992)		
Last Season	1 cap	8
Career	1 cap	8

Serious injuries: Damaged ankle ligaments (missed Wales Youth against France Juniors)

Notable landmarks in rugby career: Son of Derek (23 Welsh caps: 1972–80; 5 Lions Tests: 1971 NZ[3], 1977 NZ[2,3], 1980 SA[1,2]) who represented Welsh Schools U-18s, Wales Youth (four tries against 1990/91 England Colts), Wales U-19s and Wales U-21s, for whom scored two tries on his debut against Scotland U-21s at Bridgehaugh, Stirling. At club level represented Llanelli Youth before, last season, making himself at home in the senior back row, playing in the 16–7 Schweppes Challenge Cup final win over Swansea (Cardiff, 16 May 1992)

Touchlines: All sport, girlfriend (Nicola)

Rayer, M. A.   Wales

Full Name: Michael Anthony Rayer
1991/92 International category: Wales Full
Club: Cardiff
Position: Fullback
Height: 5'10" **Weight:** 13st 2lbs
Occupation: Metal worker/fabricator
Born: Cardiff, 21.7.65
Family: Married
Family links with rugby: Father (Alec) played for Penarth, Cardiff Athletic and Llandudno
Former club: Llandudno
International debut: Wales 13, Western Samoa 16, 1991
Five Nations' debut: England 24, Wales 0, 1992
Best moment in rugby: Landing dropped goal in extra-time of 1987 Schweppes Cup final against Swansea to put Cardiff in winning position

Worst moment in rugby: Dislocating elbow against Pontypool in 1988 (out for ten weeks)

Most embarrassing moment: Aquaplaning 20 feet with ball in sodden conditions at St Helen's playing for Cardiff against Swansea

Most respected opponent: Jean-Baptiste Lafond (Racing Club & France)

Serious injuries: Dislocated elbow, sprung shoulder joint, damaged ribs, torn hamstring, ankle and knee ligaments

Other sporting achievements: Captained Wales B baseball team (1990/91)

Best memory last season: Breaking into Wales side and starting game for first time against Argentina in World Cup

Suggestions to improve rugby: Develop more professional attitude. Disband 'old school tie' committees and stop living in past

Notable landmarks in rugby career: Captained Wales Youth (1983–85) at fullback prior to joining

	apps	pts
Wales B (1987)		
Last Season	0 caps	0
Career	2 caps	0
Wales (1991)		
Last Season	4 caps	3
Career	4 caps	3

Caps (4): **1991** wc-WS(R), Arg, A(R) **1992** E(R)

Points (3 – 1p): **1991** wc-Arg(1p)

Cardiff in 1984/85. Played twice for Wales B, as a replacement against France B at Bègles (lost 0–26, 17 Oct 1987) and then from the start against the same opposition at La Teste two years later (won 28–15, 12 Nov 1989). Toured Namibia with Wales (1990) but was unable to shift Paul Thorburn from fullback slot, despite scoring 28 points in 67–9 defeat of North Region (Tsumeb, 6 Jun 1990). Top scored on tour with 64 points from 3 appearances. Knee surgery in August 1991 further delayed his entry into big time, but day finally arrived when replacing Tony Clement during World Cup defeat by Western Samoa. Started following game against Argentina (kicking penalty) before topping up four-cap tally with replacement appearances against Australia (79th minute) and England (40th minute, for Five Nations' debut)

Thou shalt not pass. Rob Andrew tries in vain to halt John Kirwan's progress in the World Cup opener at Twickenham. New Zealand beat England 18–12

Redman, N. C.   England

Full Name: Nigel Charles Redman
1991/92 International category:
England Full
Club: Bath
Position: Lock
Height: 6'4" **Weight:** 17st 2lbs
Occupation: Electrician with
MITIE Engineering (Bristol)
Born: Cardiff, 16.8.64
Family: Lorinda (wife)
Family links with rugby: Younger
brother (Paul) plays No.8 for
Weston-super-Mare
Former club: Weston-super-Mare
International debut: England 3,
Australia 19, 1984
Five Nations' debut: Scotland 33,
England 6, 1986
Best moment in rugby: Being
involved with England's 1991 World
Cup squad; achieving 1991/92
League and Cup double with Bath
Worst moment in rugby: Being left
out of Bath Cup final team in
1988/89 after playing in all other
games. Being dropped by club is
harder to take than by country
because that is your bread and
butter. It hurt more than anything
Most embarrassing moment:
South Australia v. England (1988) –
only occasion in which English team was not on pitch while National Anthem
was being played, because I was on the toilet
Most respected opponent: Robert Norster (ex-Cardiff & Wales) –
considered short for middle jumper but is still one of best
Biggest influence on career: Jack Rowell (Bath coach)
Serious injuries: Having both elbows operated on after England's 1990 tour
of Argentina
Best memory last season: The World Cup final – I played in the 1987
tournament but the 1991 event showed just how much the game has taken
off as a world sporting spectacle
Suggestions to improve rugby: *On-field* – New regulations are good in

	apps	pts
England B (**1986**)		
Last Season	0 caps	0
England (**1984**)		
Last Season	3 caps	0
Career	13 caps	4

Caps (13): **1984** A **1986** S(R) **1987** I,
S wc-A, J, W(b) **1988** Fj **1990**
Arg(1,2) **1991** Fj wc-It, US

Points (4 – 1t): **1987** wc-J(1t)

189

principle. Welcome lineout spacing because it was a lottery before. Scrap 90-degree wheel law. Stricter control of refereeing. Work harder to establish uniformity in interpretations. During 1991 World Cup all the referees looked out of the same pair of eyes and there was not a dull game as a result of the players knowing where they stood

Notable landmarks in rugby career: Played in both World Cup tournaments, scoring only international try in 60–7 defeat of Japan in Sydney, Australia during 1987 event. Toured Argentina (1990) and Australia/Fiji (1991) with England. First-choice lock for England B in 1990/91, playing five matches (v. Emerging Australians, Sp, I, F and It). After Argentine tour missed 1991 Five Nations' campaign but returned for Test in Fiji on summer sortie Down Under and featured against Italy and the USA in the ensuing World Cup. Played in six out of the possible seven Cup final wins since joining Bath in 1983 (1984–85–86–87–90–92). Aged 19 when played in 1984 final against Bristol, scored two tries in 19–12 final defeat of Wasps (1987), and one in 48–6 final defeat of Gloucester (1990). Captained England U-23 to 15–10 win over Spain (Twickenham, 9 Apr 1986)

Touchlines: Volleyball, swimming, golf, DIY

Player to watch: Ben Clarke (Bath)

Player of the year: Dewi Morris (England)

Redpath, B. W. Scotland

Full Name: Bryan William Redpath
1991/92 International category:
Scotland U-21
Club: Melrose
Position: Scrum-half
Height: 5′7″ **Weight:** 10st 10lbs
Occupation: Joiner
Born: Galashiels, 2.7.71
Family: Single
Family links with rugby: Andrew (brother) has played for Scotland U-18s and U-21s, Craig (brother) for Scotland U-21s, and B. Lynne (sister) plays for Scotland women U-21s
International debut (U-21): Wales 23, Scotland 15, 1991
Best moment in rugby: Winning 1991/92 McEwan's Championship with Melrose

Most respected opponent: Gary Armstrong (Jedforest & Scotland)
Other sporting achievements: Cricket for St Boswells
Best memories last season: Winning League title, and selection for second U-21 cap

	apps	pts
Scotland U-21 (**1991**)		
Last Season	1 cap	0
Career	2 caps	0

Suggestions to improve rugby: *On-field* – Reduce value of penalty goal to make for more entertaining spectacle. *Off-field* – Get more youngsters involved in rugby. Instruct Melrose coach Jim Telfer not to train us so hard
Notable landmarks in rugby career: Replacement for Scotland U-18s and U-19s before making U-21 debut in loss to Wales at Llanelli (20 Apr 1991). Added second cap against Welsh at Bridgehaugh, Stirling (lost 19–28, 18 Apr 1992). Melrose's first-choice scrum-half in triumphant 1991/92 Championship campaign which featured 11 wins and a draw from 13 starts
Touchlines: Golf, cricket
Player to watch: Stuart Reid (Boroughmuir)

Rees, G. W. England

Full Name: Gary William Rees
1991/92 International category: England Full
Club: Nottingham
Position: Flanker
Height: 6′ **Weight:** 15st
Occupation: Managing director of Omniway (Nottingham)
Born: Long Eaton, 2.5.60
Family: Single
International debut: South Africa 35, England 9, 1984
Five Nations' debut: England 25, Ireland 20, 1986
Best moment in rugby: Making England debut as replacement in second Test at Ellis Park
Worst moment in rugby: Nottingham losing to Harlequins in extra time in 1990/91 Pilkington Cup semi-final

Most embarrassing moment: Left-footed touch finder against Orrell in final game of 1990/91 season – it found their No.8!
Most respected opponent: Simon Poidevin (NSW & Australia)

Biggest influence on career: Alan Davies (Nottingham coach) – who in 1980 recommended that I switched from fullback to flanker
Serious injuries: Recurring dislocated shoulder
Other sporting achievements: County Schools hockey and cricket
Best memory last season: Being part of England's World Cup squad
Suggestions to improve rugby: *On-field* – Two referees for all representative games. Stop referees answering players back. Consult players before making rules. *Off-field* – Players should reap some sort of benefit from playing at very top level. Elsewhere, continue playing for the love. If you attain international status a bit of a financial carrot would not be a bad thing. Each year the pot could be divided up by those involved

	apps	pts
England B (1988)		
Last Season	0 caps	0
England (1984)		
Last Season	3 caps	0
Career	24 caps	8

Caps (24): **1984** SA(2R), A **1986** I, F **1987** F, W(a), S wc-A, J, US, W(b) **1988** S(R), I(1,2), A(1,2), Fj **1989** W(R), R(R), Fj(R) **1990** Arg(b:R) **1991** Fj, A(a) wc-US

Points (8 – 2t): **1987** wc-J **1988** I(1:1t)

Notable landmarks in rugby career: Joined Nottingham in 1978 as fullback or scrum-half but moved to flanker and was quickly snapped up by Notts, Lincs & Derby and England U-23s in Italy (1982). Helped Midlands beat 1983 All Blacks. Represented England in 1987 World Cup and on tour in Australia (1988 and 1991). Participated in both World Cup tournaments. Crossed for tries in 60–7 win over Japan in 1987 World Cup (Sydney, 30 May 1987) and in 35–3 defeat of Ireland (Twickenham, 19 Mar 1988). After two years (1989–90) of appearing only as a replacement, he enjoyed a successful 1991 tour to Australia and Fiji, starting both Tests, and was included in World Cup squad, turning out in No.7 jersey for 37–9 win over United States (Twickenham, 11 Oct 1991)
Touchlines: Golf (handicap 24), more golf
Player to watch: Martin Pepper (Nottingham)
Player of the year: Dewi Morris (England)

Reid, S. J.   Scotland

Full Name: Stuart James Reid
1991/92 International category:
Scotland B
Club: Boroughmuir
Positions: No.8, flanker
Height: 6'3 1/2" **Weight:** 15st 11lbs
Occupation: Bank officer with Bank
of Scotland
Born: Kendal, 31.1.70
Family: Single
International debut (B): Ireland
16, Scotland 0, 1990
Best moment in rugby: Scoring
two tries for Scotland XV in 41–12
win over United States (Hartford, 18
May 1991)
Worst moment in rugby: Loss of
form in club rugby during 1991/92
season which cost me a place in the
Scotland Trial
Most respected opponent: Finlay
Calder (Stewart's-Melville &
ex-Scotland)
Biggest influence on career: Bruce
Hay (Boroughmuir coach)
Serious injuries: Knee operation to
decompress tendons in left knee
(1991/92)
Best memory last season:
Selection for Scotland's summer
tour to Australia

	apps	pts
Scotland U-21 (**1990**)		
Last Season	0 cap	0
Career	2 caps	0
Scotland B (**1990**)		
Last Season	1 cap	0
Career	3 caps	0
Scotland A (**1991**)		
Last Season	1 cap	0
Career	1 cap	0
Scotland 1992	Tour to Australia	

Suggestions to improve rugby: *On-field* – Cannot see the sense in increasing try-value to five points. It would have been better to reduce value of 'kicking' points. *Off-field* – Allow players to benefit from rugby-related activities
Notable landmarks in rugby career: Represented Scotland at U-19 (1989), U-21 (1989–91) and B levels. Played in both B games in 1990/ 91 seasons (against Ireland and France) before gaining selection to Scotland senior tour to North America. Turned out in both non-cap 'Tests', against US Eagles (scoring two tries in 41–12 win) and Canada (one try in 19–24 defeat), as well as against Alberta (one try in 76–7 win) and Rugby East. Suffered dip in form last season but still added third B cap (in 18–27 loss to France B, Albi 3 Feb 1992) and first Scotland A cap (in 36–16 defeat of Spain,

193

Murrayfield 28 Dec 1991). Also helped Boroughmuir win Alloa Brewery Cup (beating Currie in final), before embarking with Scotland on 1992 tour to Australia
Touchlines: Fishing
Player to watch: Gregor Townsend (Gala)
Player of the year: Andy Nicol (Scotland)

Richards, D.   England

Full Name: Dean Richards
1991/92 International category: England Full
Club: Leicester
Position: No.8
Height: 6′3″ **Weight:** 17st 7lbs
Occupation: Policeman
Born: Nuneaton, 11.7.63
Family: Nicky (wife)
Family links with rugby: Father (Brian) played for Nuneaton
Former club: Roanne (France)
International debut: England 25, Ireland 20, 1986
Five Nations' debut: As above
Best moment in rugby: Winning decisive third Test with 1989 Lions
Worst moments in rugby: Losing four front teeth whilst in action; England losing to Wales in Cardiff (1989)
Most respected opponent: Brian Moore (Harlequins & England)
Biggest influence on career: My work
Serious injuries: Recurring dislocated shoulder (1989/90)
Best memory last season: Completing second straight Grand Slam with England
Suggestions to improve rugby: *On-field* – Home Unions must guard against taking on new laws just because they suit the Southern

	apps	pts
England (**1986**)		
Last Season	8 caps	0
Career	33 caps	24
Lions (**1989**)	3 Tests	0

Caps (33): **1986** I, F **1987** S wc-A, J, US, W **1988** F, W, S, I(1), A(a1, a2), Fj, A(b) **1989** S, I, F, W, R. Lions-A(1,2,3) **1990** Arg **1991** W, S, I, F, F j, A(a) wc-NZ, It, US **1992** S(R), F, W

Points (24 – 6t): **1986** I(2t) **1987** wc-J(1t) **1988** A(a2:1t) **1989** I(1t), R(1t)

Hemisphere nations. *Off-field* – Reduce maximum age of committee men to 55. Allow players to prosper from non-rugby related activities, as they do everywhere else in the world

Notable landmarks in rugby career: Joined Leicester in 1982 after season playing in France. Played for England Schools at lock, before graduating to England U-23s (against Romania). Also represented Leicestershire (would like to play county rugby again after international career) and Midlands Division. Scored two tries on international debut against Ireland but it was one of his worst performances. Played in 1987 World Cup and returned to Australia with 1989 Lions, playing in all three Tests of 2–1 series win. Shoulder injury ruled out 1989/90 season. Linchpin of England's 1991 Grand Slam success. Scored one of England XV's two tries in 18–16 defeat of centenary Barbarians at Twickenham (29 Sep 1990). Voted 1990/91 Whitbread/*Rugby World* Player of Year. Toured Fiji/Australia (1991) and played in three World Cup Pool games before Mike Teague took over at No.8 for knock-out stages. Returned in 1992 Five Nations' Championship, helping England to second Grand Slam

Touchlines: Squash, five-a-side soccer

Ridge, M. P.   Ireland

Full Name: Martin Patrick Ridge
1991/92 International category:
Ireland B/Full(NZ tour)
Club: Blackrock College
Position: Centre
Height: 6'1 1/2" **Weight:** 13st 3lbs
Occupation: Marketing student
Born: Dublin, 8.10.70
Family: Single
Family links with rugby: Father
(Martin snr) played for Bective
Rangers and London Irish
International debut (B): Scotland
19, Ireland 29, 1991
Best moment in rugby: Scoring
tries on both B appearances
Worst moment in rugby: Losing
1988/89 Leinster Schools Senior
Cup final
Most respected opponent: Sean Lineen (Boroughmuir & Scotland B)
Other sporting achievements: Sailing instructor, represents Royal Irish Yacht Club

Best memory last season: Selection for senior Ireland tour to New Zealand
Suggestions to improve rugby: *On-field* – More sympathetic refereeing to provide freer flowing games
Notable landmarks in rugby career: Selected for Ireland's (1992)

	apps	pts
Ireland U-21 (**1991**)		
Last Season	2 caps	0
Career	2 caps	0
Ireland B (**1991**)		
Last Season	2 caps	8
Career	2 caps	8
Ireland 1992	Tour to New Zealand	

tour to New Zealand after season in which he broke first into the national U-21 side, for the games against Wales (lost 15–22, Newport 16 Oct 1991) and England (won 19–10, Dublin 23 Oct 1991), and then the B side, scoring one try in the 29–19 defeat of Scotland B (Murrayfield, 28 Dec 1991) and another in the 15–47 loss to England (Richmond, 31 Jan 1992). Previously, represented Leinster and Ireland at Schools and U-20 grades and the province at senior level. Won Leinster Junior and Senior Cup medals
Touchlines: Sailing, golf (handicap 15)
Player to watch: Victor Costello (Blackrock College)
Player of the year: Brendan Mullin (Ireland)

Rigney, B. J.   Ireland

Full Name: Brian Joseph Rigney
1991/92 International category: Ireland Full
Club: Greystones
Position: Lock
Height: 6'4" **Weight:** 17st 8lbs
Occupation: Brewers' representative
Born: Portlaoise, 22.9.63
Family: Single
Family links with rugby: Four brothers play for Portlaoise
Former clubs: Portlaoise, Highfield, Bective Rangers
International debut: Ireland 13, France 21, 1991
Five Nations' debut: As above
Best moment in rugby: Winning first senior cap against French

Worst moment in rugby: Being sent off after 14 minutes playing for Ireland

B against Scotland B in Belfast (22 Dec 1990) for throwing a silly punch; knee ligament injury sustained in Namibia 1991

Most embarrassing moment: Belfast dismissal

Most respected opponent: Donal Lenihan (Cork Constitution & ex-Ireland) – tremendous dedication and application

Serious injuries: Broken ankle (missed 1987 Munster Cup final as a result); torn knee ligaments (1991)

	apps	pts
Ireland B (1989)		
Last Season	1 cap	0
Career	3 caps	0
Ireland (1991)		
Last Season	2 caps	0
Career	6 caps	0

Caps (6): **1991** F, W, E, S, Na(1)
        1992 F

Points: Nil

Other sporting achievements: Won honours for Gaelic football and hurling with Portlaoise. Various swimming achievements as boy

Best memory last season: Returning to Ireland side, first for French trip in Championship, then for New Zealand tour

Suggestions to improve rugby: *Off-field* – Standardise Northern and Southern Hemisphere Unions' attitudes towards amateurism. Reimburse employers for time lost to rugby. Form a players' committee at top level

Notable landmarks in rugby career: Severe knee-ligament injury during 1991 Namibia tour put him out of World Cup and three-quarters of Five Nations' Championship. Returned for 12–44 loss to France in 1992 Five Nations' Championship and then toured New Zealand. Did not begin playing rugby until aged 19, preferring Gaelic and hurling. Joined Bective Rangers before settling down with Greystones. Capped in third season by Leinster. Picked for Ireland XV v. Wales and US Eagles during 1989 North American tour. Although no caps awarded to Ireland, both opponents received caps. Made Ireland B debut in 22–22 draw with Scotland (1989/90) and won second cap in ill-fated match against same opponents the following season. Called into Ireland's 1991 Five Nations' squad and played full campaign

Player to watch: Nick Popplewell (Greystones)

Robertson, G. B.   Scotland

Full Name: George Brian Robertson
1991/92 International category:
Scotland B
Club: Stirling County
Position: Tighthead prop
Height: 6′ **Weight:** 16st 3lbs
Occupation: Potato merchant with
Robertsons Potatoes (Tillicoutry)
Born: Falkirk, 9.8.59
Family: Morag (wife) and Craig
(son)
Best moments in rugby: Winning
1989/90 Inter-District
Championship with Glasgow and
putting on Scotland jersey for first
time
Worst moment in rugby:
Damaging knee ligaments so badly
on Glasgow's Irish tour (1989) that
thought career was over
Most respected opponent: David
Sole (Edinburgh Academicals &
Scotland)
Biggest influence on career:
Logan family who enticed me down
to Stirling

	apps	pts
Scotland B (1990)		
Last Season	2 caps	0
Career	3 caps	0

Serious injuries: Knee ligaments (operation on tendons)
Best memory last season: Helping underdog Reds beat Blues in Scotland
Trial
Suggestions to improve rugby: *On-field* – Reduce penalty goals to two
points. *Off-field* – Broken time payments
Notable landmarks in rugby career: Only took up rugby at age of 22.
Represented Glasgow since 1985 and toured with them to Holland and
Belgium (1985), and Ireland (1989). Joined Stirling when in McEwan's
League division three. Made debut for Scotland B in 0–16 loss to Ireland B
(Ravenhill, 22 Dec 1990) and, last season, added caps against Ireland B (lost
19–29, Murrayfield 28 Dec 1991) and France B (lost 18–27, Albi 3 Feb 1992)
Player to watch: Gregor Townsend (Gala)
Player of the year: Andy Nicol (Scotland)

Robinson, B. F.   Ireland

Full Name: Brian Francis Robinson
1991/92 International category:
Ireland Full
Club: Ballymena
Position: No.8
Height: 6'4" **Weight:** 15st
Occupation: PE teacher at Belfast
Royal Academy
Born: Belfast, 20.3.66
Family: Single
International debut: Ireland 13,
France 21, 1991
Five Nations' debut: As above
Best moment in rugby: Breaking
Irish single-match try-scoring record
with four against Zimbabwe in 1991
World Cup

Worst moment in rugby: Tearing
cruciate and medial ligaments in first
match after touring Zimbabwe with
Ulster (1986/87) and missing next
18 months
Most respected opponent: Zinzan
Brooke (Auckland & New Zealand)
Serious injuries: As above
Best memory last season: Scoring
four tries against Zimbabwe
Suggestions to improve rugby:
On-field – Pleased to see more points
awarded for tries. *Off-field* – Relax
amateur rules to allow players to earn
money away from rugby. Reimburse employers for time lost

	apps	pts
Ireland B (**1989**)		
Last Season	0 caps	0
Career	2 caps	0
Ireland (**1991**)		
Last Season	9 caps	16
Career	13 caps	20

Caps (13): **1991** F, W, E, S, Na(1,2)
wc-Z, S, A **1992** W, E, S, F

Points (20 – 5t): **1991** S(1t) wc-Z(4t)

Notable landmarks in rugby career: Played for Irish Wolfhounds Seven in
Sicily (1989/90), and Ireland U-25s against US Eagles (1989/90). Previously
represented Combined Irish Provinces (aged 20). Played for Ulster against
1989 All Blacks. Made Ireland B debut in 22–22 draw with Scotland B
(1989/90) and, last season, after warming B bench against Argentina (won
27–12), helped Ireland B beat Scots 16–0 at Ravenhill (22 Dec 1990). Ever
present in Ireland's back row since making full debut against France in first
match of 1991 Five Nations' Championship. Scored first international try in
25–28 loss to Scotland at Murrayfield (16 Mar 1991) and entered history
books with four-try haul in 55–11 World Cup defeat of Zimbabwe (Dublin,

6 Oct 1991). Previous best haul was three, by six different players including Keith Crossan (v. Romania, 1986) and Brendan Mullin (v. Tonga, 1987)
Touchlines: Sub-aqua diving, keep-fit
Player to watch: Simon Geoghegan (London Irish)

Rodber, T. A. K. England

Full Name: Timothy Andrew Keith Rodber
1991/92 International category: England Full
Clubs: Northampton & Army
Position: No.8
Height: 6'6" **Weight:** 16st 8lbs
Occupation: Second Lieutenant in army
Born: Richmond, Yorkshire, 2.7.69
Family: Single
Family links with rugby: Father played
Former clubs: Oxford Old Boys, Petersfield
International debut: Scotland 7, England 25, 1992
Five Nations' debut: As above
Best moment in rugby: Selection for start of 1992 Five Nations' Championship
Worst moment in rugby: Being injured by foul play against Plymouth Albion
Most respected opponent: Dean Richards (Leicester & England) – awesome in every department
Serious injuries: Popped ribs
Other sporting achievements: Hampshire Schools County hockey and cricket
Best memory last season: Winning two full caps

	apps	pts
England U-21 (**1989**)		
Last Season	0 caps	0
Career	1 cap	0
England B (**1990**)		
Last Season	0 caps	0
Career	4 caps	8
England (**1992**)		
Last Season	2 caps	0
Career	2 caps	0
	1995 Development squad	

Caps (2): **1992** S, I
Points: Nil

Suggestions to improve rugby: Anything to take away stagnant play (i.e. Gloucester scrums, etc)
Notable landmarks in rugby career: Joined Northampton from Oxford OBs

and represented original England U-21 side which dismantled Romanian opposition on a sunny May afternoon in Bucharest in 1989 (won 54–13, 13 May 1989). Represented Saints in 1991 Pilkington Cup final, the season after he toured Argentina (1990) with England's senior squad, turning out against Tucuman Selection (won 19–14), Cuyo Selection (lost 21–22) and Cordoba Selection (won 15–12). In 1990/91 he scored tries for England B in 31–16 defeat of Namibia and in 10–24 loss to Ireland B. Also played against France B (as on debut in 1990). Helped England XV beat Italy in 1990 (won 33–15) and, last season, graduated to full status with Championship appearances against Scotland and Ireland

Touchlines: Active interest in army

Rolland, A. C. P.   Ireland

Full Name: Alain Colm Pierre Rolland
1991/92 International category: Ireland B
Club: Blackrock College
Position: Scrum-half
Height: 5'10" **Weight:** 11st 9lbs
Occupation: Bank official
Born: Dublin, 22.8.66
Family: Single
International debut: Ireland 20, Argentina 18, 1990
Best moments in rugby: Blackrock beating Trinity in 1988 Leinster Senior Cup final, having been given no chance. Winning first cap
Worst moment in rugby: Blackrock losing Senior Schools Cup to De La Salle, aged 18
Most embarrassing moment: Concussed playing for Leinster U-20s and talking absolute nonsense while being helped off field
Most respected opponent: Fergus Aherne (Lansdowne & Ireland)
Best memory last season: Selection for Ireland B against England B

	apps	pts
Ireland B (**1989**)		
Last Season	1 cap	0
Career	2 caps	0
Ireland (**1990**)		
Last Season	0 caps	0
Career	1 cap	0

Caps (1): **1990** Arg
Points: Nil

201

Suggestions to improve rugby: None. Very happy with game as it is
Notable landmarks in rugby career: Played two seasons with Leinster U-20s. Three full caps for Leinster (1988/89). 1989/90 replacement for Ireland U-25s against US Eagles. First Ireland B cap came in 22–22 draw with Scotland (Murrayfield, 9 Dec 1989), with second following last season in 15–47 loss to England B at Richmond (31 Jan 1992). Made full Ireland bow in 20–18 defeat of Argentina (Dublin, 27 Oct 1990) but relegated to bench reserve throughout 1991 Five Nations' Championship
Touchlines: Half-French: speak language fluently and have dual nationality. Enjoy cycling and running

---

Rooney, S. V. J.   Ireland

Full Name: Stephen Vincent John Rooney
1991/92 International category: Ireland U-21
Club: Univ College Dublin
Position: Flanker
Height: 6'2" **Weight:** 15st
Occupation: Commerce student
Born: Dublin, 19.11.70
Family: Single
International debut: Netherlands 21, Ireland U-21 7, 1990
Best moment in rugby: Beating England U-21s at Moseley (1990/91)
Worst moment in rugby: Playing for St Michael's College in 1988 Schools Senior Cup final defeat
Best memory last season: Beating England U-21s again
Suggestions to improve rugby: *On-field* – Abandon 90-degree scrummage wheel law
Notable landmarks in rugby career: Spent two years playing for Ireland Schools (winning seven caps), before graduating to Ireland U-21s (eligible again this season), with whom went on two-match tour of Netherlands (playing against Dutch A and B sides) and then played in 22–16 win over England (Moseley, 29 Oct 1990). Also represented Leinster at U-19, U-20 and senior squad levels. Added third cap in 19–10 win over England B (Dublin, 23 Oct 1991)

	apps	pts
Ireland U-21 (**1990**)		
Last Season	1 cap	0
Career	3 caps	0

Touchlines: Any sports, music
Player to watch: Gabriel Fulcher (Univ College Dublin)

Rowntree, G. C.   England

Full Name: Graham Christopher Rowntree
1991/92 International category: England U-21
Club: Leicester
Position: Prop
Height: 6' **Weight:** 16st 10lbs
Occupation: Insurance broker
Born: Stockton-on-Tees, 18.4.71
Family: Single
Family links with rugby: Two brothers, like myself, Dean Richards and Barry Evans, represented John Cleveland College
Former club: Nuneaton
International debut (U-21): England 16, Ireland 22, 1990
Best moment in rugby: Winning first England recognition – for 16-Group back in 1987
Worst moment in rugby: England Colts' 12–6 loss to Wales at Wrexham in 1989/90 season
Most respected opponent: Gary Holmes (Wasps & England B)

	apps	pts
England U-21 (**1990**)		
Last Season	3 caps	0
Career	5 caps	0

Best memory last season: Winning three more England U-21 caps
Suggestions to improve rugby: *On-field* – Revert to old scrummaging laws. *Off-field* – Relax compensation laws
Notable landmarks in rugby career: Broke into Leicester Tigers first team aged 19. Played in all four matches for 1989/90 England Colts. Graduated to England U-21s in 1990/91 season, coming on as replacement for debut in 16–22 loss to Ireland, and starting match in 7–9 loss to French Armed Forces. Added a further three caps last season, against Belgium (won 94–0, Wolverhampton 1 Sep 1991), Ireland U-21 (lost 10–19, Donnybrook 23 Oct 1991) and French Armed Forces (drew 21–21, Twickenham 3 May 1992)
Touchlines: Music, synchronised swimming
Player to watch: Neil Back (Leicester)

Saunders, R.   Ireland

Full Name: Rob Saunders
1991/92 International category:
Ireland Full
Club: London Irish
Position: Scrum-half
Height: 5'10" **Weight:** 13st
Occupation: Marketing executive
with M. F Kent
Born: Nottingham, 5.8.68
Family: Single
Family links with rugby: Father
(Eric) a Scottish trialist who played
for Edinburgh and Leicester, and
captained Glasgow
Former club: Queen's Univ, Belfast
International debut: Ireland 13,
France 21, 1991
Five Nations' debut: As above
Best moment in rugby: Leading
Ireland out as captain on my
international debut at Lansdowne
Road
Worst moment in rugby: Being
dropped for Ireland U-21s' 13–13
draw against New Zealand (1990)
Other sporting achievements:
Ireland U-16 squash team. Ulster
Schools shotput champion
Most respected opponent:
Richard Hill (Bath & England)
Best memory last season: London
Irish retaining status in Courage
League division one

	apps	pts
Ireland U-21 (**1989**)		
Career	1 cap	0
Ireland B (**1990**)		
Last Season	0 caps	0
Career	1 cap	0
Ireland (**1991**)		
Last Season	7 caps	0
Career	11 caps	0

Caps (11): **1991** F, W, E, S, Na(1,2)
    wc-Z, J, S, A **1992** W

Points: Nil

Suggestions to improve rugby: *On-field* – Greater awareness of fitness. More
professional approach by referees (massive gap between standards). Reduce
value of penalty goal to encourage more open play. *Off-field* – Relax amateur
status. Players should be allowed to earn money from the game (e.g. writing
for papers, appearances, etc) but should not earn from a direct salary basis
Notable landmarks in rugby career: Captained Ulster Schools, Irish Schools
(v. Australia, 1987), Irish Universities and QUB. Made Ireland U-21 debut
in 10–9 away win in Italy (1989) but was dropped for 13–13 draw v. New
Zealand (1990). Rose to prominence in 1990/91 season as one of seven players

promoted from Ireland B after 16–0 defeat of Scotland B at Ravenhill (22 Dec 1990). Not only played entire 1991 Five Nations' Championship but captained side in each of four internationals. At 22 he became the third youngest captain in the history of Irish rugby (only the fifth to captain Ireland on his debut), before the experienced Phil Matthews took over for 1991 tour to Namibia. Lost place to Fergus Aherne after run of 11 consecutive internationals which covered 1991 World Cup campaign

Touchlines: Squash, golf, watching any sport

Scott, M. W. Scotland

Full Name: Martin William Scott
1991/92 International category: Scotland B
Club: Dunfermline
Position: Hooker
Height: 6′ **Weight:** 15st 7lbs
Occupation: Civil servant
Born: Falkirk, 5.7.66
Family: Karen (wife), Robyn and Ashley (daughters)
Former clubs: Rosyth and District
International debut: Scotland B 19, Ireland B 29, 1991
Best moment in rugby: Scoring try for Edinburgh Borderers against Scotland XV at Murrayfield (1990/91)
Worst moment in rugby: Tearing ankle ligaments against Watsonians in 1990
Most respected opponent: Kenny Milne (Heriot's FP & Scotland)
Biggest influence on career: Ian McNeill (Dunfermline fitness coach)
Serious injuries: Torn ankle ligaments
Best memory last season: Running out at Murrayfield in Scotland B jersey

	apps	pts
Scotland U-21 (**1987**)		
Career	1 cap	0
Scotland B (**1991**)		
Last Season	2 caps	0
Career	2 caps	0
Scotland 1992	Tour to Australia	

Suggestions to improve rugby: *On-field* – Sceptical about new maul law. *Off-field* – Sort out trust funds, especially for self-employed players who really stand to lose out from increased commitments to rugby

Notable landmarks in rugby career: Represented Scotland B against Ireland B (28 Dec 1991) and France B (lost 18–27, Albi 3 Feb 1992) during 1991/92 season. Put on standby for Scotland's 1992 tour to Australia after John Allan withdrew and Ian Corcoran was drafted. Took up rugby at age of 15. Represented North and Midlands U-21s (at lock) and senior XV. One appearance for Scotland U-21s came in 19–39 loss to Wales at Wrexham (1987)
Touchlines: Golf, football
Player to watch: Dave Barrett (West of Scotland)
Player of the year: Andy Nicol (Scotland)

Scott, R. Scotland

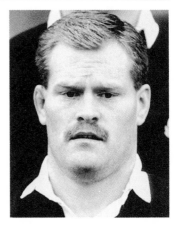

Full Name: Robb Scott
1991/92 International category: Scotland B
Club: London Scottish
Position: Lock
Height: 6'6" **Weight:** 18st 7lbs
Occupation: Area sales manager with Deceuninck Ltd
Born: Hong Kong, 25.4.66
Family: Anita (wife)
Former clubs: Heriot's FP, Dorking, Selkirk
International debut: Scotland B 19, Ireland B 29, 1991
Best moment in rugby: 50-metre sprint up Murrayfield to set up try for Derek Busby during Scottish Schools' game against Scotland U-18s (1984)
Most respected opponent: Alan Tomes (Hawick & Scotland)
Other sporting achievements: Threw discus for Scotland at Junior level (U-20 and U-21)
Serious injuries: Torn cruciate ligaments in left knee, prolapsed disc in lower back (out of rugby for two years) which required six months' full-time rehabilitation at RAF Headley Court
Best memories last season: Winning promotion to first division with

	apps	pts
Scotland B (**1991**)		
Last Season	2 caps	0
Career	2 caps	0

London Scottish; helping Reds (possibles) beat Blues (probables) in 1992 Scotland Trial

Suggestions to improve rugby: *On-field* – Abandon frustrating 90-degree wheel law. Take whatever steps are necessary to sort out lineouts. *Off-field* – Reduce points available for kicks at goal to encourage more entertaining rugby

Notable landmarks in rugby career: Represented 1984 Scottish Schools against Ireland and Wales, Hong Kong Police (1985/86) and Scotland B last season against Ireland B (lost 19–29, Murrayfield 28 Dec 1991) and France B lost 18–27, Albi 3 Feb 1992). Helped London Scottish win 1991/92 Courage League second division championship

Touchlines: Tennis, fitness training (weights coach)

Player to watch: Shade Munro (Glasgow High/Kelvinside)

Player of the Year: David McIvor (Scotland)

Scully, D. A.   England

Full Name: David Andrew Scully
1991/92 International category: England B
Club: Wakefield
Position: Scrum-half
Height: 5′8″ **Weight:** 12st
Occupation: Fireman at Edlington Fire Station
Born: Doncaster, 7.8.65
Family: Angela (wife) and Shaun (son)
Former club: Wheatley Hills
International debut: Italy B 10, England B 16, 1992
Best moment in rugby: Making B debut as 20th-minute replacement in Rome
Most respected opponent: Dewi Morris (Orrell & England)
Biggest influence on career: Tony Dunkley (chairman at Wheatley Hills)
Best memory last season: Scoring try on England B debut
Suggestions to improve rugby: *On-field* – Change new maul law,

England B (1992)	apps	pts
Last Season	1 cap	4
1992	Tour to New Zealand	
Career	1 cap	4

incites people to indulge in negative tactic of killing the ball. *Off-field* – More compensation for employers

Notable landmarks in rugby career: Replaced Steve Bates after 20 minutes of England B's match against Italy B in Rome last season and contributed try to 16–10 win which clinched Grand Slam for national second string. Joined Wakefield in 1986. Represented Yorkshire Colts, U-21 and senior teams as well as North in Divisional Championship. Captain of English Fire Service team and of Wakefield. Toured New Zealand with England B last summer

Touchlines: All sports

Players to watch: Jonathan Sleightholme, Richard Bramley (both Wakefield)

Player of the year: Peter Winterbottom (England)

Shepherd, R. J. S.   Scotland

Full Name: Rowen James Stanley Shepherd

1991/92 International category: Scotland U-21

Club: Edinburgh Academicals

Positions: Outside-half, centre

Height: 6′ **Weight:** 13st 8lbs

Occupation: PE student

Born: Edinburgh, 25.12.70

Family: Single

Family links with rugby: Father played for Caithness

Former club: Caithness

International debut (U-21): Wales 23, Scotland 15, 1991

Best moment in rugby: Scoring for Accies against Randwick at 1990 Melrose Sevens

Worst moment in rugby: Arguing with dad while playing Sevens

Best memory last season: Retained place in Scotland U-21 side

Suggestions to improve rugby: *On-field* – Alter regulation regarding rolling mauls to rule against obstructing players. *Off-field* – None. Things are okay

	apps	pts
Scotland U-21 (**1991**)		
Last Season	1 cap	0
Career	2 cap	3
Scotland 1991	Tour to North America	

Notable landmarks in rugby career: Toured North America with Scotland in summer of 1991 after Scott Nichol withdrew through injury, turning out in 76–7 win over Alberta in Edmonton (11 May 1991) and in 24–12 defeat of Rugby East four days later in New York City. Represented Scotland at Students and U-21 level. Kicked penalty goal for U-21s in 15–23 loss to Wales U-21s at Llanelli (20 Apr 1991) and, last season, played against England Students U-21s and Wales U-21s at Bridgehaugh, Stirling (lost 19–28, 18 Apr 1991)

Touchlines: Tennis, golf
Player to watch: Scott Nichol (Selkirk)

Shiel, A. G.   Scotland

Full Name: Andrew Graham Shiel
1991/92 International category:
Scotland Full
Club: Melrose
Positions: Outside-half, centre
Height: 5′10″ **Weight:** 13st
Occupation: Apprentice
stonemason with Historic Scotland
(Melrose)
Born: Galashiels, 13.8.70
Family: Single
Family links with rugby: Father
(Andrew) played for Melrose GS
International debut: Scotland 24,
Ireland 15, 1991
Five Nations' debut: None
Best moment in rugby: Scoring
winning try against Ireland on
Scotland debut after coming on as
43rd-minute replacement in 1991
World Cup match at Murrayfield

Worst moment in rugby: Not making the Scottish Schools XV to play New Zealand in 1988
Most embarrassing moment: Ball toppled over in front of posts before I kicked it during 1990 Hawick Sevens
Most respected opponent: Sean Lineen (Boroughmuir)
Biggest influences on career: Ian McGeechan, Jim Telfer
Serious injuries: Straining inner and exterior quadriceps and adductor muscle (1988/89) and missing over four months' rugby. Pelvic strain (Nov 1990) – three months out
Other sporting achievements: Athletics for Borders Schools and Borders AAA

Best memory last season: Winning McEwan's Championship for second time in three seasons with Melrose

Suggestions to improve rugby: *On-field* – Playing standards need to be improved at club level in Scotland – inferior to England and Wales. Still too forward-orientated in Scotland at present (lack of running ability). *Off-field* – Treat players better for all they put into game

Notable landmarks in rugby career: Represented Scottish Schools three times, Scotland U-19s

	apps	pts
Scotland U-21 (**1990**)		
Career	2 caps	6
Scotland A (**1991**)		
Last Season	1 cap	0
Career	1 cap	0
Scotland (**1991**)		
Last Season	2 caps	4
1992	Tour to Australia	
Career	2 caps	4

Caps (2): **1991** wc-I(R), WS

Points (4 – 1t): **1991** wc-I(R:1t)

and U-21s (twice). Scored six points in 1989/90 defeat (10–24) by Wales U-21 and played in 15–23 loss to same opposition (1990/91). Toured with Scotland to New Zealand (1990), North America and Canada (1991) and Australia (1992): made four appearances in New Zealand (Wellington, Nelson Bays/Marlborough, Southland and Manawatu) and five games out of six (including non-cap Tests against US Eagles and Canada) in North America. Represented European Saltires against South Pacific Barbarians in XVs prior to 1991 Hong Kong Sevens. Having been included in Scotland's 1991 World Cup squad, was given debut against Ireland as a 43rd-minute replacement for outside-half Craig Chalmers. Scored try as Scotland came from behind to win. Seven days later won second cap (as centre) in quarter-final against Western Samoa when knee injury ruled out Sean Lineen. Reverted to bench reserve thereafter. Remained in Australia after 1992 tour to spend summer playing with Manly

Touchlines: Social golf, cricket, swimming

Player to watch: Derek Bain (Melrose)

Player of the year: David Sole (Scotland)

Sims, D.   England

Full Name: David Sims
1991/92 International category:
England B
Club: Gloucester
Positions: Lock, No.8
Height: 6'8" **Weight:** 16st 6lbs
Occupation: Student
Born: Gloucester, 22.11.69
Family: Single
Family links with rugby:
Grandfather (Thomas Price) played
for England (1948–49)
Former clubs: Longlevens,
Sunnybank (Aus)
International debut: Spain 3,
England B 34, 1992
Best moment in rugby: Winning
regular place in 1991/92 England B
side
Worst moment in rugby:
Watching 1990 Pilkington Cup final
defeat to Bath from Gloucester
replacements' bench
Most respected opponent: John
Gadd (Gloucester)
Serious injuries: Damaged neck
muscles
Other sporting achievements:
Basketball for Gloucester Jets

	apps	pts
England U-21 (**1990**)		
Last Season	1 cap	4
Career	5 caps	4
England B (**1992**)		
Last Season	4 caps	0
1992	Tour to New Zealand	
Career	4 caps	0

Notable landmarks in rugby career: Attended England Schools (16-Group) and Colts final trials. Played for South West U-21s before graduating to senior team. Won England Students cap against Combined Services and made England U-21 debut in 24–3 win over Netherlands in Hilversum (24 Apr 1990). Played for Brisbane club Sunnybank in summer of 1990 before returning to play for England U-21s in 16–22 loss to Ireland U-21s at Moseley (29 Oct 1990), 20–18 win over Netherlands ('s-Hertogenbosch, 18 May 1991) and 7–9 loss to French Armed Forces (22 May 1991). Last season scored try in 94–0 rout of Belgium's senior side before graduating to England B squad and a place in their four-game Grand Slam side, with winning appearances put in against Spain, Ireland B, France B and Italy B. Toured New Zealand with B party in summer of 1992
Touchlines: Swimming, training, music

Skinner, M. G.   England

Full Name: Michael Gordon
Skinner
1991/92 International category:
England Full
Club: Blackheath
Positions: Flanker (6 or 7), No.8
Height: 6'4" **Weight:** 16st 6lbs
Occupation: Freelance computer
consultant with Unisys
Born: Newcastle upon Tyne,
26.11.58
Family: Single
Former clubs: Blaydon,
Blackheath, Harlequins
International debut: France 10,
England 9, 1988
Five Nations' debut: As above
Best moment in rugby: Mike
Teague's admission to being on a
mission from God
Worst moment in rugby: Referee
Fred Howard awarding Nottingham
a kickable penalty in our 1990/91
Pilkington Cup semi-final, with the
scores at 15–15 in extra-time. Guess
who it was given against?
Most embarrassing moment:
Playing blind-side for Barbarians v.
NZ Barbarians (1987/88). Still
bound to scrum when Michael Jones
was scoring on blind side from
10-yard scrum. The worst feeling I
have ever had

	apps	pts
England B (1987)		
Last Season	0 caps	0
England (1988)		
Last Season	9 caps	8
Career	21 caps	12

Caps (21): **1988** F, W, S, I(1,2) **1989** Fj **1990** I, F, W, S, Arg(a1, a2) **1991** Fj(R) wc-US, F(b), S(b), A(b) **1992** S, I, F, W

Points (12 – 3t): **1989** Fj(1t) **1991** wc-US(1t) **1992** W(1t)

Most respected opponent: Billy 'Skipper' Mordue, captain and No.8 of Ryton RFC – great commitment and loyalty to club
Biggest influences on career: Bobby Bartle (Blaydon player/coach), Des Diamond (ex-Blackheath coach), and Dick Best (Harlequins & England coach)
Serious injuries: Knee operation – file and drill knee cap
Other sporting achievements: Catching a 10lb salmon on River Tweed
Best memory last season: 1991 World Cup campaign – culmination of three years working together as a squad

Suggestions to improve rugby: *On-field* – Improve standards of refereeing. Encourage more players to become referees. Refs are not keeping up with the professional standards set by the players. Advantage law is not played half as much as it should be. If referees learned to play it we would have no need for half the new rules. That is my big gripe. I did not come into the game for all these law changes. It was a good game when I started playing. *Off-field* – Prevent rugby players from making fools of themselves on charity fund-raising TV shows!

Notable landmarks in rugby career: Scored winning try on debut for Blaydon at Stockton (1975/76) and received hero's welcome afterwards on return from having eye stitched at hospital. Started career as centre at school, and played No.8 and flanker for Northumberland Colts. Joined Blackheath in 1979 and represented Kent in 1986 County Championship final. Became fixture in London divisional team after moving to Harlequins. Made England B debut in 1987 match against France. Ever present on England bench during 1991 Grand Slam prior to touring Australia last summer. Came on as a replacement against Fiji. Benefited from Mike Teague's switch to No.8 during World Cup, moving into vacated blindside berth and scoring on first outing against USA. Was an ever present thereafter, featuring in World Cup final and throughout 1992 Grand Slam. However, because of own experience, 'I never forgot the bench reserves – christened the Bullet Holes – and shook each of their hands after each game as they put in just as much work away from pitch and never see the limelight.' Returned to old club, Blackheath, over summer

Touchlines: Cuddling girlfriend Anna Palmer (Hong Kong Sevens), fishing, squash, DIY, drinking, golf

Player to watch: Andy Mullins (Harlequins)

Player of the year: Jason Leonard (England)

Smith, I. R.   Scotland

Full Name: Ian Richard Smith
1991/92 International category:
Scotland Full
Club: Gloucester
Position: Flanker
Height: 6′ **Weight:** 14st
Occupation: Civil engineering
technician with Gloucestershire
Design
Born: Gloucester, 16.3.65
Family: Karen (wife)
Family links with rugby: Father
(Dick) was an England trialist who
played for (and captained)
Gloucester and Barbarians
Former club: Longlevens
International debut (England):
Spanish Select 15, England B 32,
1989

International debut (Scotland):
Ireland B 16, Scotland B 0, 1990
Best moment in rugby: Running
out at Murrayfield for first Scotland
cap against England
Worst moment in rugby: Losing
1989/90 Pilkington Cup final 6–48
to Bath
Most embarrassing moment:
Above match – we were humiliated
Most respected opponent: Neath
flanker Lyn Jones
Biggest influences on career:
Father and Derek Cook (coach at
Longlevens)

	apps	pts
England B (1989/90)		Tour to Spain
(1990/91)	1 rep	
Scotland B (**1990**)		
Last Season	1 cap	0
Career	3 caps	0
Scotland (**1992**)		
Last Season	3 caps	0
1992	Tour to Australia	
Career	3 caps	0

Caps (3): **1992** E, I, W
Points: Nil

Best memory last season: Gloucester beating Orrell in Pilkington Cup
quarter-finals
Suggestions to improve rugby: *On-field* – More consistency in refereeing.
Perhaps set up refereeing seminars where they can get together with players
and coaches to work things out. *Off-field* – Reimburse employers for
employee's time lost to rugby. It's not that we want to profit from rugby, it's
that we, and our bosses, don't want to be out of pocket. Relax amateur laws
Notable landmarks in rugby career: England 18-Group trialist. Played

200th game for Gloucester in 1989/90 Pilkington Cup final. Spent 1988 Australian season playing in Wollongong. Toured Spain with England B (1990) and was selected to England's 1991 World Cup squad, having spent summer of 1990 on standby for Argentine tour, but then decided to switch allegiances to Scotland (Scottish grandparents on father's side) and played twice for Scotland B in 1990/91 (v. Ireland and France) before leading side in 19–29 home loss to Ireland in 1991/92, a season in which also captained Gloucester (as in 1992/93) and broke into Scotland team for Five Nations' Championship. Missed only French visit to Murrayfield, due to a badly cut hand. Toured to Australia with Scotland over summer of 1992

Touchlines: Shooting, squash, trout fishing
Player to watch: Andy Nicol (Dundee HSFP)
Player of the Year: Derek White (Scotland)

Smith, S. J.   Ireland

Full Name: Stephen James Smith
1991/92 International category: Ireland Full
Club: Ballymena
Position: Hooker
Height: 6' **Weight:** 16st
Occupation: Sports representative with Edge Sports (Ballymena)
Born: Belfast, 18.7.59
Family: Single
Family links with rugby: Brother (Oliver) plays for Ballymena
International debut: Ireland 10, England 21, 1988
Five Nations' debut: Ireland 21, France 26, 1989
Best moment in rugby: Selection for 1989 Lions
Worst moment in rugby: Losing to Australia in last seconds of 1991 World Cup quarter-final in Dublin
Most respected opponent: Sean Fitzpatrick (Auckland & New Zealand)
Biggest influence on career: Sid Millar (ex-Ballymena, Ireland & Lions)
Serious injuries: Damaged rib cartilage (1990)
Best memory last season: Ireland's performance against Australia
Suggestions to improve rugby: *On-field* – Welcome any laws to speed up game. However, success of new rules will depend on the referees'

interpretations. *Off-field* – More professional approach away from field to match greater commitment being made by players. Pace of change is moving faster on pitch than off it

Notable landmarks in rugby career: Called out to 1987 World Cup as Ireland's second replacement hooker but did not feature. Following season broke into Ireland team and became first Irishman to mark debut with a try since Hugo MacNeill in 1981. Represented Barbarians

	apps	pts
Ireland B (1990/91)	1 rep	
Ireland (**1988**)		
Last Season	9 caps	0
1992	Tour to New Zealand	
Career	22 caps	8
Lions 1989		

Caps (22): **1988** E(b), WS, It **1989** F, W, E, S, NZ **1990** E **1991** F, W, E, S, Na(1,2) wc-Z, S, A **1992** W, E, S, F

Points (8 – 2t): **1988** E(b:1t) **1991** F(1t)

against 1988 Wallabies, 1989 Home Unions against France, and 1989 Lions in Australia, playing five games and scoring two tries. Toured South Africa with 1989 World XV and found experience awe-inspiring – a real eye-opener. Helped Ballymena win 1989/90 Ulster League and Cup double for second consecutive season (first team to achieve feat since 1907). Although only bench reserve for Ireland B against Argentina in early 1990/91, was a regular for Ireland in ensuing Five Nations' Championship, scoring try in loss to France. Toured Namibia in summer of 1991 and played in all but the Japan World Cup-tie last season (nine caps) before accepting an invitation to join the 1992 tour to New Zealand

Touchlines: Golf (handicap 15)
Player to watch: Dean McCartney (Ballymena)
Player of the year: David Campese (Australia)

France centre Franck Mesnel spills the ball with a little help from Scotland hooker Kenny Milne. The Scots maintained their recent dominance in the fixture at Murrayfield with a 10–6 triumph

Soden, P. J.   Ireland

Full Name: Philip Joseph Soden
1991/92 International category:
Ireland B
Club: Cork Constitution
Position: Loosehead prop
Height: 6' **Weight:** 16st 10lbs
Occupation: Own dry-cleaning
business
Born: London, 6.9.69
Family: Single
Former club: Christian Brothers
College (Cork)
International debut (B): Ireland
16, Scotland 0, 1990
Best moment in rugby: Playing in
above match
Best memory last season:
Retaining Ireland B place for
Scotland game in Edinburgh
**Notable landmarks in rugby
career:** Played for Irish Schools
(1986–88) and Munster at Schools
and U-20 level, before graduating to
U-21 team in 1989 for 13–13 draw
with touring New Zealand XV. Won
second U-21 cap in 22–16 defeat of
England at Moseley (29 Oct 1990)
before graduating to B team for two
matches against Scotland: 16–0 win at Ravenhill (22 Dec 1990) and 29–19
win at Murrayfield (28 Dec 1991)
Touchlines: Golf, swimming
Player to watch: Paul McCarthy (Cork Constitution)

	apps	pts
Ireland U-21 (**1989**)		
Last Season	0 caps	0
Career	2 caps	0
Ireland B (**1990**)		
Last Season	1 cap	0
Career	2 caps	0

Stanger, A. G.   Scotland

Full Name: Anthony George Stanger

1991/92 International category: Scotland Full

Club: Hawick

Position: Wing

Height: 6'2" **Weight:** 13st 7lbs

Occupation: Bank officer with Royal Bank of Scotland (Galashiels)

Born: Hawick, 14.5.68

Family: Laura (wife)

Family links with rugby: Peter (brother) plays for Hawick and Scotland U-18s

International debut: Scotland 38, Fiji 17, 1989

Five Nations' debut: Ireland 10, Scotland 13, 1990

Best moment in rugby: Scoring winning try in 1990 Grand Slam decider against England

Worst moment in rugby: Getting dropped by Hawick in 1986/87 as an 18-year-old

Most respected opponents: Keith Crossan (Instonians & Ireland), Patrice Lagisquet (Bayonne & France)

Biggest influence on career: Hawick RFC – a way of life

Other sporting achievements: Hawick High School athletics champion (three times)

Best memory last season: Winning Gala Sevens with Hawick

Suggestions to improve rugby:

	apps	pts
Scotland A (**1991**)		
Last Season	1 cap	0
Career	1 cap	0
Scotland (**1989**)		
Last Season	11 caps	16
Career	24 caps	56

Caps (24): **1989** Fj, R **1990** I, F, W, E, NZ(1,2), Arg **1991** F, W, E, I, R wc-J, Z, I, WS, E, NZ **1992** E, I, F, W

Points (56 – 14t): **1989** Fj(2t), R(3t) **1990** E(1t), NZ(2:1t), Arg(2t) **1991** I(1t) wc-J(1t), Z(1t), WS(1t) **1992** I(1t)

On-field – Pleased they increased value of a try but feel they should still reduce value of penalty goal. No real complaints with new rules as long as they give them a chance and do not just get rid of them at the end of the season when we are just becoming familiar with them. *Off-field* – Do not try to bring about too much change too quickly. The SRU are doing very well, but they must ensure that everyone is treated equally when it comes to peripheral benefits. Not much money in Scottish game

Notable landmarks in rugby career: Scored six tries in first six internationals (two on debut against Fiji, three against Romania and one against England in Grand Slam decider). Toured with Scotland to Japan (1989), New Zealand (1990), North America (1991) and Australia (1992). Made debut for Hawick while 17-year-old student. Earned five caps for Scottish Schools at centre in 1985/86, followed by two for Scotland U-21s. Began 1990/91 season with two tries in 49–3 defeat of Argentina, taking try-tally to nine in as many games. Could not sustain that prolific pace through last season's 11 games but did not do badly. Ever present (including playing in 16–16 draw with Barbarians at Murrayfield), he managed four tries: three in the World Cup tournament and one against Ireland in Championship for second consecutive season. Also turned out for Scotland A in 36–16 win over Spain (Murrayfield, 28 Dec 1991)

Touchlines: Social golf
Player to watch: Peter Stanger (Hawick)
Player of the year: Dewi Morris (England)

Staples, J. E.   Ireland

Full Name: James (**Jim**) Edward Staples
1991/92 International category: Ireland Full
Club: London Irish
Positions: Fullback, wing
Height: 6′2″ **Weight:** 13st 7lbs
Occupation: Commercial property agent with Richard Ellis
Born: London, 20.10.65
Family: Single
Family links with rugby: Younger brother (David) plays for Westcombe Park
Former clubs: St Mary's, Bromley, Sidcup
International debut: Wales 21, Ireland 21, 1991
Five Nations' debut: As above

Best moment in rugby: Making Ireland debut in Cardiff last season
Worst moments in rugby: Michael Lynagh's last-gasp try for Australia in

our World Cup quarter-final. Missing out on promotion to English First Division with London Irish in 1988/89 after losing 22–21 to last-minute dropped goal by Blackheath, having led 21–0 at half-time

Most embarrassing moment: Missing flight home from Spain on first county senior trip

Most respected opponent: Gavin Hastings (Watsonians & Scotland) – strong, fast and always a threat

Biggest influences on career: John O'Driscoll (Connacht: got me involved in the provincial scene), Roy White (schoolteacher: took me along to Sidcup where he was captain)

	apps	pts
Ireland U-25 (**1990**)		
Last Season	0 caps	0
Career	2 caps	0
Ireland B (**1989**)		
Last Season	0 caps	0
Career	1 cap	0
Ireland (**1991**)		
Last Season	8 caps	12
1992	Tour to New Zealand	
Career	11 caps	16

Caps (11): 1991 W, E, S, Na(1,2) wc-Z, J, S, A 1992 W, E

Points (16 – 3t,2c): 1991 W(1t), Na(2:1t,2c) wc-J(1t)

Serious injuries: Prolapsed disc in back, broken nose

Other sporting achievements: Played in same forward line as Arsenal and England striker Ian Wright for Greenwich Borough

Best memory last season: World Cup campaign

Suggestions to improve rugby: *On-field* – By increasing try value I fear the ball just won't come out and there will be a lot more penalties conceded. No kicks to be allowed into touch on full, even those taken inside own 22. *Off-field* – Act to compensate players from losing out in terms of career development

Notable landmarks in rugby career: Took over from former Ireland fullback Hugo MacNeill at No.15 in London Irish team. Represented Connacht against 1989 All Blacks and Irish Wolfhounds in 1988/89 Hong Kong Sevens. Played twice for Ireland U-25s before reaching B grade in 1989/90 with appearance in 22–22 draw with Scotland. Selected for senior bench against France in 1991 Five Nations' opener before playing in next three games, scoring try in 21–21 draw with Wales. Toured with Ireland to Namibia (1991) and New Zealand (1992) and in between established himself as first-choice fullback

Touchlines: Soccer, most other sports

Player to watch: Ian Hunter (Northampton & England B)

Player of the year: Andy Nicol (Scotland)

Stark, D. A.   Scotland

Full Name: Derek Alexander Stark
1991/92 International category:
Scotland B
Club: Boroughmuir
Position: Wing
Height: 6'2" **Weight:** 14st
Occupation: Chef in Foxbar Hotel,
Kilmarnock
Born: Johnstone, 13.4.66
Family: Single
Former club: Kilmarnock, Ayr
International debut (B): France
12, Scotland 18, 1988
Best moment in rugby: Going to
Hong Kong Sevens with Barbarians
Worst moment in rugby: Not
playing in above tournament due to
injury
Most embarrassing moment:
Having shorts ripped off playing for
Kilmarnock with nothing
underneath to spare my blushes. Ran
straight off pitch
Most respected opponent: Matt
Duncan (West of Scotland &
Scotland)

	apps	pts
Scotland U-21 (**1987**)		
Career	1 cap	8
Scotland B (**1988**)		
Last Season	2 caps	4
Career	5 caps	
Scotland 1992	Tour to Australia	

Biggest influence on career: Matt
Duncan – a great help in showing me
the ropes
Serious injuries: Broken collarbone, fingers, ribs; ripped ear; displaced
vertebrae in back
Other sporting achievements: Athletics – Scottish international sprinter
(100m in 10.6sec, 200m in 21.5sec)
Best memory last season: Returning to form and confidence level of past
Suggestions to improve rugby: *On-field* – Reduce points-value of kicks. Too
often an average side with a good kicker win games. *Off-field* – Reimbursement
for loss of earnings
Notable landmarks in rugby career: Aged 18 before played rugby yet
represented Scotland U-21s in 1987, scoring two tries in 19–39 loss to Wales
U-21s at Wrexham. Played football whilst training for hotel business in
London, taking two years away from rugby. Continued athletics with good
friend Brian Whittle (British Olympic runner). Made Scotland B debut in

18–12 defeat of France (Chalon-sur-Saône) and added to B tally with appearances against France B (won 14–12, Melrose 18 Feb 1989), Italy B (won 26–3, L'Aquila 4 Dec 1988), Ireland B, last season (lost 19–29, scored try, Murrayfield 28 Dec 1991) and France B (lost 18–27, Albi 3 Feb 1992). Toured with Scotland to Zimbabwe (1988) and Australia (1992)
Touchlines: Golf (handicap 10)
Player of the year: Andy Nicol (Scotland)

Stephens, C. J. Wales

Full Name: Colin John Stephens
1991/92 International category: Wales Full
Club: Llanelli
Position: Outside-half
Height: 5′7″ **Weight:** 12st
Born: Morriston, 29.11.69
Occupation: Area supervisor for Cleanshine Ltd (Llanelli)
Family: Single
International debut: Ireland 15, Wales 16, 1992
Five Nations' debut: As above
Best moment in rugby: Being picked for Wales in 1992 Five Nations' Championship
Worst moment in rugby: Being dropped three-quarters of way through above Championship
Most respected opponent: Paul Turner (Newport & Wales)
Biggest influences on career: Llanelli club coaches over last four years
Serious injuries: Hamstring tears
Other sporting achievements: Cricket for Wales (six games in Minor Counties) and Llanelli. Opening bowler. Had trials with Worcestershire 2nd XI against Gloucestershire and took four wickets
Best memory last season: Landing dropped goal which beat Ireland in Championship

	apps	pts
Wales U-21 (1988)		
Career	1 cap	14
Wales B (1989)		
Last Season	0 caps	0
Career	1 cap	4
Wales (1992)		
Last Season	3 caps	3
Career	3 caps	3

Caps (3): 1992 I, F, E
Points: (3 – 1dg): 1992 I(1dg)

Suggestions to improve rugby: *On-field* – Make game more exciting. Place greater emphasis on running with the ball. *Off-field* – Make sure players do not lose out for time away from work playing rugby. At present rewards are considerably lower than time put in

Notable landmarks in rugby career: Played two seasons for Welsh Schools (1986–87), touring New Zealand, and went on to represent Welsh Univs and Colleges. Scored 14 points on U-21 debut at Murrayfield in 20–13 defeat of Scots U-21s (1988). Toured Canada with Wales B (1989), playing against Nova Scotia, Saskatchewan, British Columbia and Canada. Scored try in latter (Edmonton, 3 Jun 1989) as Wales B won 31–29. Began season at Murrayfield representing centenary-celebrating Barbarians in last two minutes of 16–16 draw with Scotland. Broke into senior squad in 1992 Five Nations' Championship, playing against Ireland, France and England

Players to watch: Neil Boobyer, Wayne Proctor (both Llanelli)

Player of the year: Jonathan Webb (England)

Teague, M.   England

Full Name: Michael Clive Teague
1991/92 International category:
England Full
Club: Moseley
Positions: No.8, flanker
Height: 6'3" **Weight:** 16st 4lbs
Occupation: Self-employed
bricklayer
Family: Lorraine (wife)
Family links with rugby:
Grandfather played for
Gloucestershire
Former clubs: Cardiff, Gloucester
Old Blues, Gloucester
International debut: France 32,
England 18, 1984
Five Nations' debut: As above
Best moment in rugby: 1989 Lions
winning decisive third Test against
Australia

Worst moment in rugby: England losing 1990 Grand Slam decider to Scotland

Most embarrassing moment: Giving Wales three seconds of hell in 1989 and then being carried off

Most respected opponent: Murray Mexted (Wellington & New Zealand)

Serious injuries: Torn shoulder, knee ligaments
Best memory last season: Winning second Grand Slam with England
Suggestions to improve rugby: *On-field* – Cannot improve the game that much, it's improving itself. Pleased about five points for a try; perhaps less for a penalty goal, too
Notable landmarks in rugby career: Represented England at U-23 and B levels. Spent four years in international wilderness (1985–89) after moving from Gloucester to Cardiff. Returned in 1989 and at the end of that season gained selection for Lions in Australia, where voted 'Player of the Series'. Lost England place to John Hall for Argentina game (3 Nov 1990) but regained it throughout 1991 Five Nations' Grand Slam campaign, and contributed vital tries against Wales and Ireland. Also represented England B in 12–12 draw with Emerging Australians. Toured with England to South Africa (1984), New Zealand (1985) and Fiji/Australia (1991). Played in 1991 World Cup final at No.8 having begun tournament at blindside wing-forward
Touchlines: Motocross
Players to watch: David Sims, Neil Matthews (Gloucester)

	apps	pts
England B (**1981**)		
Last Season	0 caps	0
England (**1985**)		
Last Season	7 caps	0
Career	22 caps	12
Lions 1989	2 Tests	0

Caps (22): **1985** F(R), NZ(1,2) **1989** S, I, F, W, R. Lions-(2,3) **1990** F, W, S **1991** W, S(a), I, F(a), Fj, A(a) wc-NZ, It, F(b), S(b), A(b)

Points (12 – 3t): **1985** NZ(1:1t) **1991** W(1t), I(1t)

Scotland outside-half Craig Chalmers weighs up his options as opposite number Neil Jenkins gets to grips, during Wales' 15–12 Championship win at the Arms Park

Townsend, G. P. J.   Scotland

Full Name: Gregor Peter John Townsend
1991/92 International category: Scotland B
Club: Gala
Position: Outside-half
Height: 5'11" **Weight:** 13st 7lbs
Occupation: History/politics student (first year)
Born: Edinburgh, 26.4.73
Family: Single
Family links with rugby: Father (Peter) played twice for South of Scotland
International debut (B): Scotland 19, Ireland 29, 1991
Best moment in rugby: Gaining selection to Scotland's Australia tour (1992)
Worst moment in rugby: Having a nightmare against Ireland on debut – being intercepted and dropping ball for try
Most embarrassing moment: Dropping first four passes in Gala-Melrose League game (7 Dec 1991)
Most respected opponent: Craig Chalmers (Melrose & Scotland)

	apps	pts
Scotland U-21 (**1992**)		
Last Season	1 cap	0
Career	1 cap	0
Scotland B (**1991**)		
Last Season	2 caps	14
Career	2 caps	14
Scotland 1992	Tour to Australia	

Biggest influence on career: My father
Serious injuries: Sprung ribs at 1992 Hong Kong Sevens
Best memory last season: Being picked for Scotland B
Suggestions to improve rugby: *On-field* – Greater integration between top and bottom level of game (massive difference between club and international level in terms of facilities, etc). *Off-field* – Pump more money into Scottish game
Notable landmarks in rugby career: Painted as young star of Scottish rugby but ignored such talk: 'I did not play that well for my club. It's a question of concentration with me.' Represented Irish Wolfhounds at 1992 Hong Kong Sevens, having quickly progressed through Gala U-14, U-15 and U-16 ranks and, last season, played for Scotland U-21 in 19–28 loss to Wales U-21 (Stirling, 18 Apr 1992), and for Scotland B, against Ireland B (landed two

225

penalty goals in 19–29 loss, Murrayfield 28 Dec 1991), and France B (kicked conversion and two penalty goals in 18–27 loss, Albi 3 Feb 1992)
Touchlines: Golf (handicap 10)
Player to watch: Andy Ness (Glasgow High/Kelvinside)
Player of the year: Gavin Hastings (Watsonians & Scotland)

Tukalo, I. Scotland

Full Name: Iwan Tukalo
1991/92 International category:
Scotland Full
Club: Selkirk
Position: Left wing
Height: 5'9" **Weight:** 13st 4lbs
Occupation: Senior engineer with
British Gas, Scotland
Born: Edinburgh, 5.3.61
Family: Wife (Susan)
Former club: Royal High
International debut: Scotland 15,
Ireland 18, 1985
Five Nations' debut: As above
Best moment in rugby: Beating
England to win 1990 Grand Slam
Worst moment in rugby: First Test
against New Zealand in 1990 – I had
a shocker

Most embarrassing moment:
Running to listen to captain's instructions in Scotland's match v. Fiji (1989) and arriving too late
Most respected opponent: David Campese (Mediolanum Milan & Australia) – electrifying pace over five yards and excellent side-step
Biggest influence on career: John Rutherford (Selkirk & Scotland)
Serious injuries: Torn ligaments, ankle, elbow and knee. Torn hamstring
Best memory last season: Atmosphere at Murrayfield over three-week period covering World Cup
Suggestions to improve rugby: *On-field* – To make it more competitive, reduce size of Scottish first division to eight clubs and play matches on home and away basis. Also, Scotland desperately needs a national cup competition to bring an element of competitiveness lacking in club rugby at present. *Off-field* – Let events take their natural course. Sad for game when people just look to it for making a bit of extra money
Notable landmarks in rugby career: Succeeded Arthur Smith (33 caps,

1955–62) as Scotland's most-capped wing when made 34th appearance in 10–6 win over France at Murrayfield (7 Mar 1992). Had privilege of meeting Arthur's widow last season. Four tries in the 1991 World Cup (three v. Zimbabwe, 9 Oct 1991) lifted him into second place on Scotland's all-time try-scoring list with 15 – nine behind Ian Smith (24t in 32 games, 1924–33). Played three times at scrum-half for Scottish Schools in 1978–79, captaining side against France; toured with Scotland to Romania (1984), North America (1985), Spain and France (1986), Japan (1989), New Zealand (1990) and Australia (1992). Scored three tries for Scotland A XV in 39–7 defeat of Spain (Seville, 22 Dec 1990)

Touchlines: Squash, social golf
Player to watch: Gregor Townsend (Gala)
Player of the year: Jonathan Webb (England)

	apps	pts
Scotland B (**1982**)		
Last Season	0 caps	0
Career	5 caps	
Scotland A (**1990**)		
Last Season	0 caps	0
Career	1 cap	12
Scotland (**1985**)		
Last Season	11 caps	20
1992	Tour to Australia	
Career	35 caps	60

Caps (35): **1985** I **1987** I, F(a), W, E wc-F(b), Z, R, NZ **1988** F, W, E, A **1989** W, E, I, F, Fj **1990** I, F, W, E, NZ(1) **1991** I, R wc-J, Z, I(b), WS, E(b), NZ **1992** E, I, F, W

Points (60 – 15t): **1987** I(1t) wc-Z(2t), R(1t) **1988** F(1t) **1989** I(3t), Fj(1t) **1990** F(1t) **1991** R(1t) wc-J(1t), Z(3t)

... STOP PRESS ... STOP PRESS ... STOP PRESS ...

ENGLAND B TO NEW ZEALAND
June–July 1992 – Record: P8, W6, D0, L2, F273, A127.

Results: (1) North Otago, won 68-4; (2) Southlands, won 31-16; (3) New Zealand Universities, won 32-15; (4) Wairapa Bush, won 40-6; (5) Wanganui, won 35-9; (6) first Test: New Zealand, lost 18-24; (7) North Auckland, won 31-27; (8) second Test: New Zealand, lost 18-26.

1st Test: I Hunter (Northampton); S Hackney (Leicester), P de Glanville (Bath), D Hopley (Wasps), T Underwood (Leicester); S Barnes (Bath, capt), A Kardooni (Leicester); V Ubogu (Bath), G Dawe (Bath), G Baldwin (Northampton), N Back (Leicester), B Clarke (Bath). **Repl:** A Mullins (Harlequins) for Ubogu, 4 mins.

Scorers – Tries: Hunter 2, Hopley, Underwood. **Conversion:** Hunter.

2nd Test: Hunter; Hackney, de Glanville, Hopley, Underwood; Barnes (capt), Kardooni; M Hynes (Orrell), Dawe, Mullins, M Haag (Bath), Bayfield, S Ojomoh (Bath), Back, Clarke. **Repl:** G Thompson (Harlequins) for de Glanville, 52 mins.

Scorers – Tries: Ojomoh, de Glanville. **Conversions:** Barnes 2. **Penalty goals:** Barnes 2.

Turnbull, D. J.   Scotland

Full Name: Derek James Turnbull
1991/92 International category:
Scotland Full
Club: Hawick
Position: Flanker
Height: 6'3" **Weight:** 16st
Occupation: Police Officer in Kelso
Born: Hawick, 2.10.61
Family: Angie (wife)
Family links with rugby: Father
(Jim) is past president of Hawick
Trades RFC
Former clubs: Hawick PSA,
Hawick Trades
International debut: New Zealand
30, Scotland 3, 1987 (World Cup)
Five Nations' debut: Scotland 23,
France 12, 1988
Best moment in rugby: Coming on
as a replacement in the 1990 Grand
Slam decider against England at
Murrayfield
Worst moment in rugby: Missing
1992 Five Nations' Championship
due to broken jaw
Most embarrassing moment:
Leading a Hawick Sevens side out at
Gala Sports on 1 April 1989. The
rest of the side stayed in the dressing
room until I was out onto the pitch
myself – all by myself!
Most respected opponent: Willie
Duggan (Blackrock College &
Ireland) – he knew how to cheat well
Biggest influences on career:
Derrick Grant (Hawick & ex-Scotland coach), my father, and Norman
Suddon
Other sporting achievements: Completed London Marathon in 1982
Best memory last season: Scoring World Cup try against Zimbabwe
Suggestions to improve rugby: *On-field* – New mauling law looks too
negative for my liking. Don't allow anyone to kick the ball outside their own
22. Teams then would have to run and rugby would demand a more mobile

	apps	pts
Scotland B (1982)		
Last Season	0 caps	0
Career	6 caps	
Scotland A (1990)		
Last Season	0 caps	0
Career	1 cap	0
Scotland (1987)		
Last Season	2 caps	4
Career	10 caps	4

Caps (10): **1987** wc-NZ **1988** F, E
1990 E(R) **1991** F, W, E, I, R
wc-Z

Points (4 – 1t): **1991** wc-Z(1t)

approach. More liberal interpretations by referees, like in Southern Hemisphere. *Off-field* – Have got to have means of earning a living. SRU must compensate employers for the time their employees give up to rugby. Not just monetary aspect; you lose your holidays too

Notable landmarks in rugby career: Scotland tours to North America (1985), France and Spain (1986), World Cup (1987), Zimbabwe (1988), Japan (1989) and New Zealand (1990). Made Hawick debut as a 17-year-old against Alnwick (Dec 1978) and nine years later came on as replacement for John Jeffrey for first cap in 1987 World Cup quarter-final against New Zealand. Scored first international try in 51–12 defeat of Zimbabwe (Murrayfield, 9 Oct 1991). Won 1992 Gala Sevens with Hawick

Touchlines: Enjoy golf – especially the 19th hole

Player to watch: Keith Suddon (Hawick)

Player of the year: John Jeffrey (Scotland)

Underwood, T.   England

Full Name: Tony Underwood
1991/92 International category: England B
Clubs: Leicester, Cambridge Univ
Position: Wing
Height: 5'9" **Weight:** 13st 3lbs
Occupation: Student
Born: Ipoh, Malaysia, 17.2.69
Family: Single
Family links with rugby: Brother Rory is England's record try-scorer and most-capped player
International debut: England B 12, Fiji 20, 1989
Best moments in rugby: Playing for Barbarians against 1989 All Blacks, for Irish Wolfhounds in Hong Kong Sevens, and for Cambridge in 1991 Varsity match
Worst moments in rugby: Cambridge's 1990 Varsity match loss (12–21) to Oxford. England's 1990 Tour to Argentina
Most embarrassing moment: Post-try behaviour following my late score in 1991 Varsity match
Most respected opponents: Ian Hunter (Northampton & England B), David Campese (Mediolanum Milan & Australia)

Biggest influence on career: My mother (Anne)

Serious injuries: Broken jaw, torn hamstring and damaged knee cartilage – all in second half of 1989/90 season

Best memory last season: Playing all four England B games

	apps	pts
England B (1989)		
Last Season	4 caps	20
1992	Tour to New Zealand	
Career	7 caps	20
England	1995 Development squad	

Suggestions to improve rugby: *On-field* – Expansion of League programme to home and away. National training guidelines to filtrate down to club rugby. *Off-field* – Take necessary steps to prevent player drain to Rugby League. Greater representation of players' views in Union

Notable landmarks in rugby career: Played for England Schools (18-Group) before graduating to England team for inaugural Student World Cup (1988). Played for Barbarians in 10–21 defeat by 1989 All Blacks at Twickenham and for England in 18–16 win over Barbarians (1990/91). Represented Irish Wolfhounds in 1989 Hong Kong Sevens. Has gone on to represent Combined Students, England B, North of England and, latterly, England in 1990 summer tour of Argentina (v. Tucuman, Cuyo and Cordoba Selections). Represented England B in 1990/91 against Emerging Australians (12–12) and Ireland (lost 10–24), and scored four tries in Barbarians' Easter Tour match at Cardiff. Last season scored five tries in four England B games: three against Ireland B (won 47–15, Richmond 31 Jan 1992) and one apiece against Spain and France B. Not surprisingly, he was selected to tour with England B to New Zealand (1992)

Touchlines: Cricket, squash, golf, tennis, girlfriend Heidi

Player to watch: Adrian Davies (Cardiff & Cambridge Univ)

Player of the year: Will Carling (England)

Wainwright, R. I. Scotland

Full Name: Robert Iain Wainwright
1991/92 International category:
Scotland Full
Club: Edinburgh Academicals
Position: Flanker
Height: 6'5" **Weight:** 15st 4lbs
Occupation: Army doctor
Born: Perth, 22.3.65
Family: Single
Family links with rugby: Father (J. F. Wainwright) a 1956 Cambridge Blue
Former club: Cambridge Univ
International debut: Ireland 10, Scotland 18, 1992
Five Nations' debut: As above
Best moment in rugby: Replacing Neil Edwards against Ireland (1992) to win first cap
Worst moment in rugby: Cambridge Univ v. Durham Univ (Jan 1988)
Most respected opponent: John Jeffrey (Kelso & ex-Scotland)
Other sporting achievements: Boxing Blue at Cambridge Univ
Serious injuries: Broken cheekbone (Jan 1990), ankle (Sept 1990)

	apps	pts
Scotland B (1988)		
Last Season	1 cap	4
Career	3 caps	4
Scotland (1992)		
Last Season	2 caps	0
Career	2 caps	0

Caps (2): 1992 I(R), F
Points: Nil

Notable landmarks in rugby career: Representative career really took off in 1991/92 season when captained Scotland B, broke into senior side and toured New Zealand in summer. Came on as 78th-minute replacement against Ireland in Dublin (15 Feb 1992), and started 10–6 win over France (7 Mar 1992). Having appeared in three consecutive Varsity matches (1986–88), he made his Scotland B debut in 26–3 win over Italy at L'Aquila. Won further B caps against Ireland (lost 0–16, 22 Dec 1990) and, as captain, against France (lost 18–27, Albi 3 Feb 1992). He scored a try in the latter contest. Other career landmarks include Barbarians Easter tour (1988), Hong Kong Sevens (1988, 89), 1989 tour to Japan with Scotland (two games, two tries)
Touchlines: Wildlife, fishing, photography, whisky

Wallace, R. M.   Ireland

Full Name: Richard Michael Wallace
1991/92 International category: Ireland Full
Club: Garryowen
Position: Wing
Height: 5'11" **Weight:** 13st 7lbs
Occupation: Associate partner with K Walshe & Associates
Born: Cork, 16.1.68
Family: Single
Former club: Cork Constitution
International debut: Namibia 15, Ireland 6, 1991
Five Nations' debut: Ireland 15, Wales 16, 1992
Best moment in rugby: Selection for Ireland's 1991 Namibia tour and World Cup squad
Most respected opponent: Tony Underwood (Leicester, Cambridge Univ & England B)
Other sporting achievements: Sailed (Laser class) for Ireland at 1990 European Championships (France)
Notable landmarks in rugby career: Munster U-18s and U-21s (1988). Irish Colleges (1987/88). Scored try in 24–10 defeat of England B at Old Belvedere on second appearance for Ireland B (1

	apps	pts
Ireland B (1990)		
Last Season	1 cap	0
Career	3 caps	4
Ireland (1991)		
Last Season	5 caps	8
Career	5 caps	8

Caps (5): **1991** Na(1R) **1992** W, E, S, F

Points (8 – 2t): **1991** W(1t), S(1t)

Mar 1991). Added third B cap in 29–19 win at Murrayfield (28 Dec 1991). Broke into Ireland senior XV on 1991 tour of Namibia, when replacing Simon Geoghegan in 74th minute of first Test (Windhoek, 20 Jul 1991). Scored tour-best five tries in Namibia. Marked Five Nations' debut with try in Dublin loss to Wales (18 Jan 1992), and retained place throughout Championship (also crossing against Scotland) before touring to New Zealand (1992). Tour ended prematurely when he was punched, playing against Canterbury, sustained a hairline fracture of the jaw, and was flown home
Touchlines: Flying (hold private licence), sailing, reading, music
Player to watch: Simon Geoghegan (London Irish)

Waters, K.   Wales

Full Name: Kenneth Waters
1991/92 International category:
Wales Full
Club: Newbridge
Position: Hooker
Height: 5'10" **Weight:** 15st 12lbs
Occupation: Day Care Centre
Instructor
Born: Cwmbran, 9.10.61
Family: Yvette (wife) and Gregory
(son)
Former club: Cwmbran
International debut: Wales 13,
Western Samoa 16, 1991
Five Nations' debut: None
Best moment in rugby: Making
Wales debut in 1991 World Cup
Worst moment in rugby: Losing
1990/91 Schweppes Challenge Cup
semi-final to Llanelli
Most respected opponent: David
Fox (Llanelli & Wales bench)
Best memory last season:
Selection for World Cup squad
**Notable landmarks in rugby
career:** Within touching distance of
international action during 1990/91
season, as deputy to Kevin Phillips
on Wales replacements' bench

	apps	pts
Wales B (1990/91)	1 rep	
Wales (1991)		
Last Season	1 cap	0
Career	1 cap	0

Caps (1): **1991** wc-WS

Points: Nil

throughout 1991 Five Nations' Championship, and deputy to Andrew
Thomas for Wales B during 34–12 win over Netherlands. However, was given
a run by centenary Barbarians against Swansea, albeit as a replacement.
Reward for loyalty to national cause was invitation to tour Australia (1991),
playing against Western Australia, Australian Capital Territory and New
South Wales, before returning home to make full debut in World Cup defeat
by Western Samoa
Touchlines: Spending time with wife and child

Watt, A. G. J.   Scotland

Full Name: Alan Gordon James Watt

1991/92 International category: Scotland Full

Club: Glasgow High/Kelvinside

Position: Prop/lock

Height: 6′5′ **Weight:** 18st 10lbs

Occupation: Student at Jordanhill College

Born: Glasgow, 10.7.67

Family: Single

Family links with rugby: Father (Gordon) played for Jordanhill FP, grandfather (Jimmy Cairney) played for Hutchesons'

International debut: Scotland 51, Zimbabwe 12, 1991

Five Nations' debut: None

Best moment in rugby: Winning first cap

Worst moment in rugby: Losing to Currie in 1991/92 McEwan's League division one with last kick

Most embarrassing moment: Sprinting into a goalpost in training and knocking myself out

Most respected opponent: Stewart Hamilton (Stirling County)

Best memories last season: Beating Gala at Netherdale in League with last kick of game; Scotland debut

Suggestions to improve rugby: *On-field* – New mauling rule looks to be a nonsense. Use scrummage to restart game. Bring back double-banking in line-out, second rows would be then left alone and the whole set-piece would be a lot tidier

	apps	pts
Scotland U-21 (**1987**)		
Career	2 caps	0
Scotland B (**1991**)		
Last Season	0 caps	0
Career	1 cap	0
Scotland A (**1990**)		
Last Season	0 caps	0
Career	1 cap	0
Scotland (**1991**)		
Last Season	1 cap	0
1992	Tour to Australia	
Career	1 cap	0

Caps (1): **1991** wc-Z

Points: Nil

Notable landmarks in rugby career: Represented Scotland Schools, scoring try against Wales in 1987, and Scotland U-21s (twice v. Wales, 1987–88). Called into Scotland A team as prop for 39–7 defeat of Spain in Seville (1990) despite club position being lock. Also given Scotland B debut, in 10–31 defeat

by France at Hughenden (2 Mar 1991), before touring North America with Scotland (1991) and playing against US Eagles (won 41–12) and Canada (lost 19–24) in non-cap Tests. Also scored two tries in 76–7 win over Alberta and one in 24–12 defeat of Rugby East. Included in Scottish World Cup squad and played against Zimbabwe (9 Oct 1991), as well as being bench reserve on four occasions, including semi-final against England. Toured Australia with Scotland (1992)
Touchlines: Waterskiing
Player to watch: Derek Bain (Melrose)
Player of the year: Gord MacKinnon (Canada)

Webb, J. M.   England

Full Name: Jonathan Mark Webb
1991/92 International category: England Full
Club: Bath
Position: Fullback
Height: 6'2" **Weight:** 13st 8lbs
Occupation: Surgeon
Born: London, 24.8.63
Family: Amanda (wife), Harriet and Sophie (daughters)
Family links with rugby: Uncle (Ken Reid) played for Richmond and Barbarians
Former clubs: Bristol Univ, Northern, Bristol
International debut: England 6, Australia 19, 1987
Five Nations' debut: France 10, England 9, 1988
Best moment in rugby: Scoring first England try in 1991 World Cup win over Italy (won 36–6)
Worst moment in rugby: Wales 12, England 9 (18 Mar 1989)
Most respected opponent: Michael Lynagh (Queensland & Australia)
Biggest influences on career: Bob Reeves (Univ of Bristol) and Jack Rowell (Bath coach)
Serious injuries: Knee cartilage operation (before 1989 season)
Other sporting achievements: Golf (18-handicap)
Best memory last season: Beating France in World Cup quarter-final (and scoring 11 points)
Suggestions to improve rugby: *On-field* – All conversions should be taken

from in front of the posts (perhaps from 35 metres). I don't see why a try in the corner, which so often is a more skilful score, should be effectively penalised by a reduced chance of the extra two points. It is illogical. Greater consistency between Northern and Southern Hemisphere referees is still required. *Off-field* – Clarify financial side of game (relating to amateurism). There are still niggling confusions as to what is allowed to be done off the field

Notable landmarks in rugby career: Educated in Newcastle and played for Northern before medical studies forced move to West Country. Represented England B before making England debut as replacement for concussed Marcus Rose in 1987 World Cup. Returned to Australia on 1988 England tour. Lost England fullback slot to Simon Hodgkinson in May 1989. Moved to Bath at tail-end of 1989/90 season to revitalise career and was recalled to full England squad in 1990/91. Having graduated from doctor (Dr) to surgeon (Mr) status and become Fellow of Royal College of Surgeons (FRCS), he toured with England to Fiji/Australia in 1991 (playing in both Tests) before enjoying a record-breaking 1991/92 season. Quite apart from helping Bath win the League and Cup double, he became England's most-capped fullback (27) and England's leading points scorer (246), in the process establishing a Five Nations' record for the most points in a single campaign (67) and national bests for most points in a match (24 against Italy at Twickenham in World Cup) and a Championship encounter (22 v. Ireland, Twickenham 1 Feb 1992)

Touchlines: Playing oboe, golf

Players to watch: Adedayo Adebayo, Phil de Glanville (Bath & England B)

Player of the year: Willy Ofahengaue (Australia)

	apps	pts
England B (1987)		
Last Season	0 caps	0
England (1987)		
Last Season	11 caps	144
Career	27 caps	246

Caps (27): 1987 wc-A, J, US, W **1988** F, W, S, I(1,2), A(a1, a2), A(b) **1989** S, I, F, W **1991** Fj, A wc-NZ, It, F, S, A **1992** S, I, F, W

Points (246 – 4t,37c,52p): **1987** wc-A(1c), J(7c,2p), US(3c,4p), W(1p) **1988** F(2p), W(1p), S(2p), I(1:1c,1p), I(2:2c,3p), A(a1:1c,2p), A(b:3c,2p) **1989** S(2p) **1991** Fj(2c,2p), A(1c,3p) wc-NZ(3p), It(1t,4c,4p), F(1c,3p), S(2p), A(2p) **1992** S(1c,4p), I(2t,4c,2p), F(1t,3c,3p), W(3c,2p)

Webster, R. E.   Wales

Full Name: Richard Edward
Webster
1991/92 International category:
Wales Full
Club: Swansea
Position: Flanker
Height: 6′2″ **Weight:** 15st 8lbs
Occupation: Sales representative
with The Brickyard (Swansea)
Born: Morriston, 9.7.67
Family: Kelly (daughter)
Former club: Bonymaen
International debut: Australia 21,
Wales 22, 1987 (World Cup)
Five Nations' debut: Ireland 15,
Wales 16, 1992
Best moment in rugby: Winning
first Wales cap in World Cup third
place play-off
Worst moment in rugby: Getting
injured
Most respected opponent: Alan
Reynolds (Swansea & Wales)
Biggest influence on career: My
father (Phil) – always been there for
me

	apps	pts
Wales (**1987**)		
Last Season	6 caps	4
Career	8 caps	4

Caps (8): **1987** wc-A **1990** Ba **1991**
wc-Arg, A(b) **1992** I, F, E, S

Points (4 – 1t): **1992** S(1t)

Serious injuries: Six operations on
knee, two broken bones in hand
Best memory last season: Scoring
try against Scotland at Cardiff (21 Mar 1992)
Suggestions to improve rugby: *Off-field* – All committee members to retire
at 35. More sympathetic refereeing in rucks/mauls. Less club games in between
league matches. Clubs to be more sympathetic to players and players' needs.
WRU going in right direction
Notable landmarks in rugby career: Won six caps for Welsh Youth
(1984–86) whilst playing for Bonymaen before spending the summer of 1987
in Australia, primarily representing Canberra but also Wales against the
Aussies in the World Cup third/fourth place play-off (Rotorua, 18 Jun 1987),
having been called up as an emergency replacement. Persistent knee problems
kept him out of the international limelight until 1990 when he turned out
against the centenary Barbarians; but another injury, this time a broken hand,
meant that he missed the 1991 Five Nations' Championship. At last fit, he

toured Australia (1991), though he was not fielded in the Test, and rose to prominence first in the World Cup and then the 1992 Five Nations' Championship, during which he scored his first Test try, in the 15–12 defeat of Scotland

Touchlines: Horse riding, weightlifting, DIY
Player to watch: Simon Davies (Swansea)
Player of the year: Hugh Williams-Jones (Wales)

Weir, G. W.   Scotland

Full Name: George Wilson (Doddie) Weir
1991/92 International category: Scotland Full
Club: Melrose
Positions: No.8, lock
Height: 6'7" **Weight:** 16st
Occupation: Student at East of Scotland Agricultural College
Born: Edinburgh, 4.7.70
Family: Single
Family links with rugby: Father (John) played for Gala. Brother (Thomas) plays for Scottish Schools. Brother (Christopher) plays for Melrose U-18
International debut: Scotland 49, Argentina 3, 1990
Five Nations' debut: Scotland 7, England 25, 1992
Best moment in rugby: Getting capped against Argentina
Most embarrassing moment: Trying to kick clear and then dive on a loose ball, and missing it both times, in 1991 Melrose Sevens first round loss to Hawick
Most respected opponents: John Jeffrey (Kelso & ex-Scotland), David Sole (Edinburgh Acads & ex-Scotland)
Biggest influence on career: Jim Telfer (Melrose coach) – told me what to do, when and how
Other sporting achievements: Stow sprint champion. Completing Thirlestone cross-country (horses)
Best memory last season: Playing in all World Cup and Five Nations' games
Suggestions to improve rugby: *On-field* – Better education of referees to allow game to flow better. Abolish conversions and instead increase worth of

tries. *Off-field* – Allow players to benefit from rugby-related activities. Make beer cheaper so we can have a better time after rugby
Notable landmarks in rugby career: Toured New Zealand with Scottish Schools (1988) and Scotland (1990). Represented South of Scotland in Inter-District Championship, Scotland U-19, Scotland U-21s (v. Wales, 1990 and 1991) and Scotland B, becoming the youngest forward to represent them (at 19) in 22–22 draw with Ireland B (Murrayfield, 9 Dec 1989). Has also played in both Scotland A games against Spain (1990 and 1991). Made full debut against touring Pumas (10 Nov 1990). Toured North America with Scotland (1991), playing in all six matches (including two non-cap Tests against US Eagles and Canada). Helped Melrose win McEwan's Scottish Club Championship for second time in three seasons, and retain Border League for third consecutive season, before touring Australia (1992) with the national side
Touchlines: Horse riding (one-day eventing), clay pigeon shooting, training six days per week
Player to watch: Carl Hogg (Melrose)
Player of the year: Derek White (Scotland)

	apps	pts
Scotland U-21 (**1990**)		
Last Season	0 caps	0
Career	2 caps	0
Scotland A (**1990**)		
Last Season	1 cap	4
Career	2 caps	4
Scotland (**1990**)		
Last Season	11 caps	4
1992	Tour to Australia	
Career	12 caps	4

Caps (12): **1990** Arg **1991** R wc-J, Z, I, WS, E, NZ **1992** E, I, F, W

Points (4 – 1t): **1991** wc-Z(1t)

Michael Lynagh, the scourge of Dublin, stoops to conquer against Ireland, despite Phil Matthews' valiant efforts. The Aussie No. 10 scored the last-minute try which broke the Ireland captain's heart and sent the Wallabies into the semi-finals

239

Westwood, J.   Wales

Full Name: Jonathan Westwood
1991/92 International category:
Wales U-21
Club: Newport
Positions: Fullback, wing
Height: 5'11" **Weight:** 12st 4lbs
Occupation: Sales representative
with Welsh Brewers
Born: Pontypool 14.7.71
Family: Single
Family links with rugby: Father
(Keith) and uncle (Ray Knott) both
played for Ebbw Vale and
Newbridge
Former clubs: Abercarn,
Newbridge
International debut (U-21): Wales
23, Scotland 15, 1991

Best moment in rugby: Gaining
Youth and U-21 caps for Wales
Worst moment in rugby: Getting
injured and missing start to Newport
career

	apps	pts
Wales U-21 (**1991**)		
Last Season	1 cap	9
Career	2 caps	9

Most embarrassing moment:
Running into a tree during squad
session in Cardiff
Most respected opponent: Sebastien Viars (Brive & France)
Serious injuries: Broken bone in foot
Best memory last season: Scoring both tries to beat Cardiff in Schweppes
Challenge Cup
Suggestions to improve rugby: *On-field* – Less whistle-happy referees. Less
points for a penalty goal. *Off-field* – Payment for loss of wages through rugby
commitments. Look after players better
Notable landmarks in rugby career: Represented South Monmouthshire
Youth, Wales Youth, Welsh Colleges, Wales U-20, Crawshays, Gwent County
and Estiddfoed XV. Contributed nine points to Wales U-21s' 28–19 defeat
of Scotland U-21 at Bridgehaugh (Stirling, 18 Apr 1992), having previously
turned out for the side in the corresponding fixture at Llanelli in 1990/91 and
for the Welsh President's XV against the New Zealand Zealand U-21 XV.
Switched from Newbridge to Newport at start of 1991/92 season
Touchlines: Indian food, horse racing, golf, cricket
Players to watch: Jason Strange (Ebbw Vale)/Richard Brown (Newbridge)

Wilkinson, C. R.   Ireland

Full Name: Colin Robert Wilkinson
1991/92 International category:
Ireland B
Club: Malone
Positions: Fullback, outside-half,
centre
Height: 5'11" **Weight:** 13st 7lbs
Occupation: Solicitor with James
Murlend & Co
Born: Belfast 4.4.61
Family: Claire (wife) and Ben (son)
Family links with rugby:
Brother-in-law (John Martin) is the
Ireland physio
International debut (B): Ireland B
27, Argentina 12, 1990
Best moment in rugby: Selection
to Ireland's 1991 World Cup squad
as an over–30 – big thrill
Worst moment in rugby:
Captaining Malone to defeat by
Ballymena in 1989/90 Ulster Senior
Cup Final

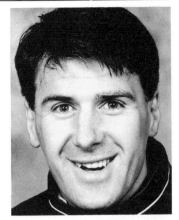

	apps	pts
Ireland B (**1990**)		
Last Season	2 caps	4
Career	5 caps	9

Most respected opponent: Keith
Crossan (Instonians & Ireland)
Biggest influence on career:
Chuck Evans (schoolteacher) – converted me from No.8 to centre
Best memory last season: Anticipation of winning first full cap against
England when Jim Staples was declared an injury doubt and I was put on
standby
Suggestions to improve rugby: *On-field* – More consistency in refereeing.
Off-field – Reimbursement for time lost to rugby
Notable landmarks in rugby career: Played for Ulster at Schools, U-19,
U-20, U-21, U-23 and senior levels. Landed conversion and penalty goal for
Ireland B in 24–10 defeat of England B at Old Belvedere (1 Mar 1991) and
added a try in the corresponding fixture at Richmond last season (31 Jan
1992) when England won 47–15. Figured also in B wins over Argentina
(27–12, Limerick 20 Oct 1990) and, twice, Scotland B (16–0, Ravenhill 22
Dec 1990; 29–19, Murrayfield 28 Dec 1991). Included in Ireland's

preliminary squad for 1991 World Cup but omitted from final 26. Helped Malone win the 1991 Melrose Sevens
Touchlines: Golf (Handicap 18)
Player to watch: Jim Fallon (Bath)
Player of the year: Jean-Luc Sadourny (France)

Williams, S. M. Wales

Full Name: Steven Michael Williams
1991/92 International category: Wales U-21
Club: Neath
Position: No.8, flanker, lock
Height: 6'5' **Weight:** 17st
Occupation: Student
Born: Neath, 3.10.70
Family: Single
Family links with rugby: Mother washes my kit, father shouts advice, brothers laugh when I miss a tackle
Former clubs: Bryncoch, Swansea
International debut: Netherlands 12, Wales B 34, 1990
Best moments in rugby: Scoring try for Wales against Singapore in Hong Kong Sevens and going on to beat Australia
Worst moments in rugby: Being dropped from Welsh Schools squad. 1991 senior Namibian tour – did not go as planned
Most embarrassing moment: Opening my bag in the Swansea changing room before my first game and discovering that my brother had put his toys on top of my kit – good for the image!

	apps	pts
Wales U-21 (**1990**)		
Last Season	2 caps	4
Career	4 caps	4
Wales B (**1990**)		
Last Season	0 caps	0
Career	1 cap	0

Most respected opponent: Dean Oswold (Pontypool)
Serious injuries: Torn ankle ligaments (1989/90), dislocated thumb (1990/91), getting hair cut while on tour with Neath – left mental scars
Other sporting achievements: Welsh junior shot put champion
Best memory last season: Beating Swansea at the Gnoll
Suggestions to improve rugby: *On-field* – Pick me for Wales. Improve

playing surfaces. Change training times from evenings to mornings. Simplify rules: don't know if coming or going at present. *Off-field* – Stop selling beer in rugby clubs! Preserve midweek games: don't allow Leagues to demean them

Notable landmarks in rugby career: Played for Welsh Schools and Welsh Tertiary Colleges. Captained Wales U-21s for two seasons (1990–92), making four appearances: v. Scotland U-21 – won 24–10 (1990), won 23–15 (1991), won 28–19 (1992); v. Ireland U-21 – won 22–15 (1992). Scored try in victory over Ireland U-21 at Newport (16 Oct 1991). Also played for WRU President's XV in 34–13 win over New Zealand U-21 XV (Pontypridd, 8 Nov 1990). Toured Namibia with Wales (1990) and represented Wales at 1990 Hong Kong Sevens. Missed two-and-half months of 1990/91 after operation to repair dislocated thumb. Made Wales B debut in 34–12 defeat of Holland in Leiden (2 Dec 1990) before switching clubs from Swansea to Neath at tail-end of 1990/91 season

Touchlines: Weightwatchers, break dancing
Player to watch: Geraint Davies (Swansea)
Player of the year: Dewi Morris (England)

Williams-Jones, H. Wales

Full Name: Hugh Williams-Jones
1991/92 International category:
Wales Full
Club: South Wales Police
Position: Prop
Height: 6′ **Weight:** 16st 4lbs
Occupation: Police officer,
Bridgend Traffic Department
Born: Bryncethin, 10.1.63
Family: Karyn (wife), Lloyd (son)
and Nia (daughter)
Family links with rugby: Brother
(Richard) in Grade III WRU referee
Former clubs: Bryncethin Youth,
Bridgend, Llanelli, Pontypridd
International debut: Scotland 23,
Wales 7, 1989
Five Nations' debut: As above
Best moment in rugby: Winning
first full cap

Worst moment in rugby: Australia tour 1991 – being thrashed by New South Wales (8–71) and Australia (6–63)
Most embarrassing moment: South Wales Police's Welsh Cup quarter-final

defeat against Llanharan in 1988/89

Most respected opponent: Scotland prop David Sole

Biggest influence on career: Brian Nicholas (my coach at Bryncethin and Bridgend) – sorted my head out

Other sporting achievements: Glamorgan County Cricket U-15 cap

Best memory last season: Helping Wales beat Scotland (15–12) in Cardiff

	apps	pts
Wales B (1989)		
Last Season	0 caps	0
Wales (1989)		
Last Season	2 caps	0
Career	5 caps	0

Caps (5): 1989 S(R) 1990 F(R), I 1991 A(a) 1992 S

Points: Nil

Suggestions to improve rugby: *On-field* – Abolish 90-degree wheel law altogether as it is too negative. *Off-field* – IRB must clarify regulations relating to amateurism and then insist on worldwide adherence. Things are slowly moving in the right direction

Notable landmarks in rugby career: Capped twice by Welsh Youth in 1982 (v. England Colts and France Juniors) whilst with Bryncethin. Toured to Italy (1986) and Canada (1989) with Wales B. Capped in 15–28 loss to France B (La Teste, 12 Nov 1989). Also toured to New Zealand (1988) with Combined Services and Australia (1991) with Wales. Missed 1990 trip to Namibia due to family commitments. Past captain of Glamorgan County and representative of Crawshays and British Police. Spent 17 days in Hong Kong last summer in company of SWP RFC

Touchlines: Cricket for Police divisional side, social golf

Player to watch: Scott Quinnell (Llanelli)

Player of the year: Will Carling (England)

Wilson, G. D.   Scotland

Full Name: Grant Douglas Wilson
1991/92 International category:
Scotland B
Club: Boroughmuir
Position: Loosehead prop
Height: 5'11" **Weight:** 16st 7lbs
Occupation: Police officer
Born: Edinburgh, 10.11.66
Family: Single
Family links with rugby: Named
after great Hawick rugby brothers of
Jake, Oliver and Derrick Grant
Former club: Preston Lodge
International debut (B): Scotland
22, Ireland 22, 1989
Best moment in rugby: Being
selected by Scotland at tighthead for
non-cap Test against Japan in Tokyo
(1989) in front of specialist
tight-heads

Worst moment in rugby: Losing
9–31 to France B (Oyonnax, 21 Jan
1990)

	apps	pts
Scotland B (**1989**)		
Last Season	1 cap	0 pts
Career	3 caps	0 pts

Most embarrassing moment:
Catching ball inside own 22,
somebody else calling 'mark', and taking resulting kick myself
Most respected opponents: Iain Milne (Heriot's FP & Scotland), David Sole
(Edinburgh Acads & ex-Scotland)
Other sporting achievements: 1989 Scottish Youth sprint and marathon
canoeing champion
Best memory last season: Winning third Scotland B cap against Irish
Suggestions to improve rugby: Establish a Scottish knock-out cup
competition and reduce size of First Division from fourteen to ten clubs
Notable landmarks in rugby career: Played for South of Scotland U-16s,
Edinburgh and Scotland U-18s (1983–85), U-21s (1985–89), British Police,
and Edinburgh District side. During busy 1989/90 season represented
Scotland XV against Japan (playing also against Kyushu and Kansai on tour),
Scotland B against Ireland and France, and was on replacements' bench for
Scotland against Fiji. Toured North America with Scotland (1991), appearing
in defeats of British Columbia (29–9) and Ontario (43–3), scoring a try against
the latter. Won third B cap during 1991/92 season in 19–29 loss to Ireland B

(Murrayfield, 28 Dec 1991) and was unused replacement in Albi where France B won 27–18 (3 Feb 1992)

Wilson, R. K.   Ireland

Full Name: Roger Kyle Wilson
1991/92 International category:
Ireland U-21
Club: Instonians
Position: No.8
Height: 6'5' **Weight:** 15st
Occupation: Medicine student at Queen's Univ, Belfast
Born: Belfast, 5.5.72
Family: Single
International debut (U-21): Wales 22, Ireland 15, 1991
Best moment in rugby: Winning Triple Crown with Irish Schools in 1990 (first time Ireland has achieved feat) and beating English at Oxford
Most respected opponent: Willie Anderson (Dungannon & ex-Ireland)
Serious injuries: Cartilage operation on right knee (March 1991)
Best memory last season: Ireland U-21s beating England U-21s in Dublin

	apps	pts
Ireland U-21 (**1991**)		
Last Season	2 caps	0
Career	2 caps	0

Suggestions to improve rugby: *On-field* – Reduce value of dropped goal to two points and ban kicking at goal inside the 22 to try and open up game
Notable landmarks in rugby career: Studied at Royal Belfast Academical Institute and was a part of the most successful ever Irish Schools side in 1990. In 1989/90 season had turned out for Ulster Schools and the province's U-20 side. In 1991/92 graduated to national U-21 side, making debut in loss to Wales U-21 at Newport, before helping beat England U-21 19–10 at Donnybrook (23 Oct 1991)
Touchlines: Golf
Player to watch: Martin Ridge (Blackrock College)
Player of the year: David Campese (Australia)

Winterbottom, P. J.   England

Full Name: Peter James
Winterbottom
1991/92 International category:
England Full
Club: Harlequins
Position: Flanker
Height: 6' **Weight:** 14st 10lbs
Occupation: Inter-dealer
Euro-bond broker with Tullett and
Tokyo
Born: Horsforth, Leeds, 31.5.60
Family: Single
Family links with rugby: Father
played for Headingley and is
secretary and past president
Former clubs: Fleetwood,
Headingley, Exeter, Napier HS OBs
(NZ), Hawkes Bay (NZ), Durban
HS OBs (SA), Merolomas
(Vancouver, Can)
International debut: England 15,
Australia 11, 1982
Five Nations' debut: Scotland 9,
England 9, 1982
Best moment in rugby: Playing in
1991 World Cup Final
Worst moments in rugby: Losing
1991 World Cup Final. Losing to
Bath with last kick of extra-time in
1992 Pilkington Cup Final
Most embarrassing moment:
Being caught from behind by Gareth
Chilcott, playing touch rugby
Most respected opponent: Former
French flanker Jean-Pierre Rives – a
legend
Biggest influence on career: My
father

	apps	pts
England B (**1981**)		
Last Season	0 caps	0
England (**1982**)		
Last Season	11 caps	0
Career	52 caps	8
Lions 1983	4 Tests	0

Caps (52): **1982** A, S, I, F, W **1983** F,
W, S, I, NZ. Lions-NZ(1,2,3,4)
1984 S, F, W, SA(1,2) **1986** W,
S, I, F **1987** I, F, W wc-A, J,
US, W **1988** F, W, S **1989** R, Fj
1990 I, F, W, S, Arg(a1, a2),
Arg(b) **1991** W, S, I, F, A
wc-NZ, It, F, S, A **1992** S, I, F,
W

Points (8 – 2t): **1987** wc-US(2t)

Serious injuries: My brain
Other sporting achievements: School U-16 tennis champion
Best memory last season: Winning in Paris in World Cup quarter-final
Suggestions to improve rugby: Consult players before introducing rules. I

cannot understand why these new rules have been brought in. I do not think the maul rule will work – it will be too easy for people to find ways round it. Nothing wrong with the law as it stands at the moment. If a side has the ball you know they have to release it

Notable landmarks in rugby career: England's most-capped forward (52 since debut in 1982) and second-most capped player behind Rory Underwood (55). Much travelled player who shot up the representative ranks following impressive displays for Yorkshire, and England against France in 1981 B International. Represented England Colts at No.8, before switching to flanker, where played for Yorkshire. Tours include New Zealand with 1983 Lions, and South Africa (1984), World Cup (1987, scoring two tries against USA), Argentina (1990) and Fiji/Australia (1991) with England. Played club rugby all over world, including for Hawke's Bay in New Zealand. Ever present during back-to-back Grand Slams (1991–92), making 50th appearance in 38–9 win over Ireland at Twickenham (1 Feb 1992). Harlequins captain in 1990/91 and 1991/92 seasons, leading team to successive Pilkington Cup Finals (winning in 1991 against Northampton)

Touchlines: Golf, squash

Player to watch: Mark Russell (Harlequins)

Player of the year: Jonathan Webb (England)

Wyllie, D. S.   Scotland

Full Name: Douglas Stewart Wyllie
1991/92 International category:
Scotland Full
Club: Stewart's-Melville FP
Positions: Outside-half, centre
Height: 6'1" **Weight:** 13st 10lbs
Occupation: Sales representative
with Nike Ltd
Born: Edinburgh, 20.5.63
Family: Jennifer (wife)
International debut: Scotland 12,
Australia 37, 1984
Five Nations' debut: Scotland 21,
Wales 25, 1985
Best moment in rugby: Winning
1982 Middlesex Sevens at
Twickenham with
Stewart's-Melville as an 18-year-old
Worst moment in rugby: Playing

in Scotland XV which lost 1989 'Test' 24–28 to Japan in Tokyo – we took them for granted

Most embarrassing moment: As above

Most respected opponents: Jim Renwick (ex-Hawick & Scotland), John Beattie (ex-Glasgow Acads & Scotland) – the most aggressive player I have ever come up against

Biggest influence on career: Dougie Morgan (Stewart's-Melville FP coach)

Serious injury: Broken bone in foot (1987/88)

Other sporting achievements: Soccer for England U-13 Schoolboys

	apps	pts
Scotland B (**1984**)		
Last Season	0 caps	0
Career	3 caps	
Scotland A (**1990**)		
Last Season	1 cap	4
Career	2 caps	4
Scotland (**1984**)		
Last Season	3 caps	3
Career	13 caps	3

Caps (13): **1984** A **1985** W(R), E **1987** I, F wc-F, Z, R, NZ **1989** R **1991** R wc-J(R), Z

Points (3 – 1dg): **1991** wc-Z(1dg)

Best memory last season: Winning Hawick Sevens with Stew-Mel

Suggestions to improve rugby: *On-field* – Fairly happy with the game before new rules. If the scrum goes down when the ball is at the No.8's feet, let play continue. Finish Scottish League programme before Christmas – New Year diary is too cluttered at present. *Off-field* – Allow game at top level to go semi-pro. Standards would improve immeasurably if players had longer to spend on their skills. Clarify amateur laws and allow players to benefit from rugby-related activities (e.g. speech-making). Look after international players better and, within that category, spread benefits around equally. The English boys get a better deal but the standard of club rugby is better down South. I would join an English club if I felt strongly enough about the matter

Notable landmarks in rugby career: Called into Scotland senior squad aged 19, having twice represented Scotland B in 1982. Selected to Scotland bench in 1983. Spent early years in England, where was educated at Dulwich College in south London. Did not take up rugby until aged 14. Ever present for Scotland in 1987 World Cup, moving from centre to outside-half after John Rutherford broke down in opening match. Captained Scotland on 1991 tour to North America, playing in all six games (including non-cap Tests against US Eagles and Canada). Represented Scotland A against Spain in 1990 and 1991, scoring try on latter occasion. Having turned out for Scotland in 12–18 Bucharest loss to Romania (31 Aug 1991), he played twice in 1991 World Cup, against Japan and Zimbabwe. Dropped goal landed against Zimbabwe (Murrayfield, 9 Oct 1991) brought first senior Scotland points in seven years of trying. Captained Stewart's-Melville FP and Edinburgh last season

Touchlines: Golf (handicap 15 at Baberton GC), Hearts soccer fan

Player to watch: Kenny Milligan (Stewart's-Melville FP)

Player of the year: Ally McCoist (Rangers)! /Dewi Morris (England)

FRANCE

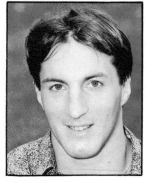

Philippe Sella
(In conversation with Chris Thau)

'When it comes to the '*Tournoi des Cinq Nations*', two wins has long been the minimum requirement of France. We achieved that in 1992 with a much-changed team, so, in that respect, we can go forward in good heart, but I remain concerned – worried about team selection. I was left out of the match against Romania at Le Havre (May 1992), ten years after I began my international career against the same team in Bucharest, and then overlooked for the squad to tour Argentina.

I do not think I am finished yet. There is still a lot of rugby left in me and the prospect of playing against the Springboks this autumn, for example, greatly excites me. But the management's view was that I should take a few months off while France toured Argentina. I was told that I was exhausted and that, together with Jean-Baptiste Lafond and Franck Mesnel, I needed a rest. I strongly disagreed with this

❛I am still confused about what happened that day in Paris against England...I do not want to excuse anyone but it is safe to say that that was not French rugby at its best and we all know it...There has never been any acrimony between us and British rugby❜

view and I said so. They (coach Pierre Berbizier and manager Robert Paparemborde) said that I needed time to recharge my batteries, but I said that I was as fresh as ever. I am the one who knows best, who should say whether I can play or not.

We (France) had just started to get things together as a team, having beaten Ireland 44-12 with an encouraging display at the Parc des Princes in our final game of a Championship which had begun, also with a win, against Wales (12-9) in Cardiff. I was naturally pleased that we beat the Welsh in my first match as captain. The victory provided the team with much-needed confidence for the future after what had been a disappointing World Cup campaign (beat Romania 30-3, beat Fiji 33-9, beat Canada 19-13, lost England 10-19), and I praised the boys for their spirit and attitude.

We managed to withstand spells of ferocious Welsh pressure which we had prepared for after the match at Cardiff back in September (won 22-9) when they threw everything at us. Their performance that night had left us quite worried going into the Championship match, and this made our victory all the more satisfying – especially bearing in mind that we had so many new players in the team. It was a real baptism of fire for the likes of Fabien Galthie, Alain Penaud, Sebastien Viars and Jean-Francois Tordo. Sure, we suffered in the forwards but that was understandable as we had so many new boys and they needed time to develop.

> ❝ While I have heard much criticism of the team, of me as a captain and even of my performance as a player, none of it has ever been made directly to my face ❞

Our next match was against England and I am still confused about what happened that day in Paris; a day which saw two of our players – prop Gregoire Lascube and hooker Vincent Moscato – sent off. The game had not been too bad up to the moment I went off injured after 55 minutes. England were definitely controlling the forward battle but we had been running at them from everywhere. Obviously the mayhem that followed after I had left the field had to do with the extraordinary series of accidents, in which I, my replacement Jean-Luc Sadourny and Christophe Mougeot all went off injured in a nine-minute period. I do not want to excuse anyone but it is safe to say that that was not French rugby at its best and we all know it.

There has never been any acrimony between us and British rugby. And while I have heard much criticism of the team, of me as a captain and even of my performance as a player, none of it has ever been made directly to my face.

Against Scotland in Edinburgh (lost 6-10) we got what we deserved. You deserve to lose when you have so much possession and you squander it, as we did with such lack of respect for the ball the forwards had won. With so much possession we should have won the game easily. There was absolutely no excuse for the defeat.

Thankfully, we showed against Ireland more of what we are capable, and although there is still a lot to be done with the team, our win was exactly what French rugby needed and exactly what the French public demanded. The team is still not perfectly tuned, still not perfectly developed, but we won two Five Nations' matches out of four, and should have won a third. The Championship was far from an unqualified success but I believe we made progress.

And that despite the fact that we play too much rugby in France. The season is too long, with ten months of solid rugby, weekend after weekend. International players have hardly any time to recuperate. There is no time to prepare for matches. Players get injured because of that and the quality of the game suffers.

> ❛ We play too much rugby in France. The season is too long ... international players have hardly any time to recuperate. There is no time to prepare for matches ... and the quality of the game suffers ❜

So what of the future? The management decided to go to Argentina last summer without me, without Jean-Baptiste [Lafond] and without Franck [Mesnel]. Where does that leave us? I was told that I will be expected to play against South Africa, but what then happens with the boys who played in Argentina. If they were successful, and I wished them well, will they be dropped for the Springboks game to let the three of us back in?

Being on tour is very important for improving, both as an individual and as a side. You train better and concentrate on the game. You train, sleep, play, eat and train again. You live rugby. It is a more professional way of approaching the game. Also, from an emotional point of view, you establish stronger bonds with the players, develop that elusive esprit de corps. Besides, as captain it would be important for me to be able to help the younger players develop. I have to admit that I am very disappointed not to be going to Argentina.'

Sella is acutely aware that the unceremonious demise of his team mates Didier Camberabero and Patrice Lagisquet is an explicit and ominous warning that the new management is ruthless in its determination to make France a credible force at the 1995 World Cup. Camberabero was injured when the Five Nations' campaign started in Cardiff and Alain Penaud – who had gambled by turning down a Student cap in the hope he would make the full team – wore the No.10 jersey throughout the Championship.

Sella is also aware that there are many other hungry young wolves waiting in the wings for his downfall: Christophe Deylaud, Michel Marfaing, Herve Couffignal, Pierre Lupuyau, Philippe Bernat-Salles and Fredric Saint-Sardos to name but a few. In truth, none of them can match his overall ability, vision and punch, not to mention experience. However, French rugby is littered with examples of great players who were victims of circumstances, or of events beyond their control. Two of Sella's previous partners – Didier Codorniou and Denis Charvet – found themselves out in the cold in similar circumstances.

Sella had an uneasy relationship with Berbizier while the French coach was captain at Agen. Last year, following Agen's dismal performance in the French Club Championship – for the first time since 1960 the most successful club in the post-war history of French rugby failed to reach the knock-out stages of the Championship – the club was split apart into two factions, and Sella and Berbizier found themselves at opposing ends of the argument. Berbizier and his faction lost the battle and the scrum-half found himself without a club. Soon after, his former ally and partner Daniel Dubroca dropped him from the French team.

Yet, when Berbizier was asked to take over and rescue the French team from the doldrums of the mismanaged World Cup campaign he unhesitatingly named Sella as his captain.

'Pierre and I spoke on the phone and we agreed that what united us was far more important than past disagreements. We both love the game and, in spite of our differences, we respect each other.'

That mutual respect, one suspects, will be tested over the coming months.

FRANCE'S INTERNATIONAL SEASON 1991/92

FRANCE (P12, W8, D0, L4, F241, A180):

(A)	v. Romania (Bucharest, 22.6.91)	won	33-21
(A)	v. United States (Denver, 13.7.91)	won	41-9
(A)	v. United States (Colorado Springs, 20.7.91)	won	10-3*
(A)	v. Wales (Cardiff, 4.9.91)	won	22-9

* Abandoned at half time due to lightning

World Cup

(H)	v. Romania (Beziers, 4.10.91)	won	30-3
(H)	v. Fiji (Grenoble, 8.10.91)	won	33-9
(H)	v. Canada (Agen, 13.10.91)	won	19-13
(H)	v. England (q/f: Paris, 19.10.91)	lost	10-19

Five Nations' Championship

(A)	v. Wales (Cardiff, 1.2.92)	won	12-9
(H)	v. England (Paris, 15.2.92)	lost	13-31
(A)	v. Scotland (Edinburgh, 7.3.92)	lost	6-10
(H)	v. Ireland (Paris, 21.3.92)	lost	12-44

France A (FIRA: P4, W4, D0, L0, F141, A39):

(H)	v. Italy (Tarbes, 16.2.92)	won	21-18
(H)	v. Spain (Bordeaux, 23.2.92)	won	59-3
(A)	v. Soviet Union (Moscow, 8.5.92)	won	36-15
(H)	v. Romania (Le Havre, 28.5.92)	won	25-3

France B (P2, W1, D0, L1, F45, A40):

(H)	v. Scotland B (Albi, 2.2.92)	won	27-18
(H)	v. England B (Paris, 15.2.92)	lost	18-22

France Students (P3, W3, D0, L0, F70, A24):

(A)	v. Wales (Swansea, 31.1.92)	won	26-6
(H)	v. England (Toulouse, 14.2.92)	won	22-9
(A)	v. Scotland (Boroughmuir, 4.3.92)	won	22-9

France Juniors (P2, W2, D0, L0, F46, A27):

(H)	v. Wales Youth (Dax, 14.3.92)	won	23-9
(A)	v. England Colts (Bournemouth, 25.4.92)	won	23-18

France Schools U-18 (P3, W1, D0, L2, F22, A25):

(A)	v. Scotland (Edinburgh, 21.12.91)	lost	6-10
(H)	v. England (Billancourt, 18.4.92)	lost	9-12
(A)	v. Wales (Maesteg, 22.4.92)	won	7-3

French Armed Forces (P1, W0, D1, L0, F21, A21):

(A)	v. England U-21 (Twickenham, 2.5.92)	drew	21-21

Armary, L.   France

Full Name: Louis Armary
Club: Lourdes
Positions: Prop, hooker
Height: 6′ **Weight:** 15st 12lbs
Occupation: Business executive
Born: Lourdes, 24.7.63
International debut: France 55, Romania 12, 1987
Five Nations' debut: Scotland 23, France 12, 1988
Notable landmarks in rugby career: Scored his one and only international try for France in their 48–31 second Test reversal at the hands of Australia at the Ballymore Oval, Brisbane (24 Jun 1990). Represented France in two different positions last season: at hooker against Wales in floodlit international, and at loosehead prop at Murrayfield and in Paris against Ireland after first-choice Gregoire Lascube was suspended for his dismissal against England. Has in all played in 12 cap internationals at prop and 11 at hooker. Member of the 1991 World Cup squad but did not get off the bench. First turned out for Lourdes as a 17-year-old. Also captained France B to 27–18 win over Scotland B in Albi. Former skipper of France A in FIRA Championship

	apps	pts
France (**1987**)		
Last Season	3 caps	0
Career	23 caps	4

Caps (23): **1987** wc-R(a). R(b) **1988** S, I, W, Arg(b1, b2), R **1989** W, S, A(1,2) **1990** W, E, S, I, A(1,2,3), NZ(1) **1991** W(b) **1992** S, I

Points (4 – 1t): **1990** A(2)

Benazzi, A.   France

Full Name: Abdelatif Benazzi
Club: Agen
Positions: No.8, flanker
Height: 6'6" **Weight:** 17st 4lbs
Occupation: Sales representative
Born: Oujda, Morocco, 20.8.68
Former club: Cahors
International debut: Australia 21, France 9, 1990
Five Nations' debut: England 21, France 19, 1991
Notable landmarks in rugby career: Sent off after 14 minutes of full debut in first Test against Australia in Sydney. But modest 14-day ban meant he was able to play in the next two Tests of the series at flanker. Switched to second row for the visit of the All Blacks to Nantes (3 Nov 1990) and it was six internationals before he finally adopted his favoured No.8 berth. Came to France by way of Czechoslovakia where, while on tour with Morocco, he met up with a touring fourth-division French club. On learning he wanted to play in France, they advised him to join second-division Cahors. This he did

	apps	pts
France (**1990**)		
Last Season	5 caps	0
Career	11 caps	0

Caps   (11): **1990** A(1,2,3), NZ(1,2) **1991** E(a), US(1R,2) wc-R, Fj, C

Points: Nil

before switching, a year later, to Agen, for whom he appeared in the 1990 French Club Championship final. Represented Morocco in the African zone of the 1991 World Cup qualifying rounds, against Belgium in Casablanca, and then France in the final stages. Became the first Moroccan to play at Twickenham when making his Five Nations' debut for France in the 1991 Grand Slam decider. Suspended indefinitely last season by the French Federation after being sent off for fighting with Eric Champ in an Agen-Toulon Cup match on 2 May. The ban ruled him out of France's summer tour of Argentina

Benetton, P. France

Full Name: Philippe Benetton
Club: Agen
Positions: Flanker, No.8
Height: 6'3" **Weight:** 15st 2lbs
Occupation: Council worker
Born: Cahors, 17.5.68
Former club: Cahors
International debut: France 27, British Lions 29, 1989
Notable landmarks in rugby career: Marked his senior debut with a try against the 1989 British Lions, masquerading as a Home Unions XV, in the Paris floodlit international staged to mark the bicentenary of the French Revolution. In common with Abdel Benazzi, Michel Courtiols and Denis Charvet, he started out with Cahors before switching to Agen in 1988. At international level Philippe graduated through the U-21 and B set-ups. He missed out on the 1990 and 1991 Five Nations' Championships, unable in the latter to displace Xavier Blond from the blindside berth. However, he

	apps	pts
France (**1989**)		
Last Season	1 cap	0
Career	2 caps	4

Caps (2): **1989** BL **1991** US(2)
Points (4 – 1t): **1989** BL(1t)

re-emerged on France's 1991 tour to North America, winning his second cap in the 10–3 second Test win over the US Eagles. The match, staged in Colorado Springs, was abandoned at half-time due to lightning. Although included in the 26-man World Cup squad, he remained redundant through France's four matches, as he has been since clubmate Pierre Berbizier succeeded Jacques Fouroux as national coach

Blanco, S.   France

Full Name: Serge Blanco
Club: Biarritz Olympique
Position: Fullback
Height: 6' **Weight:** 13st 6lbs
Occupation: Public relations officer
Born: Caracas, Venezuela, 31.8.58
International debut: South Africa
37, France 15, 1980
Five Nations' debut: France 16,
Scotland 9, 1981
**Notable landmarks in rugby
career:** The world's most-capped
player, with 93 international
appearances to his name when he
bowed out of the game following
France's quarter-final elimination by
England in the 1991 World Cup. His
total of 38 tries would also constitute
a global best were it not for a certain
David Campese. Try-spread: 6 –
Wales, Argentina; 5 – Scotland,
Australia; 4 – Ireland, Romania; 3 –
New Zealand, USA; 1 – England,
British Lions. Remarkably durable,
Serge missed precious few games
after making his debut in 15–37 loss
in Pretoria (8 Nov 1980) to South
Africa, the only major nation he
failed to score against. Had made his
France B debut the previous
December, scoring 19 points (2t, 1c,
3p) in 31–18 win over Wales B at
Aberavon. On Five Nations' debut
against Scotland in 1981 he scored a
try with the very first pass he
received. Appointed France captain
for 1990 tour to Australia and
retained honour for 17 games until
his retirement on 19 Oct 1991

	apps	pts
France **(1980)**		
Last Season	8 caps	20
Career	93 caps	233

Caps (93): **1980** SA, R **1981** S, W, E,
A(1,2), R, NZ(1,2) **1982** W, E,
S, I, R, Arg(1,2) **1983** E, S, I,
W **1984** I, W, E, S, NZ(1,2), R
1985 E, S, I, W, Arg(1,2) **1986**
S, I, W, E, R(a), Arg, A, NZ(a),
R(b), NZ(b1, b2) **1987** W, E,
S(a), I wc-S(b), R(a), Fj, A,
NZ. R(b) **1988** E, S, I, W,
Arg(a1, a2). Arg(b1, b2), R
1989 I, W, E, S, NZ(1,2), BL,
A(1) **1990** E, S, I, R, A(1,2,3),
NZ(1,2) **1991** S, I, W(a), E(a),
R(a), US(1,2), W(b) wc-R(b),
Fj, C, E(b)

Points (233 – 38t,6c,21p,2dg): **1981**
S(1t), A(1:1p), R(1t), NZ(2:1p)
1982 W(1t), I(1t,2p),
Arg(1:1t,1p), Arg(2:1t) **1983**
E(2c), S(1c,3p), I(1t,1c,2p),

(continued opposite)

W(3p) **1984** NZ(1:1t) **1985** S(2t), Arg(1:1t), Arg(2:1t) **1986** I(1p),
W(1t), E(1t), A(2t), R(b:1t) **1987** E(1dg) wc-S(1t,1c,2p), A(1t) **1988**
I(1t), Arg(b1:2t), R(1t) **1989** I(1t), W(2t), S(1t), NZ(1:2t), NZ(2:4p),
BL(1t) **1990** A(2:2t), A(3:1p) **1991** S(1dg), W(1t,1c), R(1t), US(1:2t),
US(2:1t), W(1t)

Cabannes, L. France

Full Name: Laurent Cabannes
Club: Racing Club de France
Position: Flanker
Height: 6'2" **Weight:** 14st 2lbs
Occupation: Company
representative
Born: Rheims, 6.2.64
Former club: Pau
International debut: France 12,
New Zealand 30, 1990
Five Nations' debut: France 15,
Scotland 9, 1991
**Notable landmarks in rugby
career:** Would likely be one of the
most prolific scorers in world rugby
if France were to play Ireland in
every international. Or so he might
have you believe. His two outings
against the Emerald Isle have yielded
as many tries and neither effort has
been a gimme – each requiring
significant leg-work in open-field.
An outstanding contributor to the
Gallic cause last season – he was ever
present throughout World Cup and
Five Nations' Championship –
Laurent has travelled far and wide in
rugby pursuit, playing club rugby in
South Africa and in the south-west

	apps	pts
France **(1990)**		
Last Season	10 caps	4
Career	15 caps	8

Caps (15): 1990 NZ(2R) **1991** S, I,
W(a), E(a), US(2), W(b)
wc-R(b), Fj, C, E(b) **1992** W,
E, S, I

Points (8 – 2t): **1991** I(1t) **1992** I(1t)

region of France for Pau. But it was
with Racing that his representative career burgeoned, scoring a try as the Paris
side won the 1990 French Club Championship; their first success in 31 years.
Four years earlier he had started playing France B rugby (against Wales B at
Pontypridd) but it was only in November 1990 that he broke into the senior
ranks as a replacement for Abdel Benazzi in the second Test against New
Zealand in Paris

Cadieu, J.-M.   France

Full Name: Jean-Marie Cadieu
Club: Toulouse
Position: Lock
Height: 6'4" **Weight:** 16st 1lbs
Occupation: PE/sports instructor
Born: Tulle, 16.10.63
Former club: Tulle
International debut: Romania 21, France 33, 1991
Five Nations' debut: Wales 9, France 12, 1992
Notable landmarks in rugby career: A regular in the France B team, having turned out against the second strings of England and Scotland for three straight seasons: won 35–16 and lost 12–14 respectively in 1988/89, drew 15–15 and won 31–9 in 1989/90, won 10–6 and 31–10 in 1990/91. He did not contribute a point in those six games, nor against Scotland in the 1985 and 1986 losses at Murrayfield and Villefranche-sur-Saône. Won three Championship medals with Toulouse (1985, 1986 and 1989). An impressive performance for the French Barbarians against New

	apps	pts
France (**1991**)		
Last Season	8 caps	0
Career	8 caps	0

Caps (8): **1991** R(a), US(1) wc-R(b), Fj, C, E(b) **1992** W, I

Points: Nil

Zealand in 1990 prompted his promotion to the senior team when he was one of six new caps blooded against Romania in Bucharest during the summer of 1991. A permanent fixture during France's disappointing 1991 World Cup campaign, he lost his place after the unconvincing Five Nations' win over Wales in Cardiff, only to be recalled, after two games warming the bench, for the 44–12 defeat of Ireland

Camberabero, D.   France

Full Name: Didier Camberabero
Club: Béziers
Position: Outside-half
Height: 5'8" **Weight:** 11st 5lbs
Occupation: Public relations executive
Born: La Voulte, 9.11.61
Family links with rugby: Father (Guy) was capped 14 times for France between 1961 and 1968; Brother (Gilles) is former captain of La Voulte
Former club: La Voulte
International debut: Romania 13, France 9, 1982
Five Nations' debut: England 15, France 19, 1983
Notable landmarks in rugby career: Record French points scorer in internationals, with total 332 (surpassing Jean-Pierre Romeu's 265) and world record holder for most points in a single match, with 30 against Zimbabwe (three tries, nine conversions) in Auckland during the 1987 World Cup. Made his France debut on the wing in Bucharest against Romania in 1982, having previously represented French Universities and France A in the FIRA Championship. Despite scoring 32 points (28 with the boot) in three World Cup ties last season, he was not fond of the Adidas ball. 'It is a mixture of a bar of soap and a balloon... it flies like a loose rocket... it's a flying object identified only by the International Rugby Board.' World Cup campaign ended prematurely for the son of Guy, with whom he shares the French record for most conversions in an

	apps	pts
France (**1982**)		
Last Season	7 caps	78
Career	33 caps	332

Caps (33): **1982** R, Arg(1,2) **1983** E, W **1987** wc-R(a:R), Z, Fj(R), A, NZ **1988** I **1989** BL, A(1) **1990** W, S, I, R, A(1,2,3), NZ(1,2) **1991** S, I, W(a), E(a), R(a), US(1,2), W(b) wc-R(b), Fj, C

Points (332 – 12t, 46c, 54p, 10dg): **1982** R(1c,1dg) Arg(1:1p,1dg), Arg(2:1c,1p) **1983** E(1p), W(1dg) **1987** wc-R(1t), Z(3t,9c), A(4c,2p), NZ(1c,1p) **1988** I(1t,1p) **1989** BL(1t,3c,3p), A(4p,1dg) **1990** W(1t,3c,1p), I(2c,5p), A(1:3p), A(2:3c,3p), A(3:1t,1c,2p,3dg), NZ(1:1p), NZ(2 :3p,1dg) **1991** S(2p,2dg), I(2c,3p), W(a:2c,2p), E(a:1t,2c,1p), R(a:1t,1c,5p), US(1:3c,1p), US(2:1c), W(b:1t,2c,2p) wc-R(b:1c,4p), Fj(1t,3c,1p), C(1c,1p)

international (nine), when he sustained a hairline rib fracture playing against Canada. First Thierry Lacroix deputised, for the quarter-final against England, and then Alain Penaud stepped up, for the duration of the Five Nations' Championship

Cécillon, M.   France

Full Name: Marc Cécillon
Club: Bourgoin-Jallieu
Positions: No.8, flanker, lock
Height: 6'3" **Weight:** 15st 2lbs
Occupation: Schoolmaster
Born: Bourgoin-Jallieu, 30.7.59
International debut: France 25,
Ireland 6, 1988
Five Nations' debut: As above
Notable landmarks in rugby career: Had to wait more than eight years between first representing France B – in December 1979 against Wales (won 33–12) in Bourg-en-Bresse – and making his full debut against Ireland in Paris in 1988. In between he busied himself with regular tours of duty for France A in the FIRA Championship, before embarking on a cap-less world tour with France in 1986. A Jack of virtually all scrummage trades and master of a good many, Marc's 22 caps include eleven at flanker, eight at No.8 and three at lock, the position he occupied against England and Scotland last season, sandwiched between outings at No.8 (his position for Bourgoin) against Wales and Ireland. Appeared only sporadically before 1991, collecting just four Championship caps in three seasons. All that changed last season

	apps	pts
France (**1988**)		
Last Season	8 caps	12
Career	23 caps	28

Caps (23): **1988** I, W, Arg(a2), Arg(b1, b2), R **1989** R, I, E, NZ(1,2), A(1) **1990** S, I, E(R) **1991** R(a), US(1), W(b) wc-E(b) **1992** W, E, S, I

Points (28 – 7t): **1988** Arg(b1:1t), Arg(b2:1t) **1989** NZ(1:1t), NZ(2:1t) **1991** R(a:1t), US(1:1t) **1992** I(1t)

when he was considered a vital member of the French squad, as well as the oldest. Indeed, so highly was he regarded that a place was made for him in the 26-man World Cup party despite coach Jean Trillo's awareness that a torn thigh muscle would rule him out of the three Pool games

Champ, E.   France

Full Name: Eric Champ
Club: Toulon
Position: Flanker
Height: 6'5" **Weight:** 15st 4lbs
Occupation: Marketing manager
Born: Toulon, 8.6.62
Family: Married, with one child
International debut: Argentina 24, France 16, 1985
Five Nations' debut: France 29, Ireland 9, 1986
Notable landmarks in rugby career: One of only two French forwards (Pascal Ondarts being the other) surviving from the 1987 World Cup final to last year's tournament, in which he was French pack leader. Switched to flank from No.8, the position he occupied during his days with France Schools and Juniors. Made his full debut in June 1985 when France lost 24–16 to Argentina in Buenos Aires. Scored two tries against Ireland which secured the 1987 Grand Slam with 19–13 Dublin win, but then had to wait 21 matches for his next score, in the 41–9 defeat of the United States in Denver (13 July 1991). In recent seasons he has been one of many to be affected by the selectors' indecision over back row combinations. Has not featured in the last two Five Nations' Championships and played only two

	apps	pts
France **(1985)**		
Last Season	6 caps	4
Career	42 caps	12

Caps (42): **1985** Arg(1,2) **1986** I, W, E, R(a), Arg(1,2), A, NZ(a), R(b), NZ(b1, b2) **1987** W, E, S(a), I wc-S(b), R(a), Fj, A, NZ. R(b) **1988** E, S, Arg(a1, a2), Arg(b1), R **1989** W, S, A(1,2) **1990** W, E, NZ(1) **1991** R(a), US(1) wc-R(b), Fj, C, E(b)

Points (12 – 3t): **1987** I(2t) **1991** US(1:1t)

of the four matches in each of the three campaigns prior to 1990. Yet has still collected 42 caps, 27 against non-Home Union opposition. A perennially tough and uncompromising presence at the tail of the line-out: who can forget his tête-à-tête with Mickey Skinner in the 1991 World Cup quarter-final?

Courtiols, M.   France

Full Name: Michel Courtiols
Club: Bègles-Bordeaux
Position: Flanker
Height: 6'3" **Weight:** 15st 2lbs
Occupation: Student
Born: Fumel, 27.4.65
Former club: Cahors
International debut: Romania 21, France 33, 1991
Five Nations' debut: None
Notable landmarks in rugby career: One of a long list to have benefited from Bègles-Bordeaux's French Championship triumph in 1991. Scored Bègles' first try in the 19–10 final defeat of Toulouse. Given his debut, along with three club colleagues, in Bucharest against Romania (22 Jun 1991), he touched down his first international try the following month on his next outing in the first Test against the United States in Denver (won 41–9). Despite winning his third cap in the floodlit contest against Wales at Cardiff and earning selection to France's 26-man World Cup squad

	apps	pts
France (**1991**)		
Last Season	3 caps	4
Career	3 caps	4

Caps (3): 1991 R(a), US(1), W(b)
Points (4 – 1t): 1991 US(1:1t)

(ahead of Racing's Xavier Blond), Courtiols did not figure in the French campaign. Neither was he required for the 1992 Five Nations' Championship. Added instead to his tally of B caps with an appearance in the 27–18 win over Scotland B at Albi, having turned out against England B (won 10–6) and Scotland B (won 31–10), at Bristol and Hughenden respectively, during the 1990/91 season

Devergie, T.   France

Full Name: Thierry Devergie
Club: Nîmes
Position: Lock
Height: 6'6" **Weight:** 17st 4lbs
Occupation: Public relations
executive
Born: Marseille, 27.7.66
International debut: Romania 12,
France 16, 1988
Five Nations' debut: Wales 19,
France 29, 1990
**Notable landmarks in rugby
career:** Only started rugby at the age
of 16 after a childhood spent playing
handball. Quickly acquired
representative honours, graduating
through Schools, Junior, Army and B
levels. Broke into the French team in
1988 but had to wait two years to
make his Five Nations'
Championship bow (against Wales
in Cardiff) due to a broken jaw
sustained in 1989. Happily, he
recovered in time to tour New
Zealand in 1989. Switched to No.8
for the second Test against Australia
that same year before reverting to
lock thereafter, including an
appearance against the British Lions

	apps	pts
France (**1988**)		
Last Season	2 caps	0
Career	15 caps	0

Caps (15): **1988** R **1989** NZ(1,2), BL, A(2) **1990** W, E, S, I, R, A(1,2,3) **1991** US(2), W(b)

Points: Nil

XV under the Parc des Princes lights in the French Revolution Bicentenary
match (4 Oct 1989). After a full international diary in 1990, including the
three-Test series against Australia, Thierry was overlooked for the 1991 Five
Nations' Championship, returning for the North American tour and another
floodlit contest, this time in Cardiff, before playing the role of redundant
member in the French World Cup squad

Gallart, P.   France

Full Name: Philippe Gallart
Club: Béziers
Position: Prop
Height: 6'0½" **Weight:** 18st 1lbs
Occupation: International
computer company representative
Born: Pezenas, 18.12.62
Former club: Pezenas
International debut: France 6,
Romania 12, 1990
Five Nations' debut: Scotland 10,
France 6, 1992
**Notable landmarks in rugby
career:** Keen saxophonist who was
recalled in place of Philippe Gimbert
against Scotland last season, for the
first time since being sent off by
Clive Norling for punching Tim
Gavin in the 48th minute of the
28–19 third Test win against
Australia in Sydney (30 Jun 1990).
For that misdemeanour a
four-month suspension was meted
out, ensuring that he played no part
in the 1991 Five Nations' campaign
when only England stood between
France and a fifth Grand Slam.
Despite touring North America last

	apps	pts
France (**1990**)		
Last Season	2 caps	0
Career	6 caps	0

Caps   (6): **1990** R, A(1,2R,3) **1992** S, I
Points: Nil

summer he was no less redundant, and failed to make the 26-man World
Cup squad. However, the Paris débâcle, which wrote Gimbert and Lascube
out of the international script, allowed Philippe to restore a representative
career which had begun, in Stade Patrice Brocas, Auch, with defeat against
Romania (24 May 1990). Injury forced him from the field prematurely, to be
replaced by Pascal Ondarts, although he returned Down Under to play in two
and a half Tests against the Wallabies

Galthie, F.   France

Full Name: Fabien Galthie
Club: Colomiers
Position: Scrum-half
Height: 5'10½" **Weight:** 12st 4lbs
Occupation: Student
Born: Cahors, 20.3.69
International debut: Romania 21,
France 33, 1991
Five Nations' debut: Wales 9,
France 12, 1992
**Notable landmarks in rugby
career:** Became the first player from
the Colomiers club (Paris suburb) to
be capped when, to the surprise of
many, he succeeded Pierre Berbizier
at No.9. It had been widely
anticipated that Henri Sanz, a former
France B captain and long-standing
understudy to *le patron*, would step
up, but erstwhile coach Daniel
Dubroca thought differently, and
successor Berbizier himself agreed.
Fabien was consequently given his
debut in Bucharest (22 Jun 1991)
and remained on the field for eight of
the next ten internationals, before
Toulon's Aubin Hueber took over
for Ireland's Championship visit to
Paris following mounting criticism of

	apps	pts
France (**1991**)		
Last Season	9 caps	0
Career	9 caps	0

Caps (9): **1991** R(a), US(1) wc-R(b),
Fj, C, E(b) **1992** W, E, S

Points: Nil

the incumbent. In his defence, Fabien was unable to settle into a half-back
understanding because the stand-off's identity kept changing – Didier
Camberabero, Thierry Lacroix and Alain Penaud all being given a shot. Even
captained France for part of the Five Nations' game against England last
season when Philippe Sella was injured

Genet, J.- P.   France

Full Name: Jean-Pierre Genet
Club: Racing Club de France
Position: Hooker
Height: 5'11½" **Weight:** 14st
Born: Chatellerault, 15.10.62
Former clubs: Espinay-sur-Orge,
C. A. S. G.
International debut: Scotland 10,
France 6, 1992
Five Nations' debut: As above
**Notable landmarks in rugby
career:** One of the few to owe a debt
of gratitude to Vincent Moscato.
The latter's dismissal against
England and subsequent ban paved
the way for Genet's upgrading from
France A and B representative
rugby, in which he had participated
in the FIRA Championship and the
27–18 win over Scotland B
respectively, for the Five Nations'
trip to Murrayfield, where Lions'
loosehead David Sole was his
illustrious opponent. Had the
comfort at least of packing down
alongside prop Louis Armary, his
captain and front row cohort at A

	apps	pts
France (**1992**)		
Last Season	2 caps	0
Career	2 caps	0
Caps (2): **1992** S, I		
Points: Nil		

and B level. A member of Racing's French Championship-winning side of
1990, having previously experienced the dejection of defeat in the 1987 final
to Toulon, Jean-Pierre retained his tighthead berth for the Paris match against
Ireland, but failed to get his name on any of France's seven tries

Gimbert, P.   France

Full Name: Philippe Gimbert
Club: Bègles-Bordeaux
Position: Prop
Height: 6′1″ **Weight:** 17st 8lbs
Occupation: Public relations officer
Born: Firminy, 20.3.66
Former club: Biarritz
International debut: Romania 21,
France 33, 1991
Five Nations' debut: Wales 9,
France 12, 1992
**Notable landmarks in rugby
career:** Formed one-third of
Bègles-Bordeaux's fearsome front
row, along with Serge Simon and
Vincent Moscato, which was
selected *en-bloc* for debut
international duty in Bucharest last
season (22 Jun 1991). The trio were
retained for the 41–9 first Test
victory over the US Eagles in Denver
(13 Jul 1991), but he alone was
invited to join France's 26-man
World Cup squad. It was of little
benefit for he was was unable to oust
Pascal Ondarts from the tighthead
berth, sitting idly on the sidelines
until new coach Pierre Berbizier
called him into his front

	apps	pts
France (**1991**)		
Last Season	4 caps	0
Career	4 caps	0

Caps (4): **1991** R(a), US(1) **1992** W, E

Points: Nil

row for the Five Nations' games against Wales and England. The fiery latter
contest proved to be his most recent outing for he was dropped, along with
front row colleagues Moscato and Gregoire Lascube, despite being the only
one to hear the final whistle. Spent the last two Saturdays of the Championship
season watching from the bench as Philippe Gallart turned out against
Scotland and Ireland

Hontas, P. France

Full Name: Pierre Hontas
Club: Biarritz Olympique
Position: Wing
Height: 6′ **Weight:** 12st 12lbs
Occupation: PE student
Born: Biarritz, 19.7.66
Family: Single
International debut: Scotland 21,
France 0, 1990
Five Nations' debut: As above
**Notable landmarks in rugby
career:** A virtual stranger to the
British Isles, having appeared on the
other side of the channel just the
once, when France lost 21–0 to
Grand Slam champions-elect
Scotland (17 Feb 1990) at
Murrayfield on his debut. It was not
a particularly auspicious
performance, neither by France,
who had Alain Carminati sent off for
stamping on John Jeffrey, nor by
Pierre, who failed to prevent
opposite number Iwan Tukalo from
slipping through his defensive cover
to score. A clubmate of Serge Blanco
at Biarritz, he retained his place on
the right wing for the 31–12 Paris

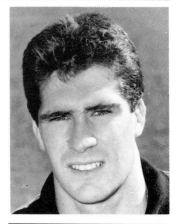

	apps	pts
France **(1990)**		
Last Season	1 cap	0
Career	4 caps	0

Caps (4): **1990** S, I, R **1991** R(a)
Points: Nil

victory over Ireland but again failed to score, as has been the case on his two
outings since, both against Romania. The last of these, as a left wing in the
33–21 win in Bucharest (22 Jun 1991), preceded a spell in the international
wilderness as Jean-Baptiste Lafond, Patrice Lagisquet, Philippe Saint-André
and, most recently, Sebastien Viars carved up the wing duties

Hueber, A.   France

Full Name: Aubin Hueber
Club: Lourdes
Position: Scrum-half
Height: 5'8" **Weight:** 12st
Occupation: Sales representative
Born: Tarbes, 5.4.67
International debut: Australia 19,
France 28, 1990
Five Nations' debut: None
**Notable landmarks in rugby
career:** Succeeded Henri Sanz as
France B scrum-half at Brecon (29
Oct 1988) when Wales B were
defeated 18–12. Again partnered
Thierry Lacroix at half-back when
the second string were undone
14–12 by Scotland B at Melrose (18
Feb 1989), and was captain when
Wales B were beaten 28–15 in La
Teste (12 Nov 1989). A year earlier
he had appeared at Auch in a
non-cap match against Ireland and
moved a step nearer cap-recognition
when selected to represent the Rest
of Europe against the Four Home
Unions (lost 43–18) at Twickenham
in a match organized to raise money
for the Romania appeal (22 Apr

	apps	pts
France (**1990**)		
Last Season	2 caps	0
Career	4 caps	0

Caps (4): **1990** A(3), NZ(1) **1991**
US(2) **1992** I

Points: Nil

1990). Again understudied Sanz when   France toured Australia in 1990 and
was given his long-awaited chance in the third Test, Jacques Fouroux's last
match as coach, which the visitors won 28–19 (30 Jun 1990), despite the
dismissal of Philippe Gallart. Went on to play in the first Test against New
Zealand (3 Nov 1990) but was replaced by Sanz after France lost 3–24. A
third cap followed, however, in the lightning-shortened second Test win over
the United States on France's pre-World Cup tour and, although Fabien
Galthie was pulled in for the World Cup, Aubin was again recalled for the
Championship concluder against Ireland

Lacroix, T. France

Full Name: Thierry Lacroix
Club: Dax
Position: Outside-half
Height: 6'1" **Weight:** 13st 2lbs
Occupation: Physiotherapy student
Born: Nogaro, 2.3.67
International debut: France 15,
Australia 32, 1989
Five Nations' debut: France 36,
Wales 3, 1991
**Notable landmarks in rugby
career:** Burst onto the international
scene with 17 points – five penalty
goals and a conversion – on his first
start in France's 25–19 defeat of
Australia in the second Test in Lille.
Debut had come in the first Test as a
replacement for Didier
Camberabero. In spite of his prolific
start Lacroix had to wait until the
1991 Five Nations' Championship
for his third cap, when replacing
Philippe Sella in the 36–3 win over
Wales (2 Mar 1991). Again replaced
Sella against Wales in the contest to
celebrate the Arms Park's new
floodlights (4 Sep 1991) before
further profiting from another's
misfortune in the World Cup –

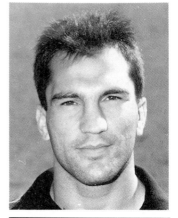

	apps	pts
France **(1989)**		
Last Season	4 caps	12
Career	6 caps	29

Caps (6): **1989** A(1R,2) **1991** W(a:R)
wc-R(b), C(R), E(b)

Points (29 – 1c,9p): **1989** A(2:1c,5p)
1991 wc-C(2p), E(b:2p)

injury to Camberabero allowing him three further caps (one at centre against
Romania) and the opportunity to kick four penalty goals, two each against
Canada and quarter-final opponents England. Did not feature in Pierre
Berbizier's 1992 Five Nations' plans. Representing France B in 1988/89, he
kicked ten points (2c, 2p) in the 18–12 defeat of Wales B in Brecon (29 Oct
1988), and all 12 (4p) in the 14–12 loss to Scotland B at Melrose (18 Feb
1989)

Lafond, J.-B. — France

Full Name: Jean-Baptiste Lafond
Club: Racing Club de France
Positions: Fullback, wing
Height: 5'11" **Weight:** 13st
Occupation: Businessman
Born: Paris, 29.12.61
Family links with rugby:
Grandfather played for France in 1922
International debut: France 15, Australia 15, 1983
Five Nations' debut: Scotland 18, France 17, 1986
Notable landmarks in rugby career: Finally established himself as a regular in the French team last season when appearing in 11 of the 12 matches, even if for the last of those, against Ireland, he was relegated to replacement and was only brought into the fray ten minutes from time. Prior to 1991, injuries and selection restricted the outings of Jean-Baptiste, a most versatile and exciting back – plays wing, centre and fullback with equal dexterity – and it was not until 1986 that he made his Championship debut. In seven years, from his debut (marked with a dropped goal) in the 15–15 draw with Australia at Clermont-Ferrand in 1983, he turned out just 16 times, 1986 representing his only complete Five Nations' campaign. Has always been a prolific scorer – ten tries on the 1986 tour in Australia, having crossed for six in two non-cap Tests

	apps	pts
France (1983)		
Last Season	11 caps	36
Career	31 caps	94

Caps (31): 1983 A(1) **1985** Arg(1,2) **1986** S, I, W, E, R **1987** I(R) **1988** W **1989** I, W, E **1990** W, A(3R), NZ(2) **1991** S, I, W(a), E(a), R(a), US(1), W(b) wc-R(b:R), Fj, C, E(b) **1992** W, E, S, I(R)

Points (94 – 13t,6c,8p,2dg): 1983 A(1dg) **1985** Arg(1:1t) **1986** I(1dg), W(2t) **1988** W(2p) **1989** I(1t,2c,2p), W(3c,2p) **1990** W(1t) **1991** W(a:1t), US(1:1t) wc-R(bR:1t), Fj(3t), C(1t), E(b:1t) **1992** W(1c), S(2p)

against Japan (four in the 50–0 win in Dax and two in Nantes when Japan were crushed 52–0) the previous year. Must surely rate Wales as his favourite opponents, having scored in all six France–Wales Five Nations' contests (36 points) in which he has appeared

Lagisquet, P.   France

Full Name: Patrice Lagisquet
Club: Bayonne
Position: Wing
Height: 6′ **Weight:** 12st 6lbs
Occupation: Insurance director
Born: Arcachon, 4.9.62
International debut: France 15, Australia 15, 1983
Five Nations' debut: France 25, Ireland 12, 1984
Notable landmarks in rugby career: Nicknamed the Bayonne Express (he has clocked 10.6sec for the 100m), Patrice is the most capped French wing: 46 appearances in a career dating back to 1983 when he made his full debut, along with Jean-Baptiste Lafond, in the first Test against the touring Australians at Clermont-Ferrand. Turned out in the same year for France B against Scotland at Dundee. Scored seven tries in France's 106–12 win over Paraguay in 1988, establishing national records for the most tries in a tour match and most points in a tour match (28). Originally a centre before joining Bayonne, his commitment to charity fund-raising saw him quickly accept an invitation to represent the Rest of Europe against the Four Home Unions in the 1990 Romania Appeal match at Twickenham. Among his plethora of international tries was one against Australia in the never-to-be-forgotten 1987 World Cup semi-final, which the French

	apps	pts
France (**1983**)		
Last Season	2 caps	0
Career	46 caps	76

Caps (46): **1983** A(1,2), R **1984** I, W, NZ(1,2) **1986** R(aR), Arg(1,2), A, NZ(a) **1987** wc-S(b), R(a), Fj, A, NZ. R(b) **1988** S, I, W, Arg(a1, a2), Arg(b1, b2), R **1989** I, W, E, S, NZ(1,2), BL, A(1,2) **1990** W, E, S, I, A(1,2,3) **1991** S, I, US(2) wc-R(b)

Points (76 – 19t): **1986** R(1t) **1987** wc-R(a:2t), Fj(1t), A(1t). R(b:2t) **1988** S(1t), I(1t), Arg(b1:1t), R(1t) **1989** I(2t), S(1t), A(2:1t) **1990** W(1t), E(1t), I(1t) **1991** I(1t)

edged 30–24. Unfortunately for France, he failed to trouble the scorers in the ensuing final which New Zealand won 29–9

Lascube, G.   France

Full Name: Gregoire Lascube
Club: Agen
Position: Prop
Height: 6'1" **Weight:** 16st 3lbs
Occupation: Police interrogator
Born: Lourdes, 3.4.62
International debut: France 15, Scotland 9, 1991
Five Nations' debut: As above
Notable landmarks in rugby career: Just when Gregoire looked as though he had made the loosehead slot his own he went and spoiled all the good work put in during eight consecutive international appearances, 12 out of a possible 14 between 19 Jan 1991 and 15 Feb 1992, by stamping on Martin Bayfield and becoming one of two Frenchmen sent off in the 13–31 Paris Five Nations' loss to England. Was promptly suspended for six months, a period he spent constructively, refereeing junior games. A familiar face in the south-west of France where he partakes in a Basque version of the Highland Games, Gregoire was a relatively late arrival on the

	apps	pts
France (**1991**)		
Last Season	8 caps	0
Career	12 caps	0

Caps (12): **1991** S, I, W(a), E(a), US(2), W(b) wc-R(b), Fj, C, E(b) **1992** W, E

Points: Nil

international scene, breaking into the France B side as a 27-year-old in the 28–15 defeat of Wales B at La Teste (12 Nov 1989), having risen to prominence in the 1988 Agen side that won the French Club Championship final. Despite appearing only as replacement hooker in the 1990 Club final, he gave Richard Loe a thoroughly uncomfortable afternoon in the Côte Basque's famous 18–12 win over the All Blacks at Bayonne (30 Oct 1990), from where the only way was up. His full debut came, aged 28, against Scotland in Paris in the 1991 Five Nations' curtain-raiser. From there until his dismissal the only games he missed were pre-World Cup engagements with Romania and the United States (first Test) when Serge Simon was given a run

Marocco, P.   France

Full Name: Philippe Marocco
Club: Montferrand
Position: Hooker
Height: 5'11" **Weight:** 16st 5lbs
Occupation: Sales representative
Born: Cintegabelle, 14.6.60
International debut: Scotland 18,
France 17, 1986
Five Nations' debut: As above
**Notable landmarks in rugby
career:** Hookers are not renowned
for their try-scoring exploits and
Philippe, a former boxer, is no
exception. Notched his only
international try on his second of 21
appearances, a 29–9 win over Ireland
in Paris in the 1986 Five Nations'
Championship. The only French
forward from his debut game in 1986
– when another newcomer, Gavin
Hastings, kicked Scotland to an
18–17 win at Murrayfield – to
remain in the top echelon come the
1991/92 season, even if
three-quarters Serge Blanco,
Jean-Baptiste Lafond and Philippe
Sella all managed it. Prior to his
Edinburgh debut, Philippe turned

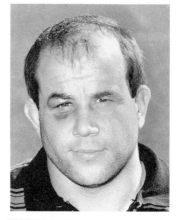

	apps	pts
France **(1990)**		
Last Season	1 cap	0
Career	6 caps	0

Caps (6): **1990** I(R), A(1,2,3), NZ(1)
1991 US(2)

Points: Nil

out at tighthead prop in the non-cap international with Japan at Nantes (26
Oct 1985), which France sneaked 52–0. Also in 1985 he represented France
B at Murrayfield against Scotland B (lost 21–12) and at Sainte-Foy-la-Grande
against Wales B (won 30–13). After a full and active role in the 1991 World
Cup, his international licence was not renewed by new coach Pierre Berbizier

Melville, E.   France

Full Name: Eric Melville
Club: Toulon
Positions: No.8, flanker
Height: 6'5" **Weight:** 16st 4lbs
Occupation: Public relations officer
Born: South Africa, 27.6.61
International debut: France 31,
Ireland 12, 1990
Five Nations' debut: As above
**Notable landmarks in rugby
career:** One of only four foreign
players to represent France since the
War – the others being
Venezuelan-born Serge Blanco,
Moroccan Abdelatif Benazzi and
fellow South African Andries van
Heerden – Eric made his debut as a
replacement for Jean-Marie Lhermet
in the 31–12 win over Ireland in Paris
(3 Mar 1990). Thereafter, he was
selected for the 1990 tour to
Australia and was an ever present in
the three-Test series, which Australia
took 2–1 (France losing 9–21 and
31–48, before winning 'dead' rubber
28–19). Eric retained his spot for
New Zealand's 3–24 winning visit to
Nantes' Stade Beaujoire (3 Nov
1990) but, bar a 40-minute outing in
the second Test against hosts the
United States (20 Jul 1991) –

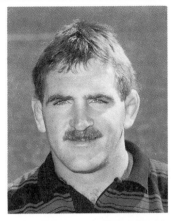

	apps	pts
France (**1986**)		
Last Season	5 caps	0
Career	21 caps	4

Caps (21): **1986** S, I, W, E, R(1),
Arg(1,2), A **1988** Arg(b2) **1989**
I **1990** E(R), NZ(1R) **1991** S, I,
W(a), E(a), US(2) wc-R(b), Fj,
C, E(b)

Points (4 – 1t): **1986** I(1t)

abandoned at half-time due to lightning, with France 10–3 to the good – he
has not played since

Mesnel, F.   France

Full Name: Franck Mesnel
Club: Racing Club de France
Positions: Centre, outside-half
Height: 5'11" **Weight:** 14st 2lbs
Occupation: Architect
Born: Neuilly-sur-Seine, 30.6.61
Former club: St Germain-en-Laye
International debut: France 7,
New Zealand 19, 1986
Five Nations' debut: France 16,
Wales 9, 1987
Notable landmarks in rugby career: Shares with Philippe Sella the French record for a centre partnership of 20 games, having passed the old mark when France lost in Edinburgh during last season's Five Nations' Championship. Ironically, Franck had been dropped for that game, following England's win in Paris, but he was reinstated 24 hours before kick-off because of injury to Sebastien Viars. His appearance at Murrayfield maintained a unique attendance record. Since missing the 21–9 first-Test loss to Australia at Sydney (9 Jun 1990), he has been a permanent fixture in the French line-up. Twenty matches played since, 20 caps for the Mesnel hatstand. Of his 48 career caps, 22 have been won at outside-half, the position he occupied in 1987 when France won the Grand Slam and reached the World Cup final, and 26 at centre. His first cap came against New Zealand when replacing the

	apps	pts
France (**1986**)		
Last Season	12 caps	8
Career	48 caps	41

Caps (48): **1986** NZ(1R,2) **1987** W, E, S(a), I wc-S(b), Z, Fj, A, NZ. R(b) **1988** E, Arg(1,2), Arg(1,2), R **1989** I, W, E, S, NZ(1), A(1,2) **1990** E, S, I, A(2,3), NZ(1,2) **1991** S, I, W(a), E(a), R(a), US(1,2), W(b) wc-R(b), Fj, C, E(b) **1992** W, E, S, I

Points (41 – 8t,3dg): **1987** W(1t), E(1dg), S(a:1dg) **1989** W(1dg) **1990** I(2t), A(3:1t) **1991** W(a:1t), E(a:1t), US(1:1t), US(2:1t)

injured Jean-Patrick Lescarboura two minutes from the end of the All Black's 19–7 triumph in Toulouse (8 Nov 1986). Kept his place for the second Test the following week, in Nantes when France scored a famous 16–3 win, and has barely looked back since

Montlaur, P.   France

Full Name: Pierre Montlaur
Club: Agen
Position: Outside-half
Height: 5'8" **Weight:** 11st 12lbs
Occupation: Contractor
Born: Castelsarrasin, 7.2.63
Former club: Castelsarrasin
International debut: France 13,
England 31, 1992
Five Nations' debut: As above
Notable landmarks in rugby career: The long-time half-back partner of French coach Pierre Berbizier at Agen, he broke into the France side as one of three replacements used by Berbizier the coach in the traumatic 13–31 Five Nations' loss to England at Parc des Princes. Had previously displayed prolific form for France B during the 1990/91 season: 19 points (2c, 4p, 1dg from eight pots at goal) in the comprehensive 31–10 defeat of Scotland B at Hughenden, and six points (2dg) in the 10–6 win over England's second string at Bristol. Spent his formative years

	apps	pts
France (1992)		
Last Season	1 cap	0
Career	1 cap	0
Caps (1): 1992 E(R)		
Points: Nil		

representing France Juniors and the Army before helping Agen to win the 1988 French Club Championship and reach the final two years later. Also represented the French Barbarians against the All Blacks (27 Oct 1990), landing a dropped goal and conversion in a 23–13 losing cause. His big chance came during England's Championship visit to Paris last season when he was called off the bench in the 64th minute to replace the concussed Jean-Luc Sadourny, himself a replacement just nine minutes earlier. But with Alain Penaud keeping hold of the No.10 jersey, it was back to the bench for the visit to Scotland three Saturdays later

Moscato, V.   France

Full Name: Vincent Moscato
Club: Bègles-Bordeaux
Position: Hooker
Height: 5'10" **Weight:** 15st 4lbs
Occupation: Municipal employee
Born: Paris, 28.7.65
International debut: Romania 21,
France 33, 1991
Five Nations' debut: Wales 9,
France 12, 1992
**Notable landmarks in rugby
career:** An amateur boxer, who was
handed a six-month ban for
exercising his 'art' and more besides
when England visited Paris last
season. Irish referee Stephen
Hilditch dismissed him for
head-butting in the later stages of
France's 13–31 Five Nations' defeat
at the Parc des Princes. His response
was to return to legitimate pugilism.
A product of the rise of
Bègles-Bordeaux, whom he helped
to lift the Brennus Shield by winning
the 1991 French Club
Championship final 19–10 over
Toulouse, Vincent was given his
debut along with front row

	apps	pts
France (**1991**)		
Last Season	4 caps	0
Career	4 caps	0

Caps (4): **1991** R(a), US(1) **1992** W,
E

Points: Nil

clubmates Serge Simon and Philippe Gimbert in the 33–21 defeat of Romania
in Bucharest (22 Jun 1991). The unit kept their places for the next outing, a
41–9 first Test win over the United States in Denver, but he and Simon were
then excluded by national coaches Jean Trillo and Daniel Dubroca from the
26-man World Cup squad. New coach Pierre Berbizier restored Vincent's
career by bringing him back for the 1992 Five Nations' but, after maintaining
his 100 per cent winning record in a French jersey against Wales, Vincent
saw red against England and paid the price

Mougeot, C.   France

Full Name: Christophe Mougeot
Club: Bègles-Bordeaux
Position: Lock
Height: 6'5" **Weight:** 16st 7lbs
Occupation: PE teacher
Born: Dijon, 22.11.63
Former club: Is-sur-Tille
International debut: Wales 9,
France 12, 1992
Five Nations' debut: As above
**Notable landmarks in rugby
career:** Brought into the French
team when new coach Pierre
Berbizier began his tenure of office
in the 1992 Five Nations'
Championship. Started games
against Wales and England yet
completed neither. In the first there
were allegations of 'tactical
substitution' as he made way for
Olivier Roumat midway through the
contest, while France was getting
cleaned out in the line-out, but
against England there was little
doubt he had torn a thigh muscle.
First caught the eye when scoring a
try in Bègles-Bordeaux's 1991

	apps	pts
France (1992)		
Last Season	2 caps	0
Career	2 caps	0

Caps (2): **1992** W, E
Points: Nil

French Club Championship final win over Toulouse (won 19–10). Also in
the 1990/92 season he helped France B humiliate Scotland B 31–10 at
Hughenden. Prior to that he played junior rugby near Dijon and impressed
playing at No.8 for France A against the touring All Blacks at La Rochelle,
despite being on the wrong end of a 22–15 scoreline. Missed out on the World
Cup when Jean-Marie Cadieu took preference

Ondarts, P. — France

Full Name: Pascal Ondarts
Club: Biarritz Olympique
Position: Prop
Height: 5'10" **Weight:** 15st 10lbs
Born: Meharin, 1.4.56
International debut: France 16,
New Zealand 3, 1986
Five Nations' debut: France 16,
Wales 9, 1987
**Notable landmarks in rugby
career:** The most flexible of front
rows, having propped on either side
of the French scrum and also hooked
on occasion, although at that time
France were concentrating more on
steamrollering over opposition packs
with their three-prop front rows.
Coincided his senior debut with the
famous 16–3 French win over the All
Blacks in Nantes – their biggest-ever
margin of victory against New
Zealand – and he reappeared in the
fixture 12 months later when the
1987 inaugural Webb Ellis Cup was
directly at stake to the winner.
Pascal's solitary scoring memory is of
Agen (11 Nov 1987), after the 1987
World Cup, when he put his initials
on the sixth of France's seven tries in
a 49–3 rout of Romania before a
crowd of almost 13,000. A
folksinging Basque, he was discarded
by France when Pierre Berbizier, his
long-time national teammate and
captain, took up the coaching reins
following the 1991 World Cup

	apps	pts
France (**1986**)		
Last Season	6 caps	0
Career	42 caps	4

Caps (42): **1986** NZ(b2) **1987** W, E,
S(a), I wc-S(b), Z, Fj, A, NZ.
R(b) **1988** E, I, W, Arg(a1, a2),
Arg(b1, b2), R **1989** I, W, E,
NZ(1,2), A(2) **1990** W, E, S, I,
R, NZ(1,2) **1991** S, I, W(a),
E(a), US(2), W(b) wc-R(b), Fj,
C, E(b)

Points (4 – 1t): **1987** R(1t)

Penaud, A.   France

Full Name: Alain Penaud
Club: Brive
Position: Outside-half
Height: 5'11" **Weight:** 14st 2lbs
Occupation: Military student
Born: Juillac, 19.7.69
Former club: Objat
International debut: Wales 9,
France 12, 1992
Five Nations' debut: As above
**Notable landmarks in rugby
career:** Made a strong impression
after being given his chance out of
the blue by new coach Pierre
Berbizier in the 1992 Five Nations'
Championship. Having dropped a
goal in France's three-point defeat of
Wales in Cardiff on his debut (1 Feb
1992), he managed a try against
England in a 31–13 losing cause next
time out (15 Feb 1992), after
charging down Will Carling's
attempted clearance in the 66th
minute. Drew a blank in Edinburgh,
but ended the season with a two-try
flourish against Ireland: starting and
finishing the seven-try rout with
touchdowns in the 2nd and 85th

	apps	pts
France (**1992**)		
Last Season	4 caps	15
Career	4 caps	15

Caps (4): **1992** W, E, S, I

Points (15 – 3t,1dg): **1992** W(1dg),
E(1t), I(2t)

minutes. Originally made a name for himself when guiding French Schools
to the 1987 Triple Crown with 18 points in wins against Scotland, Wales and
England. From there he graduated to France A and the FIRA Championship,
in which he tasted triumph when scoring the try that inspired a 22–14 victory
over the Soviet Union and gave France A the title on try-difference

Roumat, O.

France

Full Name: Olivier Roumat
Club: Dax
Position: Lock
Height: 6'6" **Weight:** 17st 4lbs
Occupation: Surveyor
Born: Mont-de-Marsan, 16.6.66
Family links with rugby: Father played in Mont-de-Marsan back row
International debut: New Zealand 34, France 20, 1989
Five Nations' debut: Wales 19, France 29, 1990
Notable landmarks in rugby career: A funny old season for Olivier, in that he was widely reckoned to be France's only genuine line-out jumper. All went pretty much according to plan up until Christmas, then Pierre Berbizier took over as coach and Christophe Mougeot was brought in for the 1992 Five Nations' Championship. It did not cost Olivier a cap, for Mougeot failed to last the course against Wales and England, and the Dax surveyor was sent into the fray in the 40th and 64th minutes respectively. Brought back against Scotland and Ireland, he then toured New Zealand with the World XV and, at Athletic Park, Wellington, lasted only nine minutes

	apps	pts
France **(1989)**		
Last Season	11 caps	4
Career	27 caps	8

Caps (27): **1989** NZ(2R), BL **1990** W, E, S, I, R, A(1,2,3), NZ(1,2) **1991** S, I, W(a), E(a), R(a), US(1), W(b) wc-R(b), Fj, C, E(b) **1992** W(R), E(R), S, I

Points (8 – 2t): **1991** W(a:1t) wc-R(b:1t)

of the World's 54–26 second Test defeat before Kiwi referee David Bishop dismissed him for illegal use of the shoe. Banned for four weeks. Formerly a flanker, his position against the British Lions XV who helped celebrate the bicentenary of the French Revolution in 1989, he built himself an impressive reputation in the 1988 Student World Cup and helped France B beat Wales B 28–15 in La Teste (12 Nov 1989), four months after replacing Marc Cécillon against New Zealand in Auckland for his first cap

Sadourny, J.-L.   France

Full Name: Jean-Luc Sadourny
Club: Colomiers
Positions: Wing, fullback
Height: 6'1" **Weight:** 13st 9lbs
Occupation: Public relations officer
Born: Toulouse, 26.8.66
International debut: Wales 9,
France 22, 1991
Five Nations' debut: France 13,
England 31, 1992
**Notable landmarks in rugby
career:** Acquainted himself with
British rugby during the 1990/91
season when he represented France
B against Scotland and England
counterparts, scoring a try in the
31–10 defeat of the Scots at
Hughenden, and suffering
concussion in the 10–6 win over the
English at Bristol. Lightning struck
twice for the unfortunate Jean-Luc
because he lasted just nine minutes
on his Five Nations' debut against
England in Paris last season. Having
replaced injured captain Philippe
Sella in the 55th minute he was then
involved in a head-on collision with
outside-half Alain Penaud

	apps	pts
France (**1991**)		
Last Season	5 caps	4
Career	5 caps	4

Caps (5): **1991** W(b:R) wc-C(R)
1992 E(R), S, I

Points (4 – 1t): **1992** I(1t)

attempting a scissors movement and was led groggily from the arena. His first cap (following the 1991 US tour during which he scored two tries against USA B) came as a 76th minute replacement for Serge Blanco in the floodlit international against Wales at the Arms Park (4 Sep 1991) and it was yet again as a replacement, this time against Canada in the vital World Cup pool game, that he made his second appearance, given 30 minutes after Sella retired from the fray. It was a novelty for Jean-Luc to start the following game at Murrayfield and then in Paris where he scored a try in the 44–12 win over Ireland

Saint-André, P.   France

Full Name: Philippe Saint-André
Club: Montferrand
Position: Wing
Height: 5'11" **Weight:** 13st 5lbs
Occupation: Self-employed
sponsorship agent
Born: Romans, 19.4.67
Former clubs: Romans,
Clermont-Ferrand
International debut: France 6,
Romania 12, 1990
Five Nations' debut: Ireland 13,
France 21, 1991
**Notable landmarks in rugby
career:** If he never achieved
anything else in rugby, the try
Philippe scored against England in
the 1991 Grand Slam decider would
ensure his place in the annals of
Championship rugby. However, he
has achieved much more since
rounding off The Try under the
opposite posts from where the move
was initiated by Serge Blanco and
fed, via Jean-Baptiste Lafond, Didier
Camberabero, Philippe Sella and
then Camberabero's boot behind
enemy lines where the wing, who has
clocked 10.9sec over 100m,
scorched through to apply the *coup
de grâce*. Seven tries in all have been
registered in the name of

	apps	pts
France (**1990**)		
Last Season	11 caps	20
Career	18 caps	28

Caps (18): **1990** R, A(3), NZ(1,2)
1991 I(R), W(a), E(a), US(1,2),
W(b) wc-R(b), Fj, C, E(b) **1992**
W, E, S, I

Points (28 – 7t): **1991** W(a:1t), E(a:1t),
US(1:1t), W(b:1t) wc-R(b:1t),
C(1t) **1992** W(1t)

Saint-André, all coming in a ten-game period between the 1991 and 1992
Five Nations' Championship games with Wales, who kindly donated a try per
game to Philippe's collection. A prolific try-scorer in French club rugby for
Montferrand, he also represented France A and B before stepping into the
top flight at Stade Patrice Brocas, Auch (24 May 1990) as a centre for the
visit of Romania, who triumphed (12–6) on French soil for the first time

Sanz, H.   France

Full Name: Henri Sanz
Club: Narbonne
Position: Scrum-half
Height: 5'8" **Weight:** 11st 9lbs
Occupation: Commercial attaché
Born: Versailles, 17.1.63
Former club: Graulhet
International debut: France 29,
Argentina 9, 1988
Five Nations' debut: Scotland 21,
France 0, 1990
**Notable landmarks in rugby
career:** Made his senior bow in the
first Test defeat of touring Argentina
at the Beaujoire Stadium, Nantes (5
Nov 1988) and scored his first
international try in the following
week's second Test when France
won 28–18 in Lille. Captained
France B to a 15–9 victory over
Scotland B (7 Feb 1987) at St
Andrews and in defeat against Wales
B (10–13 at Pontypridd, 25 Oct
1986) and England B (9–22 at Bath,
20 Feb 1987) during 1986/87.
Weighed in with two tries the
following season as France B beat
Wales B 26–0 in Bègles (17 Oct
1987). Looked finally to have

	apps	pts
France (**1988**)		
Last Season	1 cap	0
Career	11 caps	4

Caps (11): **1988** Arg(b1, b2), R **1989**
A(2) **1990** S, I, R, A(1,2),
NZ(2) **1991** W(b)

Points (4 – 1t): **1988** Arg(b2:1t)

become first-choice No.9 when captaining France in the 25–17 second-Test
win over Australia in Lille's Stade Grimpooris (11 Nov 1989). But, despite
starting against Scotland and Ireland in the 1990 Five Nations' Championship
and adding a further four caps against summer opponents Romania, Australia
(twice) and New Zealand, following a knee operation that summer and missing
the North American tour, he found himself relegated by Pierre Berbizier
behind Fabien Galthie in the pecking order. Although he collected his 11th
cap under the new Arms Park lights against Welsh opposition (won 22–9, 4
Sep 1991), Galthie took over for the World Cup and beyond. To compound
his misery, when Galthie was dropped Aubin Hueber got the nod

Sella, P.   France

Full Name: Philippe Sella
Club: Agen
Position: Centre
Height: 5'11" **Weight:** 13st 4lbs
Occupation: Businessman
Born: Clairac, 14.2.62
International debut: Romania 13,
France 9, 1982
Five Nations' debut: England 15,
France 19, 1983
**Notable landmarks in rugby
career:** French captain since Pierre
Berbizier retired to become national
coach, Philippe is the world's
most-capped centre three-quarter.
Only Serge Blanco's 93-cap haul
exceeds his own tally of 83
(including six caps at wing and one
at fullback), amassed since his debut
in the 1982 defeat by Romania. On
his next appearance, in the first Test
against Argentina, he scored the first
two of his 25 international tries. He
played 45 consecutive Tests until
injury ruled him out of the 49–3 win
over Romania, a match played on his
own Agen pitch (11 Nov 1987). It
was but a temporary blip for a man
who had also represented France at
Schools, Juniors and Universities
grade. In 1986 he scored a try in
every Championship match,
equalling a feat achieved only by
compatriate Patrick Estève (1983),
Johnny Wallace (Scotland, 1925) and
Carston Catcheside (England,
1924). That same year he was alone
in playing all 12 French
internationals and represented the
Five Nations' in a 13–32 defeat by
the Overseas Unions in the IRB
Centenary match at Twickenham

	apps	pts
France (1982)		
Last Season	11 caps	8
Career	83 caps	100

Caps (83): 1982 R, Arg(1,2) 1983 E,
S, I, W, A(1,2), R 1984 I, W, E,
S, NZ(1,2), R 1985 E, S, I, W,
Arg(1,2) 1986 S, I, W, E, R(a),
Arg(1,2), A, NZ, R(b), NZ(1,2)
1987 W, E, S(a), I wc-S(b),
R(a), Z(R), Fj, A, NZ 1988 E,
S, I, W, Arg(a1, a2), Arg(b1,
b2), R 1989 I, W, E, S,
NZ(1,2), BL, A(1,2) 1990 W,
E, S, I, A(1,2,3) 1991 W(a),
E(a), R(a), US(1,2), W(b)
wc-Fj, C, E(b) 1992 W, E, S, I

Points (100 – 25t): 1982 Arg(1:2t)
1983 E(1t) 1984 I(1t), W(1t),
E(1t), R(1t) 1986 S(1t), I(1t),
W(1t), E(1t), R(a:1t), Arg(2:1t),
A(1t), NZ(1:1t) 1987 E(1t),
wc-S(b:1t), R(a:1t), A(1t) 1988
I(1t), Arg(4:1t) 1990 W(1t)
1991 W(a:1t) wc-Fj(2t)

(19 Apr 1986). Played a key role the next season in France's run to the World Cup final. A torn thigh muscle accounted for his absence from the 1991 World Cup opener against Romania but, typically, he returned with two dazzling tries in the following match against Fiji. His first match as captain was against Wales (1 Feb 1992)

Simon, S.   France

Full Name: Serge Simon
Club: Bègles-Bordeaux
Position: Prop
Height: 6'2" **Weight:** 15st 2lbs
Occupation: Doctor
Born: 3.7.67
International debut: Romania 21, France 33, 1991
Five Nations' debut: None
Notable landmarks in rugby career: One of the posse of players to rise to prominence out of the success of 1991 French Club champions Bègles-Bordeaux. Selectors opted for Bègles front row *en masse* when France played in Bucharest (22 Jun 1991) prior to 1991 World Cup, so Serge was chosen along with Vincent Moscato and Philippe Gimbert. Although he marked his debut in Romania's 33–21 defeat with a try, and was retained for the first Test against the United States in Denver (won 41–9, 13 Jul 1991) on France's summer tour, Serge was omitted from the 26-man World Cup squad and,

	apps	pts
France (**1991**)		
Last Season	2 caps	4
Career	2 caps	4

Caps (2): 1991 R, US(1)
Points (4 – 1t): **1991** R(1t)

following Pierre Berbizier's succession to Daniel Dubroca's coaching post, remained in the international wilderness for the 1992 Five Nations' Championship, when first Gregoire Lascube, then Louis Armary were handed the loosehead duties

Tordo, J.- F.   France

Full Name: Jean-François Tordo
Club: Nice
Positions: Flanker, hooker
Height: 6′1″ **Weight:** 14st 10lbs
Occupation: Building foreman
Born: Nice, 1.8.64
Former club: Toulon
International debut: United States
9, France 41, 1991
Five Nations' debut: Wales 9,
France 12, 1992
**Notable landmarks in rugby
career:** A true utility forward,
varying between blindside
wing-forward and hooker. He
hooked France B to a 28–15 win over
Wales B at La Teste (12 Nov 1989),
reverted to back row for France B's
31–10 defeat of Scotland B at
Hughenden (2 Mar 1991), but then
went and reclaimed the No.2 jersey
for the 10–6 win over England B a
fortnight later. Promoted to the
senior XV on the 1991 tour of the
United States, he made his debut as a
73rd-minute replacement for Michel
Courtiols in the 41–9 win at Denver
(13 Jul 1991). Although excluded

		apps	pts
France **(1991)**			
Last Season		5 caps	0
Career		5 caps	0

Caps (5): **1991** US(1R) **1992** W, E,
    S, I

Points: Nil

from the French World Cup squad, he returned for the 1992 Five Nations'
Championship, occupying the No.6 jersey throughout the campaign. Tasted
the high life as a teenager when, aged 18, he won a runners-up medal after
coming on as a second-half replacement for Nice in the 1983 French Club
Championship final. Thereafter joined Toulon but returned north along the
Riviera to Nice in September 1990, having toured New Zealand with France
in 1989, hooking against Manawatu and flanking in the wins over Bay of
Plenty and a Seddon Shield XV. Has also hooked for France A in the FIRA
Championship

Van Heerden, A.   France

Full Name: Andries Van Heerden
Club: Tarbes
Position: No.8
Height: 6'5½" **Weight:** 16st 2lbs
Occupation: Air-traffic controller
(Lourdes-Tarbes Airport)
Born: Cape Town, South Africa,
6.10.61
Family: Noelle (wife)
Former club: Stellenbosch Univ
(SA)
International debut: France 13,
England 31, 1992
Five Nations' debut: As above
**Notable landmarks in rugby
career:** Only the fourth foreign-born
player to represent France since the
war (Morocco's Abdelatif Benazzi,
Venezuelan-born Serge Blanco and
fellow South African Eric Melville
making up the list), his selection
against England in last season's Five
Nations' Championship caught the
opposition by surprise. 'He is totally
unknown to us,' confessed manager
Geoff Cooke. Dries, as he is more
commonly known, left South Africa

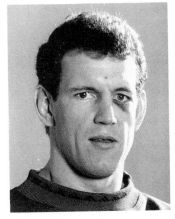

	apps	pts
France (**1992**)		
Last Season	2 caps	0
Career	2 caps	0

Caps (2): **1992** E, S
Points: Nil

for France in 1986 on the advice of his coach at Stellenbosch Univ, believing he could never play international rugby for the Springboks. Having studied agriculture at Stellenbosch, he entered the business in Tarbes before later turning his attention to controlling air traffic. A flanker in Tarbes' 9–3 French Club Championship final loss to Agen in 1988, he married a French girl, Noelle, and became a French citizen in 1990. Called into the French squad when Eric Champ declined the invitation, Dries warmed the bench in the Championship opener against Wales before turning out against England and Scotland. He reverted to the bench for the season's finale against Ireland, when Marc Cécillon was moved back from lock to No.8

Viars, S.   France

Full Name: Sebastien Viars
Club: Brive
Position: Wing
Height: 5′10½″ **Weight:** 11st 11lbs
Occupation: Military student
Born: Aurillac, 24.6.71
International debut: Wales 9, France 12, 1992
Five Nations' debut: As above
Notable landmarks in rugby career: Surely the find of last season for the French, Sebastien hinted at his potential when scoring a quite outstanding try in France B's 10–6 win over England B at Bristol (15 Mar 1991), having represented the French second strings in the 31–10 win over Scotland B at Hughenden two weeks earlier. Not required for duty during the World Cup – although he toured North America in July 1991, scoring four tries against Western Unions and USA B – he had to wait until last season's Five Nations' Championship to step up in class. He responded by marking his debut in Cardiff with a penalty goal in the 12–9 win over Wales before

	apps	pts
France (**1992**)		
Last Season	3 caps	36
Career	3 caps	36

Caps (3): **1992** W, E, I
Points (36 – 3t,6c,4p): **1992** W(1p), E(1t,1c,1p), I(2t,5c,2p)

notching his first try (as well as a penalty and conversion) on his Paris debut against England (lost 13–31) a fortnight later. However, his most spectacular was still to come. Injury robbed him of a third cap and further points, against Scotland, but he made amends with a Championship-record 24 points in the 44–12 win over Ireland on a delightful sunny afternoon in Parc des Princes. His history-making haul included two tries, five conversions and two penalty goals. Early career featured Schools caps in 1989, Junior honours in 1990 (landing four goals against Wales Youth) and the 1991 Hong Kong Sevens with France

APPENDIX

ADAM, Douglas Russell Wallace. **1991/92 International category**: Scotland A (bench). **Position**: Centre. **Club**: Edinburgh Acads. **Debut**: Scotland U-21 10, Wales U-21 24, 1990. **U-21 caps**: 2 (also: 15–23 v. Wales U-21, April 1991. Bench – 1A,1B). **U-21 points**: 4 (1t v. W, 1991). **Born**: 20.7.70. **Height**: 6'. **Weight**: 13st 5lbs. **Occupation**: Student.

ADEBAYO, Adedayo Adeyemi. **1991/92 International category**: England. **Position**: Wing. **Club**: Bath. **U-21 Debut**: England U-21 94, Belgium 0, 1991. **U-21 caps**: 1. **U-21 points**: 8 (2t). **B Debut**: England B 50, Spain 6, 1991. **B caps**: 3 (also: v. France B, 1991; v. Italy B, 1991). B points: 8 (2t v. Spain). **Born**: 30.11.70. **Height**: 5'11". **Weight**: 14st.

AINSCOUGH, Gerry Christopher. **1991/92 International category**: England B (bench). **Positions**: Centre, outside-half. **Club**: Leicester. **Debut**: Spain 9, England B 31, 1989. **Caps**: 1 (bench – 3B). **Points**: 0. **Born**: Wigan, 7.8.64. **Height**: 5'11". **Weight**: 11st 7lbs. **Occupation**: Mechanical engineer. Family: Karen (wife).

ALEXANDER, Jeffrey. **1991/92 International category**: England U-21. **Position**: Centre. **Club**: Harlequins. **Debut**: Netherlands 12, England U-21 48, 1992. **Caps**: 1. **Points**: 0. **Height**: 6'2". **Weight**: 13st 10lbs. **Rep**: Old Tiffinians, Harlequins, Surrey County (1990/91), Surrey U-21 (1991/92), London U-21 (1992).

ALLEN, Kevin W. **1991/92 International category**: Wales U-21. **Position**: Tighthead prop. **Club**: Aberavon. **Debut**: Scotland U-21 19, Wales U-21 28, 1992. **U-21 caps**: 1. **Points**: 0. **Born**: 17.8.71. **Height**: 6'1". **Weight**: 17st. **Occupation**: Carpenter.

ALLINGHAM, Michael James De Grey. **1991/92 International category**: Scotland B. **Position**: Scrum-half. **Club**: Heriot's FP. **Debut**: Scotland B 19, Ireland B 29, 1992 (58th-min. replacement. Bench – 2B). **Born**: 6.1.65. **Height**: 6'0½". **Weight**: 14st. **Occupation**: Sports coach. **Other sports**: Scotland cricket team.

AMOS, John Peter. **1991/92 International category**: Scotland A (bench). **Position**: Flanker. **Club**: Gala. **Debut**: None (bench – 1A: Scotland A 36, Spain 16, 1991). **Born**: Bergen, Norway, 25.1.68. **Height**: 6'. **Weight**: 14st. **Occupation**: Joiner. **Landmarks**: Centre for Scotland U-18s. Toured North America (1991) with Scotland (1991).

BARRETT, David. **1991/92 International category**: Scotland B (bench). **Position**: Fullback. **Club**: West of Scotland. **Debut**: Scotland B 22, Ireland B 22, 1989. **Caps**: 3 (1989 v. Ireland B, 22–22; 1990: v. France B, 9–31; v. Ireland B, 0–16. **Points**: 12 (4p: 1p v. I, 1989; 3p v. Fr). **Born**: London, 25.7.63. **Height**: 5'10". **Weight**: 12st 6lbs.

BOOTH, Andrew Howell. **1991/92 International category**: Wales Full (bench). **Position**: Scrum-half. **Club**: Cardiff. **Debut**: France B 28, Wales B 15, 1989. **B caps**: 1 (bench – 5F). **Points**: 0. **Born**: 8.12.68. **Height**: 5'10". **Weight**: 13st. **Occupation**: Financial sales consultant. **Landmarks**: Former Welsh Students captain. 1989 Cambridge Blue.

BRAMLEY, Richard. **1991/92 International category**: England U-21. **Position**: Lock. **Club**: Wakefield. **Debut**: Ireland U-21 19, England U-21 10, 1991. **U-21 caps**: 2 (also: 21–21 v. French Armed Forces, 1992). **Points**: 0. **Height**: 6'5". **Weight**: 17st. **Rep**: England U-16, U-18, U-19, U-21, Students.

BROMLEY, Spencer. **1991/92 International category**: England U-21. **Position**: Wing. **Club**: Liverpool St Helens. **Debut**: England U-21 16, Ireland U-21 22, 1990. **Caps**: 2 (also: England U-21 94, Belgium 0, 1991). **Points**: 12 (3t v. Belgium). **Height**: 6'1". **Weight**: 14st 7lbs. **Rep**: Rochdale, Bath, Liverpool Poly, England U-21, Students.

BRYCE, Robert. **1991/92 International category**: England U-21. **Position**: Wing. **Club**: Sale. **Debut**: England U-21 21, French Armed Forces 21, 1992. **Caps**: 1. **Points**: 0. **Height**: 6'1". **Weight**: 14st. **Rep**: Redcar (1987–89), West Hartlepool (1989–91), Yorkshire & North U-19 (1989/90), Sale (1991-), Yorkshire & North U-21 (1990–92).

BULLOCK, Warwick. **1991/92 International category**: England U-21. **Position**: Lock. **Club**: Coventry. **Debut**: Netherlands 18, England U-21 20, 1991. **Caps**: 2 (also: England U-21 94, Belgium 0, Sept 1991). **Points**: 0. **Born**: 9.2.70. **Height**: 6'. **Weight**: 16st 6lbs. **Occupation**: Family garage salesman.

BURNS, Graeme G. **1991/92 International category**: Scotland U-21 (bench). **Position**: Scrum-half. **Club**: Stewart's-Melville FP. **Debut**: None (bench: Scotland U-21 19, Wales U-21 28, 1992). **Born**: 29.10.71. **Height**: 5'9". **Weight**: 11st 4lbs. **Occupation**: Agriculture student. **Rep**: Scotland U-18 and U-19.

CAREY, Ronald. **1991/92 International category**: Ireland B. **Position**: Right wing. **Club**: Dungannon. **Debut**: England B 47, Ireland B 15, 1992. **Caps**: 1. **Points**: 0. **Born**: 6.8.65. **Height**: 5'8". **Weight**: 12st 6lbs. **Occupation**: Civil Servant.

CHILDS, Graham Christopher. **1991/92 International category**: England B (NZ tour). **Position**: Centre. **Club**: Wasps. **Debut**: None (bench v. Namibia, 2.11.90). **Born**: 3.4.68. **Height**: 6'. **Weight**: 13st 10lbs. **Landmark**: Toured Argentina with England (1990), playing against Cuyo (lost 22–21, 24.7.91) and Cordoba (won 15–12, 31.7.90).

CLARK, Christopher. **1991/92 International category**: England U-21. **Position**: Loosehead prop. **Clubs**: Rosslyn Park, Swansea Univ. **Debut**: Ireland U-21 19, England U-21 10, 1991. **U-21 caps**: 2 (also: v. French Armed Forces, 1992). **Points**: 0. **Height**: 6'. **Weight**: 16st. **Rep**: England Schools (1989), Colts (1990), Students and U-21 (1991/92).

CLINKENBEARD, John M. **1991/92 International category**: Scotland U-21. **Position**: Blindside flanker. **Club**: Currie. **Debut**: Scotland U-21 19, Wales U-21 28, 1992. **U-21 caps**: 1 (also: won 19–16 v. English Students U-21s, non-cap). **Points**: 0. **Born**: 27.2.71. **Height**: 6'2". **Weight**: 15st. **Rep**: Scotland U-18.

COCKERILL, Richard. **1991/92 International category**: England U-21/B (bench). **Position**: Hooker. **Club**: Coventry. **Debut**: Netherlands 18, England U-21 20, 1991. **U-21 caps**: 3 (also: won 94–0 v. Belgium, 1991; lost 10–19 to Ireland U-21, 1991). Bench – 2B. **U-21 points**: 4 (1t v. B). **Born**: 16.12.70. **Height**: 5'10". **Weight**: 14st.

CORCORAN, Ian. **1991/92 International category**: Scotland B (bench). **Position**: Hooker. **Club**: Gala. **Debut**: France B 31, Scotland B 9, Jan 1990. **B caps**: 1 (bench – 2F,2B: 38–17 v. Fiji, 1990; 32–0 v. Romania, 1990; 0–16 v. Ireland B, 1990; 10–31 v. France B, 1991). **Points**: 0. **Born**: Edinburgh, 11.5.63. **Height**: 5'11". **Weight**: 13st 5lbs.

COSTELLO, Richard. **1991/92 International category**: Ireland Full (NZ tour). **Position**: Lock. **Club**: Garryowen. **Debut**: None. **Born**: 8.3.64. **Height**: 6'7". **Weight**: 16st 7lbs. **Occupation**: Publican. **Landmark**: Selected to tour New Zealand (1992) with Ireland.

COUGHLIN, Timothy. **1991/92 International category**: Ireland B. **Position**: Lock. **Club**: Old Belvedere. **Debut**: England B 47, Ireland B 15, 1992. **Caps**: 1. **Points**: 0. **Born**: 21.5.65. **Height**: 6'5". **Weight**: 16st 6lbs. **Occupation**: Marketing executive.

COUSAR, Graham S. **1991/92 International category**: Scotland U-21 (bench). **Position**: Flanker. **Club**: Stirling County. **Debut**: None (bench: Scotland U-21 19, Wales U-21 28, 1992). **Born**: 12.3.71. **Height**: 6'. **Weight**: 13st. **Occupation**: Geography student. **Landmark**: Helped Stirling U-18 win 1988 Scottish Youth Cup.

CLANCY, Tom P. J. **1991/92 International category**: Ireland Full (NZ tour). **Position**: Loosehead prop. **Club**: London Irish. **Debut**: Ireland 9, Wales 12, 1988. Caps (9): 1988 W, E(1,2), WS, It 1989 F, W, E, S. **Points**: 0. **Born**: 15.3.62. **Height**: 6'2". **Weight**: 17st 5lbs. **Occupation**: Transport manager.

COWAN, Christopher J. **1991/92 International category**: Scotland U-21. **Position**: Hooker. **Club**: Dundee HSFP. **Debut**: Scotland U-21 19, Wales U-21 28, 1992. **U-21 caps**: 1. **Points**: 0. **Born**: 14.4.71. **Height**: 5'11". **Weight**: 14st 7lbs. **Rep**: Scottish Schools (squad), Royal Navy, Combined Services.

CROMPTON, Darren. **1991/92 International category**: England U-21. **Position**: Loosehead prop. **Club**: Bath. **Debut**: Netherlands 12, England U-21 48, 1992. **Caps**: 1. **Points**: 0. **Height**: 6'1". **Weight**: 17st. **Rep**: England U-16 (1989), U-18 (1990–91), U-21 (1992), Exeter (1992). **Landmark**: Captained England U-18.

DALLAGLIO, Lawrence Bruno. **1991/92 International category**: England U-21. **Position**: No.8. **Club**: Wasps. **Debut**: Netherlands 12, England U-21 48, 1992. **Caps**: 1. **Points**: 0. **Born**: 10.8.72. **Height**: 6'4". **Weight**: 15st 7lbs. **Occupation**: Trainee travel management. **Rep**: England Colts (5 caps), 18-Group squad, London U-21.

DAVIES, Geraint. **1991/92 International category**: Wales U-21. **Position**: Hooker. **Club**: Bridgend. **Debut**: Wales U-21 22, Ireland U-21 15, 1991. **Caps**: 1. **Points**: 0. **Born**: 20.5.71. **Height**: 5'10". **Weight**: 13st 12lbs. **Occupation**: Employed with Ford Engine Plant (Bridgend).

DAWSON, Matthew. **1991/92 International category**: England U-21. **Position**: Centre. **Club**: Northampton. **Debut**: England U-21 21, French A rmed Forces 21. **Caps**: 1. **Points**: 4 (1t). **Height**: 5'10". **Weight**: 13st. **Rep**: Marlow (1981–90), England U-16 squad (1989 tour to Italy), U-18 (1991: 5 caps).

DESMOND, Ian. **1991/92 International category**: England U-21. **Position**: Flanker. **Club**: Harlequins. **Debut**: England 21, French Armed Forces 21, 1992. **Caps**: 1. **Points**: 0. **Born**: 5.3.71. **Height**: 6'3". **Weight**: 16st. **Rep**: Racing Club de France (1990/91); Surrey U-16, U-18, U-21; London U-18, U-21. **Landmark**: 2t on Quins debut v. Llanelli.

DIPROSE, Anthony. **1991/92 International category**: England U-21. **Positions**: Lock, No.8, flanker. **Club**: Loughborough Students. **Debut**: Netherlands 12, England U-21 48, 1992. **Caps**: 1. **Points**: 0. **Height**: 6'5". **Weight**: 16st. **Rep**: Saracens, London Division U-21, England 18-Group (1990/91), Students U-21 (1991/92).

DUNN, Kevin Anthony. **1991/92 International category**: England B (NZ tour). **Position**: Hooker. **Club**: Gloucester. **Debut**: England B 9, Australia 37, 1988. **Caps**: 4 (also: 89:F, It, Fj). **Points**: 4 (1t v. F). **Height**: 5'9". **Weight**: 13st 10lbs. **Landmarks**: Unused repl when England beat Australia 28–19 (5.11.88), and 9 times for England B.

ETHERIDGE, John. **1991/92 International category**: Ireland Full (NZ tour squad). **Position**: Lock. **Club**: Northampton. **Ireland debut**: None. **England B Debut**: Italy B 0, England B 44, 1989. **England B caps**: 2 (also: won 18–10 v. USSR, 1989). **Points**: 0. **Born**: Gloucester, 8.6.65. **Height**: 6'6". **Weight**: 16st 7lbs. **Rep**: England B (1989 tour to Spain).

EVANS, Jonathan. **1991/92 International category**: Wales U-21 (bench). **Position**: Hooker. **Club**: Bryncoch. **Debut**: None (bench: Scotland U-21 19, Wales U-21 28, 1992). **Born**: 5.4.72. **Height**: 5'8". **Weight**: 13st 2lbs. **Occupation**: Student.

FLOCKHART, Gareth N. **1991/92 International category**: Scotland U-21. **Position**: No.8. **Club**: Stirling County. **Debut**: Scotland U-21 19, Wales U-21 28, 1992. **U-21 caps**: 1. **Points**: 0. **Born**: 11.5.72. **Height**: 6'3". **Weight**: 15st 5lbs. **Rep**: Scotland U-19. **Touchline**: Member of the Young Farmers.

FLOOD, Jonathan **Paul**. **1991/92 International category**: England U-21. **Position**: Centre. **Club**: Bridgend. **Debut**: Netherlands 18, England U-21 20, 1991. **Caps**: 5 (also: 1991 v. FAF, Belg, I; 1992 v. Neth). **Points**: 8 (2t: 1991 1vB, 1vI). **Born**: 25.11.70. **Height**: 6'. **Weight**: 13st 9lbs. **Rep**: England Schools (4 caps), Students. **Landmark**: Captain v. Neth (3.5.92).

FULCHER, Gabriel Mark. **1991/92 International category**: Ireland B. **Position**: Lock. **Club**: UC Dublin. **Debut**: Scotland B 19, Ireland B 29, 1991. **B caps**: 1. **B points**: 0. **U-21 caps**: 2 (lost 7–21 v. Netherlands, Leiden 21.9.90; won 22–16 v. England U-21, Moseley 29.10.90). **U-21 points**: 0. **Born**: 27.11.69. **Height**: 6'5". **Weight**: 16st 7lbs.

FURLONG, Neville. **1991/92 International category**: Ireland B/Full (NZ tour). **Position**: Wing. **Club**: UC Galway. **Debut**: Scotland B 19, Ireland B 29, 1991. **Caps**: 2 (also: England B 47, Ireland B 15, 1992). **Points**: 0. **Born**: 10.7.68. **Height**: 6'2". **Weight**: 14st 5lbs. **Occupation**: Army officer cadet at UC Galway.

FRASER, A. Murray. **1991/92 International category**: Scotland U-21 (bench). **Position**: Fullback. **Club**: Highland. **Debut**: None (bench: Scotland U-21 19, Wales U-21 28, 1992). **Born**: 25.12.70. **Height**: 5'10". **Weight**: 13st 7lbs. **Rep**: North & Mids U-18 and U-21, Scotland U-18.

GIBBS, Andrew. **1991/92 International category**: Wales U-21. **Position**: Blindside flanker. **Club**: Newbridge. **Debut**: Scotland U-21 19, Wales U-21 28, 1992. **U-21 caps**: 1. **Points**: 0. **Born**: 20.3.72. **Height**: 6'3". **Weight**: 16st. **Occupation**: Apprentice engineer (Parke Davis Warner Lambert). **Landmarks**: Wales Youth, U-19s.

GLASGOW, Iain Cameron. **1991/92 International category**: Scotland B (bench). **Positions**: Fullback, wing. **Debut**: Scotland B 10, France B 31, 1991. **B caps**: 1 (bench – 2F,3B). **Points**: 6 (2p). **Club**: Heriot's FP. **Born**: 24.2.66. **Height**: 5'7½". **Weight**: 11st 7lbs. **Landmark**: 39 points for Scotland XV in 91–8 win v. Kanto (Japan 1989).

GOODEY, Richard. **1991/92 International category**: Wales Full (Aus tour). **Position**: Lock. **Club**: Pontypool. **Debut**: None (bench: France B 28, Wales B 15). **Born**: 17.7.65. **Height**: 6'4". **Weight**: 16st. **Occupation**: Postman. Family: Helen (wife). **Landmark**: Toured Australia (1991) with Wales, playing v. W. Aus and Queensland County.

GOODWIN, Clark. **1991/92 International category**: Wales U-21. **Position**: Blindside flanker. **Club**: Cardiff Institute. **Debut**: Wales U-21 22, Ireland U-21 15, 1991. **Caps**: 1. **Points**: 0. **Born**: 19.8.71. **Height**: 6'3". **Weight**: 15st 2lbs. **Occupation**: Student.

GRAYSON, Paul James. **1991/92 International category**: England U-21. **Position**: Outside-half. **Club**: Preston Grasshoppers. **Debut**: England U-21 21, FAF 21, 1992. **Caps**: 1. **Points**: 17 (1c,3p,2dg). **Height**: 6'. **Weight**: 12st 4lbs. **Landmarks**: Captained North U-21; 5pts in Lancs' 9–6 County final win over Cornwall (18.4.92).

GREENWOOD, Matthew. **1991/92 International category**: England B. **Position**: Blindside flanker. **Club**: Nottingham. **Debut**: Spain 3, England B 34, 1992. **Caps**: 4 (also: won 47–15 v. Ireland B, 31.1.92; won 22–18 v. France B, 15.2.92; won 16–10 v. Italy B, 7.3.92). **Points**: 0. **Landmark**: Toured to New Zealand with England (1992).

GRIFFITHS, Matthew. **1991/92 International category**: England U-21. **Position**: Wing. **Club**: Blackheath. **Debut**: Netherlands 12, England U-21 48, 1992. **Caps**: 1. **Points**: 4 (1t). **Height**: 5'8½". **Weight**: 11st 10lbs. **Rep**: Sidcup (1987–90), London & Kent U-18, Colts, U-21; Kent Senior XV (1992).

HAMILTON, David R. **1991/92 International category**: Scotland U-21 (bench). **Position**: Centre. **Club**: Dundee HSFP. **Debut**: None (bench: Scotland U-21 19, Wales U-21 28, 1992. **Born**: 15.12.71. **Height**: 6'. **Weight**: 13st. **Occupation**: Law student. **Rep**: Scotland U-18 and U-19.

HARRIMAN, Andrew Tuoyo. **1991/92 International category**: England B tour (NZ). **Position**: Wing. **Club**: Harlequins. **Debut**: England 28, Australia 19, 1988. **Caps**: 1. **Points**: 0. **Born**: 13.7.64. **Height**: 6'2". **Weight**: 12st 8lbs. **Touchlines**: GB U-16 tennis doubles champion; double Cambridge Blue (athletics/rugby).

HASTINGS, Richard K. **1991/92 International category**: Scotland U-21. **Position**: Tighthead prop. **Club**: West of Scotland. **Debut**: Scotland U-21 19, Wales U-21 28, 1992. **U-21 caps**: 1. **Points**: 0. **Born**: 9.3.72. **Height**: 5'11". **Weight**: 17st 8lbs. **Rep**: Scottish Schools (U-15 and U-18), Scotland U-19 (squad), Scottish Students.

HAY, James Alan. **1991/92 International category**: Scotland A (bench). **Position**: Hooker. **Club**: Hawick. **Debut**: Scotland B 14, France B 12, 1989. **B caps**: 2 (also: v. France, 1991). **Bench** – 1F,2A. **Points**: 0. **Born**: 8.8.64. **Height**: 5'10". **Weight**: 14st 4lbs. Family: Susan (wife). **Landmark**: Toured with Scotland to Zimbabwe (1988) and Japan (1989).

HEMBROW, Ian Lee. **1991/92 International category**: Wales Full (Australia tour squad). **Position**: No.8. **Club**: Cardiff. **Debut**: None. **Born**: 21.6.69. **Height**: 6'3". **Weight**: 17st 4lbs. **Occupation**: Gas Board service engineer. **Landmark**: Selected to tour with Wales after only eight club games, but did not play in Australia.

HOGG, Carl David. **1991/92 International category**: Scotland Full (tour squad). **Positions**: No.8, lock, flanker. **Club**: Melrose. **Debut**: Scotland B 10, France B 31, 1991. **B caps**: 1. **Points**: 0. **U-21 caps**: 1 (Scotland U-21 10, Wales U-21 24, 1990 – captain). **Points**: 0. **Born**: 5.7.69. **Height**: 6'4". **Weight**: 15st 7lbs. **Landmark**: Toured Australia (1992).

HOPLEY, Damian Paul. **1991/92 International category**: England B (NZ tour). **Position**: Centre. **Club**: Wasps. **Debut**: England B 12, Emerging Australians 12, Nov 1990. **B caps**: 1 (bench – 1F: Wales 6, England 25, 19.1.91). **Points**: 0. **Born**: 12.4.70. **Height**: 6'2". **Weight**: 14st 10lbs. **Landmark**: Toured Fiji/Australia with England (1991).

HUNTER, Richie. **1991/92 International category**: Ireland U-21. **Position**: Centre. **Club**: Loughborough Students. **Debut**: Wales U-21 22, Ireland U-21 15, 1991. **Caps**: 1. **Points**: 0. **Born**: 7.7.72. **Height**: 6'. **Weight**: 13st 3lbs.

ISAAC, Gary Ronald. **1991/92 International category**: Scotland B (bench). **Position**: Prop. **Club**: Gala. **Debut**: Spain 7, Scotland A 39, 1990. **Caps**: 1A, 1U21 (Italy 6, Scotland 22, 1986) (bench: 1B). **Points**: 0. **Born**: 15.2.66. **Height**: 5'10". **Weight**: 15st 8lbs. **Occupation**: Surveyor. Family: Antonya (wife). **Touchline**: Tug-of-war for Elgin.

JONES, Derwyn. **1991/92 International category**: Wales U-21. **Position**: Lock. **Club**: Llanelli. **Debut**: Wales U-21 22, Ireland U-21 15, 1991. **U-21 caps**: 2 (also: 28–19 v. Scotland 1992). **Points**: 0. **Born**: 14.11.70. **Height**: 6'10". **Weight**: 19st. **Occupation**: Student. **Landmarks**: Welsh Students, English/GB Universities.

JONES, Paul. **1991/92 International category**: Wales U-21 (bench). **Positions**: Lock, No.8. **Club**: Neath. **Debut**: None. **Born**: 19.6.72. **Height**: 6'8". **Weight**: 16st. **Occupation**: Trainee electrician. **Other sports**: Wales U-15 basketball. **Landmarks**: Wales U-19 (1991 tour of Canada).

JONES, Rhodri Jason. **1991/92 International category**: Wales U-21 (bench). **Position**: Scrum-half. **Club**: Neath. **Debut**: None. **Born**: 22.8.71. **Height**: 5'9". **Weight**: 12st 7lbs. **Occupation**: Apprentice plumber (W G Beynon & Sons Ltd). **Family links**: Brother of Wales scrum-half Robert (Swansea), and Anthony (SWP).

JONES, Rhys. **1991/92 International category**: Wales U-21 (bench). **Position**: Prop. **Club**: Newcastle Emlyn. **Debut**: None. **Born**: 4.2.72. **Height**: 6'. **Weight**: 16st. **Occupation**: Carpenter. **Rep**: Pembrokeshire Youth, Wales Youth, U-19 (1991 tour of Canada).

JOSEPH, David (Dai). **1991/92 International category**: Wales full (bench). **Position**: Prop. **Club**: Swansea. **B Debut**: Italy 12, Wales 24, Treviso 1986. **B caps**: 1. **Points**: 0. **Born**: 20.9.63. **Height**: 6'1". **Weight**: 17st. **Landmark**: Ever present on Wales bench during 1992 Championship. **Touchline**: Unbeaten as an amateur boxer.

KARDOONI, Aadel. **1991/92 International category**: England B (NZ tour). **Position**: Scrum-half. **Club**: Leicester. **Debut**: None (bench v. Ireland B and France B in 1990/91). **Born**: Tehran, Iran, 17.5.68. **Height**: 5'8". **Weight**: 11st 8lbs. **Landmark**: Represented Leicester v. Bath in 1988 Pilkington Cup final.

KELLAM, Robert. **1991/92 International category**: England U-21. **Position**: Hooker. **Club**: Newbury. **Debut**: Netherlands 12, England U-21 48, 1992. **Caps**: 1. **Points**: 0. **Height**: 5'10". **Weight**: 15st. **Rep**: Wasps Colts (1989/90); South West Colts, U-21; England Students U-21; British Polytechnics (1991/92).

KERNOHAN, Michael. **1991/92 International category**: Ireland U-21. **Position**: Hooker. **Club**: Glasgow University. **Debut**: Ireland U-21 19, England U-21 10, 1991. **Caps**: 1. **Points**: 0. **Born**: 18.5.71. **Height**: 5'10". **Weight**: 13st 4lbs.

KNIGHT, Steven. **1991/92 International category**: England B (bench). **Position**: Scrum-half. **Club**: Bath. **Debut**: None. **Born**: 8.12.64. **Height**: 5′10″. **Weight**: 13st. **Rep**: Bath for past ten years, collecting 1990 Pilkington Cup winners' medal and warming bench in 1992 final.

LANGLEY, Colin. **1991/92 International category**: Wales U-21. **Position**: Lock. **Club**: Cardiff. **Debut**: Wales U-21 23, Scotland U-21 15, 1991. **U-21 caps**: 2 (also: Wales 22, Ireland 15, 1991). **Points**: 0. **Born**: 17.10.71. **Height**: 6′6″. **Weight**: 17st 2lbs. **Occupation**: Student.

LEWIS, Iestyn. **1991/92 International category**: Wales U-21. **Position**: Centre. **Club**: Bath. **Debut**: Wales U-21 22, Ireland U-21 15, 1991. **Caps**: 1. **Points**: 0. **Born**: 1.11.71. **Height**: 6′. **Weight**: 13st. **Occupation**: Student at Bath University. **Rep**: Welsh Students. **Landmark**: Bench reserve for 1992 Pilkington Cup final.

LILEY, Robert James. **1991/92 International category**: England U-21. **Position**: Fullback. **Club**: Wakefield. **Debut**: French Armed Forces 9, England U-21 7, 1991. **Caps**: 2 (also: 94–0 v. Belgium, 1991). **Points**: 26 (1t,11c v. Belgium). **Born**: 3.4.70. **Height**: 6′. **Weight**: 12st 6lbs. **Rep**: Cahors (Fra).

LLOYD, Owain Stradling. **1991/92 International category**: Wales U-21. **Position**: Flanker. **Club**: Bridgend. **Debut**: Wales U-21 23, Scotland U-21 15, 1991. **U-21 caps**: 2. **Points**: 0 (also: Scotland 19, Wales 28, 1992). **Born**: 26.9.70. **Height**: 6′3″. **Weight**: 16st. **Occupation**: Human movements student.

LONGWELL, Gary. **1991/92 International category**: Ireland U-21. **Position**: Lock. **Club**: Queen's University, Belfast. **Debut**: Wales U-21 22, Ireland U-21 15, 1991. **Caps**: 2 (also: Ireland U-21 19, England U-21 10, 1991). **Points**: 4 (1t v. Wales). **Born**: 30.7.71. **Height**: 6′6″. **Weight**: 17st 10lbs.

McCALL, Mark. **1991/92 International category**: Ireland B/Full (NZ tour). **Position**: Centre. **Club**: Bangor. **Debut**: Scotland B 19, Ireland B 29, 1991. **Caps**: 2 (also: England B 47, Ireland B 15, 1992). **Points**: 0. **Born**: 29.11.67. **Height**: 5′10″. **Weight**: 12st 3lbs. **Occupation**: Public servant with independent commission for police complaints.

McCARTHY, Matthew. **1991/92 International category**: Wales U-21. **Position**: Outside-half. **Club**: Neath. **Debut**: Scotland U-21 19, Wales U-21 28, 1992. **Caps**: 1. **Points**: 3 (1p). **Born**: 16.4.71. **Height**: 5′8″. **Weight**: 11st 3lbs. **Occupation**: Student.

301

McCARTNEY, Dean. **1991/92 International category**: Ireland B. **Position**: Flanker. **Club**: Ballymena. **Debut**: Scotland B 19, Ireland B 29, 1991. **Caps**: 2 (also: England B 47, Ireland B 15, 1992). **Points**: 0. **Born**: 5.5.69. **Height**: 6'3". **Weight**: 15st 8lbs. **Occupation**: Sales representative.

McCLUSKEY, Graeme. **1991/92 International category**: Ireland U-21. **Position**: Left wing. **Club**: Portadown. **Debut**: Wales U-21 22, Ireland U-21 15, 1991. **Caps**: 1. **Points**: 0. **Born**: 5.8.71. **Height**: 5'8". **Weight**: 11st 10lbs.

McDERMOTT, Mark. **1991/92 International category**: Ireland U-21. **Position**: Hooker. **Club**: Blackrock College. **Debut**: Wales U-21 22, Ireland U-21 15, 1991. **Caps**: 2 (also: Ireland U-21 19, England U-21 10, 1991). **Points**: 0. **Born**: 10.6.71. **Height**: 5'9". **Weight**: 12st 2lbs.

McNULTY, Ross B. **1991/92 International category**: Scotland U-21. **Position**: Loosehead prop. **Club**: Stewart's-Melville FP. **Debut**: Scotland U-21 19, Wales U-21 28, 1992. **U-21 caps**: 1. **Points**: 0. **Born**: 28.10.71. **Height**: 6'1". **Weight**: 15st 7lbs. **Rep**: Scotland U-18 and U-19.

McVIE, Malcolm J. **1991/92 International category**: Scotland U-21. **Position**: Lock. **Club**: Edinburgh Academicals. **Debut**: Scotland U-21 19, Wales U-21 28, 1992. **U-21 caps**: 1. **Points**: 0. **Born**: 24.6.71. **Height**: 6'6". **Weight**: 14st. **Rep**: Scottish Schools. **Touchline**: 1990 Scottish Schools high jump champion.

MAPLETOFT, Mark. **1991/92 International category**: England U-21. **Position**: Fullback. **Club**: Rugby. **Debut**: Ireland U-21 19, England U-21 10, 1991. **U-21 caps**: 2 (also: 21–21 v. French Armed Forces, 1992). **Points**: 0. **Height**: 5'8". **Weight**: 12st 7lbs. **Rep**: England Schools. **Landmark**: 280 points for Rugby 1991/92 (9th best in England).

MEADOWS, Alastair. **1991/92 International category**: England U-21. **Position**: Lock. **Club**: Newcastle Gosforth. **Debut**: Netherlands 12, England U-21 48, 1992. **Caps**: 1. **Points**: 4 (1t). **Height**: 6'5". **Weight**: 16st 6lbs. **Rep**: Yorkshire & North Schools (1989), Northumberland & North U-21, English Univs & Students U-21.

MILLAR, Peter. **1991/92 International category**: Ireland B. **Position**: Tighthead prop. **Club**: Ballymena. **Debut**: England B 47, Ireland B 15, 1992. **Caps**: 1. **Points**: 0. **Born**: 8.6.62. **Height**: 6'1". **Weight**: 16st 6lbs. **Occupation**: Bank official.

MILLARD, David Bruce. **1991/92 International category**: Scotland Full (Australia tour). **Position**: Scrum-half. **Club**: London Scottish. **Debut**: None. **Born**: Guildford, 19.9.64. **Height**: 6'1½". **Weight**: 14st 4lbs. **Occupation**: Student osteopath. **Scottish links**: Mother – Glasgow; father – Stirling. **Landmark**: Capt Scotland Students 1988 World Cup.

MILLHOUSE, Craig. **1991/92 International category**: England U-21. **Position**: Openside flanker. **Club**: Bristol. **Debut**: Netherlands 12, England U-21 48, 1992. **Caps**: 1. **Points**: 0. **Height**: 6'. **Weight**: 14st. **Rep**: Gloucestershire U-21, South-South West U-21, English Colleges (1991/92).

MILLIGAN, Kenneth R. **1991/92 International category**: Scotland U-21. **Positions**: Wing, centre. **Club**: Stewart's-Melville FP. **Debut**: Scotland U-21 19, Wales U-21 28, 1992. **U-21 caps**: 1. **Points**: 0. **Born**: 19.7.72. **Height**: 5'10". **Weight**: 12st 7lbs. **Rep**: Scottish Schools (2 seasons), and U-19.

MOLLOY, Darren. **1991/92 International category**: England U-21. **Position**: Loosehead prop. **Club**: Wasps. **Debut**: Netherlands 12, England U-21 48, 1992. **Caps**: 1. **Points**: 0. **Born**: 31.8.72. **Height**: 6'2". **Weight**: 17st 7lbs. **Occupation**: Bricklayer. **Rep**: Old Gaytonians, England Colts (1990/91 v. S, F), London U-21.

MURPHY, John. **1991/92 International category**: Ireland B. **Position**: Hooker. **Club**: Greystones. **Debut**: Scotland B 19, Ireland B 29, 1991. **Caps**: 1 (also bench – 1B: England B 47, Ireland B 15, 1992). **Points**: 0. **Born**: 2.8.63. **Height**: 6'. **Weight**: 15st 7lbs. **Occupation**: Sales representative.

MURPHY, Leo. **1991/92 International category**: Ireland U-21. **Position**: Loosehead prop. **Club**: University College Cork. **Debut**: Wales U-21 22, Ireland U-21 15, 1991. **Caps**: 2 (also: Ireland U-21 19, England U-21 10, 1991). **Points**: 0. **Born**: 21.4.71. **Height**: 5'10". **Weight**: 13st 5lbs. **Landmark**: Toured to Netherlands with Ireland U-21s.

NEWTON, Jonathan. **1991/92 International category**: Scotland U-21. **Positions**: Outside-half, wing. **Club**: Dundee HSFP. **Debut**: Scotland U-21 19, Wales U-21 28. **Caps**: 1. **Points**: 15 (5p). **Born**: 23.4.71. **Height**: 5'11". **Weight**: 12st. **Landmark**: Set new British record for points scored in a season with 527 (16t, 107c, 77p, 6dg) in 1991/92.

NICHOL, Scott Alan. **1991/92 International category**: Scotland B (bench). **Position**: Outside-half. **Club**: Selkirk. **Debut**: Ireland B 16, Scotland B 0, 1990. **B caps**: 2 (also: v. France, 1991). **Points**: 0. **U-21 caps**: 2 (v. Wales, 1990; v. Wales, 1991). **Points**: 4 (1t, 1991). **Born**: 18.6.70. **Height**: 5'10". **Weight**: 11st 7lbs. **Occupation**: Fireman.

O'CALLAGHAN, Ultan. **1991/92 International category**: Ireland U-21. **Position**: Lock. **Club**: Highfield. **Debut**: Wales U-21 22, Ireland U-21 15, 1991. **Caps**: 1. **Points**: 0. **Born**: 24.3.71. **Height**: 6'2". **Weight**: 18st 7lbs.

PEARSON, Joel Timothy Vernon Pearson. **1991/92 International category**: England U-21. **Position**: Flanker. **Club**: Bristol. **Debut**: Netherlands 18, England U-21 20, 1991. **Caps**: 3 (also: 7–9 v. FAF, 1991; 94–0 v. Belgium, 1991). **Points**: 4 (1t: v. B). **Club**: Bristol. **Born**: 8.3.70. **Height**: 6'. **Weight**: 14st 6lbs.

PHILLIPS, Adrian. **1991/92 International category**: Wales U-21. **Position**: Hooker. **Club**: Bridgend Athletic. **Debut**: Scotland U-21 19, Wales U-21 28. **Caps**: 1. **Points**: 0. **Born**: 1.8.71. **Height**: 5'9". **Weight**: 14st. **Occupation**: Upholsterer.

POTTS, Kevin. **1991/92 International category**: Ireland B. **Position**: Lock. **Club**: St Mary's College. **Debut**: Scotland B 19, Ireland B 29, 1991. **Caps**: 1. **Points**: 4 (1t). **Born**: 6.11.66. **Height**: 6'4". **Weight**: 16st 12lbs. **Occupation**: Accountant.

RAVENSCROFT, Stephen. **1991/92 International category**: England U-21. **Position**: Centre. **Club**: Saracens. **Debut**: Ireland U-21 19, England U-21 10, 1991. **Caps**: 2 (also: 21–21 v. FAF, 1992). **Points**: 0. **Height**: 5'11". **Weight**: 13st 7lbs. **Rep**: Bradford & Bingley, Northcote (NZ–1990), England Schools, Students.

REDRUP, Justin. **1991/92 International category**: Wales U-21. **Position**: Centre. **Club**: Bristol. **Debut**: Scotland U-21 19, Wales U-21 28, 1992. **Caps**: 1. **Points**: 4 (1t). **Born**: 19.3.72. **Height**: 6'2". **Weight**: 15st 7lbs. **Occupation**: Bar manager.

RENNELL, Mark Ian. **1991/92 International category**: England U-21. **Positions**: No.8, flanker. **Club**: Bedford. **Debut**: FAF 9, England U-21 7, 1991. **Caps**: 4 (also: 1991/92 v. Belgium, Ireland, French Armed Forces). **Points**: 8 (2t: v. Belgium). **Club**: Bedford. **Born**: 17.1.71. **Height**: 6'2". **Weight**: 16st 7lbs. **Rep**: England U-16, Colts.

ROY, Stuart. **1991/92 International category**: Wales Full (bench). **Position**: Lock. **Club**: Cardiff. **Debut**: None. U-21 caps: 1 (Scotland 10, Wales 24, 28.4.90). **Points**: 0. **Born**: 25.12.68. **Height**: 6'6". **Weight**: 17st 4lbs. **Occupation**: Medical student. **Landmark**: Ever present on Wales bench in 1992 Five Nations' Championship.

RUSSELL, Mark. **1991/92 International category**: England B (NZ tour squad). **Position**: Flanker. **Club**: Harlequins. **Debut**: None. **Born**: Nairobi, Kenya, 16.12.65. **Height**: 6'4". **Weight**: 17st. **Family links**: Brother Stuart played for Wales (v. US Eagles, 1987). **Rep**: Univ of Capetown (SA), Western Province (SA), London (1991 Australia tour).

RUSSELL, Peter. **1991/92 International category**: Ireland Full (tour squad). **Position**: Outside-half. **Club**: Instonians. **Born**: 22.2.62. **Height**: 5'9". **Weight**: 12st. **Occupation**: Bank official. **Debut**: England 23, Ireland 0, 1990. **Caps**: 1. **Points**: 0. **B caps**: 1 (Scotland 22, Ireland 22, 1989). B points: 14 (1c,4p). **Touchline**: Tennis for Ulster Schools.

RYAN, Dean. **1991/92 International category**: England B (NZ tour). **Positions**: Flanker, No.8. **Club**: Wasps. Full debut: Argentina 12, England 25, 1990. Full caps: 2 (also: lost 13–15 v. Argentina, 4.8.90). Full points: 4 (1t on debut). **B caps**: 5 (v. 88:A, 90:Em. A, 91:Sp, I, F). B points: 4 (1t: v. Sp, 20.1.91). **Height**: 6'6". **Weight**: 17st.

SANDERS, Ian. **1991/92 International category**: England U-21. **Position**: Scrum-half. **Club**: Bath. **Debut**: Netherlands 12, England U-21 48, 1992. **Caps**: 1. **Points**: 4 (1t). **Height**: 5'9". **Weight**: 12st 10lbs. **Rep**: St Ives (1989/90), England 16-Group (1986/87), Colts (1989/90); South West Division (1991/92).

SCOTT, Peter. **1991/92 International category**: Ireland U-21. **Position**: Blindside flanker. **Club**: University College Cork. **Debut**: Wales U-21 22, Ireland U-21 15, 1991. **Caps**: 1. **Points**: 0. **Born**: 13.1.71. **Height**: 6'. **Weight**: 13st 1lb.

SCOTT, Stephen. **1991/92 International category**: Scotland U-21 (bench). **Position**: Hooker. **Club**: Melrose. **Debut**: None (bench: Scotland U-21 19, Wales U-21 28, 1992). **Born**: 26.7.73. **Height**: 6'. **Weight**: 14st. **Rep**: South of Scotland U-15, U-18, U-19, U-21.

SLEIGHTHOLME, Jonathan. **1991/92 International category**: England U-21. **Position**: Wing. **Club**: Wakefield. **Debut**: Ireland U-21 19, England U-21 10, 1991. **Caps**: 2 (also: 21–21 v. French Armed Forces. **Points**: 0. **Height**: 5'11". **Weight**: 13st 6lbs. **Rep**: Hull Ionians, Yorkshire-North-England Colts, England U-21, Students.

SMITH, Thomas J. **1991/92 International category**: Scotland U-21 (bench). **Position**: Prop. **Club**: Dundee HSFP. **Debut**: None (bench: Scotland U-21 19, Wales U-21 28, 1992). **Born**: 31.10.71. **Height**: 5'10". **Weight**: 15st 7lbs. **Rep**: Scottish Schools (two seasons).

STEELE, John. **1991/92 International category**: England B (NZ tour). **Position**: Outside-half. **Club**: Northampton. **Debut**: England B 31, Namibia 16 (2.11.90). **Caps**: 1. **Points**: 0. **Born**: 9.8.64. **Height**: 5'10". **Weight**: 13st. **Rep**: Army (capt in Royal Artillery), Combined Services, Midlands.

THOMAS, Damon. **1991/92 International category**: Wales U-21. **Position**: Loosehead prop. **Club**: Pontypool. **Debut**: Wales U-21 22, Ireland U-21 15, 1991. **Caps**: 1. **Points**: 0. **Born**: 22.11.71. **Height**: 5'9". **Weight**: 14st 10lbs.

THOMSON, Murray M. **1991/92 International category**: Scotland U-21. **Position**: Fullback. **Club**: Stewart's-Melville FP. **Debut**: Scotland U-21 19, Wales U-21 28, 1992. **Caps**: 1. **Points**: 0. **Born**: 10.1.72. **Height**: 6'3". **Weight**: 15st. **Rep**: Scottish Schools and Scotland U-19.

THOMPSON, Christopher. **1991/92 International category**: England U-21. **Position**: Fullback. **Club**: Sheffield. **Debut**: Netherlands 12, England U-21 48, 1992. **Caps**: 1. **Points**: 20 (1t,5c,2p). **Height**: 6'. **Weight**: 11st 3lbs. **Rep**: Cheshire & North U-21 (1991–92); English Universities (1991/92), Students U-21 (1991/92).

THOMPSON, Gavin John. **1991/92 International category**: England B bench. **Position**: Centre. **Club**: Harlequins. **B caps**: 5 (v. Em. A, Sp, I, F, It). **B points**: 0. **U-21 caps**: 3. **U-21 points**: 12 (3t: v. R, Neth, FAF). **Born**: 30.8.69. **Height**: 6'. **Weight**: 13st 6lbs. **Landmarks**: Capt England U-21s (1989/90 v. R/Neth). Toured Arg with Eng (1990).

THORNEYCROFT, Harvey Spencer. **1991/92 International category**: England B (NZ tour). **Position**: Wing. **Club**: Northampton. **U-21 Debut**: Romania U-21 13, England U-21 54, 1989. **U-21 caps**: 3 (also: 24–3 v. Neth, 29.4.90; 23–16 v. FAF, 12.5.90). **Points**: 12 (3t: 1vR,2vN). **Born**: 22.2.69. **Height**: 6'. **Weight**: 14st.

TOLAND, Liam Thomas. **1991/92 International category**: Ireland U-21. **Positions**: Flanker, No.8. **Club**: Old Crescent. **Debut**: Wales U-21 22, Ireland U-21 15, 1991. **Caps**: 2 (also: 19–10 v. Eng, 1991). **Points**: 0. **Born**: 18.6.72. **Height**: 6'2". **Weight**: 14st 7lbs. **Rep**: Munster Schools (1988–90), Irish Schools (1989/90), Munster U-20 (1990–92).

TONKIN, W Marrack. **1991/92 International category**: Scotland U-21. **Position**: Centre. **Club**: Currie. **Debut**: Scotland U-21 19, Wales U-21 28, 1992. **Caps**: 1. **Points**: 0. **Born**: 5.2.72. **Height**: 5'9". **Weight**: 12st 10lbs. **Rep**: Scottish Schools (U-15) and Scotland U-18.

UBOGU, Victor Eriakpo. **1991/92 International category**: England B (bench). **Position**: Loosehead prop. **Club**: Bath. **Debut**: England B 12, Emerging Australians 12, 1990. **Caps**: 2 (also: England B 50, Spain 6, Jan 1991). **Points**: 8 (2t v. Spain). **Born**: Lagos, Nigeria, 8.9.64. **Height**: 5'9". **Weight**: 16st. **Occupation**: Surveyor.

WALLACE, Paul. **1991/92 International category**: Ireland U-21. **Position**: Tighthead prop. **Club**: University College Cork. **Debut**: Wales U-21 22, Ireland U-21 15, 1991. **Caps**: 2 (also: Ireland U-21 19, England U-21 10, 1991). **Points**: 0. **Born**: 30.12.71. **Height**: 5'11". **Weight**: 14st 8lbs.

WEST, Richard John. **1991/92 International category**: England U-21. **Position**: Lock. **Club**: Gloucester. **Debut**: Netherlands 20, England U-21 20, 1991. **Caps**: 3 (also: 1991/92 v. Ireland, French Armed Forces). **Points**: 0. **Born**: 20.3.71. **Height**: 6'8". **Weight**: 16st 7lbs. **Occupation**: Agricultural student.

WILLIAMS, Andrew. **1991/92 International category**: Wales U-21. **Position**: Lock. **Club**: Maesteg. **Debut**: Wales U-21 22, Ireland U-21 15, 1991. **Caps**: 1. **Points**: 0. **Born**: 31.3.71. **Height**: 6'3". **Weight**: 15st 7lbs. **Occupation**: Emcee Systems (Bridgend).

WILLIAMS, Jason Alan. **1991/92 International category**: Wales U-21. **Position**: Outside-half. **Club**: Abertillery. **Debut**: Scotland U-21 19, Wales U-21 28, 1992. **U-21 caps**: 1. **Points**: 0. **Born**: 5.8.72. **Height**: 5'11". **Weight**: 11st 12lbs. **Occupation**: Labourer (Warwills Ltd).

WILLS, Stephen Richard. **1991/92 International category**: England U-21. **Positions**: Wing, fullback. **Club**: Leicester. **Debut**: Netherlands 18, England U-21 20, 1991. **Caps**: 3 (also: 10–19 v. Ire, 1991; 48–12 v. FAF, 1992). **Points**: 22 (1t v. Neth, 3t v. FAF, 2p v. Ire). **Born**: 26.12.70. **Height**: 5'10". **Weight**: 12st 10lbs.

WOODS, Niall. **1991/92 International category**: Ireland U-21. **Position**: Wing. **Club**: Blackrock College. **Debut**: Wales U-21 22, Ireland U-21 15, 1991. **Caps**: 2 (also: Ireland U-21 19, England U-21 10, 1991). **Points**: 19 (1t,2c,1p v. Wales; 1c,2p v. England). **Born**: 21.6.71. **Height**: 5'11". **Weight**: 11st 8lbs.

RETIREES

Ackford, P. J. — England

Full Name: Paul John Ackford
1991/92 International category:
England Full
Club: Harlequins
Position: Lock
Height: 6′6′ **Weight:** 17st 4lbs
Occupation: Police officer, New
Scotland Yard
Born: Hanover, West Germany,
26.2.58
Family: Suzie (wife)
Family links with rugby: Father
(Colin) played for Army
Former clubs: Plymouth Albion,
Rosslyn Park, Met Police
International debut: England 28,
Australia 19, 1988
Five Nations' debut: England 12,
Scotland 12, 1989
Best moments in rugby: Final
whistle in decisive third Test,
Australia against 1989 Lions.
Winning 1991 Grand Slam
Worst moments in rugby: Losing
1992 Pilkington Cup final to Bath
with last kick of extra time. Losing
1990 Grand Slam decider to
Scotland
Most embarrassing moment:
Losing ball to Rob Andrew in
mauling practice
Most respected opponent:
England lock Wade Dooley –
because he's bigger than me
Biggest influence on career: Phil

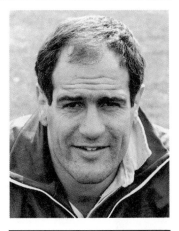

	apps	pts
England B (**1979**)		
Last Season	0 caps	0
England (**1988**)		
Last Season	6 caps	0
Career	22 caps	4
Lions 1989	3 Tests	0

Caps (22): 1988 A 1989 S, I, F, W,
R, Fj. Lions-A(1,2,3) 1990 I, F,
W, S, Arg(b) 1991 W, S(a), I,
F(a), A(a) wc-NZ, It, F(b),
S(b), A(b)

Points (4 – 1t): 1989 Fj(1t)

Keith-Roach (taught me about tight forward play on my first excursion into senior rugby)

Serious injuries: Assorted shoulder and rib injuries

Other sporting achievements: Worst Celebrity-Am golfer on the circuit

Best memory last season: Beating France in the World Cup quarter-final

Suggestions to improve rugby: *On-field* – Let the game evolve naturally. Resist television and administrators' trying to force the pace. *Off-field* – Introduce a compulsory retiring age of 55 for all alickadoos

Notable landmarks in rugby career: Spotting former *Daily Mail* rugby correspondent Terry O'Connor buying a drink. Being complimented by a back – it must happen one day. Had to wait until aged 30 for England debut, 28–19 win over touring Australians at Twickenham (5 Nov 1988). From there, quickly earned reputation as the world's premier number two line-out jumper and by the end of his first senior international season was in the 1989 Lions team which defeated Australia 2–1 in test series Down Under. A 1979 Cambridge Blue, he represented England B that same season against France (Sep 1979) and London from 1981 onwards. Was a member of England's 1991 Grand Slam and World Cup final sides before retiring on 23 Nov 1991. Came out of retirement to answer Quins' SOS call and play in 1992 Pilkington Cup final against Bath, three days after representing Clapham Police Division in Dowswell Cup final. Lost both matches by combined total of just four points!

Touchlines: Cooking, eating, social golf, keep-fit

Player to watch: Andy Mullins (Harlequins)

Player of the year: John Eales (Australia)

Mickey Skinner finds his progress blocked by Ireland hooker Steve Smith during England's 38–9 win at Twickenham

Calder, F.   Scotland

Full Name: Finlay Calder, OBE
1991/92 International category:
Scotland Full
Club: Stewart's-Melville FP
Position: Flanker
Height: 6'1" **Weight:** 15st 7lbs
Occupation: Grain shipper with
Ceres (UK) Ltd
Born: Haddington, 20.8.57
Family: Liz (wife), David (son) and
Hazel (daughter)
Former club: Melrose
International debut: Scotland 18,
France 17, 1986
Five Nations' debut: As above
Best moment in rugby: Winding
up John Jeffrey prior to 1990 Grand
Slam decider against England
Worst moment in rugby: Being
referred to as 'Buftie' by younger
members of club
Most respected opponent: Michael
Jones (Auckland & New Zealand) –
quite simply the best
Biggest influence on career: Jim
Telfer (Scotland coach)
Other sporting achievements:
Birdie 3 at second hole at Lauder
Golf Club
Best memory last season: Seeing
Pierre Berbizier playing in my guest
team in a game on the Orkney Islands
Suggestions to improve rugby:
On-field – Administrators must
consult those who are playing about

	apps	pts
Scotland B (**1983**)		
Career	2 caps	0
Scotland (**1986**)		
Last Season	6 caps	0
v. Barbarians	1 app	4
Career	34 caps	8
Lions 1989	3 Tests	0

Caps (34): **1986** F, W, E, I, R **1987** I,
F, W, E wc-F, Z, R, NZ **1988** I,
F, W, E **1989** W, E, I, F, R
1990 I, F, W, E, NZ(1,2) **1991**
R wc-J, I, WS, E, NZ

Points (8 – 2t): **1988** W(1t) **1990** F(1t)

rule-changes rather than present them with *faits accomplis*. Speak *with* players
not *to* them. Someone like England hooker Brian Moore is so eloquent and
well-versed. His thoughts should not be ignored. Referees need to be more
sympathetic to keeping games going. Follow example of French and Southern
Hemisphere officials: far more liberal stances and interested in keeping games
alive for benefit of fans rather than refereeing panels. Too many are out to
score points for themselves these days. Uniformity in laws between two

hemispheres. Take rucking: what is permitted in New Zealand is deemed foul in Scotland. But good rucking, although it looks ferocious, is as safe as anything. Referees must acquire a genuine understanding of rugby to be able to distinguish. *Off-field* – Uniformity desperately needed over amateurism debate. Work towards a more liberal stance and clear up present grey areas

Notable landmarks in rugby career: 1989 Scotland captain. Captained 1989 British Lions to 2–1 Test series win in Australia (Lions first for 15 years). Retired from game after Scotland's 1990 summer tour to New Zealand but personal request from Scotland coach Ian McGeechan led to comeback in 1991 World Cup, during which made five appearances. Also represented Scotland in 12–18 loss to Romania in Bucharest and caused near hysteria at Murrayfield when scoring try in non-cap match against centenary Barbarians which ended in 16–16 draw

Touchlines: Golf

Player to watch: Laurent Cabannes (Racing Club de France) – far and away the most exciting player in 1992 Five Nations' Championship

Player of the year: Laurent Cabannes (France)

Fallon, J. A. England

Full Name: James (**Jim**) Anthony Fallon

1991/92 International category: England B

Club: Bath

Position: Wing

Height: 6'1" **Weight:** 15st

Occupation: Rugby League player with Leeds RLFC

Born: Windsor, 27.3.65

Family: Single

Family links with rugby: Father (Terry) won Oxford Blues 1953–55, was travelling reserve for Ireland and coach to England 16-Group

Former clubs: Tinmouth, Oxford Polytechnic, Libourne (Fr), Richmond

International debut (B): France 15, England 15, 1990

Best moment in rugby: Winning 1991/92 Courage Championship with Bath

Worst moment in rugby: Bath being docked a point by the RFU for fielding an ineligible player during 1991/92 League season − could have cost us the title

Most respected opponent: Rory Underwood (Leicester, RAF & England)

	apps	pts
England B (1990)		
Last Season	4 caps	12
Career	5 caps	12

Best memory last season: Scoring two tries in Bath's 27–18 extra-time Pilkington Cup semi-final win over Gloucester

Suggestions to improve rugby: *On-field* − New maul law will suit those teams with a more expansive game but not convinced it is a good move. But as a wing, well pleased with five points for a try. *Off-field* − Relax amateur laws

Notable landmarks in rugby career: Played for Tinmouth first team as a Colt. Joined Richmond when came to London for work and, from there, won divisional and national B honours before joining Bath in summer of 1990. An everpresent in England B's 1991/92 'Grand Slam' (v. S, I, F, It), scoring two tries against Ireland B (won 47–15, Richmond 31 Jan 1992) and one in the 22–18 defeat of France B (Paris 15 Feb 1992), he managed 30 tries in his 44 Bath appearances, including 20 in 25 outings last season. His most precious two came in the Cup semi-final defeat of Gloucester. Selected to tour New Zealand with England B last summer, he instead accepted a five-year £200,000 deal from Leeds RLFC to switch codes in May 1992

Halliday, S. J.   England

Full Name: Simon John Halliday
1991/92 International category: England Full
Club: Harlequins
Positions: Centre, wing
Height: 6′ **Weight:** 14st
Occupation: Stockbroker with UBS Phillips and Drew
Born: Haverfordwest, 13.7.60
Family: Suzanne (wife) and Sophie (daughter)
Family links with rugby: Father (Gordon) played for Norfolk and Royal Navy
Former clubs: Oxford University, Bath
International debut: England 28, Canada 0, 1983

Five Nations' debut: England 21, Wales 18, 1986

Best moment in rugby: Final whistle of England 28, Australia 19 (5 Nov 1988)

Worst moment in rugby: Losing 6–33 to Scotland (15 Feb 1986)

Most embarrassing moments: Having hairstyle criticised by Will Carling in commentary of Romania/England match (1989); leg bandage slipping down to my ankle as I broke through to score for England against Australia (1988). Had my journey been any longer the support would have tripped me up!

Most respected opponent: Ray Gravell (Llanelli & Wales) – very tough to knock down

Biggest influences on career: Jack Rowell (Bath coach), Jon Horton (Bath)

Serious injuries: Fractured dislocation of left foot, playing for Somerset v. Middlesex in 1983 County Championship (cost me three years of International rugby), torn hamstrings

Other sporting achievements: Oxford cricket Blue (1980). Proud owner of first-class century (113 n.o. v. Kent). Played for Dorset and Minor Counties

Best memory last season: Selection for World Cup semi-final against Scotland and final whistle of that match (I am half-Scottish)

Suggestions to improve rugby: *On-field* – Kicks at goal to be restricted to foul play and deliberate offside. Introduce home and away League fixtures but reduce other commitments. England structure is so good now that we can afford to do away with the Divisional Championship which serves no useful purpose. *Off-field* – Recognition of time players spend away from work – pro-rata compensation. Show players what they are doing is appreciated. Present situation is still embarrassing, though less so than a year ago. However, still not the level of communication and rapport between adminstrators and players that I would like to see

Notable landmarks in rugby career: Played for Dorset & Wilts U-19s. Won three Blues for rugby at Oxford (1979,80,81) and one for cricket. Captained South West to victories over USA and Australia (both 1988). After six winning Cup finals – five with Bath (1985–86–87–89–90), one with Harlequins (1991) – finally emerged a loser last season when Quins were beaten by Stuart Barnes' late dropped goal for Bath. Retired from club and country afterwards, having contributed to England's two Grand Slams (1991–92) and run to 1991 World Cup final, playing in climax against Australia

Touchlines: Golf, DIY

Player to watch: Ian Hunter (Northampton)

Player of the year: Jon Webb (England)

	apps	pts
England B (1985)		
Last Season	0 caps	0
England (1986)		
Last Season	7 caps	4
Career	23 caps	8

Caps (23): **1986** W, S **1987** S **1988** S, I(1,2), A(a1), A(b) **1989** S, I, F, W, Ro, Fj(R) **1990** W, S **1991** wc-US, S, A **1992** S, I, F, W

Points (8 – 2t): **1988** A(b:1t) **1992** I(1t)

Jeffrey, J.   Scotland

Full Name: John Jeffrey
1991/92 International category:
Scotland Full
Club: Kelso
Positions: Flanker, No.8
Height: 6′4″ **Weight:** 14st 5lbs
Occupation: Farmer
Born: Kelso, 25.3.59
Family: Single
International debut: Scotland 12,
Australia 37, 1984
Five Nations' debut: Scotland 15,
Ireland 18, 1985
Best moment in rugby: Winning
1990 Five Nations' Grand Slam with
Scotland
Worst moment in rugby: Scotland
losing 6–9 to England (October
1991) at Murrayfield in World Cup
semi-final. We let the supporters
down by not playing well. We could
have won the game if we had played
it right
Most embarrassing moment:
Being 'wound-up' by Fin Calder the
day before the 1990 Grand Slam
decider against England
Most respected opponent: Gary
Armstrong (Jedforest & Scotland)
Serious injuries: Cartilage
operation whilst at school, senility!
Best memory last season: Scotland
reaching semi-finals of World Cup
Suggestions to improve rugby:
On-field – Work harder on fitness
and enjoy the game more. Do not
lose sight of the fact that we play
rugby for enjoyment. *Off-field –*
None. Too many people indulge in

	apps	pts
Scotland B (**1983**)		
Last Season	0 caps	0
Career	3 caps	
Scotland (**1984**)		
Last Season	5 caps	8
Career	40 caps	44
Lions 1986		
1989		

Caps (40): **1984** A **1985** I, E **1986** F,
W, E, I, R **1987** I, F, W, E
wc-F, Z, R **1988** I, W, A **1989**
W, E, I, F, Fj, R **1990** I, F, W,
E, NZ(1,2), Arg **1991** F, W, E,
I wc-J, I, WS, E, NZ

Points (44 – 11t): **1986** W(1t), R(1t)
1987 W(1t) wc-Z(1t), R(3t)
1989 E(1t), I(1t) **1991**
wc-WS(2t)

chucking oil on the fire over the amateurism question. Progress in Scotland
is being made and we have a good relationship with the SRU
Notable landmarks in rugby career: Shares with Derek White the Scottish

forward try-scoring record with 11 tries in cap Internationals. Member of both British Lions and Five Nations' teams in the 1986 IRB celebration matches. Captained Kelso to McEwan's Scottish League division one title in 1988/89. Most capped Kelso International, with 40. Played five times for 1989 British Lions' midweek team in Australia and represented 1990 Home Unions XV against Europe in Romania Appeal match at Twickenham. Scored two tries in Scotland's 28–6 quarter-final World Cup defeat of Western Samoa. Retired from international rugby following Scotland's campaign, with defeat by New Zealand in the third place play-off representing his final appearance
Touchlines: Golf, skiing
Player to watch: Gregor Townsend (Gala)
Player of the year: Timo Tagaloa (Western Samoa)

Kiernan, M. J.   Ireland

Full Name: Michael Joseph Kiernan
1991/92 International category: Retired
Club: Dolphin
Positions: Centre, wing
Height: 6′ **Weight:** 14st
Occupation: Director of Parfrey Murphy Financial Services
Born: Cork, 17.1.61
Family: Anne (wife) and Alison (daughter)
Family links with rugby: Father (Tom) is Ireland's most-capped fullback with 54 appearances between 1960–73
Former club: Lansdowne
International debut: Ireland 20, Wales 12, 1982
Five Nations' debut: As above
Best moment in rugby: Winning Triple Crown in 1985
Worst moment in rugby: British Lions losing 6–38 to New Zealand in fourth Test (1983)
Most respected opponent: Joe Stanley (Auckland & New Zealand)
Serious injuries: Depressed cheekbone (1988)
Other sporting achievements: National 200m sprint champion (1981)
Suggestions to improve rugby: *On-field* – Increase actual playing time (time ball is in play). *Off-field* – Address amateur dilemma. Danger that if left alone

sooner or later it will come to an unpleasant head. IRB must govern – at present there is a lack of cohesion between it and member unions

Notable landmarks in rugby career: Record points scorer for Ireland, having taken tally to 308 since winning first cap in 1982 as a replacement against Wales. Set Irish record for overseas tour with 65 on 1985 tour of Japan. Began representative career with Schools cap in 1979 and toured South Africa with Ireland in 1981 and North America (scoring 61 points) in 1989. Scored two tries for World XV in 38–42 loss to Australia in Australian Bicentennial match (May 1988). Landed penalty for Ireland B in 24–10 win over England B last season at Old Belvedere

Touchlines: Golf (handicap 14), tennis, athletics

Player to watch: Jack Clarke (Dolphin)

	apps	pts
Ireland B (**1991**)		
Last Season	1 cap	3
Career	1 cap	3
Ireland (**1982**)		
Last Season	2 caps	25
Career	43 caps	308
Lions 1983 1986	3 Tests	0

Caps (43): **1982** W(R), E, S, F **1983** S, F, W, E. Lions-NZ(2,3,4) **1984** E, S, A **1985** S, F, W, E **1986** F, W, E, S, R **1987** E, S, F, W(a) wc-W(b), C, A **1988** S, F, W, E(a, b), WS **1989** F, W, E, S **1990** E, S, F, W, Arg **1991** F

Points (308 – 6t,40c,62p,6dg): **1983** S(1t) **1984** S(1t), A(3p) **1985** S(2c,1p,1dg), F(5p), W(2c,3p), E(2p,1dg) **1986** F(3p), W(1c,2p), E(1c,2p), S(1c,1p), R(7c,2p) **1987** E(1t,1c,1p), S(1c,1p,1dg), F(1c,1p), W(a:2c,1p) wc-W(b:2p), C(5c,2p,1dg), A(1t,2c,1p) **1988** S(2c,1p,1dg), F(2p), W(1c,1p), E(a:1dg), E(b:1c), WS(1t,4c,2p) **1989** F(1c,5p), W(1c,3p), E(1p), S(3c,1p) **1990** S(2p), F(4p), I(1c), Arg(1t,4p) **1991** F(3p)

Lenihan, D. G.   Ireland

Full Name: Donal Gerald Lenihan
1991/92 International category:
Ireland Full
Club: Cork Constitution
Position: Lock
Height: 6'4" **Weight:** 17st
Occupation: Building Society
manager
Born: Cork, 12.9.59
Family: Married with son
Former club: Univ College, Cork
International debut: Ireland 12,
Australia 16, 1981
Five Nations' debut: Ireland 20,
Wales 12, 1982
Best moments in rugby: Winning
two Triple Crowns with Ireland and
1990/91 All-Ireland League success
with Cork Constitution
Most respected opponent: Former
England lock Maurice Colclough
Best memory last season: Taking
part in World Cup tournament
Serious injuries: Broken nose,
finger
Suggestions to improve rugby:
On-field – Standardise refereeing
interpretations in Southern and
Northern Hemispheres
**Notable landmarks in rugby
career:** Made Ireland debut for
Schools (1977) and within four years
had graduated through U-23s
(1979) and Ireland B (1980) to full
status (1981). Shared in
Constitution's 1990/91 All-Ireland
League triumph and, in same season,
captained Ireland to 20–18 defeat

	apps	pts
Ireland B (**1980**)		
Last Season	0 caps	0
Ireland (**1981**)		
Last Season	5 caps	0
Career	52 caps	4
Lions 1983		
1986		
1989		

Caps (52): **1981** A **1982** W, E, S, F
1983 S, F, W, E **1984** F, W, E,
S, A **1985** S, F, W, E **1986** F,
W, E, S, R **1987** E, S, F, W(a)
wc-W(b), C, T, A **1988** S, F,
W, E(a, b), WS, It **1989** F, W,
E, S, NZ **1990** S, F, W, Arg
1991 Na(2) wc-Z, S, A **1992** W

Points (4 – 1t): **1987** S(1t)

over Argentina in Dublin before sustaining season-ending injury. Flew out to
replace injured Brian Rigney in Namibia (1991), playing in second Test as
prelude to three World Cup appearances and the 1992 Five Nations' loss to
Wales in Dublin, after which he retired. Tally of 52 caps makes him sixth

most-capped Irishman behind Mike Gibson (69), Willie John McBride (63), Fergus Slattery (61), Phil Orr (58) and Tom Kiernan (54)

Mullin, B. J.   Ireland

Full Name: Brendan John Mullin
1991/92 International category:
Ireland Full
Club: Blackrock College
Position: Centre
Height: 6'1" **Weight:** 13st
Occupation: Stockbroker with J & E
Davy (Dublin)
Born: Israel, 31.10.63
Family: Sharon (wife)
Former clubs: Trinity College
Dublin, Oxford Univ, London Irish
International debut: Ireland 9,
Australia 16, 1984
Five Nations' debut: Scotland 15,
Ireland 18, 1985
Best moment in rugby: Selection
for 1989 Lions

Worst moment in rugby: Ireland's
dreadful campaign at 1987 World
Cup
Most respected opponents: Brett
Papworth (ex-NSW & Australia)
and Jeremy Guscott (Bath &
England)
Biggest influence on career: Jim
Burns (school hurdles coach)
Serious injuries: Operation on knee
cartilage (1989/90)
Other sporting achievements:
International hurdling for Ireland
Best memory last season: Coming
so close to beating Australia in
quarter-finals of World Cup
Suggestions to improve rugby:
Off-field – Rugby Union must try not
to compete with Rugby League.
Changing the face of the game is no

	apps	pts
Ireland B (**1983**)		
Last Season	0 caps	0
Ireland (**1984**)		
Last Season	8 caps	2
Career	45 caps	62
Lions 1986		
1989	1 Test	0

Caps (45): **1984** A **1985** S, W, E **1986**
F, W, E, S, R **1987** E, S, F, W
wc-W, C, T, A **1988** S, F, W,
E(a, b), WS, It **1989** F, W, E, S,
NZ. Lions-A(1) **1990** E, S, W,
Arg **1991** F, W, E, S, Na(1,2)
wc-J, S, A **1992** W, E, S

Points (62 – 15t,1c): **1985** E(1t) **1986**
E(1t), R(2t) **1987** W(1t)
wc-T(3t) **1988** S(1t), WS(1t)
1989 F(1t), S(2t) **1991** W(1t),
S(1t), Na(1:1c)

solution to anything. More important than ever that the administration of the game is carried out on a more accurate and professional basis. International Rugby Board must offer some direction and leadership. Rugby has outgrown what the archaic IRB was set up to administer. Digressionary element handed to Unions by IRB is ridiculous – has led to utter confusion

Notable landmarks in rugby career: Representative career began when played six times for Irish Schools (1981–82), three as captain. Made B debut against Scotland in 1983 and following season broke into full team. Played for 1986 Lions against The Rest in Cardiff to mark centenary of IRB. Scored three tries against Tonga in 1987 World Cup. Won two Oxford Blues (1986, 87). Voted 1988/89 Irish Player of Year. Leading try-scorer for 1989 Lions with seven. Played for Lions in first Test against Australia (lost 12–30), and against the ANZAC XV (won 19–15), and for 1989 Home Unions in 29–27 defeat of France. Set Irish try-scoring record with No.15 in 25–28 loss to Scotland at Murrayfield in 1991 Championship (16 Mar 1991), having scored first back in 1985 against England on fourth appearance. Sequence of 29 consecutive appearances broken when missed 1990 Paris match and he missed that same fixture two years after taking decision to retire, three-quarters of the way through 1992 Championship, citing personal and business reasons

Touchlines: Tennis

Player to watch: Richard Wallace (Garryowen)

Player of the year: Will Carling (England)

Rendall, P. A. G.   England

Full Name: Paul Anthony George Rendall

1991/92 International category: England Full

Club: Wasps

Position: Loosehead prop

Height: 5′11″ **Weight:** 16st 8lbs

Occupation: Paid administrator to Bracknell RFC/self-employed with RPG Engineering

Born: London, 18.2.54

Family: Sue (wife), Kim (daughter) and Daniel (son)

Former club: Slough (1970–75)

International debut: England 15, Wales 24, 1984

Five Nations' debut: As above

Best moment in rugby: England beating France 26–7 in Paris (1990)
Worst moments in rugby: Not being selected for 1989 British Lions. Losing 1990 Grand Slam decider to Scotland
Most embarrassing moment: Being asked to pay for extra breakfast after England v. France 1989 (ate three)
Most respected opponent: Jeff Probyn (Wasps & England) – a boring so-and-so!
Biggest influence on career: Geoff Cooke (England manager)

	apps	pts
England B (1981)		
Last Season	0 caps	0
England (1984)		
Last Season	1 cap	0
	5 reps	
Career	28 caps	0

Caps (28): **1984** W, SA(2) **1986** W, S **1987** I, F, S wc-A, J, W **1988** F, W, S, I(a, b), A(a1, a2), A(b) **1989** S, I, F, W, R **1990** I, F, W, S **1991** wc-It(R)

Points: Nil

Best memory last season: England's run to World Cup Final
Suggestions to improve rugby: *On-field* – Rugby did not need the new laws. It would have been better to have concentrated on improving standards of refereeing. Implement two-referee system. *Off-field* – Pay for broken time. Take away fence which RFU are sitting on so it has to make a decision one way or another. International Rugby Board should start making decisions on world rugby
Notable landmarks in rugby career: Gained first cap aged 30 against Wales (1984). Played for World XV against New Zealand (Tokyo 1987) and in South Africa (1989). Toured with England to Australia, Argentina, USA, Canada, South Africa and Italy, as well as 1987 World Cup. Only International points came from a try in non-cap match against USA (1982). Represented centenary Barbarians in 31–24 win over Wales in 1990/91. Joined Askeans along with Jeff Probyn prior to World Cup but returned to Wasps after tournament. Selected for England's 1991 World Cup squad and turned out as a 53rd-minute replacement for Probyn against Italy (8 Oct 1991)
Touchlines: Reading Halsbury
Player to watch: David Pears (Harlequins)
Player of the year: Wade Dooley (England)

Ring, M. G.   Wales

Full Name: Mark Gerard Ring
1991/92 International category:
Wales Full
Club: Cardiff
Positions: Centre, fullback
Height: 6′ **Weight:** 13st 10lbs
Occupation: Company director
with Ringdale Industrial Roofing Ltd
Born: Cardiff, 15.10.62
Family: Single
Family links with rugby: Father
(Brian) played for Leicester,
Maesteg, Glamorgan Wanderers
and Tredegar
Former club: Pontypool
International debut: Wales 13,
England 13, 1983
Five Nations' debut: As above
Best moment in rugby: Welsh
Rugby Player of Year 1985
Worst moment in rugby: Injury to
left knee which meant two barren
seasons
Most embarrassing moment:
Showing off in Sevens. Ran to
try-line with ball behind back. When
placed ball over try line it slipped
from my grasp
Most respected opponents:
Warwick Taylor (Canterbury &
New Zealand) – showed me a new
dimension to centre play – and
Jeremy Guscott (Bath & England)
Biggest influence in career: My
father
Serious injuries: Torn ligaments in
both knees; arthritic right knee

	apps	pts
Wales B (1983)		
Career	2 caps	23
Wales (1983)		
Last Season	4 caps	22
Career	32 caps	34

Caps (32): **1983** E **1984** A **1985** S, I,
F **1987** I(a) wc-I(b), T, A. US
1988 E, S, I, F, NZ(1,2) **1989**
NZ **1990** F, E, S, I, Na(1,2), Ba
1991 E, S, I, F(a), F(b) wc-WS,
Arg, A

Points (34 – 1t,3c,8p): **1987** wc-I(b:1t)
1988 NZ(1:1p), NZ(2:1c,1p)
1991 F(b:1c,1p) wc-WS(1c,1p),
Arg(3p), A(1p)

Other sporting achievements: Welsh baseball international (four caps)
Best memory last season: My latest comeback
Suggestions to improve rugby: *On-field* – Leave rules alone. Most back
divisions have enough difficulty executing the basics like passing down the
line. Give touch judges more authority in offside laws around fringes. Referees

invariably guess. In line-out, return to double-banking and lifting as prevalent in shambolic 1970s (far better). Relax and enjoy every game. Take advice from coaches and fellow players. Study videos of great players. *Off-field* – Administrators are botching up the game completely. Learn from Rugby League in way they market their game. Too many people in charge are out of touch with the modern game. Invite younger men to join set-up. Time to move a step nearer full professionalism. Look at me: I am retired at 29 with an old man's knee, having played solidly since I was seven. I have nothing to show for my playing career. Top players should benefit for all the effort they put in, and their bosses should not lose out either. As an employer I could not afford to employ a rugby player who did nothing

Notable landmarks in rugby career: Played outside-half for Wales Youth before Cardiff (first spell) moved him to centre. Bagged three Welsh Cup winners' medals. Played in Cardiff's 1984 defeat of Australia, for Barbarians against Australia in 1988 and for World XV v. South Africa (1989). Toured with Wales to New Zealand (1988) and Namibia (1990) but was overlooked for 1991 trip to Australia. Benefited from Alan Davies' appointment as coach at the start of the 1991/92 season: starting each of Wales' three World Cup games, against Western Samoa, Argentina and Australia and kicking six penalty goals and a conversion

Touchlines: Horse racing fanatic. Becoming a fan of Rugby League (esp. Wigan). Play Sunday soccer. Interested in Brazilian soccer players who are given bad names because of off-field habits

Touchlines: All sport, especially baseball and soccer

Player to watch: Ian McKim (Cardiff)

Player of the year: David Campese (Australia)

Sole, D. M. B. Scotland

Full Name: David Michael Barclay Sole
1991/92 International category: Scotland Full
Club: Edinburgh Academicals
Position: Prop
Height: 5'11" **Weight:** 16st 4lbs
Occupation: Grain buyer for United Distillers
Born: Aylesbury, 8.5.62
Family: Jane (wife), Jamie (son) and Gemma (daughter)
Former clubs: Exeter Univ, Toronto Scottish, Bath
International debut: Scotland 18, France 17, 1986
Five Nations' debut: As above
Best moment in rugby: Captaining Scotland to 1990 Five Nations' Grand Slam
Worst moments in rugby: Coming so close to winning second Test against New Zealand (Auckland, 23 Jun 1990) before losing 18–21
Most respected opponents: Iain Milne (Heriot's FP & Scotland) and Jean-Pierre Garuet (Lourdes & France) – two of the world's strongest scrummagers, who don't bend the rules, but use their strength to succeed
Biggest influence on career: Four years spent at Bath RFC
Serious injuries: Broken nose and cheekbone playing in Bath's 12–3 win against Moseley in 1987 John Player Cup quarter-final

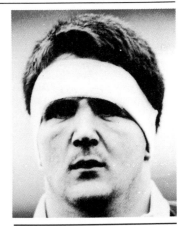

	apps	pts
Scotland B (**1983**)		
Last Season	0 caps	0
Career	5 caps	
Scotland (**1986**)		
Last Season	12 caps	4
1992	Tour to Australia	
Career	44 caps	12
Scotland VII (**1991**)	Hong Kong Sevens	
Lions 1989	3 Tests	0

Caps (44): 1986 F, W 1987 I, F, W, E wc-F, Z, R, NZ 1988 I, F, W, E, A 1989 W, E, I, F, Fj, R. Lions-A(1,2,3) 1990 I, F, W, E, NZ(1,2), Arg 1991 F, W, E, I, R wc-J, I, WS, E, NZ 1992 E, I, F, W, A(1,2)

Points (12 – 3t): 1989 R(1t) 1990 NZ(1:1t) 1992 A(2:1t)

Best memory last season: Half-time team talk as captain of the Barbarians against the East Midlands (1991/92 Mobbs Memorial match) when I told the team they were not smiling enough
Suggestions to improve rugby: *On-field* – Pleased to see more points

awarded for a try. Hopefully that will have the effect of taking the emphasis off kicking. *Off-field* – The question of amateurism needs urgent attention. For a start where is the line drawn between rugby-related and non-rugby-related activities? Surely there is no difference. Players' commitment to international rugby is becoming ever greater but at our own expense. Yet the set-up is totally different for the Southern Hemisphere nations. The IRB must make and enforce universal regulations.

Notable landmarks in rugby career: Won 1987 John Player Cup winners' medal with Bath (won 19–12 v. Wasps, 2 May 1987). Made Scotland debut as one of six newcomers against France (won 18–17, Murrayfield, 17 Jan 1986). Appointed Scotland captain for Scotland 38, Fiji 17 (Murrayfield, 28 Oct 1989) and went on to become Scotland's most capped leader with 23 starts prior to the 1992 tour to Australia, including the 1990 Grand Slam decider when he led Scotland slowly onto the field prior to beating England. Also captained Lions against New South Wales B (won 39–19, Dubbo 27 Jun 1989) and the Anzacs (won 19–15, Queensland 23 Jul 1989) during 1989 tour of Australia, Barbarians against 1989 All Blacks (lost 10–21, Twickenham 25 Nov 1989) and Home Unions against Europe in aid of the Romanian Appeal (won 43–18, Twickenham 22 Apr 1990). Recalls with great affection the £2 fine he imposed on anyone who kicked to touch during 1991 Barbarians' Easter Tour match at Cardiff. Ended playing career with try in second of two tests against Australia last summer

Player to watch: Eroni Clarke (Auckland)

Thorburn, P. H.   Wales

Full Name: Paul Huw Thorburn
1991/92 International category:
Wales Full
Club: Neath
Position: Fullback
Height: 6′ **Weight:** 13st 5lbs
Occupation: Sales manager for telecom company
Born: Rheindalen, West Germany, 24.11.62
Family: Ann (wife) and Kelly (daughter)
Family links with rugby: Father played for Cardiff 2nd XV. Brother had England Schools Trial
Former clubs: Swansea Univ, Ebbw Vale
International debut: France 14, Wales 3, 1985
Five Nations' debut: As above
Best moments in rugby: Kicking last-minute goal which beat Australia 22–21 and gave Wales third place in 1987 World Cup. Scoring first ever try for Wales against Namibia (1991)
Worst moment in rugby: Being dropped by Wales for 1988 game against England
Most embarrassing moment: Taking easy penalty kick for Neath against Sale. Scoreboard was directly behind posts and as I was about to strike ball it registered 3 extra points. I promptly missed
Most respected opponent: Serge Blanco (Biarritz & France)
Serious injuries: Broken leg, collarbone. Dislocated shoulder
Other sporting achievements: Cricket for Hereford and Worcester
Suggestions to improve rugby: Make it easier for players to compete

Wales B (1984)	apps	pts
Career	2 caps	32
Wales (1984)		
Last Season	1 cap	3
Career	37 caps	304

Caps (37): **1985** F, E, Fj **1986** E, S, I, F **1987** F, US wc-I, T, C, E, NZ, A **1988** S, I, F, WS, R(R) **1989** S, I, F, E, NZ **1990** F, E, S, I, Na(1,2), Ba **1991** E, S, I, F(a), A(a)

Points (304 – 2t, 43c, 70p): **1985** F(1p), E(2c,3p), Fj(3c,2p) **1986** E(1c,3p), S(5p), I(1c,3p), F(5p) **1987** F(3p), US(4c,2p) wc-I(1p), T(2c,2p), C(4c), E(2c), NZ(1c), A(2c,2p) **1988** S(2c,1p), I(1c,1p), F(1c,1p), WS(4c), R(R:1c,1p) **1989** I(3p), F(4p), E(1c,2p), NZ(3p) **1990** F(4p), E(1c), S(1c,1p), Na(1: 1t, 2c, 2p), Na(2:3c,3p), Ba(1t,1c,5p) **1991** E(1p), S(1c,2p), I(2c,2p), F(a:1p), A(a:1p)

in events all over world by compensating employers for time away from work
Notable landmarks in rugby career: Born in Europe, grew up in England, but played for Welsh Univs, UAU and Ebbw Vale before joining Neath. Record points scorer in Welsh rugby (304). Failed to score only twice in 37 appearances for Wales (v. Scotland 1989 and Ireland 1990). Set Welsh record when scoring 52 points in 1986 Five Nations' Championship. Among other fondest memories are 70-yard penalty goal which helped Wales beat Scotland in 1986, and injury-time kick that beat Ireland in 1988 to secure Welsh Triple Crown. Captained Wales ten times (won 1, drew 1, lost 8), including throughout 1990/91 five-match schedule. Broke Welsh single-match points-scoring record with 21 points (try, conversion and five penalty goals) in 24–31 loss to centenary Barbarians (caps awarded, 6 Oct 1990). Previous best (19) held by Jack Bancroft, Keith Jarrett and Phil Bennett. Toured to Australia in 1991 but proved an unhappy experience and he retired from international rugby on arrival home
Touchlines: Waterskiing, squash, golf
Player to watch: Scott Gibbs (Swansea)

Underwood, R.   England

Full Name: Rory Underwood
1991/92 International category: England Full
Club: Leicester & RAF
Position: Wing
Height: 5'9" **Weight:** 13st 7lbs
Occupation: RAF pilot
Born: Middlesbrough, 19.6.63
Family: Wendy (wife), Rebecca and Alexandra (daughters)
Family links with rugby: Brother (Tony) plays for Leicester, Cambridge Univ and England B
Former club: Middlesbrough
International debut: England 12, Ireland 9, 1984
Five Nations' debut: As above
Best moment in rugby: Winning first (1991) Grand Slam with England

Worst moment in rugby: England's 9–12 loss to Wales at Cardiff (1989)
Most embarrassing moment: Making error which led to Wales scoring crucial try against England in above match
Most respected opponent: Patrice Lagisquet (Bayonne & France)

Biggest influence on career: Geoff Cooke (England manager)
Other sporting achievements: Swam and played cricket for Barnard Castle School, which England team-mate Rob Andrew also attended
Best memory last season: England's second Grand Slam
Suggestions to improve rugby: *On-field* – RFU Committee working more with players in the future. At present some do, some do not. *Off-field* – Continued improvement by Unions in looking after players and wives. International Board must make unambiguous rulings concerning amateurism. Only reward should be in playing for natural enjoyment
Notable landmarks in rugby career: England's most-capped player (55) and record try-scorer (35). Scored two tries for Leicester

	apps	pts
England B (1982)		
Last Season	0 caps	0
England (1984)		
Last Season	12 caps	32
Career	55 caps	140
Lions 1986		
1989	3 Tests	0

Caps (55): **1984** I, F, W, A **1985** R, F, S, I, W **1986** W, I, F **1987** I, F, W, S wc-A, J, W **1988** F, W, S, I(1,2), A(a1, a2), Fj, A(b) **1989** S, I, F, W, R, Fj **1990** I, F, W, S, Arg(b) **1991** W, S, I, F, Fj, A wc-NZ, It, US, F, S, A **1992** S, I, F, W

Points (140 – 35t): **1984** F(1t) **1985** I(1t) **1987** wc-J(2t) **1988** I(1:2t), I(2:1t), A(a1:1t), A(a2:1t), Fj(2t), A(b:2t) **1989** Fj(5t) **1990** I(1t), F(1t), W(2t), Arg(b:3t) **1991** I(1t), F(1t), Fj(1t) wc-It(1t), US(2t), F(1t) **1992** S(1t), I(1t), F(1t)

against Barbarians in 1983 and, three months later, was in England team. Missed tour to Argentina in summer of 1990, due to RAF commitments, having already become England's most-capped back and highest try-scorer during 1989/90 season. Equalled Dan Lambert's 1907 England record of five tries in an international, against Fiji (won 58–23, Twickenham 4 Nov 1989). Previously played for England Colts, U-23 and B teams. Toured Australia with 1989 Lions, playing in all three Tests. Try scored in 16–7 defeat of Ireland during 1990/91 Grand Slam was most important of career (No.26). Also scored in 21–19 win over France (1991 Grand Slam decider). Last season notched a further eight tries: including four en route to World Cup Final and three *en route* to 1992 Grand Slam. Retired from international arena once back-to-back Grand Slams were safely in the bag
Touchlines: Crosswords, reading
Players to watch: Neil Back/Tony Underwood (both Leicester)
Player of the year: Dewi Morris (England)

White, D. B.   Scotland

Full Name: Derek Bolton White
1991/92 International category:
Scotland Full
Club: London Scottish
Positions: No.8/lock, flanker
Height: 6'4" **Weight:** 16st 4lbs
Occupation: Investment consultant
with Investors Advisory Services Ltd
of Guildford
Born: Haddington, 30.1.58
Family: Audrey (wife) and one child
Family links with rugby: Brother
(Kenyan) plays for Harlequins
Former clubs: Dunbar,
Haddington, Gala
International debut: Scotland 16,
France 7, 1982
Five Nations' debut: As above
Best moment in rugby: Winning
1990 Grand Slam
Worst moment in rugby: 1989
Lions' first Test defeat (12–30) v.
Australia
Most embarrassing moment:
Missing an opponent and hitting
John Jeffrey instead
Most respected opponent: John
Beattie (Glasgow Acads & Scotland)
– combined strength, skill, and a
determination to win with a really
mean streak
Serious injuries: Severed medial
ligament in left knee (New Zealand,
1981), broken cheekbone (1990/91)
Best memory last season:
Atmosphere at Murrayfield for
Scotland-England World Cup
semi-final
Suggestions to improve rugby:
On-field – Shorten second half of
matches! *Off-field* – Get the Unions

	apps	pts
Scotland B (**1982**)		
Career	1 cap	0
Scotland A (**1990**)		
Career	1 cap	0
Scotland (**1982**)		
Last Season	11 caps	12
Career	41 caps	44
Scotland VII (**1991**)	Hong Kong Sevens	
Lions 1989	1 Test	0

Caps (41): **1982** F, W, A(1,2) **1987**
W, E wc-F, R, NZ **1988** I, F,
W, E, A **1989** W, E, I, F, Fj, R
Lions A(1) **1990** I, F, W, E,
NZ(1,2) **1991** F, W, E, I, R
wc-J, Z, I, WS, E, NZ **1992** E,
I, F, W

Points (44 – 11t): **1982** W(1t) **1987**
wc-F(1t) **1989** W(1t), R(1t)
1990 I(2t) **1991** W(2t) wc-J(1t),
Z(1t) **1992** E(1t)

into the 20th century. Appoint team managers. Allow payments for books, articles, appearances, etc. More promotion of rugby at grass roots level

Notable landmarks in rugby career: Toured with Scotland to New Zealand (1981), Australia (1982), France (1986) and World Cup (1987), and went to Australia (1989) with Lions. Played in each of back-five forward positions for Scotland. Played in seven games for 1989 Lions, scoring one try. Scotland replacement 13 times. Played Inter-District rugby for Edinburgh, the South and Anglo-Scots. Three tries scored last season (third, against England in 1992 Five Nations' Championship) gave him a career total of 11 which gave him a share (with John Jeffrey) of the national forward try-scoring record. Ever present throughout Scotland's World Cup and Five Nations' campaigns last season

Touchlines: Mountaineering, walking – plan to walk the West Highland Way
Player to watch: Mark Moncrieff (Gala) – possesses pace, skill and dedication
Player of the year: Will Carling (England)

... STOP PRESS ... STOP PRESS ... STOP PRESS ...

IRELAND TO NEW ZEALAND
May-June 1992 – Record: P8, W3, D0, L5, F153, A287.

Results: South Canterbury, won 21-16; (2) Canterbury, lost 13-38; (3) Bay of Plenty, won 39-23; (4) Auckland, lost 7-62; (5) Poverty Bay-East Coast, won 22-7; (6) first Test: New Zealand, lost 21-24; (7) Manawatu, lost 24-58; (8) second Test: New Zealand, lost 6-59.

1st Test: J Staples (London Irish); R Carey (Dungannon), V Cunningham (St Mary's College), P Danaher (Garryowen, capt), N Furlong (UCG); P Russell (Instonians), M Bradley (Cork Con); N Popplewell (Greystones), S Smith (Ballymena), P McCarthy (Cork Con), M Galwey (Shannon), P Johns (Dungannon), K Leahy (Wanderers), M Fitzgibbon (Shannon), B Robinson (Ballymena). **Repl:** M McCall (Bangor) for Danaher, 37 mins; B Rigney (Greystones) for Leahy, 40 mins.

Scorers – Tries: Cunningham 2, Staples. **Conversions:** Russell 3. **Penalty goal:** Russell.

2nd Test: Staples; Carey, Cunningham, McCall, Furlong; Russell, Bradley (capt); Popplewell, Smith, McCarthy, Galwey, Johns, Rigney, Fitzgibbon, Robinson. **Repl:** P Kenny (Wanderers) for Fitzgibbon, 18 mins; K Murphy (Cork Con) for Staples, 40 mins; J Clarke (Dolphin) for Russell, 45 mins.

Scorers – Try: Furlong. **Conversion:** Russell.

THE 1991 WORLD CUP

The second World Cup was launched in a 'fanfare of obscurity', or so said RFU secretary Dudley Wood. Yet, whilst apposite at the time, such words could not possibly be applied once the tournament's final stages kicked off in England, Ireland, Scotland, Wales and France, accompanied by a level of media saturation previously alien to the sport.

Four years after New Zealand had beaten France on home soil to capture the inaugural Webb Ellis Cup, the All Blacks open the competition, and with it their defence, at Twickenham, the headquarters of the game, against England. Many believe, after the hosts are usurped with a stunning second-half display of ball preservation by the Blacks, that only one of the sides can possibly expect to return for the final a month later. That assertion proves correct; the selection of most, however, does not.

England capture the hearts of the nation, à la 1966. In spite of their opening day loss, they rally wonderfully, surging forward on a wave of public goodwill, if against a tide of media criticism. Playing to what the management considers to be their strengths, namely the titanic pack, is frowned upon in so many quarters. This is nothing new, as criticism seems to go perversely hand in hand with triumph where Britain or anything or anyone made therein, is concerned.

The counter argument favours utilising the talented back division sooner, indeed, just as soon as a firm forward platform has been established – even though the chances of England triumphing in either Paris or Edinburgh would likely be reduced by such a cavalier option. So England keep faith with their tight 'game-strangling' style – that which had won them the 1991 Grand Slam – and profit mightily. A place in the final of the biggest sporting event to be held in Britain since the 1966 World Cup, against Australia, the most attractive side in the tournament, is their reward.

Billed as Beauty (Australia) against the Beast (England), the match has 13.6 million viewers tuned into Independent Television's live coverage to witness a game which exceeds every expectation. Australia win – and every congratulation to them for they are, indeed, the tournament's outstanding side – but England play their part to the full in front of Her Majesty Queen Elizabeth and, on the day, can consider themselves a mite unfortunate. The Aussies might have triumphed but the game of rugby football truly wins the day and that, for the future interests of the sport, has to be what matters most.

To see Football League clubs bringing forward kick-off times so that their fans and, no doubt, players too, can get back in time for the 'rugger final', and to see the words of England's adopted anthem, 'Swing Low Sweet Chariot', along with a front page headline 'Cry God for Will, England & Saint George', plastered across the *The Sun* on 2 November, 1991, are sights which somehow provide the ultimate confirmation – Rugby Union, the game devised by frustrated footballer William Webb Ellis at Rugby School all those years ago, will never be the same again.

SQUADS

Squads are listed in alphabetical order with players' clubs bracketed directly after their names, followed by the initial(s) of countries played against. An * denotes an appearance as captain. Any points scored by the individual are listed in brackets (t = try, c = conversion, p = penalty, dg = dropped goal) directly after the relevant match.

Nation abbreviations: Arg – Argentina, Aus – Australia, C – Canada, E – England, Fj – Fiji, F – France, I – Ireland, It – Italy, J – Japan, NZ – New Zealand, R – Romania, S – Scotland, US – United States, W – Wales, WS – Western Samoa, Z – Zimbabwe.

ARGENTINA: M Aguirre (Asociacion Alumni) *WS;* M Allen (Atletico San Isidro); G Angaut (La Plata) *WS;* L Arbizu (Belgrano Athletic) *Aus(2dg), W, WS(1c,1p);* M Bosch (Olivos) *Aus(R), WS;* P Buabse (Los Tarcos, Tucuman) *WS;* G Camardon (Alumni) *Aus, W, WS;* M Carreras (Olivos) *Aus, W, WS(R);* D Cash (San Isidro) *Aus, WS;* D Cuesta Silva (San Isidro) *Aus, W, WS;* G del Castillo (Rosario) *Aus(1p,1c), W(1p);* H Garcia Simon (Pueyrredon) *Aus, W(1t), WS;* P Garreton (Circulo Universitario) *Aus*, W*, WS*;* F Irazaval (Cardenel Newman) *WS;* G Jorge (Pucara); E Laborde (Pucara) *Aus, W, WS(1p);* R le Fort (Tucuman) *Aus, W;* G Llanes (La Plata) *Aus, W;* M Lombardi (Alumni); F Mendez (Mendoza) *Aus, W;* S Meson (Tucuman) *WS(R);* L Molina (Tucuman) *W;* J Santamarina (Tucuman) *Aus, W, WS;* P Sporleder (Curupayti) *Aus, W, WS;* M Teran Nouges (Tucuman) *Aus(2t), W, WS(1t);* A Zanoni (Pueyrredon). **Manager**: F Alvarez. **Coach**: L Gradin.

AUSTRALIA: D Campese (Randwick) *Arg(2t), WS, W(1t), I(2t), NZ(1t), E;* T Coker (Western Districts) *Arg, WS, NZ, E;* D Crowley (Southern Districts) *WS;* S Cutler (Gordon) *WS;* A Daly (Eastern Suburbs) *Arg, W, I, NZ, E(1t);* J Eales (Brothers) *Arg, WS, W, I, NZ, E;* R Egerton (Sydney Univ) *Arg, W, I, NZ, E;* N Farr-Jones (Sydney Univ) *Arg*, WS*, I*, NZ*, E*;* J Flett (Randwick) *WS;* A Herbert (GPS) *WS;* T Horan (Southern Districts) *Arg(2t), WS, W(1t), I, NZ(1t), E;* P Kearns (Randwick) *Arg(1t), WS, W, I, NZ, E;* D Knox (Randwick); C Lillicrap (Queensland Univ) *WS;* J Little (Southern Districts) *Arg, W, I, NZ, E;* M Lynagh (Queensland Univ) *Arg(3c,2p), WS(3p), W(1t,4c,2p), I(2t,2c,1p), NZ(1c,2p), E(1c,2p);* R McCall (Brothers) *Arg, W, I, NZ, E;* E McKenzie (Randwick) *Arg, W, I, NZ, E;* J Miller (Queensland Univ) *WS, W, I;* B Nasser (Queensland Univ) *WS;* D Nucifora (Queensland Univ) *Arg(R);* V Ofahengaue (Manly) *Arg, W, I, NZ, E;* S Poidevin (Randwick) *Arg, W, I, NZ, E;* M Roebuck (Eastwood) *Arg, WS, W(2t), I, NZ, E;* P Slattery (Queensland Univ) *WS(R), W(1t), I(R);* R Tombs (Northern Suburbs). **Manager**: J Breen. **Coach**: R Dwyer.

CANADA: B Breen (Meralomas) *R;* A Charron (Ottawa Irish) *Fj, F, NZ(1t);* G Dukelow (Cowichan) *Fj, R, NZ;* G Ennis (Kats) *Fj*, R(1t), F, NZ;* E Evans (UBCOB) *Fj, R, F, NZ;* J Graf (UBCOB) *R;* S Gray (Kats) *Fj, F, NZ;* N Hadley (UBCOB) *Fj, R, F, NZ;* D Jackart (UBCOB) *Fj, R, E;* J Knauer (Meralomas); J Lecky (Meralomas) *Fj, R;* D Lougheed (Toronto Welsh); G MacKinnon (Ex Britannia Lions) *NZ;* E CTynan (Meralomas) *Fj, F, NZ(1t);* R Van den Brink (Kats) *R, F(R), NZ;* T Woods (James Bay) *F, NZ;* M Wyatt (Velox Valhallians) *R*(1c,2p), F*(1t,1p), NZ(1p).* **Manager**: M Luke. **Coach**: I Birtwell.

331

ENGLAND: P Ackford (Harlequins) *NZ, It, F, S, Aus;* R Andrew (Wasps) *NZ(1dg), It, US, F, S(1dg), Aus;* W Carling (Harlequins) *NZ*, It*, US*(1t), F(1t)*, S*, Aus*;* W Dooley (Preston Grasshoppers) *NZ, US, F, S, Aus;* J Guscott (Bath) *NZ, It(2t), F, S, Aus;* S Halliday (Harlequins) *US, S, Aus;* N Heslop (Orrell) *US(1t), F;* R Hill (Bath) *NZ, It, US, F, S, Aus;* S Hodgkinson (Nottingham) *US(4c,3p);* J Leonard (Harlequins) *NZ, It, US, F, S, Aus;* B Moore (Harlequins) *NZ, It, F, S, Aus;* D Morris (Orrell); J Olver (Northampton) *It;* C Oti (Wasps) *NZ, It;* G Pearce (Northampton) *US;* D Pears (Harlequins); J Probyn (Askeans) *NZ, It, F, S, Aus;* N Redman (Bath) *It, US;* G Rees (Nottingham) *US;* P Rendall (Askeans) *It(R);* D Richards (Leicester) *NZ, It, US;* M Skinner (Harlequins) *US(1t), F, S, Aus;* M Teague (Gloucester) *NZ, It, F, S, Aus;* R Underwood (Leicester & RAF) *NZ, It(1t), US(2t), F(1t), S, Aus;* J Webb (Bath) *NZ(3p), It(1t,4c,4p), F(1c,3p), S(2p), Aus(2p);* P Winterbottom (Harlequins) *NZ, It, F, S, Aus.* **Manager:** G Cooke. **Coach:** R Uttley.

FIJI: S Aria (Regent) *C, F;* D Baleiwai (Duavata) *C(R)F, R;* A Dere (Army) *C, F, R*;* S Domoni Jnr (Waimanu) *C, F;* L Kato (Saunaka) *C, F(R);* S Koroduadua (Police) *C, F(1c,1p);* T Lovo (QVSOB) *C, F;* A Nadolo (QVSOB) *R;* N Nadruku (Hyatt) *C, R;* K Naisoro (FCS) *F, R;* E Naituivau (Army) *C, R(R);* S Naiwilawasa (Police Union) *C;* P Naruma (Police) *F(1t), R(R);* M Ollsson (St Johns) *R;* T Rabaka (Mt St Marys) *R(2dg);* I Savai (Regent) *C, F, R;* W Serevi (Nabua) *C(1dg), F;* F Seru (Nabua) *C, F, R;* P Tabulutu (Nabua) *C, F(R), R;* M Taga (QVSOB) *C*, F*;* I Tawake (Yalovata) *C, F, R;* O Turuva (Yavusania) *R(2p,1dg);* P Volavola (Brothers) *F, R;* T Vonolagi (Army) *R;* M Vosanbola (Army) *F;* N Vuli (PWD) *F, R.* **Manager:** Dr J Taka. **Coach:** S Viriviri.

FRANCE: L Armary (Lourdes); A Benazzi (Agen) *R, Fj, C;* P Benetton (Agen) *S;* Blanco (Biarritz) *R*, Fj*, C*, E*;* L Cabannes (Racing Club de Paris) *R, Fj, C, E;* J-M Cadieu (Toulouse) *R, Fj, C, E;* D Camberabero (Beziers) *R(1c,4p), Fj(1t,3c,1p), C(1c,1p);* M Cecillon (Bourgoin) *E;* E Champ (Toulon) *R, Fj, C, E;* M Courtiols (Begles); T Devergie (Nimes); F Galthie (Colomiers) *R, Fj, C, E;* P Gimbert (Begles); P Hontas (Biarritz); T Lacroix (Dax) *R, C(R,2p), E(2p);* J-B Lafond (Racing Club de Paris) *R(R,1t), Fj(3t), C(1t), E(1t);* P Lagisquet (Bayonne) *R;* G Lascube (Agen) *R, Fj, C, E;* P Marocco (Montferrand) *R, Fj, C, E;* F Mesnel (Racing Club de Paris) *R, Fj, C, E;* P Ondarts (Biarritz) *R, Fj, C, E;* O Roumat (Dax) *R(1t), Fj, C, E;* J-L Sadourny (Colomiers) *C(R);* P Saint-Andre (Montferrand) *R(1t), Fj, C(1t), E;* H Sanz (Narbonne); P Sella (Agen) *Fj(2t), C, E.* **Manager:** H Foures. **Coach:** D Dubroca.

IRELAND: F Aherne (Lansdowne); J Clarke (Dolphin) *J, Aus;* K Crossan (Instonians) *Z, J, S;* V Cunningham (St Mary's College) *Z, J(R);* D Curtis (London Irish) *Z(1t), J, S, Aus;* P Danaher (Garryowen); D Fitzgerald (De La Salle Palmerston) *Z, S, Aus;* J Fitzgerald (Young Munster) *J;* N Francis (Blackrock College) *Z, J, S, Aus;* M Galwey (Shannon) *J;* S Geoghegan (London Irish) *Z(1t), S, Aus;* G Halpin (London Irish) *J;* G Hamilton (Ballymena) *Z, J, S, Aus(1t);* R Keyes (Cork Constitution) *Z(4c,5p), J(2c,4p), S(4p,1dg), Aus(1c,3p,1dg);* T Kingston (Dolphin) *J*;* D Lenihan (Cork Constitution) *Z, S, Aus;* N Mannion (Lansdowne) *J(2t);* P Matthews (Wanderers, captain) *Z*, S*, Aus*;* B Mullin (Blackrock College) *J, S, Aus;* K Murphy (Cork Constitution); P O'Hara (Cork Constitution) *J(1t);* N Popplewell (Greystones) *Z(2t), S, Aus;* B Robinson (Ballymena) *Z(4t), S, Aus;* R Saunders (London Irish) *Z, J, S, Aus;* S Smith (Ballymena) *Z, S, Aus;* J Staples (London Irish) *Z, J(1t), S, Aus.* **Manager:** K Reid. **Coach:** C Fitzgerald.

ITALY: S Barba (Amatori Medio) *US(1t), E;* M Bonomi (Amatori Medio) *E(R), NZ(1t);* S Bordon (Cagnoni Rovigo); A Bottacchiari (Scavolini L'Aquila) *NZ;* C Checchinato (Cagnoni Rovigo) *NZ;* A Colella (Scavolini L'Aquila); G Croci (Amatori Medio) *US,*

E, NZ; Marcello Cuttitta (Amatori Medio) *US, E(1t), NZ(1t);* Massimo Cuttitta (Amatori Medio) *US, E, NZ;* D Dominguez (Amatori Medio) *US(4c,2p), E(1c), NZ(2c,3p);* F Favaro (Benetton Treviso) *US, E, NZ;* I Francescato (Pastajolly Tarvisium) *US(1t), E, NZ;* F Gaetaniello (Ecomar Liv) *US(1t), E, NZ;* M Giovanelli (Amatori Medio) *E, NZ;* G Grespan (Benetton Treviso) *NZ(R);* C Orlandi (Bilboa Piacenza); F Pietrosanti (Scavolini L'Aquila); G Pivetta (Iranian Loom San) *US, E, NZ*;* F Properzi Curti (Amatori Medio) *US, E, NZ;* G Rossi (Delicius Parma); R Saetti (Petrarca Padova) *US, E;* D Tebaldi (Officine Savi Noceto); L Troiani (Scavolini L'Aquila) *US, E;* P Vaccari (Nutrilinea Calvisano) *US(1t), E, NZ;* E Venturi (Cagnoni Rovigo) *NZ;* G Zanon (Benetton Treviso) *US*, E*.* **Manager:** G Dondi. **Coach:** B Fourcade.

JAPAN: S Aoki (Ricoh) *I;* T Fujita (IBM) *I;* T Hayashi (Kobe Steel) *S, I(1t), Z;* S Hirao (Kobe Steel) *S*, I*, Z*;* M Horikoshi (Kobe Steel) *I, Z(1t);* T Hosokawa (Kobe Steel) *S(1t,1c,1dg), I(2c), Z(5c,2p);* H Kajihara (Toshiba Fuchu) *S, I(1t), Z;* K Kimura (Toyota); M Kunda (Toshiba Fuchu) *S, I(R), Z;* E Kutsuki (Toyota) *S, I, Z(2t);* S Latu (Sanyo) *S, I, Z;* T Maeda (NTT Kansai) *S, I, Z(2t);* T Masuho (Waseda Univ) *S, I, Z(2t);* T Matsuda (Kanto Gakuen Univ); K Matsuo (World) *S, I, Z(1t);* K Miyamoto (Sanyo) *I(R);* Y Motoki (Meiji Univ); W Murata (Toshiba Fuchu) *S;* S Nakashima (Nihon Denki) *S;* O Ota (Nihon Denki) *S, I, Z;* H Ouchi (Ryukoku Univ); A Oyagi (Kobe Steel) *I, Z;* K Takahashi (Toyota); M Takura (Mitsubishi Jiko Kyoto) *S, I, Z;* E Tifaga (Niko Niko Do) *S, I, Z(1t);* Y Yoshida (Isetan) *S, I(1t), Z(2t).* **Manager:** S Konno. **Coach:** H Shukuzawa.

NEW ZEALAND: G Bachop (Canterbury) *E, US, C, Aus, S;* Z Brooke (Auckland) *E, It(1t), C(1t), Aus, S;* M Carter (Auckland) *It, Aus;* K Crowley (Taranaki) *Aus;* G Dowd (North Auckland); A Earl (Canterbury) *E(R), US(1t), S;* S Fitzpatrick (Auckland) *E, US, It, C, Aus, S;* G Fox (Auckland) *E(1c,4p), It(3c,3p), C(3c,1p), Aus(2p);* S Gordon (Waikaro); P Henderson (Otago) *C;* J Hewett (Auckland) *It(1t);* C Innes (Auckland) *E, US(1t), It(1t), C, Aus, S;* I Jones (North Auckland) *E, US, It, C, Aus, S;* M Jones (Auckland) *E(1t), US, S;* J Kirwan (Auckland) *E, It, C(1t), Aus, S;* W Little (North Harbour) *It, S(1t);* R Loe (Waikaro) *E, It, C, Aus, S;* B McCahill (Auckland) *E, US, C(1t), Aus;* S McDowell (Auckland) *E, US, It, C, Aus, S;* S Philpott (Canterbury) *It(R), S(R);* J Preston (Canterbury) *US(4c,2p), S(3p);* G Purvis (Waikaro) *US(1t);* J Timu (Otago) *E, US(1t), C(2t), Aus;* V Tuigamala (Auckland) *US(1t), It(1t), C, S;* A Whetton (Auckland) *E, US, It, C, Aus;* G Whetton (Auckland) *E*, US*, It*, C*, Aus*, S*;* T Wright (Auckland) *E, US(3t), It, S.* **Manager:** J Sturgeon. **Co-Coaches:** A Wyllie/J Hart.

ROMANIA: T Brinza (RC Grivita) *C(R);* S Ciorascu (SC Angouleme) *F, C, Fj;* C Cojocariu (CS Dinamo) *F, C, Fj;* I Colceriu (CS Steaua) *Fj;* G Dinu (Grivita) *F, C, Fj;* I Doja (CS Dinamo) *C;* H Dumitras (AS Pau) *F*, C*, Fj*(1t);* M Dumitru (CS Rapid Metrou) *F, C;* M Foca (CS Farul Constanta); N Fulina (CS Farul) *C, Fj;* C Gheorghe (Grivita); A Guranescu (CS Dinamo) *F;* G Ion (CS Dinamo) *F, C, Fj(1t);* V Ionescu (CS Rapid Metrou); I Ivanciuc (CSM Suceava) *Fj(R);* G Leonte (Olimpique Mielan) *F, C;* A Lungu (CS Dinamo) *F, C(1t), Fj;* N Marin (CS Farul) *Fj;* D Neaga (CS Dinamo) *F, C, Fj;* N Nichitean (CS Stiinta Cemin) *F(1p), C(1p), Fj(1p);* N Racean (CS University) *F, C, Fj(1c);* C Sasu (CS Farul) *F, C(1t), Fj(1t);* G Sava (CS Stiinta Cemin) *F, C(R);* C Stan (AS Contactoare) *F, C, Fj;* S Tofan (CS Dinamo); G Vlad (Grivita) *C(R), Fj.* **Manager:** A Bojinescu. **Coach:** P Ianusevici.

SCOTLAND: J Allan (Edinburgh Academicals) *J, I, WS, E, NZ;* G Armstrong (Jed-Forest) *J, I(1t), WS, E, NZ;* P Burnell (London Scottish) *J, Z, I, WS, E, NZ;* F Calder (Stewart's-Melville FP) *J, I, WS, E, NZ;* C Chalmers (Melrose) *J(1t,1p), Z(R),*

I(1dg), *WS*, *E*, *NZ;* D Cronin (Bath) *Z;* P Dods (Gala) *Z*(5c,2p)*, *NZ(R);* C Gray (Nottingham) *J*, *I*, *WS*, *E*, *NZ;* G Hastings (Watsonians) *J(1t,5c,2p)*, *I(2c,3p)*, *WS(2c,4p)*, *E(2p)*, *NZ(2p);* S Hastings (Watsonians) *J(1t)*, *Z(1t)*, *I*, *WS*, *E*, *NZ;* J Jeffrey (Kelso) *J*, *I*, *WS(2t)*, *E*, *NZ;* S Lineen (Boroughmuir) *J*, *Z*, *I*, *E*, *NZ;* G Marshall (Selkirk) *Z;* D Milne (Heriot's FP) *J(R);* K Milne (Heriot's FP) *Z;* M Moncrieff (Gala); G Oliver (Hawick) *Z;* G Shiel (Melrose) *I(R)(1t)*, *WS;* D Sole (Edinburgh Academicals) *J**, *I**, *WS**, *E**, *NZ*;* A Stanger (Hawick) *J(1t)*, *Z(1t)*, *I*, *WS(1t)*, *E*, *NZ;* I Tukalo (Selkirk) *J(1t)*, *Z(3t)*, *I*, *WS*, *E*, *NZ;* D Turnbull (Hawick) *Z(1t);* A Watt (Glasgow High/Kelvinside) *Z;* G Weir (Melrose) *J*, *Z(1t)*, *I*, *WS*, *E*, *NZ;* D White (London Scottish) *J(1t)*, *Z(1t)*, *I*, *WS*, *E*, *NZ;* D Wyllie (Stewart's-Melville FP) *J(R)*, *Z(1dg)*. **Manager:** D Paterson. **Coach:** I McGeechan.

UNITED STATES: J Burke (Albany Knicks) *NZ;* B Daily (San Jose Seahawks) *It;* M De Jong (Denver Barbarians) *It*, *E(R);* R Farley (Phil Whitemarch) *It*, *E;* T Flay (Jersey Shore) *It*, *E;* G Hein (Old Blues, Berkeley) *It*, *NZ*, *E;* K Higgins (Old Blues, Berkeley) *It*, *E;* P Johnson (Louisville) *NZ;* B Leversee (OMBAC, San Diego) *It;* S Lipman (Santa Monica) *It(R)*, *NZ*, *E;* C Lippert (OMBAC, San Diego) *It*, *NZ;* L Manga (South Jersey) *NZ(R)*, *E;* N Mottram (Boulder, Colorado) *NZ*, *E;* R Nelson (Belmont Shore) *It*, *E(1t);* C O'Brien (Old Blues, Berkeley) *NZ*, *E;* F Paoli (Denver Barbarians) *It;* M Pidcock (Pensacola, Florida) *NZ*, *E;* T Ridnell (Old Puget Sound) *It*, *NZ*, *E;* M Sawicki (Chicago Lions) *NZ;* P Sheehy (Washington DC) *NZ*, *E;* K Swords (Beacon Hill, Boston) *It(1t)*, *NZ**, *E*;* C Tunnacliffe (Belmont Shore) *NZ*, *E;* B Vizard (OMBAC, San Diego) *It*;* E Whitaker (Old Blues, Berkeley) *It*, *NZ;* J Wilkerson (Belmont Shore) *E(R);* M Williams (Aspen, Colorado) *It(1c,1p)*, *NZ(2p)*, *E(1c,1p)*. **Manager:** E Schram. **Coach:** J Perkins.

WALES: P Arnold (Swansea) *Arg(1t)*, *Aus;* A Booth (Cardiff); A Clement (Swansea) *WS*, *Aus;* R Collins (Cardiff) *WS;* A Davies (Cambridge Univ); P Davies (Llanelli) *WS*, *Arg*, *Aus;* M Davis (Newport); L Delaney (Llanelli) *WS*, *Arg*, *Aus;* A Emyr (Cardiff) *WS(1t)*, *Arg*, *Aus;* D Evans (Cardiff) *Aus(R);* I Evans (Llanelli) *WS*(1t)*, *Arg**, *Aus*;* S Ford (Cardiff); S Gibbs (Neath) *WS*, *Arg*, *Aus;* M Griffiths (Cardiff) *WS*, *Arg*, *Aus;* M Hall (Cardiff) *WS*, *Arg*, *Aus;* G Jenkins (Pontypool) *WS(R)*, *Arg*, *Aus;* R Jones (Swansea) *WS*, *Arg*, *Aus;* E Lewis (Llanelli) *WS*, *Arg*, *Aus;* P May (Llanelli) *WS;* M Morris (Neath) *WS(R);* K Moseley (Newport) *WS*, *Arg*, *Aus;* M Rayer (Cardiff) *Arg(1p)*, *Aus(R);* M Ring (Cardiff) *WS(1c,1p)*, *Arg(3p)*, *Aus(1p);* K Waters (Newbridge) *WS;* R Webster (Swansea) *Arg*, *Aus;* H Williams-Jones (South Wales Police). **Manager:** R Norster. **Coach:** A Davies.

WESTERN SAMOA: A Aiolupo (Moat'a) *W*, *Aus*, *Arg*, *S;* V Alaalatoa (Apia/Manly) *W*, *Aus*, *Arg*, *S;* A Alilomaiava (Marist-St Joseph's); S Bachop (Canterbury) *W*, *Aus*, *Arg(1t)*, *S(1dg);* M Birtwhistle (Hutt OB) *W*, *Aus*, *Arg*, *S;* F Bunce (Helensville) *W*, *Aus*, *Arg(1t)*, *S;* T Fa'amasino (Vaimoso/Oriental-Rongotai) *Aus;* P Fatialofa (Ponsonby) *W**, *Aus**, *Arg**, *S*;* E Ioane (Ponsonby) *S;* D Kaleopa (Marist-Auckland) *Aus;* M Keenan (Univ of Auckland) *W*, *Aus*, *Arg;* P Lam (Marist-Auckland) *W*, *Arg*, *S;* S Lemamea (Lefaga/Western Suburbs); B Lima (Marist-St Peter's/Marist-St Joseph's) *W*, *Aus*, *Arg(2t)*, *S;* T Nu'ualiitia (Patumahoe); J Paramore (Manuwera) *Aus;* A Perelini (Ponsonby) *W*, *Aus*, *Arg*, *S;* F Saena (Moata'a); K Sio (SCOPA); T Sio (Marist-St Joseph's/Northern Suburbs); T Tagaloa (Wellington) *W*, *Aus(R)*, *Arg(2t)*, *S;* S To'omalatai (Vaiala/Marist-St Patrick's) *W*, *Aus*, *Arg*, *S;* F Tuilagi (Marist-St Joseph's); M Vaea (Marist-St Joseph's) *W(1c,2p)*, *Aus(1p)*, *Arg(4c,1p)*, *S(1p);* T Vaega (Taradale) *W(1t)*, *Aus*, *Arg*, *S;* S Vaifale (Marist-St Joseph's) *W(1t)*, *Arg*, *S*. **Manager:** T Simi. **Coach:** P Schuster.

ZIMBABWE: B Beattie (Old Miltonians) *I, S, J;* C Botha (Old Hararians) *I, J;* C Brown (Harare Sports) *I, S, J;* B Catterall (Old Hararians) *I, S, J;* E Chimbima (Old Hararians) *S(R);* B Currin (Old Hararians) *I*, S*(2c), J*;* B Dawson (Old Miltonians) *I(1t), S, J;* R Demblon (Old Hararians) *I;* A Ferreira (Old Georgians) *I(1p);* A Garvey (Old Miltonians) *I, S(2t), J;* R Hunter (Old Miltonians) *I, S(R);* R Kuhn (Old Hararians) *I;* M Letcher (Karoi) *I, S, J;* E MacMillan (Old Hararians) *S, J;* B Marais (Old Hararians); M Martin (Harare Sports) *I, S, J;* D Muirhead (Old Miltonians) *S;* H Nguruve (Old Georgians) *S, J(1t);* A Nicholls (Old Hararians) *S, J;* I Noble (Old Miltonians); M Nyala (Old Hararians); C Roberts (Harare Sports) *S(R);* W Schultz (Karoi) *I(R,1t), S, J;* G Snyder (Harare Sports) *J(R);* R Tsimba (Old Hararians) *I, S, J(1t);* D Walters (Karoi) *I, S, J.* **Manager:** A Woldemar. **Coach:** I Buchanan.

POOL MATCHES

POOL 1

As a competitive eliminator, Pool One is over within 80 minutes of the opening ceremony. Once New Zealand have recovered a 9-12 half-time deficit to beat England 18-12 in the tournament's inaugural match, the Pool's outcome is a foregone conclusion, with respect to Italy and the United States. Yet there is a theory, hinted at by the Italians, that the All Blacks are rather closer to their sell-by date than had previously been thought. *Winners: New Zealand.* **Runners-up:** *England.*

England (12) 12, New Zealand (9) 18
Twickenham, 3 October 1991
England: Webb; Underwood, Carling (capt), Guscott, Oti; Andrew, Hill; Leonard, Moore, Probyn, Ackford, Dooley, Teague, Winterbottom, Richards.
   Scorers – *Penalty goals:* Webb 3. *Dropped goal:* Andrew.

New Zealand: Wright; Kirwan, Innes, McCahill, Timu; Fox, Bachop; McDowell, Fitzpatrick, Loe, I Jones, G Whetton (capt), A Whetton, M Jones, Brooke (Earl 70).
   Scorers – *Try:* M Jones. *Conversion:* Fox. *Penalty goals:* Fox 4.

Referee: J M Fleming (Scotland).

Series score: Played 16, England 3, NZ 13.

Italy (9) 30, United States (3) 9
Otley, 5 October 1991
Italy: Troiani; Vaccari, Gaetaniello, Barba, Marcello Cuttitta; Dominguez, Francescato; Massimo Cuttitta, Pivetta, Properzi Curti, Favaro, Croci, Saetti, Checchinato, Zanon (capt).
   Scorers – *Tries:* Barba, Francescato, Vaccari, Gaetaniello. *Conversions:* Dominguez 4. *Penalty goals:* Dominguez 2.

United States: Nelson; Hein, Williams, Higgins, Whitaker; De Jong, Daily; Lippert, Flay, Paoli, Swords, Leversee, Vizard (capt) (Lipman 57), Ridnell, Farley.
   Scorers – *Try:* Swords. *Conversion:* Williams. *Penalty goal:* Williams.

Referee: O E Doyle (Ireland).

Series score: Played 1, Italy 1, USA 0.

New Zealand (20) 46, USA (3) 6
Gloucester, 8 October 1991
New Zealand: Wright; Timu, Innes, McCahill, Tuigamala; Preston, Bachop; McDowell, Fitzpatrick, Purvis, A Whetton, I Jones, G Whetton (capt), M Jones, Earl.
    Scorers – *Tries:* Wright 3, Earl, Purvis, Timu, Tuigamala, Innes. *Conversions:* Preston 4. *Penalty goals:* Preston 2.

United States: Sheehy; Hein, Williams, Burke, Higgins; O'Brien, Pidcock; Lippert (Manga 51), Johnson, Mottram, Sawicki, Swords (capt), Tunnacliffe, Lipman, Ridnell.
    Scorers – *Penalty goals:* Williams 2.

Referee: E Sklar (Argentina).

Series score: Played 3, NZ 3, USA 0.

England (24) 36, Italy (0) 6
Twickenham, 8 October 1991
England: Webb; Oti, Carling (capt), Guscott, Underwood; Andrew, Hill; Leonard, Moore, Probyn (Rendall 53), Ackford, Redman, Teague, Winterbottom, Richards.
    Scorers – *Tries:* Underwood, Guscott 2, Webb. *Conversions:* Webb 4. *Penalty goals:* Webb 4.

Italy: Troiani (Bonomi 48); Vaccari, Gaetaniello, Barba, Marcello Cuttitta; Dominguez, Francescato; Massimo Cuttitta, Pivetta, Properzi Curti, Favoro, Croci, Saetti, Giovanelli, Zanon (capt).
    Scorers – *Try:* Marcello Cuttitta. *Conversion:* Dominguez.

Referee: J B Anderson (Scotland).

Series score: Played 1, England 1, Italy 0.

England (21) 37, United States (3) 9
Twickenham, 11 October 1991
England: Hodgkinson; Heslop, Carling (capt), Halliday, Underwood; Andrew, Hill; Leonard, Olver, Pearce, Dooley, Redman, Skinner, Rees, Richards.
    Scorers – *Tries:* Underwood 2, Carling, Skinner, Heslop. *Conversions:* Hodgkinson 4. *Penalty goals:* Hodgkinson 3.

United States: Nelson; Hein, Williams, Higgins (De Jong 40), Sheehy; O'Brien, Pidcock; Manga, Flay, Mottram, Tunnacliffe, Swords (capt), Lipman, Farley (Wilkerson 76), Ridnell.
    Scorers – *Try:* Nelson. *Conversion:* Williams. *Penalty goal:* Williams.

Referee: L Peard (Wales).

Series score: Played 4, England 4, USA 0.

New Zealand (16) 31, Italy (3) 21
Leicester, 13 October 1991
New Zealand: Wright (Philpott 73); Kirwan, Innes, Little, Tuigamala; Fox, Hewett; McDowell, Fitzpatrick, Loe, I Jones, G Whetton (capt), A Whetton, Carter, Brooke.
    Scorers – *Tries:* Innes, Brooke, Tuigamala, Hewitt. *Conversions:* Fox 3. *Penalty goals:* Fox 3.

Italy: Vaccari; Venturi, Gaetaniello, Dominguez, Marcello Cuttitta; Bonomi, Francescato; Massimo Cuttitta, Pivetta (capt), Properzi Curti (Grespan 44), Favaro, Croci, Bottacchiari, Giovanelli, Checchinato.

    Scorers – *Tries:* Marcella Cuttitta, Bonomi. *Conversions:* Dominguez 2. *Penalty goals:* Dominguez 3.

Referee: K Fitzgerald (Australia).

Series score: Played 3, NZ 3, Italy 0.

	P	W	D	L	F	A	Pts
New Zealand	3	3	0	0	95	39	9
England	3	2	0	1	85	33	7
Italy	3	1	0	2	57	76	5
USA	3	0	0	3	24	113	3

POOL 2

As in Pool One, there is a showdown but, unlike Pool One, it is saved for last, thus allowing the Scottish and Irish public a week to savour the enticing prospect of their Murrayfield battle. The wait – punctuated by comfortable victories for both sides over Zimbabwe and Japan – proves worthwhile as Edinburgh serves up a classic, at least in Northern Hemisphere terms. We are not talking David Campese-style flowing extravagance, rather intense close-quarter grind. It is captivating stuff nonetheless. Both nations receive due recompense for their efforts in the form of home quarter-final ties although, as 24-15 victors, Scotland are granted a rather more appetising engagement with Western Samoa. Australia are booked in at Dublin. **Winners: Scotland. Runners-up: Ireland.**

Scotland (17) 47, Japan (9) 9
Edinburgh, 5 October 1991
Scotland: G Hastings; Stanger, S Hastings, Lineen, Tukalo; Chalmers (Wyllie 70), Armstrong; Sole (capt) (D Milne 75), Allan, Burnell, Weir, Gray, Jeffrey, Calder, White.

    Scorers – *Tries:* S Hastings, Stanger, Chalmers, penalty try, White, Tukalo, G Hastings. *Conversions:* G Hastings 5. *Penalty goals:* Chalmers, G Hastings 2.

Japan: Hosokawa; Masuho, Kutsuki, Hirao (capt), Yoshida; Matsuo, Murata; Ota, Kunda, Takura, Hayashi, Tifaga, Kajihara, Nakashima, Latu.

    Scorers – *Try:* Hosokawa. *Conversion:* Hosokawa. *Dropped goal:* Hosokawa.

Referee: E Morrison (England).

Series score: Played 5, Scotland 4, Japan 1.

Ireland (33) 55, Zimbabwe (0) 11
Dublin, 6 October 1991
Ireland: Staples; Geoghegan, Cunningham, Curtis, Crossan; Keyes, Saunders; Popplewell, Smith, D Fitzgerald, Lenihan, Francis, Matthews (capt), Hamilton, Robinson.

    Scorers – *Tries:* Robinson 4, Popplewell 2, Geoghegan, Curtis. *Conversions:* Keyes 4. *Penalty goals:* Keyes 5.

Zimbabwe: Currin (capt); Brown, Tsimba, Letcher, Walters; Kuhn (Schultz 29), Ferreira; Hunter, Beattie, Garvey, Demblon, Martin, Botha, Dawson, Catterall.

Scorers – *Tries:* Dawson, Schultz. *Penalty goal:* Ferreira.

Referee: K H Lawrence (New Zealand).

Series score: Played 2, Ireland 2, Zimbabwe 0.

Scotland (21) 51, Zimbabwe (12) 12
Edinburgh, 9 October 1991
Scotland: Dods (capt); Stanger (Chalmers 78), S Hastings, Lineen, Tukalo; Wyllie, Oliver; Burnell, K Milne, Watt, Cronin, Weir, Turnbull, Marshall, White.

Scorers – *Tries:* Tukalo 3, Stanger, S Hastings, White, Turnbull, Weir. *Conversions:* Dods 5. *Penalty goals:* Dods 2. *Dropped goal:* Wyllie.

Zimbabwe: Currin (capt); Schultz, Tsimba, Letcher, Walters (Chimbima 56); Brown, MacMillan; Nicholls, Beattie, Garvey (Hunter 46, Roberts 78), Martin, Nguruve, Muirhead, Dawson, Catterall.

Scorers – *Tries:* Garvey 2. *Conversions:* Currin 2.

Referee: D Reordan (United States).

Series score: Played 4, Scotland 4, Zimbabwe 0.

Ireland (19) 32, Japan (6) 16
Dublin, 9 October 1991
Ireland: Staples; Clarke, Mullin, Curtis, Crossan (Cunningham 60); Keyes, Saunders; J Fitzgerald, Kingston (capt), Halpin, Galwey, Francis, O'Hara, Hamilton, Mannion.

Scorers – *Tries:* Mannion 2, O'Hara, Staples. *Conversions:* Keyes 2. *Penalty goals:* Keyes 4.

Japan: Hosokawa; Masuho, Kutsuki, Hirao (capt), Yoshida; Matsuo, Horikoshi; Ota, Fujita (Kunda 52), Takura, Hayashi, Oyagi, Tifaga (Miyamoto 73), Kajihara, Latu.

Scorers – *Tries:* Hayashi, Kajihara, Yoshida. *Conversions:* Hosokawa 2.

Referee: L Colati (Fiji).

Series score: Played 3, Ireland 3, Japan 0.

Scotland (9) 24, Ireland (12) 15
Edinburgh, 12 October 1991
Scotland: G Hastings; Stanger, S Hastings, Lineen, Tukalo; Chalmers (Shiel 43), Armstrong; Sole (capt), Allan, Burnell, Gray, Weir, Jeffrey, Calder, White.

Scorers – *Tries:* Shiel, Armstrong. *Conversion:* G Hastings. *Penalty goals:* G Hastings 3. *Dropped goal:* Chalmers.

Ireland: Staples; Geoghegan, Curtis, Mullin, Crossan; Keyes, Saunders; Popplewell, Smith, D Fitzgerald, Lenihan, Francis, Matthews (capt), Hamilton, Robinson.

Scorer – *Penalty goals:* Keyes 4. *Dropped goal:* Keyes.

Referee: F Howard (England).

Series score: Played 103, Scotland 53, Ireland 45, Drawn 4, Abandoned 1.

Japan (16) 52, Zimbabwe (4) 8
Belfast, 14 October 1991
Japan: Hosokawa; Masuho, Kutsuki, Hirao (capt), Yoshida; Matsuo, Horikoshi; Ota, Kunda, Takura, Hayashi, Oyagi, Tifaga, Kajihara, Latu.
  Scorers – *Tries:* Yoshida 2, Masuho 2, Kutzuki 2, Horikoshi, Tifaga, Matsuo. *Conversions:* Hosokawa 5. *Penalty goals:* Hosokawa 2.

Zimbabwe: Currin (capt); Schultz, Tsimba, Letcher, Walters; Brown, MacMillan; Nicholls, Beattie, Garvey (Roberts 70), Martin, Botha, Nguruve, Dawson, Catterall.
  Scorers – *Tries:* Tsimba, Nguruve.

Referee: R Hourquet (France).

Series score: Played 1, Japan 1, Zimbabwe 0.

	P	W	D	L	F	A	Pts
Scotland	3	3	0	0	122	36	9
Ireland	3	2	0	1	102	51	7
Japan	3	1	0	2	77	87	5
Zimbabwe	3	0	0	3	31	158	3

POOL 3

Hail Western Samoa, and thank-you. Not, perhaps, an exclamation prevalent in and around the Welsh valleys but one echoed around the globe by rugby neutrals. Forget Australia for the moment; their headlines are to come. Relish the success and entertainment brought by the Polynesians. Wales are first to experience the South Pacific islanders' attacking flair and ruthless tackling. Sure, everyone except referee Robin sees that To'o Vaega is beaten to the touch by Robert Jones but the Samoans are, nevertheless, worthy of their Principality-shattering triumph. All credit, too, to Wales for not voicing a syllable of complaint, a single dissenting voice at the official's honest blunder. Welsh rugby might be at its lowest ebb but, unlike in Australia over the summer, acceptance is gracious, for which the team deserves unstinting praise. Despite beating Argentina, Wales are eliminated, leaving the Samoans, who come remarkably close to beating the Wallabies in the Pontypool rain, to grace the quarter-finals. Australia, no surprise, qualify with little duress (handing Wales their record home defeat in the process), completing an unbeaten programme. **Winners:** *Australia.* **Runners-up:** *Western Samoa.*

Australia (16) 32, Argentina (7) 19
Llanelli, 4 October 1991
Australia: Roebuck; Egerton, Little, Horan, Campese; Lynagh, Farr-Jones (capt); Daly, Kearns (Nucifora 50), McKenzie, Coker, McCall, Poidevin, Ofahengaue, Eales.
  Scorers – *Tries:* Campese 2, Horan 2, Kearns. *Conversions:* Lynagh 3. *Penalty goals:* Lynagh 2.

Argentina: del Castillo; Teran Nouges, Laborde, Garcia Simon, Cuesta Silva; Arbizu, Camardon; Mendez, le Fort (Bosch 40), Cash, Sporledor, Llanes, Garreton (capt), Santamarina, Carreras.
  Scorers – *Tries:* Teran 2. *Conversion:* del Castillo. *Dropped goal:* Arbizu 2.

Referee: D J Bishop (New Zealand).

Wales (3) 13, Western Samoa (3) 16
Cardiff, 6 October 1991
Wales: Clement (Rayer 48); I Evans (capt), Gibbs, Hall, Emyr; Ring, Jones; Griffiths, Waters, Delaney, May (Morris 29), Moseley, Lewis, Collins (Jenkins 52),P Davies.
  Scorers – *Tries:* Emyr, Evans. *Conversion:* Ring. *Penalty goal:* Ring.

Western Samoa: Aiolupo; Lima, Vaega, Bunce, Tagaloa; Bachop, Vaea; Fatialofa (capt), To'omalatai, T Sio, Birtwhistle, Keenan, Vaifale, Perelini, Lam.
  Scorers – *Tries:* Vaega, Vaifale. *Conversion:* Vaea. *Penalty goals:* Vaea 2.

Referee: P Robin (France).

Series score: Played 3, Wales 2, Western Samoa 1.

Australia (6) 9, Western Samoa (0) 3
Pontypool, 9 October 1991
Australia: Roebuck; Flett, Herbert, Horan, Campese; Lynagh, Farr-Jones (capt) (Slattery 10); Lillicrap, Kearns, Crowley, Coker, Cutler, Nasser, Miller, Eales.
  Scorer – *Penalty goals:* Lynagh 3.

Western Samoa: Aiolupo; Lima (Tagaloa 52), Vaega, Bunce, Fa'amasino; Bachop, Vaca; Fatialofa (capt), To'omalatai, Alaalatoa, Birtwhistle, Keenan, Paramore, Perelini, Kaleopa.
  Scorer – *Penalty goal:* Vaea

Referee: E Morrison (England).

Series score: Played 1, Australia 1, Western Samoa 0.

Wales (9) 16, Argentina (0) 7
Cardiff, 9 October 1991
Wales: Rayer; I Evans (capt), Hall, Gibbs, Emyr; Ring, Jones; Griffiths, Jenkins, Delaney, Arnold, Moseley, Lewis, Webster, P Davies.
  Scorers – *Try:* Arnold. *Penalty goals:* Ring 3, Rayer.

Argentina: del Castillo; Teran Nouges, Laborde, Garcia Simon, Cuesta Silva; Arbizu, Camardon; Mendez, le Fort, Molina, Sporledor, Llanes, Garreton (capt), Santamarina, Carreras.
  Scorers – *Try:* Garcia Simon. *Penalty goal:* del Castillo.

Referee: R Hourquet (France).

Series score: Played 4, Wales 2, Argentina 1, Drawn 1.

Wales (3) 3, Australia (22) 38
Cardiff, 12 October 1991
Wales: Clement; I Evans (capt), Hall, Gibbs (Rayer 79), Emyr (D Evans 75); Ring, Jones; Griffiths, Jenkins, Delaney, Arnold, Moseley, Lewis, Webster, P Davies.
  Scorer – *Penalty goal:* Ring.

Australia: Roebuck; Campese, Horan, Little, Egerton; Lynagh (capt), Slattery; Daly, Kearns, McKenzie, McCall, Eales, Poidevin, Miller, Ofahengaue.

Scorers – *Tries:* Roebuck 2, Slattery, Campese, Lynagh, Horan. *Conversions:* Lynagh 4. *Penalty goals:* Lynagh 2.

Referee: K Lawrence (New Zealand).

Series score: Played 15, Wales 8, Australia 7.

Argentina (12) 12, Western Samoa (15) 35
Pontypridd, 13 October 1991

Argentina: Angaut (Meson 53); Teran Nouges, Laborde, Garcia Simon, Cuesta Silva; Arbizu, Camardon; Aguirre, Bosch, Cash, Buabse, Sporledor, Irazaval (Carreras 60), Garreton (capt), Santamarina.

Scorers – *Try:* Teran Nouges. *Conversion:* Arbizu. *Penalty goals:* Laborde, Arbizu. *Sent-off:* Sporledor (65).

Western Samoa: Aiolupo; Lima, Vaega, Bunce, Tagaloa; Bachop, Vaea; Fatialofa (capt), To'omalatai, Alalatoa, Birtwhistle, Keenan, Vaifale, Perelini, Lam.

Scorers – *Tries:* Tagaloa 2, Lima 2, Bunce, Bachop. *Conversions:* Vaea 4. *Penalty goal:* Vaea. *Sent-off:* Keenan (65).

Referee: B Anderson (Scotland) (J M Fleming 40).

Series score: Played 1, Western Samoa 1, Argentina 0.

	P	W	D	L	F	A	Pts
Australia	3	3	0	0	79	25	9
W Samoa	3	2	0	1	54	34	7
Wales	3	1	0	2	32	61	5
Argentina	3	0	0	3	38	83	3

POOL 4

The success of Canada in reaching the quarter-finals is as welcome as the progress of the Samoans. Inspired by flanker Gord MacKinnon, the Canucks produce a series of devastating forward performances which account for the enigmatic Romanians and Fijians and come very close to bidding adieu to France in Agen. It is just sad that British audiences miss out on the Canadian experience as the group's business is conducted exclusively in France. The French, save fleeting moments of brilliance behind the scrum, lack conviction, and the injury suffered by outside-half Didier Camberabero against Canada compounds their problems going into the knock-out stage. All the same, the hosts win three out of three. But what a disappointment are both Romania, victors over Scotland five weeks previously, and fifth seeds Fiji, whose only solace comes in the form of a display of quite awesome dropped goal-kicking by Tomasi Rabaka and Opeti Turuva against Romania. However, the breathtaking Fijian flair, which hallmarks their magnificent Sevens' sides, is sadly left back home in paradise. ***Winners:** France.* ***Runners-up:** Canada.*

France (6) 30, Romania (0) 3
Beziers, 4 October 1991

France: Blanco (capt); Saint-Andre, Lacroix, Mesnel, Lagisquet (Lafond 70); Camberabero, Galthie; Lascube, Marocco, Ondarts, Cadieu, Roumat, Champ, Cabannes, Benazzi.

Scorers – *Tries:* penalty try, Saint-Andre, Roumat, Lafond. *Conversion:* Camberabero. *Penalty goals:* Camberabero 4.

Romania: Dumitru; Sasu, Lungu, Sava, Racean; Nichitean, Neaga; Leonte, Ion, Stan, Ciorascu, Cojocariu, Dinu, Guranescu, Dumitras (capt).
    Scorer – *Penalty goal:* Nichetean.

Referee: L Peard (Wales).

Series score: Played 38, France 29, Romania 9.

Fiji (3) 3, Canada (7) 13
Bayonne, 5 October 1991
Fiji: Koroduadua; Seru, Aria, Nadruku, Lovo; Serevi, Tabulutu; Taga (capt), Naiwilawasa, Naituivau, Savai, Domoni, Kato, Tawake, Dere.
    Scorer – *Dropped goal:* Serevi.

Canada: S Stewart; Palmer, C Stewart, Lecky, Gray; Rees, Tynan; Evans, Speirs, Jackart, Robertson, Hadley, Charron, MacKinnon, Ennis (capt).
    Scorers – *Try:* S Stewart. *Penalty goals:* Rees 3.

Referee: K Fitzgerald (Australia).

Series score: Played 2, Fiji 1, Canada 1.

France (19) 33, Fiji (3) 9
Grenoble, 8 October 1991
France: Blanco (capt); Lafond, Sella, Mesnel, Saint-Andre; Camberabero, Galthie; Lascube, Marocco, Ondarts, Cadieu, Roumat, Champ, Cabannes, Benazzi.
    Scorers – *Tries:* Lafond 3, Sella 2, Camberabero. *Conversions:* Camberabero 3. *Penalty goal:* Camberabero.

Fiji: Koroduadua; Seru, Aria, Naisoro, Lovo; Serevi, Vosanibola (Tabulutu 40); Taga (capt) (Volavola 10), Baleiwai, Vuli, Savai, Domoni (Kato 73), Naruma, Dere, Tawake.
    Scorers – *Try:* Naruma. *Conversion:* Koroduadua. *Penalty goal:* Koroduadua.

Referee: W D Bevan (Wales).

Series score: Played 4, France 4, Fiji 0.

Canada (3) 19, Romania (3) 11
Toulouse, 9 October 1991
Canada: Wyatt (capt); Palmer, C Stewart, Lecky, S Stewart; Rees, Graf; Evans, Svoboda, Jackart, Van den Brink, Hadley, Breen, MacKinnon, Ennis.
    Scorers – *Tries:* MacKinnon, Ennis. *Conversion:* Wyatt. *Penalty goals:* Wyatt 2. *Dropped goal:* Rees.

Romania: Dumitru (Sava 33); Sasu, Lungu, Fulina, Racean; Nichitean, Neaga; Leonte (Vlad 70), Ion, Stan, Ciorascu, Cojocariu, Dinu, Doja (Brinza 15), Dumitras (capt).
    Scorers – *Tries:* Lungu, Sasu. *Penalty goal:* Nichitean.

Referee: A R MacNeill (Australia).

Series score: Played 1, Canada 1, Romania 0.

France (9) 19, Canada (7) 13
Agen, 13 October 1991

France: Blanco (capt); Lafond, Sella (Sadourny 50), Mesnel, Saint-Andre; Camberabero (Lacroix 40), Galthie; Lascube, Marocco, Ondarts, J-M Cadieu, Roumat, Champ, Cabannes, Benazzi.

Scorers – *Tries:* Lafond, Saint-Andre. *Conversion:* Camberabero. *Penalty goals:* Camberabero, Lacroix 2.

Canada: Wyatt (capt) (S Stewart 45); Palmer, C Stewart, Woods, Gray; Rees, Tynan; Evans, Svoboda, Jackart, Robertson (Van den Brink 25), Hadley, Charron, MacKinnon, Ennis.

Scorers – *Try:* Wyatt. *Dropped goal:* Rees. *Penalty goals:* Wyatt, Rees.

Referee: S Hilditch (Ireland).

Series score: Played 3, France 3, Canada 0.

Fiji (6) 15, Romania (9) 17
Brive, 13 October 1991

Fiji: Turuva; Seru, Nadruku, Naisoro, Vonolagi; Rabaka, Tabulutu; Volavola (Naituivau), Baleiwai, Vuli, Savai, Nadolo, Tawake, Dere (capt), Ollsson (Naruma).

Scorers – *Penalty goals:* Turuva 2. *Dropped goals:* Rabaka 2, Turuva.

Romania: Racean; Sasu, Lungu, Fulina, Colceriu; Nichitean (Ivanciuc), Neaga; Stan, Ion, Vlad, Cojocariu, Ciorascu, Dinu, Marin, Dumitras (capt).

Scorers – *Tries:* Ion, Dumitras, Sasu. *Conversion:* Racean. *Penalty goal:* Nichitean.

Referee: O Doyle (Ireland).

Series score: Played 1, Romania 1, Fiji 0.

	P	W	D	L	F	A	Pts
France	3	3	0	0	82	25	9
Canada	3	2	0	1	45	33	7
Romania	3	1	0	2	31	64	5
Fiji	3	0	0	3	27	63	3

QUARTER-FINALS

Scotland (13) 28, Western Samoa (3) 6
Edinburgh, 19 October 1991

Scotland and Western Samoa arrive at their quarter-final lacking one regular apiece: the Samoans without lock Ma'taafa Keenan, whose one-match suspension (meted out by an RWC disciplinary committee in the wake of his dismissal, together with Argentina's Sporledor, in the Pool 3 win over the Pumas) is upheld after appeal; the Scots minus Kiwi centre Sean Lineen who, despite a week spent predominantly in a hyperbaric oxygen chamber, fails to shake off his left knee injury. In the event Scotland, with Graham Shiel deputising, cope the better with their loss. The Samoans tackle with the bone-crunching ferocity that has become their hallmark, but the Scots, men possessed amid the Murrayfield chorus, never flinch, never shirk a challenge and, overall, are as tactically astute as they are streetwise. Coach Ian McGeechan has stressed the need to 'keep the ball moving and the target coming towards them', and the back row unit together with

Gavin Hastings, employed in his uncustomary guise as auxiliary flanker in the early exchanges before claiming 16 points, ensure his orders are obeyed to the letter. John Jeffrey, with the second of his two touchdowns, his 11th for his country, regains the Scottish forwards' try-scoring record from Derek White. But the warmest memory from this encounter is the South Sea Islanders' post-match lap of honour and emotion-charged encore of their 'manu Samoa' dance to the delight of the privileged Edinburgh crowd.

Scotland: G Hastings; Stanger, S Hastings, Shiel, Tukalo; Chalmers, Armstrong; Sole (capt), Allan, Burnell, Weir, Gray, Jeffrey, Calder, White.

Scorers – *Tries:* Jeffrey 2, Stanger. *Conversions:* G Hastings 2. *Penalty goals:* G Hastings 4.

Western Samoa: Aiolupo; Lima, Vaega, Bunce, Tagaloa; Bachop, Vaea; Fatialofa (capt), To'omalatai, Alalatoa, Birtwhistle, Ioane, Vaifale, Perelini, Lam.

Scorers – *Penalty goal:* Vaea. *Dropped goal:* Bachop.

Referee: W D Bevan (Wales).

Series score: Played 1, Scotland 1, W Samoa 0.

France (6) 10, England (10) 19
Paris, 19 October 1991

This is never going to be a contest for the faint-hearted, there is too much at stake, but that in no way can possibly excuse the cynical, downright violent behaviour of the French towards visitors England in general and New Zealand referee David Bishop in particular. England's significant achievement in progressing to the semi-finals is most regrettably overshadowed by the assaults carried out on Orrell wing Nigel Heslop by Serge Blanco (making a world record 93rd and final French appearance) and Eric Champ during the early passage of play, and on Bishop by French coach Daniel Dubroca in the players' tunnel after the official had called time on France's challenge. Physical clashes, while not to be condoned, are inherent in contact sports – such is the nature of the beast – but misdemeanours that smack of premeditated malice are totally unacceptable. Not only do they have no place in sport, they have no place in society. To their shame, the RWC committee take too long in recognising as much: despite allegations that Dubroca called Bishop a cheat, spat at him and grabbed his collar, RWC organising committee chairman Russ Thomas decides that as no official complaint has been registered, no action will be taken. It is a grave error of judgement. The referee's report later speaks of 'a serious incident' and, allied to Dubroca's later admission of guilt and written apology, triggers a letter from tournament director Ray Williams to the French Rugby Federation demanding action. Belatedly, Dubroca responds to the ever-mounting condemnation by resigning. It takes too long, but rugby union's code of honourable conduct – the referee's decision is final, no 'buts' – is belatedly preserved.

France: Blanco (capt); Saint-Andre, Sella, Mesnel, Lafond; Lacroix, Galthie; Lascube, Marocco, Ondarts, Cadieu, Roumat, Champ, Cabannes, Cecillon.

Scorers – *Try:* Lafond. *Penalty goals:* Lacroix 2.

England: Webb; Heslop, Carling (capt), Guscott, Underwood; Andrew, Hill; Leonard, Moore, Probyn, Ackford, Dooley, Skinner, Winterbottom, Teague.

Scorers – *Tries:* Underwood, Carling. *Conversion:* Webb. *Penalty goals:* Webb 3.

Referee: D J Bishop (New Zealand).

Series score: Played 67, England 36, France 24, Drawn 7.

Ireland (3) 18, Australia (6) 19
Dublin, 20 October 1991

Considering their woeful summer, Ireland surely vie with Western Samoa and Canada as the most surprising team of the tournament. Desperately unlucky to lose out to Scotland and, therefore, forced to entertain the Webb Ellis Cup favourites, the Irish come within seconds of a famous victory against a side assessed by coach Bob Dwyer as 'putting in their best performance of the tour'. The ubiquitous Campese has already poached two tries for a 15-12 Antipodean lead when, with 4 minutes remaining, Jim Staples and Jack Clarke unleash flanker Gordon Hamilton on a glory-run into Irish rugby folklore. Landsdowne Road erupts in joy, Ralph Keyes adds the conversion to his earlier dropped goal and three penalty goals, and Ireland, 18-15 to the good, await the final whistle. Australia, though, refuse to accept the seemingly inevitable and when they win an attacking position 15 metres out, Michael Lynagh rejects the opportunity of adding a second penalty to a haul which also includes two conversions and opts instead for a scrum. The ball spins right, Campese is held, but here comes Lynagh...

Ireland: Staples; Geoghegan, Curtis, Mullin, Clarke; Keyes, Saunders; Popplewell, Smith, D Fitgerald, Lenihan, Francis, Matthews (capt), Hamilton, Robinson.

    Scorers – *Try:* Hamilton. *Conversion:* Keyes. *Penalty goals:* Keyes 3. *Dropped goal:* Keyes.

Australia: Roebuck; Campese, Horan, Little, Egerton; Lynagh, Farr-Jones (capt) (Slattery 18); Daly, Kearns, McKenzie, McCall, Eales, Poidevin, Miller, Ofahengaue.

    Scorers – *Tries:* Campese 2, Lynagh. *Conversions:* Lynagh 2. *Penalty goal:* Lynagh.

Referee: J M Fleming (Scotland).

Series score: Played 13, Ireland 6, Australia 7.

New Zealand (21) 29, Canada (3) 13
Lille, 20 October 1991

It rains cats and dogs in Lille but also rucks and mauls of the very highest quality, as Canada compete on an equal footing with the All Blacks up front. The Canucks have come a long way in the 17 years since the only other meeting of two nations, when New Zealand eased to a 40-14 victory. Yet at half-time it looks as though Canada are en route to another heavy defeat as they trail 21-3, the Blacks exploiting Canada's marginally hesitant defence and capitalising on their own sure touch in the most testing of conditions. The Canadians, though, are built of sterner stuff as they demonstrate in a second period in which they outscore their opponents with their combatative back row to the fore. Like the Western Samoans before them, Canada are awarded a standing ovation as they take a lap of honour on the final whistle.

New Zealand: Timu; Kirwan, Innes, McCahill, Tuigamala; Fox, Bachop; McDowell, Fitzpatrick, Loe, I Jones, G Whetton (capt), A Whetton, P Henderson, Brooke.

    Scorers – *Tries:* Timu 2, Kirwan, Brooke, McCahill. *Conversions:* Fox 3. *Penalty goal:* Fox.

Canada: Wyatt (capt); S Stewart, C Stewart, Woods, Gray; Rees, Tynan; Evans, Speirs, Szabo, Van den Brink, Hadley, Charron, MacKinnon, Ennis.

    Scorers – *Tries:* Tynan, Charron. *Conversion:* Rees. *Penalty goal:* Wyatt.

Referee: F A Howard (England).

Series score: Played 2, NZ 2, Canada 0.

SEMI-FINALS

Scotland (6) 6, England (3) 9
Edinburgh, 26 October 1991

Nineteen months after Scotland and England contested the biggest match in Home Unions' rugby history (the 1990 Five Nations' Grand Slam decider) they reconvene for an even grander occasion. This time there is no Grand Slam, no Triple Crown, no Calcutta Cup up for grabs ... but a place in the World Cup final. Such an occasion, such an atmosphere – such a disappointing match, even given the adroit, domineering, performance of the English pack. We should not be surprised at either side's reluctance to move the ball, such are the stakes and the historical precedence in the series, but when set alongside the dish served up in the Southern Hemisphere semi-final, the Northern version is a crashing disappointment, satisfying only the blandest, least discerning palate. Indeed it is only the second match in the tournament devoid of tries (the other being Australia 9, Western Samoa 3). Rory Underwood, becoming the first Englishman to reach 50 caps, is a virtual spectator, though he enjoys watching the dropped goal by Rob Andrew (a world record-equalling 15th) which succeeds, where Gavin Hastings (with a relatively straightforward 61st minute penalty attempt) fails, in breaking a 6-6 deadlock, 7 minutes from time. Previous to that, Webb has atoned for four penalty misses with two successes to match Hastings' brace inside the opening half-hour.

Scotland: G Hastings; Stanger, S Hastings, Lineen, Tukalo; Chalmers, Armstrong; Sole (capt), Allan, Burnell, Weir, Gray, Jeffrey, Calder, White.
   Scorer – *Penalty goals:* G Hastings 2 (9,30).

England: Webb; Halliday, Carling (capt), Guscott, Underwood; Andrew, Hill; Leonard, Moore, Probyn, Ackford, Dooley, Skinner, Winterbottom, Teague.
   Scorers – *Penalty goals:* Webb 2 (32,57). *Dropped goal:* Andrew (73).

Referee: K V J Fitzgerald (Australia).

Series score: Played 108, England 52, Scotland 39, Drawn 17.

New Zealand (0) 6, Australia (13) 16
Dublin, 27 October 1991

Just when the rugby neutral's spirits are waning, desperately in need of a pick-me-up following the attrition of Murrayfield, Australia and New Zealand provide the most magnificent tonic for the troops. Just when we are beginning to believe that rugby cannot in fact be played amid the intolerable pressure imposed by a World Cup semi-final, the Australasian fraternity explode the myth, and so gloriously that the winners are rightly heralded as champions-in-waiting. David Campese, the wizard of Oz, sets the tone with a magnificent score (extending his world try-scoring record to 46) as early as the sixth minute and, before the half is out, works Tim Horan into position for the try of the tournament; instinctively sensing the whereabouts of his support before nonchalantly slipping the ball over his shoulder for the powerful midfielder to apply the *coup de grâce*. The men in Black should have sensed Campo's intentions when he juggled the ball alone under his own posts while his team mates faced the pre-match Haka – his act every bit as much a declaration of intent as the colourful Maori ritual. The world champions can only look on in awe and wonderment. Since they upheld the Webb Ellis Cup in 1987 the All Blacks have beaten Australia on seven of their ten meetings. But not this time, not when it matters most. Despite dominating possession in the second half, they are unable to shore up the Wallaby defence, which shows itself to be as prodigious as their rightly-vaunted attack; Grant Fox, whilst maintaining his record of scoring in every International in which he has played by matching Michael Lynagh's two penalty strikes, cannot save his team mates this time.

New Zealand: Crowley; Kirwan, Innes, McCahill, Timu; Fox, Bachop; McDowell, Fitzpatrick, Loe, I Jones, G Whetton (capt), A Whetton, M Carter, Z Brooke.

Scorer – *Penalty goals:* Fox 2 (42,73).

Australia: Roebuck; Egerton; Little, Horan, Campese; Lynagh, Farr-Jones (capt); Daly, Kearns, McKenzie, McCall, Eales, Poidevin, Ofahengaue, Coker.

Scorers – *Tries:* Campese (6), Horan (34). *Conversion:* Lynagh (34). *Penalty goals:* Lynagh 2 (13,61).

Referee: J M Fleming (Scotland).

Series score: Played 93, Australia 24, NZ 64, Drawn 5.

THIRD PLACE PLAY-OFF

Scotland (3) 6, New Zealand (6) 13
Cardiff, 30 October 1991
The end of an era for both nations is signalled by a match of remarkable entertainment and commitment, considering the lack of incentive, which is a credit to all involved. Regardless of the splendid fare dished up, both sides know the damage has already been done by failure to stay the course. Finlay Calder and John Jeffrey, for so long stalwarts of the Scottish back row and, as such, the heart and soul of the national cause, bow out while the All Black unit, players and management alike, heads home for drastic overhaul. The downbeat tempo of the pre-match formalities – 'Flower of Scotland' played at a ludicrously pedestrian pace – belies the intense contest to follow. Bucket-loads of pride pour out of both nations' displays but Scotland, despite the three-point lead given them by Gavin Hastings after only 4 minutes of their first match of the tournament away from Murrayfield, remain under almost continuous siege throughout. The All Blacks, growing accustomed to running into concrete defences after their semi-final, have to make do with three John Preston penalty goals until Hastings adds his second penalty 3 minutes from time to provoke a belated Kiwi revival which, with Walter Little's last-ditch try, ensures that New Zealand retain their unbroken supremacy over Scotland.

Scotland: G Hastings; Stanger (Dods 47), S Hastings, Lineen, Tukalo; Chalmers, Armstrong; Sole (capt), Allan, Burnell, Weir, Gray, Jeffrey, Calder, White.

Scorer – *Penalty goals:* G Hastings 2 (4,77).

New Zealand: Wright; Kirwan, Innes, Little, Tuigamala (Philpott 40); Preston, Bachop; McDowell, Fitzpatrick, Loe, I Jones, G Whetton (capt), Earl, M Jones, Brooke.

Scorers – *Try:* Little (80). *Penalty goals:* Preston 3 (13,33,49).

Referee: S R Hilditch (Ireland).

Series score: Played 16, Scotland 0, NZ 14, Drawn 2.

FINAL

England (0) 6, Australia (9) 12
Twickenham, 2 November 1991

Glorious failure is the phrase universally applied to England's contribution to a quite wonderful finale to the second World Cup. The Poms are ultimately denied but, just as no-one would deny Australia's right over the piece to the soubriquet 'world champions', so England richly deserve their acclaim in defeat. The all whites have been lambasted by media critics and rival nations alike for their unambitious forward approach throughout the tournament yet their final display is such a complete diversion from what has passed (or not passed!) before. With the benefit of hindsight, many of the English XV argue that by belatedly opting to entertain, they actually give Australia the last laugh; the argument being that the World Cup final is hardly the occasion to break with immediate tradition and start executing rusty expansive movements. Hindsight, though, is a nauseatingly precise science. Better to reflect on how close England actually come, employing their chosen mix of relentless effort, intense desire and undying, breathless ambition before an enthralled global audience. Australia claim the game's only try when, from a line-out inside the English 22 on the half-hour, Willie O (Ofahengaue) drives over before slipping Tony Daly the scoring pass. Nine points adrift at half-time, but still England's belief is undiminished. Jon Webb sandwiches penalty successes either side of Michael Lynagh's 68th minute effort but, in a frantic, fraught climax, Australia hold out. As the great Dan Maskell so often put it: 'Well played, well played indeed.'

England: Webb; Halliday, Carling (capt), Guscott, Underwood; Andrew, Hill; Leonard, Moore, Probyn, Ackford, Dooley, Skinner, Winterbottom, Teague. *Repls:* Pears, Heslop, Morris, Pearce, Olver, Richards.
    Scorer – *Penalty goals:* Webb 2 (62,71).

Australia: Roebuck; Egerton; Little, Horan, Campese; Lynagh, Farr-Jones (capt); Daly, Kearns, McKenzie, McCall, Eales, Poidevin, Ofahengaue, Coker. *Repls:* Flett, Herbert, Slattery, Miller, Crowley, Nucifora.
    Scorers – *Try:* Daly (30). *Conversion:* Lynagh. *Penalty goals:* Lynagh 2 (26,68).

Referee: W D Bevan (Wales). **Touch judges:** K Lawrence, D Bishop (both NZ).

MATCH FACTS (supplied by *Unisys*): ***Territorial advantage (mins):*** *England* 44, *Australia* 38. **Possession (mins):** *England* 47, *Australia* 35. **Scrums:** *England* – award 14, won 14; *Australia* – award 15, won 15. **Lineouts:** *England* – award 26, won 19, void 3; *Australia* – award 21, won 15, void 10. **Penalties/free kicks:** *England* – award 16, tap 6, goal 2, miss 2; *Australia* – award 8, tap 1, goal 2, miss 1. **Outside-halves:** Andrew *(England)* – run 0, kick 15, pass 26; Lynagh *(Australia)* – run 0, kick 13, pass 4. **Kicks at goal:** Webb *(England)* – total 4, success 2; Andrew *(England)* – total 1 (dropped goal), success 0; Lynagh *(Australia)* – total 4, success 3. **Attendance:** 60,000. **Series score:** *Played 18, England 6, Australia 12.*

LEADING SCORERS

Points:
68 – R Keyes *(Ireland: 0t,7c,16p,2dg)*
66 – M Lynagh *(Australia: 2t,11c,12p,0dg)*
61 – G Hastings *(Scotland: 1t,9c,13p,0dg)*

Tries:
6 –   D Campese *(Australia)*
       J-B Lafond *(France)*
4 –   T Horan *(Australia)*

56 – J Webb *(England: 1t,5c,14p,0dg)*   4 –   B Robinson *(Ireland)*
44 – G Fox *(New Zealand: 0t,7c,10p,0dg)*   I Tukalo *(Scotland)*
32 – D Camberabero *(France: 1t,5c,6p,0dg)*   R Underwood *(England)*

THE YEAR IN REVIEW

Details are given of every International match played during season 1991–2 (at or above U-21 level) involving the four Home Unions, the World Cup, and a selection of other matches played around the globe. Player's clubs are given in brackets. In the case of tours: results, appearances (signified by the relevant match number after the player's name), and scorers have been logged. 'R' indicates an appearance as a replacement. An * indicates an appearance as captain. For Five Nations' and World Cup last eight matches the number in brackets after scorer indicates time of score; number after scorer's name indicates quantities of score.

WALES TO AUSTRALIA
June–July 1991: P6 W3 L3 F102 A185

This tour is widely predicted as a disaster waiting to happen – and so it proves. Wales win three of their six matches but their defeats are catastrophic. To lose 71-8 to New South Wales and 63-6 to Australia (the biggest Test defeat suffered by one of the eight major IB nations) are pills too bitter to swallow for the Welsh, both at home and Down Under. Back in the Principality the call is for heads to roll and a drastic re-structuring of the sport from top to bottom, while in Australia the players resort to fighting each other at the post-International reception.

On arrival back home captain Paul Thorburn announces his retirement from international rugby and coach Ron Waldron steps down on health grounds. Nottingham's Alan Davies, the former England B coach, is voted in as Waldron's successor ahead of Tony Gray, the WRU executive committee's nominee, with the highly respected Bob Norster appointed team manager. Both engagements are intended to be temporary: for the three-month period up to and including the World Cup.

PARTY: **L Evans** (Llanelli – 5), **P Thorburn** (Neath, capt – 1,2,4,6), **A Clement** (Swansea – 3,5,6R), **I Evans** (Llanelli – 1,2,3,4,6), **I Jones** (Llanelli – 1,3), **S Ford** (Cardiff – 2,4,6), **D Evans** (Cardiff – 1,5,6R), **S Gibbs** (Neath – 1,2,3,4,6), **M Hall** (Cardiff – 2,4,5,6), **S Lewis** (Pontypridd – 3,5), **A Davies** (Neath – 1,2,5,6), **N Jenkins** (Pontypridd – 3,4), **C Bridges** (Neath – 2,5,6), **R Jones** (Swansea – 1,2R,3,4), **M Davis** (Newport – 3,4,6), **M Griffiths** (Cardiff – 1,2,5), **P Knight** (Pontypridd – 2,3), **H**

Williams-Jones (South Wales Police – 1,4,5,6), **K Phillips** (Neath – 2,5,6), **K Waters** (Newbridge – 1,3,4), **P Arnold** (Swansea – 2,3,4,6), **R Goodey** (Pontypool – 1,5), **G D Llewellyn** (Neath – 3,4,6), **G O Llewellyn** (Neath – 1,2,5,6R), **R Collins** (Cardiff – 1,3,4,5,6), **E Lewis** (Llanelli – 1,3,6), **M Morris** (Neath – 2,5), **R Webster** (Swansea – 2,4), **P Davies** (Llanelli – 1,2,4,6), **I Hembrow** (Cardiff), **S Legge** (Glamorgan Wanderers – 1,3,5).

Fixtures: (1) Western Australia 6, Wales 22 (Perth, 30 June); (2) Queensland 35, Wales 24 (Brisbane, 7 July); (3) Australian Capital Territory 3, Wales 7 (Canberra, 10 July); (4) New South Wales 71, Wales 8 (Sydney, 14 July); (5) Queensland Country 7, Wales 35 (Rockhampton, 17 July); (6) Test: **Australia 63, Wales 6** (Brisbane, 21 July).

Scorers – A Davies 19 (*1t,5dg*), D Evans 15 (*1t,1p,4c*), Hall 12 (*3t*), L Evans 8 (*2t*), R Jones 8 (*2t*), Webster 8 (*2t*), Thorburn 5 (*1c,1dg*), Clement 4 (*1t*), Ford 4 (*1t*), Legge 4 (*1t*), E Lewis 4 (*1t*), G O Llewellyn 4 (*1t*), penalty try (*4*), Jenkins 3 (*1p*).

Australia (23) 63, Wales (6) 6
Brisbane, 20 July 1991

Australia: M Roebuck; D Campese (both NSW), T Horan, J Little (both Queensland), R Egerton (NSW); M Lynagh (Queensland), N Farr-Jones (capt); A Daly, P Kearns, E McKenzie (all NSW), R McCall, J Eales, J Miller (all Queensland), V Ofahengaue, T Gavin (both NSW). *Repl:* P Slattery (Queensland) for Farr-Jones, 60 mins.

Scorers – *Tries:* Horan, Lynagh 2, Ofahengaue, Kearns 2, Roebuck, Gavin 2, Campese, Egerton, Little. *Conversions:* Lynagh 6. *Penalty goal:* Lynagh.

Wales: Thorburn (capt); I Evans, Gibbs, Hall, Ford; A Davies, Bridges; Davis, Phillips, Williams-Jones, Arnold, G D Llewellyn, Collins, E Lewis, P Davies. *Repls:* G O Llewellyn for P Davies, 20 mins; Clement for Thorburn, 38 mins; D Evans for Ford, 79 mins.

Scorers – *Penalty goal:* Thorburn. *Dropped goal:* A Davies.

Referee: F Howard (England).

Series score: Played 14, Australia 6, Wales 8.

ENGLAND TO AUSTRALIA AND FIJI
July 1991: P7 W3 D0 L4 F151 A132

England enjoy a little more success than Wales in their summer sojourn but the emphasis is on 'little' rather than 'enjoy' as they are made to work feverishly hard to overcome a Fijian side by 28-12 – the Fijians fully deserving a 12-12 scoreline after an hour's play – before succumbing to Australia and sustaining their second biggest ever away defeat (in the process New Zealand beat England 42-15 in second Test, Wellington, 1985). England forsake their conservative, ultra-disciplined 1991 Five Nations' gameplan and take on the Wallabies at their own extravagant game. The problem is that Australia, put simply, are better at it. Their manoeuvres are gloriously orchestrated whereas England's are sporadic, isolated outbursts, and critically, lacking in support.

David Campese takes his Test try-record to 40 with a brace, and Michael Lynagh extends his international points tally to 607.

PARTY: S Hodgkinson (Nottingham – 2,3,4R,6), J Webb (Bath – 1,4,5), N Heslop (Orrell – 1,4,6), I Hunter (Northampton – 2,4,6), C Oti (Wasps – 2,3,5), R Underwood (Leicester – 1,3,5), W Carling (Harlequins, capt – 1,3,5), J Guscott (Bath – 1,3,4R,5), S Halliday (Harlequins – 2,4,6), D Hopley (Wasps – 2,4,6), R Andrew (Wasps – 1,3,5), D Pears (Harlequins – 2,4,6), R Hill (Bath – 1,3,5), D Morris (Orrell – 2,4,6), J Leonard (Harlequins – 1,3,5), G Pearce (Northampton – 3,4,6), J Probyn (Wasps – 1,2,5), P Rendall (Wasps – 2,4,6), B Moore (Harlequins – 1,3,5), J Olver (Northampton – 2*,4*,6*), P Ackford (Harlequins – 1,3,6), W Dooley (Preston Grasshoppers – 1,3), N Redman (Bath – 2,4,5,6), M Bayfield (Northampton – 2,4,5), J Hall (Bath – 1,4), G Rees (Nottingham – 2,4,5), M Skinner (Harlequins – 1R,2,4,5R,6), M Teague (Gloucester – 1,3,5,6), P Winterbottom (Harlequins – 1,3,6), D Richards (Leicester – 2,3,5).

Fixtures: (1) New South Wales 21, England 19 (Sydney, 7 July); (2) Victoria President's XV 9, England 26 (Melbourne, 10 July); (3) Queensland 20, England 14 (Brisbane, 14 July); (4) Fiji B 27, England 13 (Lautoka, 16 July); (5) Test: **Fiji 12, England 28** (Suva, 20 July); (6) Emerging Australians 3, England 36 (Gosford, 23 July); (7) Test: **Australia 40 England 15** (Sydney, 27 July).

Scorers – Webb 41 (*1t,9p,5c*), Hodgkinson 17 (*1p,7c*), Andrew 10 (*1t,2dg*), Guscott 8 (*2t*), Heslop 8 (*2t*), Hopley 8 (*2t*), Hunter 8 (*2t*), Morris 8 (*2t*), Underwood 8 (*2t*), Pears 7 (*1t,1dg*), Hill 4 (*1t*), Oti 4 (*1t*), Probyn 4 (*1t*), Rees 4 (*1t*), Richards 4 (*1t*), Skinner 4 (*1t*), Teague 4 (*1t*).

Fiji (9) 12, England (12) 28
Suva, 20 July 1991
Fiji: O Turuva; T Vonolagi, J Taqaiwai, V Rauluni, F Seru; W Serevi, P Tabulutu; E Naituivau, S Naiwilawasa, M Taga (capt), S Domoni, I Savai, A Dere, I Tawake, M Olsson.

Scorers – *Try:* Seru. *Conversion:* Serevi. *Penalty goal:* Serevi. *Dropped goal:* Serevi.

England: Webb; Underwood, Guscott, Carling (capt), Oti; Andrew, Hill; Leonard, Moore, Probyn, Redman, Bayfield, Teague, Rees, Richards. *Repl:* Skinner for Teague, 40 mins.

Scorers – *Tries:* Probyn, Underwood, Andrew. *Conversions:* Webb 2. *Penalty goals:* Webb 2. *Dropped goals:* Andrew 2.

Referee: B Kinsey (Australia).

Series score: Played 6, Fiji 0, England 6.

Australia (16) 40, England (9) 15
Sydney, 27 July 1991
Australia: M Roebuck; D Campese (both NSW), T Horan, J Little (both Queensland), R Egerton (NSW); M Lynagh (Queensland), N Farr-Jones (capt); A Daly, P Kearns, E McKenzie (all NSW), R McCall, J Eales (both Queensland), S Poidevin (NSW), V Ofahengaue, T Gavin (both NSW). *Repl:* P Slattery (Queensland) for Farr-Jones, 58 mins.

Scorers – *Tries:* Roebuck, Campese 2, Ofahengaue 2. *Conversions:* Lynagh 4. *Penalty goals:* Lynagh 4.

England: Webb; Underwood, Guscott, Carling (capt), Oti; Andrew, Hill; Leonard, Moore, Probyn, Ackford, Bayfield, Teague, Rees, Richards.

Scorers – *Try:* Guscott. *Conversion:* Webb. *Penalty goals:* Webb 3.

Referee: K Lawrence (New Zealand).

Series score: Played: 17, Australia 11, England 6.

IRELAND TO NAMIBIA
July 1991: P4 W2 D0 L2 F101 A61

Ireland, led by Philip Matthews in succession to Rob Saunders, suffer the same pre-World Cup dose of dejection as England and Wales. Two Tests are lost to a Namibian side who extend their unbeaten run to nine matches, and the hope aroused by the Five Nations' Championship appears misplaced. Until independence Namibia played in the 'B' section of South Africa's Currie Cup. Yet in the ten-week period prior to Ireland's arrival they underline their hastily acquired class with wins over Spain, Portugal, Italy (twice) and Zimbabwe (twice). Ireland look unconvincing at half-back (where Saunders and Vince Cunningham earn the nod), suffer badly from a tropical bug and, most cruelly of all, lose influential lock Brian Rigney with a serious knee ligament injury which requires immediate attention in Dublin.

PARTY: J Staples (London Irish – 2,4), **K Murphy** (Constitution – 1,3), **S Geoghegan** (London Irish – 2), **B Mullin** (Blackrock Coll – 1,2,4), **D Curtis** (London Irish – 2,3,4), **K Crossan** (Instonians – 1,3,4), **R Wallace** (Garryowen – 1,2R,3), **J Clarke** (Dolphin – 1,2,3,4), **V Cunningham** (St Mary's Coll – 1,2,4), **N Barry** (Garryowen – 4R,3), **R Saunders** (London Irish – 2,4), **F Aherne** (Lansdowne – 1,3), **J Fitzgerald** (Young Munster – 3), **S Smith** (Ballymena – 1,2,4), **D Fitzgerald** (Lansdowne – 1,2,4), **N Popplewell** (Greystones – 1,2,4), **T Kingston** (Dolphin – 3), **G Halpin** (Wanderers – 3), **B Rigney** (Greystones – 2), **D Lenihan** (Constitution – 3,4), **M Galwey** (Shannon – 1,3,4R), **N Francis** (Blackrock Coll – 1,2,4), **P Matthews** (Wanderers, capt – 1,2), **G Hamilton** (NIFC – 3,4), **B Robinson** (Ballymena – 1,2,4), **P O'Hara** (Sunday's Well – 1,2,3), **N Mannion** (Lansdowne – 2R,3,4).

Fixtures: (1) Namibia B 16, Ireland 45 (Windhoek, 17 July); (2) first Test: **Namibia 15, Ireland 6** (Windhoek, 20 July); (3) Namibia South Sub-Union 4, Ireland 35 (Keetmanshop, 23 July); (4) second Test: **Namibia 26, Ireland 15** (Windhoek, 27 July).

Scorers – Wallace 20 (*5t*), Mullin 20 (*3p,4c,1dg*), Aherne 14 (*1t,2c,2p*), Staples 8 (*1t,2c*), Barry 5 (*1p,1c*), Crossan 4 (*1t*), Cunningham 4 (*1t*), D Fitzgerald 4 (*1t*), Galwey 4 (*1t*), Popplewell 4 (*1t*), Smith 4 (*1t*), penalty try (*4*), Curtis 3 (*1dg*), Murphy 3 (*1p*).

Namibia (9) 15, Ireland (0) 6
first Test: Windhoek, 20 July 1991
Namibia: A Stoop; G Mans, H Snyman, J Deysel, E Meyer; J Coetzee, B Buitendag; C Derks, W Alberts, M Grobler, A Kotze, A van der Merwe, J Barnard, W Maritz, S Losper.

Scorers – *Try:* Stoop. *Conversion:* Coetzee. *Penalty goals:* Coetzee 2.

Ireland: Staples; Geoghegan, Mullin, Curtis, Clarke; Cunningham, Saunders; Popplewell, Smith, D Fitzgerald, Rigney, Francis, Matthews (capt), O'Hara, Robinson. *Repls:* Mannion for Rigney, 22 mins; Wallace for Geoghegan, 74 mins.

Scorers – *Try:* penalty try. *Conversion:* Mullin.

Referee: C Norling (Wales).

Series score: Played 1, Namibia 1, Ireland 0.

Namibia (10) 26, Ireland (12) 15
second Test: Windhoek, 27 July 1991
Namibia: A Stoop; G Mans, H Snyman, J Deysel, E Meyer; J Coetzee, B Buitendag; C Derks, W Alberts, M Grobler, A Kotze, A van der Merwe, J Barnard, W Maritz, S Losper. *Repl:* A van Rooyen for Losper, 60 mins.

Scorers – *Tries:* Stoop, Mans, Maritz, Barnard, Coetzee. *Conversions:* Coetzee 3.

Ireland: Staples; Crossan, Mullin, Curtis, Clarke; Cunningham, Saunders; Popplewell, Smith, D Fitzgerald, Lenihan, Francis, Mannion, Hamilton, Robinson. *Repls:* Barry for Crossan, 40 mins; Galwey for Francis, 59 mins.

Scorers – *Tries:* Staples, Cunningham. *Conversions:* Staples 2. *Dropped goal:* Curtis.

Referee: C Norling (Wales).

Series score: Played 2, Namibia 2, Ireland 0.

Bledisloe Cup
August 1991: Series drawn 1-1
(Holders New Zealand retain Cup)

Match 1: Australia (9) 21, New Zealand (9) 12
Sydney, 10 August 1991
Australia's forwards dominate their All Black counterparts in ruck and maul to claim a famous win; only the second loss incurred by New Zealand in 29 matches stretching back to 1986. Having crushed Wales and England in preceding weeks, Australia are tied 9-9 at half-time, with Ian Jones bagging the opening try for the Blacks. But with Michael Lynagh tactically flawless, the Wallabies pull clear with the restart through a combination of Lynagh's boot and Rob Egerton's spectacular try.

Australia: M Roebuck; D Campese, J Little, T Horan, R Egerton; M Lynagh, N Farr-Jones (capt); T Daly, P Kearns, E McKenzie, J Eales, R McCall, S Poidevin, V Ofahengaue, T Gavin.

Scorers – *Tries:* Gavin, Egerton. *Conversions:* Lynagh 2. *Penalty goals:* Lynagh 3.

New Zealand: T Wright; J Kirwan, C Innes, W Little, J Timu; G Fox, G Bachop; S McDowell, S Fitzpatrick, R Loe, I Jones, G Whetton (capt), M Jones, A Earl, Z Brooke.

Scorers – *Try:* I Jones. *Conversion:* Fox. *Penalty goals:* Fox 2.

Referee: R Megson (Scotland).

Series score: Played 91, Australia 23, NZ 63, Drawn 5.

Match 2: New Zealand (3) 6, Australia (0) 3
Auckland, 24 August 1991

A story of missed goal kicks from usually impeccable sources – Michael Lynagh (1 success in 7) and Grant Fox (2 in 5) – in a titanic struggle between sides desperate for a psychological edge to take into the World Cup. Lynagh, perfection personified a fortnight earlier, has a straightforward penalty kick in the last minute to give Australia a series win. It is not to be. The holders split the series and thus retain.

New Zealand: T Wright; J Kirwan, C Innes, B McCahill, J Timu; G Fox, G Bachop; S McDowell, S Fitzpatrick, R Loe, I Jones, G Whetton (capt), M Jones, M Carter, Z Brooke.

Scorer – *Penalty goals:* Fox 2.

Australia: M Roebuck; D Campese, J Little, T Horan, R Egerton; M Lynagh, N Farr-Jones (capt); T Daly, P Kearns, E McKenzie, J Eales, R McCall, S Poidevin, V Ofahengaue, T Coker.

Scorer – *Penalty goal:* Lynagh.

Referee: K McCartney (Scotland).

Series score: Played 92, NZ 64, Australia 23, Drawn 5.

———————

Romania (9) 18, Scotland (6) 12
Bucharest, 30 August 1991

Had not the World Cup been just around the corner – a mere month away – Scotland might have been tempted to blame defeat against a Romanian side inactive for three months on the fact that the British season had itself hardly dawned. In mitigation Scotland are convening for the first time since victory over the Irish in March, as only six of the side played in the XV beaten by Canada on the last leg of their non-cap summer tour of North America. Finlay Calder returns to the international arena after 14 months absence. Peter Dods kicks two first-half penalty goals and converts Iwan Tukalo's 66th minute try but Scotland slide to their second loss in a series totalling six matches.

Romania: D Pitti; C Sasu, A Lungu, G Sava, L Colceriu; F Ion, D Neaga; G Leonte, G Ion, C Stan, S Ciorascu, C Cojocariu, G Dinu, A Guranescu, H Dumitras (capt).

Scorers – *Tries:* Ciorascu, Sasu. *Conversions:* F Ion 2. *Penalty goals:* F Ion 2.

Scotland: P Dods (Gala); A Stanger (Hawick), S Lineen (Boroughmuir), D Wyllie (Stewart's-Melville FP), I Tukalo (Selkirk); C Chalmers (Melrose), G Armstrong (Jed-Forest); D Sole (capt), J Allan (both Edinburgh Acads), P Burnell (London Scottish), D Cronin (Bath), G Weir (Melrose), F Calder (Stewart's-Melville FP), D Turnbull (Hawick), D White (London Scottish).

Scorers – *Try:* Tukalo. *Conversion:* Dods. *Penalty goals:* Dods 2.

Referee: A Ceccon (France).

Series score: Played 6, Romania 2, Scotland 4.

England U-21 (30) 94, Belgium 0
Wolverhampton, 1 September 1991

England U-21 coach Tony Lannaway is able to field a full-strength XV for the first time but the occasion coincides with the visit of their least accomplished opponents to date. Lannaway feels a chance has been lost to see just how good his charges are. The Belgian senior side are 30-0 adrift at the mid-point but totally capitulate in the new half as England take their try-tally to 18. The match marks the opening of the new Castlecroft complex – 'a junior Twickenham', in the words of RFU President Peter Yarranton. The refurbishment of Wolverhampton Wanderers' erstwhile training ground has cost the RFU £500,000 and includes the construction of a 486-seater stand.

England U-21: R Liley (Wakefield); A Adebayo (Bath), L Boyle (Leicester), P Flood (Bridgend), S Bromley (Liverpool St Helens); N Matthews (Gloucester), S Douglas (Newcastle Gosforth); G Rowntree (Leicester), R Cockerill, W Bullock (both Coventry), M Johnson (Leicester), D Sims (Gloucester), J Pearson (Bristol), G Adams (Bath, capt), M Rennell (Bedford). *Repl:* S Cassidy (West Hartlepool) for Pearson, 70 mins.

Scorers – *Tries:* Bromley 3, Douglas 3, Adebayo 2, Matthews 2, Rennell 2, Pearson, Boyle, Liley, Sims, Flood, Cockerill. *Conversions:* Liley 11.

Belgium: P Dorigneau; P Ernst, A Gerrard, J Blanchez, E Tijchman, T Balburg, J Smets; H Firguet, C Beuzer, L Otten, S Delelienne, C Folon, P Lalli (capt), P Burrion, T Vanhemelen. *Repls:* P Tholly for Lalli, 45 mins; N Honhon for Balburg, 60 mins.

Referee: F Howard (England).

Series score: Played 1, England U-21 1, Belgium 0.

Wales (3) 9, France (6) 22
Cardiff, 4 September 1991

Wales ring in the new with a heartening display against France in an International arranged to celebrate the inauguration of floodlights at the Arms Park. Under the spotlight as never before – metaphorically as well as literally due to their deeply depressing experiences in Australia – the Welsh produce a valiant performance brimming with character. It is not enough to avoid their tenth successive loss to the French, but the display – highlighted by Richie Collins' try and 5 points from Mark Ring's boot – sends them into the World Cup with at least a glimmer of hope.

Wales: A Clement (Swansea); I Evans (Llanelli, capt), S Gibbs (Neath), M Hall, A Emyr; M Ring (all Cardiff), R Jones (Swansea); M Griffiths (Cardiff), G Jenkins (Pontypool), L Delaney (Llanelli), K Moseley (Newport), G D Llewellyn (Neath), E Lewis (Llanelli), R Collins (Cardiff), P Davies (Llanelli). *Repls:* D Evans (Cardiff) for Ring, 73 mins; L Evans (Llanelli) for I Evans, 78 mins.

Scorers – *Try:* Collins. *Conversion:* Ring. *Penalty goal:* Ring.

France: S Blanco (Biarritz, capt); J-B Lafond (Racing), P Sella (Agen), F Mesnel (Racing), P Saint-Andre (Montferrand); D Camberabero (Beziers), H Sanz (Narbonne); G Lascube (Agen), L Armary (Lourdes), P Ondarts (Biarritz), O Roumat (Dax), T Devergie (Nimes), M Courtiols (Begles-Bordeaux), L Cabannes (Racing), M Cecillon (Bourgoin). *Repls:* T Lacroix (Dax) for Sella, 22 mins; J-L Sadourny (Colomiers) for Blanco, 76 mins.

Scorers – *Tries:* Blanco, Camberabero, Saint-Andre. *Conversions:* Camberabero 2. *Penalty goals:* Camberabero 2.

Referee: J Fleming (Scotland).

Series score: Played 65, Wales 36, France 26, Drawn 3.

England XV (22) 53, Soviet Union 0
Twickenham, 7 September 1991

The value of a nine-try World Cup warm-up over course and distance is offset by the badly sprained left ankle suffered by fullback Simon Hodgkinson – stretchered off for an X-ray in the early throes of the second period – which jeopardises his participation in the forthcoming finals. England still noticeably lack the edge to their performance that the high-stake incentive of a major tournament subconsciously induces, but they at least take the opportunity to better themselves in the noble art of try-scoring.

England: S Hodgkinson (Nottingham); R Underwood (Leicester & RAF), W Carling (Harlequins, capt), J Guscott (Bath), C Oti; R Andrew (both Wasps), R Hill (Bath); J Leonard, B Moore (both Harlequins), J Probyn (Askeans), P Ackford (Harlequins), W Dooley (Preston Grasshoppers), M Skinner (Harlequins), G Rees (Nottingham), M Teague (Gloucester). *Repls:* D Pears (Harlequins) for Hodgkinson, 48 mins; S Halliday (Harlequins) for Guscott, 56 mins.

Scorers – *Tries:* Oti 2, Guscott 2, Underwood 2, Skinner 2, Andrew. *Conversions:* Hodgkinson 3, Andrew 4. *Penalty goal:* Hodgkinson.

Soviet Union: V Voropaev; I Kuperman, S Romanov, A Gomozkhin, I Mironov; S Boldakov, A Bychkov; I Khokhlov, S Molchanov, E Kabylkin, S Sergeev, E Ganiakhin, A Tikhonov, F Negodin, A Ogryzkov.

Referee: B Anderson (Scotland).

Scotland XV (6) 16, Barbarians (10) 16
Edinburgh, 7 September 1991

Following away-day reversals in Canada (non-cap) and Romania, Scotland look to reassert themselves on their own patch where, after all, they will spend the duration of their World Cup campaign until either the final or third place play-off. With nine successive home wins under the tartan belt – an unbroken run dating back to the visit of the 1988 Wallabies – Scotland are a force to be reckoned with in Edinburgh, yet on this occasion they turn in a curate's egg of a performance: a dodgy start and conclusion sandwiching an irresistible filling either side of half-time. Non-cap status the Barbarians' visit might have been afforded, but the Scottish team is a useful one nonetheless. However, it lacks a fulcrum, such as Stuart Barnes offers the Baa-Baas, and a penetrative force which New Zealander Eric Rush provides the scratch XV. Still, the Scots do well to turn a 3-10 deficit into a 16-10 lead with tries by Kenny Milne and, to a crescendo of sound, the un-retired Finlay Calder. That should be that but the Baa-Baas have one trump card still to play: their South African connection. The wonderful Andre Joubert breaks from under his own posts and, via New Zealander Scott Pierce, sets up replacement Quentin Daniels to score at the other end. Barnes' conversion ties the scores. Before the World Cup gets underway Scotland are further troubled by Edinburgh Borderers who beat the Scotland side, masquerading as a SRU President's XV, 19-13 at Murrayfield, before the President's men rally to defeat an Anglo-Scots XV 32-4, again at the national stadium.

Scotland XV: G Hastings (Watsonians); A Stanger (Hawick), S Hastings (Watsonians), G Shiel (Melrose), M Moncrieff (Gala); C Chalmers (Melrose), G Oliver (Hawick); D Sole (Edinburgh Acads, capt), K Milne (Heriot's FP), P Burnell (London Scottish), D Cronin (Bath), G Weir (Melrose), J Jeffrey (Kelso), F Calder (Stewart's-Melville FP), G Marshall (Selkirk). *Repl:* D White (London Scottish) for Marshall, 75 mins.

Scorers – *Tries:* Milne, Calder. *Conversion:* Chalmers. *Penalty goals:* Chalmers 2.

Barbarians: A Joubert (Old Greys, SA); A Harriman (Harlequins), S Pierce (North Shore, NZ), E Blanc (Racing Club, Fra), T Underwood (Cambridge Univ); S Barnes (Bath, capt), P Berbizier (Agen, Fra); G Kebble (Durban Collegians, SA), T Lawton (Durban HSOB, SA), E Rodriguez (Warringah, NZ), A Macdonald (Heriot's FP), A Copsey (Llanelli), W Bartmann (Durban Harlequins, SA), E Rush (Otahuhu, NZ), K Tapper (Enkoping, Swe). *Repls:* Q Daniels (Cape Town Police, SA) for Underwood, 66 mins; C Stephens (Llanelli) for Joubert, 78 mins.

Scorers – *Tries:* Rush 2, Daniels. *Conversions:* Barnes 2.

Referee: F Howard (England).

Gloucester (4) 4, England XV (12) 34
Kingsholm, 14 September 1991

England experiment with No.8 Dean Richards at blindside flanker, seem indifferent as to the results, and Mike Teague swaps with the Leicester Tiger midway through the second half, whereupon England pull clear with a morale-boosting burst of 22 points to finally put paid to the aspirations of a Gloucester side which had led 4-3 after 17 minutes.

Gloucester: T Smith; D Morgan, S Morris, D Caskie, N Marment; M Hamlin, R Williams; P Jones, J Hawker, R Phillips, N Scrivens, D Sims, P Ashmead, I Smith (capt), S Masters. *Repl:* N Matthews for Morgan, 51 mins.

Scorer – *Try:* Morgan.

England XV: J Webb (Bath); N Heslop (Orrell), S Halliday, W Carling (capt, both Harlequins Northampton), C Oti (Wasps); D Pears (Harlequins), R Hill (Bath); P Rendall (Askeans), J Olver (Northampton), G Pearce (Northampton), N Redman (Bath), W Dooley (Preston Grasshoppers), D Richards (Leicester), P Winterbottom (Harlequins), M Teague (Gloucester). *Repl:* J Leonard (Harlequins) for Rendall, 40 mins.

Scorers – *Tries:* Heslop, Pears, Webb 2, Oti. *Conversions:* Webb 4. *Penalty goals:* Webb 2.

Referee: F Howard (Liverpool).

Gloucester (7) 14, Ireland XV (4) 13
Kingsholm, 21 September 1991

Hardly the kind of result to strike fear into the hearts of World Cup Pool 2 opponents Scotland, Japan and Zimbabwe, as Ireland's unconvincing build-up to the World Cup continues. As an encore to losing both Tests in Namibia they return home and defeat an International Select 25-13 before dropping record try-scorer Brendan Mullin for the 38-12 win over a Cork Constitution/Old Wesley select. Mullin is reinstated for the next outing, a slender and unconvincing 28-25 success at the expense of All-Ireland second division club Malone but, consequently, a further five changes are made for the visit to Gloucester. The West Country side, fielding 11 of the XV which played against England a week previously, lead 14-4 after 47 minutes against a virtually full-strength Ireland XV, but one which is unable to repair the damage. The alarm bells are ringing. Next stop Zimbabwe...

Gloucester: T Smith; G Perrins, D Caskie, S Morris, N Marment; N Matthews, M Hannaford; P Jones, J Hawker, R Phillips, P Miles, D Sims, P Ashmead, I Smith (capt), S Masters.

Scorers – *Tries:* Perrins, Morris. *Penalty goals:* T Smith 2.

Ireland XV: J Staples; S Geoghegan (both London Irish), B Mullin (Blackrock Coll), D Curtis (London Irish), J Clarke (Dolphin); R Keyes (Constitution), R Saunders (London Irish); N Popplewell (Greystones), S Smith (Ballymena), D Fitzgerald (Lansdowne), D Lenihan (Constitution), M Galwey (Shannon), P Matthews (Wanderers, capt), G Hamilton (NIFC), B Robinson (Ballymena). *Repls:* K Murphy (Constitution) for Staples, 39 mins; N Barry (Garryowen) for Geoghegan, 59 mins.

Scorers – *Tries:* Staples, Curtis. *Conversion:* Keyes. *Penalty goal:* Keyes.

Referee: M Bayliss (Gloucester).

England XV (17) 35, England Students 0
Cambridge, 21 September 1991

England field their World Cup pack and execute a number of their back row and three-quarter moves against opponents fighting a rearguard action from the first whistle. That is not to say the senior XV are over-impressive – too many passes go astray for comfort – but, as against the Soviet Union and Gloucester, England's superior fitness pays dividends in the last 10 minutes with 12 points bolstering the scoreline. Rupert Moon, the Students' captain and scrum-half, confirms himself as a star of the future.

England XV: J Webb (Bath); N Heslop (Orrell), S Halliday (Harlequins), J Guscott (Bath), R Underwood (Leicester & RAF); R Andrew (Wasps, capt), D Morris (Orrell); J Leonard, B Moore (both Harlequins), J Probyn (Askeans), P Ackford (Harlequins), W Dooley (Preston Grasshoppers), M Teague (Gloucester), P Winterbottom (Harlequins), D Richards (Leicester). *Repl:* P Rendall (Askeans) for Probyn, 40 mins.

Scorers – *Tries:* Winterbottom, Guscott, Underwood 2, Webb, Teague. *Conversions:* Webb 4. *Penalty goal:* Webb.

England Students: A Lumsden; A Parton, M Fielden, L Boyle, H Thorneycroft; D Willett, R Moon (capt), C Clark, T Beddow, J Mallett, A Milward, S Shortland, C Tarbuck, G Adams, E Peters.

Referee: E Morrison (Bristol).

THE 1991 WORLD CUP

3 October – 2 November 1991

See pages 330–49

Wales U-21 (16) 22, Ireland U-21 (9) 15
Newport, 16 October 1991

Wales extend their unbeaten record at this age level to 11 games with a victory made somewhat flattering by late tries from skipper Steve Williams and scrum-half Robert Howley. It is, nonetheless, no less welcome for that to a nation still reeling from its failure to make the quarter-finals in the World Cup. Neil Jenkins, left out of the World Cup squad, kicks ten points, including the conversion of outside-half Luc Evan's opening try.

Wales U-21: L Evans (Llanelli); P Harries (Cardiff Inst), I Lewis (Bath), R Brown (Newbridge), I Jones (Llanelli); N Jenkins (Pontypridd), R Howley (Bridgend); D Thomas (Pontypool), G Davies (Taffs Well), T Orrell (South Wales Police), C Langley (Cardiff), D Jones (Llanelli), A Williams (Maesteg), C Goodwin (Cardiff Inst), S Williams (Neath, capt).

Scorers – *Tries:* Evans, Williams, Howley. *Conversions:* Jenkins 2. *Penalty goals:* Jenkins 2.

Ireland U-21: C O'Shea (Lansdowne); N Woods, M Ridge (both Blackrock Coll), G Lavin (St Mary's Coll), G McCluskey (Portadown); N Malone (Loughborough Students), N Hogan (Terenure Coll); L Murphy (UC Cork), M McDermott (Blackrock Coll), P Wallace (UC Cork), U O'Callagh an (Highfield), G Longwell (Queen's Univ, Belfast), P Scott (UC Cork), R Wilson (Instonians), L Toland (Old Crescent).

Scorers – *Tries:* Woods, Longwell. *Conversions:* Longwell 2. *Penalty goal:* Woods.

Referee: L Colati (Fiji).

Series score: Played 1, Wales 1, Ireland 0.

Ireland U-21 (6) 19, England U-21 (7) 10
Donnybrook, 23 October 1991

Victor Costello turns the tide Ireland's way just when England, 10-6 to the good early in the second half, look set to avenge their defeat in last year's fixture. England's decision to keep play close to their forwards works against them in the opening period, when a little more adventure would have yielded a more emphatic half-time edge than 7-6. But just as Gloucester lock Richard West had ruled the first-half line-out, so Costello takes charge after the break and, fittingly, seals England's fate with a late try.

Ireland U-21: C O'Shea (Lansdowne); W O'Shea (Shannon), M Ridge (Blackrock Coll), R Hunter (Loughborough Students), N Woods (Blackrock Coll); N Malone (Loughborough Students), N Hogan (Terenure Coll, capt); L Murphy (UC Cork), M McDermott (Blackrock Coll), P Wallace (UC Cork), G Longwell (Queen's Univ, Belfast), V Costello (Blackrock Coll), S Rooney (UC Dublin), L Toland (Old Crescent), R Wilson (Instonians). *Repl:* M Kernohan (Glasgow Univ) for M McDermott, 3 mins.

Scorers – *Tries:* C O'Shea, Costello. *Conversion:* Woods. *Penalty goals:* Woods 2. *Dropped goal:* Malone.

England U-21: S Wills (Leicester); J Sleightholme (Wakefield), P Flood (Bridgend), S Ravenscroft (Saracens), M Lloyd (Bristol); D Willett (Bath), S Douglas (Newcastle Gosforth); C Clark (Swansea Univ), R Cockerill (Coventry), G Rowntree (Leicester), R Bramley (Wakefield), R West (Gloucester), M Rennell (Bedford), G Adams (Bath, capt), C Wilkins (Wasps). *Repl:* M Mapletoft (Rugby) for Wills, 79 mins.

Scorers – *Try:* Flood. *Penalty goals:* Wills 2.

Referee: D Davies (Wales).

Series score: Played 2, Ireland 2, England 0.

110th Varsity Match
Twickenham, 10 December 1991
Oxford Univ (4) 11, Cambridge Univ (3) 17

Wales outside-half Adrian Davies captains Cambridge to their 50th series win on his fourth Varsity appearance. His dropped goal and brace of penalty goals takes to 34 his points tally in the fixture. Only Cambridge's Alistair Hignell (45) and Rob Andrew (36) have contributed more. Tony Underwood produces the game's outstanding memory with his spectacular and decisive 77th minute try.

Oxford: N Fitzwater; C Henderson, R Jones, K Street, S Barclay; A Tapper, F du Toit; S Whiteside, M Patton, A Everett (capt), D Evans, P Thresher, R Pask, L Jones, A Milward.

Scorers – *Tries:* du Toit, Barclay. *Dropped goal:* Fitzwater.

Cambridge: A Parton; R Given, L Davies, K Price, T Underwood; A Davies (capt), M de Maid; B Davies, B Gegg, M Chapple, M Duthie, D Dix, E Peters, C Bates, C Sheasby.

Scorers – *Tries:* Underwood, Price. *Penalty goals:* A Davies 2. *Dropped goal:* A Davies.

Referee: J Fleming (Scotland).

Series score: Played 110, Cambridge 50, Oxford 47, Drawn 13.

Scotland B (12) 19, Ireland B (16) 29
Edinburgh, 28 December 1991

A match with an indirect bearing on the Five Nations' Championship in that six of the participants are promoted to senior status based on a combination of their own performances and the misfortune of incumbents. Ireland outscore the Scots by four tries to two, yet the Scots, due to an untimely spate of injuries, promote four – Andy Nicol (the scorer of a quite outstanding try), Ian Smith, David McIvor and Neil Edwards – to Ireland's two – Richard Wallace and Michael Fitzgibbon. Derek McAleese kicks Ireland into the clear with five successes from eight attempts.

Scotland B: M Appleson (London Scottish); D Stark (Ayr), F Harrold (London Scottish), I Jardine (Stirling Co), M Moncrieff (Gala); G Townsend (Gala), A Nicol (Dundee HSFP); G Wilson (Boroughmuir), M Scott (Dunfermline), B Robertson (Stirling Co), N Edwards (Harlequins), R Scott (London Scottish), D McIvor (Edinburgh Acads), I Smith (Gloucester, capt), D McIntosh (Pontypridd). *Repl:* M Allingham (Heriot's FP) for Nicol, 58 mins.

Scorers – *Tries:* Nicol, Stark. *Conversion:* Appleson. *Penalty goals:* Townsend 2, Appleson.

Ireland B: C Wilkinson (Malone); N Furlong (UC Galway), M Ridge (Blackrock), M McCall (Bangor), R Wallace (Garryowen); D McAleese (Ballymena), A Blair (Dungannon); P Soden (Constitution), J Murphy (Greystones, capt), P McCarthy (Constitution), K Potts (St Mary's Coll), G Fulcher (UC Dublin), D McCartney (Ballymena), M Fitzgibbon (Shannon), B O'Mahony (UC Cork).

Scorers – *Tries:* Potts, McCarthy, Ridge, Fitzgibbon. *Conversions:* McAleese 2. *Penalty goals:* McAleese 3.

Referee: C Thomas (Wales).

Series score: Played 7, Ireland 4, Scotland 2, Drawn 1.

Scotland A (20) 36, Spain (3) 16
Edinburgh, 28 December 1991

Scotland's A team – an entity blending a measure of senior squad members with unfortunates undone by the Scottish Rugby Union's decision to bar players from the B team once capped at senior level – allow Spain to turn an embarrassing 3-20 half-time deficit into a respectable 16-20 scoreline with just 10 minutes remaining, before a timely three-try spree saves face in the home camp.

Scotland A: P Dods (Gala, capt); A Stanger (Hawick), D Caskie (Gloucester), D Wyllie (Stewart's-Melville FP), A Moore (Edinburgh Acad); G Shiel (Melrose), G Oliver (Hawick); P Jones (Gloucester), K Milne (Heriot's FP), P Burnell (London Scottish), D Cronin (London Scottish), A Macdonald (Heriot's FP), S Reid (Boroughmuir), G Weir (Melrose).

Scorers – *Tries:* Macdonald, Dods 2, Wyllie, Weir, Moore. *Conversions:* Dods 3. *Penalty goals:* Dods 2.

Spain: O Gonzalez; P Gutierrez, A Mino, J Azkargorta, C Moreno; M Sanchez, J Macariego, J Alvarez (capt), J Alducin, J-L Moral, A Ma lo, A Gonzalez, J Etxebarria, J Gutierrez, E Illaregui. *Repl:* F Castro for Moral, 52 mins; J Rodriguez for Illaregui, 73 mins.

Scorers – *Tries:* J Gutierrez, P Gutierrez. *Conversion:* Sanchez. *Penalty goal:* Sanchez. *Dropped goal:* Sanchez.

Referee: G Simmonds (Wales).

Series score: Played 2, Scotland A 2, Spain 0.

Spain (0) 3, England B (21) 34
Madrid, 19 January 1992

Stuart Barnes marks his return to the England fold, following a self-imposed exile, with a brace of conversions in a match dominated by the English side and, in particular, their forwards. The Bath influence is thick in the air with newly appointed B coach, Bath's own Jack Rowell, steering a XV featuring six of his club charges including captain Barnes. Only two of the Spanish side did not play in the 16-36 loss to Scotland A three weeks previously.

Spain: F Puerto; P Gutierrez, J Azkargorta, A Mino, C Moreno; M Sanchez, J Macariego; A Malo (capt), J Gutierrez, J Etxebarria, H Massani, A Gonzalez, J-L Moral, F Castro, J Alvarez.

Scorer – *Penalty goal:* Moreno.

England B: I Hunter (Northampton); J Fallon (Bath), P de Glanville (Bath), J Buckton (Saracens), T Underwood (Cambridge Univ); S Barnes (Bath, capt), S Douglas (Newcastle Gosforth); G Baldwin (Northampton), G Dawe (Bath), A Mullins

(Harlequins), M Haag (Bath), D Sims (Gloucester), M Greenwood (Nottingham), N Back (Leicester), B Clarke (Bath).

Scorers – *Tries:* Hunter 2, Douglas, Clarke, Underwood, Back. *Conversions:* Barnes 2. *Penalty goal:* Barnes. *Dropped goal:* Hunter.

Referee: M Desclaux (France).

Series score: Played 4, Spain 0, England B 4.

England B 47, Ireland B 15
Richmond, 31 January 1992

Stuart Barnes, whose maverick skills have, almost unbelievably, failed to earn him a Five Nations' start, delights Richmond with a command performance against opponents unaccustomed to experiencing such repression. Barnes' vision pinpoints Ireland's defensive chinks and serves as the catalyst for his team mates' *tour de force*. Wings Tony Underwood (3) and Jim Fallon (2) share five of England's nine tries before Ireland rescue a measure of pride with late tries by Colin Wilkinson and Martin Ridge.

England B: I Hunter (Northampton); J Fallon (Bath), P de Glanville (Bath), J Buckton (Saracens), T Underwood (Cambridge Univ); S Barnes (Bath, capt), S Bates (Wasps); G Baldwin (Northampton), G Dawe (Bath), A Mullins (Harlequins), M Haag (Bath), D Sims (Gloucester), M Greenwood (Nottingham), N Back (Leicester), B Clarke (Bath).

Scorers – *Tries:* Hunter, Underwood 3, Haag, Fallon 2, Back, Clarke. *Conversions:* Barnes 4. *Penalty goal:* Barnes.

Ireland B: C Wilkinson (Malone); R Carey (Dungannon), M Ridge (Blackrock), M McCall (Bangor), N Furlong (UC Galway); P Hennebry (Terenure), A Rolland (Blackrock Coll); J Fitzgerald (Young Munster, capt), P Adair (Instonians), P Millar (Ballymena), B Rigney (Greystones), T Coughlin (Old Belvedere), K Leahy (Wanderers), D McCartney (Ballymena), P Johns (Dungannon).

Scorers – *Tries:* Wilkinson, Ridge. *Conversions:* Hennebry 2. *Penalty goal:* Hennebry.

Referee: G Gadjovich (Canada).

Series score: Played 4, England B 3, Ireland B 1.

France B (12) 27, Scotland B (0) 18
Albi, 3 February 1992

Scotland, with a performance in marked contrast to those of the 1980s when they won four of the five fixtures played in France, blow their chances of continued profit by falling 18 points adrift inside the hour as Didier Pouyau lands four penalty goals and converts Herve Couffignal's try early into the second period. The French outside-half later completes his 19-point haul with a fifth penalty and conversion of Jerome Cazalbou's close-range score. But Scotland maintain an interest by sharing the try-count at 2-2. Leading by example, captain Rob Wainwright orchestrates a belated Scottish fightback, in tandem with young Gregor Townsend who bags a brace of penalty goals. After the thrusting Ian Jardine crosses for Mark Appleson to convert, Wainwright adds the second try but, despite Townsend's conversion, it is too little too late.

France B: S Ougier (Toulouse); P Bernat-Salles (Pau), M Marfaing (Toulouse), H Couffignal (Colomiers), B Lorenzin (Albi); D Pouyau (Bayonne), J Cazalbou

(Toulouse); L Armary (Lourdes, capt), J-P Genet (Racing), R Crespy (Brive), H Miorin (Toulouse), J-F Gourragne (Beziers), P Chamayou (Narbonne), M Courtiols (Begles-Bordeaux), C Deslandes (Racing). *Repl:* F Seguier (Castres) for Cazalbou, 79 mins.

Scorers – *Tries:* Couffignal, Cazalbou. *Conversions:* Pouyau 2. *Penalty goals:* Pouyau 5.

Scotland B: M Appleson (London Scottish); D Stark (Ayr), D Caskie (Gloucester), I Jardine (Stirling Co), M Moncrieff (Gala); G Towns end (Gala), D Patterson (Edinburgh Acads); P Jones (Gloucester), M Scott (Dunfermline), B Robertson (Stirling Co), R Scott (London Scottish), A Macdonald (Heriot's FP), S Reid (Boroughmuir), R Wainwright (Edinburgh Acads, capt), D McIntosh (Pontypridd).

Scorers – *Tries:* Jardine, Wainwright. *Conversion:* Appleson, Townsend. *Penalty goals:* Townsend 2.

Referee: S Pearcy (England).

Series score: Played 20, France B 12, Scotland B 8.

France B (9) 18, England B (9) 22
Paris, 15 February 1992

England extend their unbeaten season at B level with a slender, if nonetheless deserved, victory over the French at the Stade Jean Bouin in Paris. As a foretaste of the senior International to follow there are striking similarities. Firstly, the French are more than capable with the ball in their hands; secondly, they have a tendency towards employing their hands for less savoury pursuits when the ball is elsewhere; and thirdly, England weather each and every storm and emerge triumphant. To that end, captain Stuart Barnes, once again, is the protagonist, controlling the game's pulse and kicking 14 points.

France B: J-C Langlade (Nimes); S Weller (Grenoble), E Bonneval (Toulouse), E Blanc (Racing), D Berty (Toulouse); F Velo (Grenoble), G Accoceberry (Tyrosse, capt); P Tapie (Grenoble), F Landreau (Narbonne), E Michaud (SBUC), B Bourguignon (Narbonne), J-P Revallier (Graulhet), B Dalla Riva (Toulouse), P Benetton (Agen), N Hallinger (Mazamet). *Repl:* L van der Linden (Brive) for Dalla Riva, 29 mins; P Marty (Graulhet) for Wella, 46 mins; T Devergie (Nimes) for Revallier, 65 mins.

Scorers – *Try:* Bonneval. *Conversion:* Velo. *Penalty goals:* Velo 4.

England B: I Hunter (Northampton); J Fallon (Bath), P de Glanville (Bath), J Buckton (Saracens), T Underwood (Cambridge Univ); S Barnes (Bath, capt), S Bates (Wasps); G Baldwin (Northampton), G Dawe (Bath), A Mullins (Harlequins), D Sims (Gloucester), M Johnson (Leicester), M Greenwood (Nottingham), J Cassell (Saracens), B Clarke (Bath).

Scorers – *Tries:* Underwood, Fallon. *Conversion:* Barnes. *Penalty goals:* Barnes 4.

Referee: R McDowell (Ireland).

Series score: Played 8, France B 3, England B 4, Drawn 1.

THE 1992 FIVE NATIONS' CHAMPIONSHIP

Scotland (7) 7, England (10) 25
Edinburgh, 18 January 1992

England defeat their auld enemy for the third time in 12 months – achieving their highest ever margin of victory at Murrayfield in so doing – and score their first Murrayfield tries since the 1980 Grand Slam season. The first, a 65-yard scamper by Underwood after the Scottish midfield (in which Sean Lineen and Scott Hastings are equalling Michael Kiernan/Brendan Mullin's world record for a centre pairing of 23 major internationals) are dispossessed, extends the wing's England try-scoring record to 33 but, remarkably, represents his first points against Scotland. David Sole, captaining Scotland for a record 20th time, is delighted with his side's first half effort when, against all expectations, they rule the touchlines. Martin Bayfield (6'10"), and Wade Dooley (6'8") have the height, but George Weir (6'7") and debutant Neil Edwards (6'4") possess the nous. The game's lasting memory also belongs to Scotland: when their maligned pack blows the power-packed English eight over their own try-line at such a rate of knots that No.8 Derek White is almost pulled over the startled ball. Scotland coach Ian McGeechan feels his charges should have led at the break, rather than trail by three (chiefly due to Gavin Hastings' kicking profligacy – he kicked one from five in all, compared to Jon Webb's five from eight), and England skipper Will Carling, whose 33rd cap gives him a record haul for an England centre, can hardly disagree. However, he is more satisfied with the second half showing when the whiphand is regained in the line-out and, following new cap Tim Rodber's premature departure with spinal concussion, replacement Dean Richards galvanises an English second wind which features a first internation al dropped goal for Jeremy Guscott and recalled scrum-half Dewi Morris touching down after a magnificent counter thrust by Simon Halliday.

Scotland: G Hastings (Watsonians); A Stanger (Hawick), S Hastings (Watsonians), S Lineen (Boroughmuir), I Tukalo (Selkirk); C Chalmers (Melrose), A Nicol (Dundee HSFP); D Sole (Edinburgh Acads, capt), K Milne (Heriot's FP), P Burnell (London Scottish), N Edwards (Harlequins), G Weir (Melrose), D McIvor (Edinburgh Acads), I Smith (Gloucester), D White (London Scottish).

Scorers – *Try:* White (39). *Penalty goal:* G Hastings (5).

England: J Webb (Bath); S Halliday (Harlequins), J Guscott (Bath), W Carling (Harlequins, capt), R Underwood (Leicester & RAF); R Andrew (Toulouse), D Morris (Orrell); J Leonard (Harlequins), B Moore (Harlequins), J Probyn (Wasps), M Bayfield (Northampton), W Dooley (Preston Grasshoppers), M Skinner (Harlequins), P Winterbottom (Harlequins), T Rodber (Northampton & Army). *Repl:* D Richards (Leicester) for Rodber, 63 mins.

Scorers – *Tries:* Underwood (28), Morris (78). *Conversion:* Webb (78). *Penalty goals:* Webb 4 (11,19,52,59). *Dropped goal:* Guscott (75).

Referee: D Bevan (Wales).

Series score: Played 109, England 53, Scotland 39, Drawn 17.

Ireland (9) 15, Wales (6) 16
Dublin, 18 January 1992

Wales are back. For the first time since March 1989, when England were upset in Cardiff, the Principality is given a Five Nations' victory to savour. And savour it they do. Ireland, always the most generous of hosts, extend their hospitality too far – letting slip a 15-6 lead given them by Richard Wallace's Five Nations' debut try, created magnificently by Brendan Mullin, 8 minutes into the second half. That should have been that, especially with Wales' World Cup nightmare still painfully fresh in the memory. But coach Alan Davies' side refuses to bow to adversity yet again. Instead they stare all the smiling out of the Irish eyes and go on a profitable rampage which yields ten unanswered points. It is hard to comprehend that a dozen of this Irish side, on their last outing in the World Cup quarter-finals, had come within seconds of beating champions-to-be Australia – the same Wallaby side which had handed Wales their heaviest ever Arms Park defeat earlier in the same tournament. Yet, with Anthony Clement and Robert Jones tossing inspiration among their team mates like confetti, the unthinkable happens. Debutant No.8, Stuart Davies, bulls his way over for a try, 12 minutes from time, to light the touchpaper on Welsh celebrations.

Ireland: J Staples (London Irish); R Wallace (Garryowen), B Mullin (Blackrock Coll), D Curtis (London Irish), K Crossan (Instonians); R Keyes (Cork Constitution), R Saunders (London Irish); N Popplewell (Greystones), S Smith (Ballymena), D Fitzgerald (De La Salle), D Lenihan (Constitution), N Francis (Blackrock Coll), P Matthews (Wanderers, capt), M Fitzgibbon (Shannon), B Robinson (Ballymena).

Scorers – *Try:* Wallace (48). *Penalty goals:* Keyes 3 (8,15,40). *Conversion:* Keyes.

Wales: A Clement (Swansea); I Evans (Llanelli, capt), N Jenkins (Pontypridd), S Gibbs (Neath), M Hall (Cardiff); C Stephens (Llanelli), R Jones (Swansea); M Griffiths (Cardiff), G Jenkins (Swansea), L Delaney (Llanelli), G O Llewellyn (Neath), T Copsey (Llanelli), E Lewis (Llanelli), R Webster (Swansea), S Davies (Swansea).

Scorers – *Try:* Davies (67). *Penalty goals:* Jenkins 3 (23,60,63). *Dropped goal:* Stephens (38).

Referee: C Howard (England).

Series score: Played 95, Wales 57, Ireland 32, Drawn 6.

Wales (0) 9, France (12) 12
Cardiff, 1 February 1992

When Wales beat Ireland a fortnight earlier the notion that their back division lacked pace was discreetly lost in the celebrations. After so long spent in the wilderness coach Alan Davies is not about to shuffle the first Welsh team to win a Five Nations' match since England turned belly-up in Cardiff in 1989. It proves to be a show of blind faith on Davies' part. England have dominated the European scene for some time now yet their management are not above chopping the odd wing, changing the odd scrum-half, even mixing up the back row in the name of refinement. The painful truth is driven in against France but, significantly, not by them. The Welsh have failed to avoid defeat in the fixture's ten previous meetings yet have more than enough possession to turn the screw decisively this time. That they fail is not down to the forwards, who cause such a stir in the French ranks that ineffective lock Christophe Mougeot is mysteriously replaced by Olivier Roumat at half-time, but rather to backs who are effortlessly penned throughout by their Gallic counterparts and squander one opening after another simply because the door creaks shut before they can trot through. France, in spite of their forwards' failings in the set-piece, lead by a dozen points at the interval, having served up the game's only try – presented to wing Philippe Saint-Andre by Jean-Baptiste Lafond. The Welsh, alive with the sounds of soprano Beverley Humphreys' pre-match rendering of their national anthem, rally with three penalty goals by Neil Jenkins, but it remains a lost cause.

Wales: A Clement (Swansea); I Evans (Llanelli, capt), N Jenkins (Pontypridd), S Gibbs (Neath), M Hall (Cardiff); C Stephens (Llanelli), R Jones (Swansea); M Griffiths (Cardiff), G Jenkins (Swansea), L Delaney (Llanelli), G O Llewellyn (Neath), T Copsey (Llanelli), E Lewis (Llanelli), R Webster (Swansea), S Davies (Swansea).

Scorer – *Penalty goals:* Jenkins 3 (46,59,65).

France: J-B Lafond (Racing); P Saint-Andre (Montferrand); P Sella (Agen, capt), F Mesnel (Racing), S Viars (Brive); A Penaud (Brive), F Galthie (Colomiers); G Lascube (Agen), V Moscato (Begles Bordeaux), P Gimbert (Begles-Bordeaux), J-M Cadieu (Toulouse), C Mougeot (Begles-Bordeaux), J-F Tordo (Nice), L Cabannes (Racing), M Cecillon (Bougoin). *Repl:* O Roumat (Dax) for Mougeot, 42 mins.

Scorers – *Try:* Saint-Andre (32). *Conversion:* Lafond. *Penalty goal:* Viars (3). *Dropped goal:* Penaud (36).

Referee: O Doyle (Ireland).

Series score: Played 65, Wales 36, France 26, Drawn 3.

England (24) 38, Ireland (9) 9
Twickenham, 1 February 1992

Twickenham throws a party to celebrate Peter Winterbottom becoming the first English forward to win 50 caps. And what an occasion it proves to be after Winters has been accorded the honour of leading the English XV out onto the field. Jonathan Webb equals Dan Lambert's 1911 English individual record of 22 points scored in a match as the Grand Slam holders record their highest score against Ireland in 105 matches dating back to 1875. Ireland are not even permitted a firm grip on the ball before Webb scores the first of his two tries inside 30 seconds – the fastest in the Championship's history. Phil Matthews fumbles the kick-off, England's forwards pile through, the ball is rucked back and Webb enters the line to decisive effect. Despite the comfort brought by Ralph Keyes' retaliatory try, Ireland are utterly incapable of sustaining a challenge. Will Carling and Jeremy Guscott spend the afternoon punching holes in the Irish defence for their team mates to pour through. Dewi Morris and Brian Moore combine spectacularly to put the scrum-half over, Guscott crosses after Ireland's midfield defence is bamboozled by Rory Underwood's run, the free-scoring wing bags number 34 from a tap-move, Simon Halliday twists and turns to claim his first Five Nations' try and, finally, Webb saunters over to complete the rout.

England: J Webb (Bath); S Halliday (Harlequins), J Guscott (Bath), W Carling (Harlequins, capt), R Underwood (Leicester & RAF); R Andrew (Toulouse), D Morris (Orrell); J Leonard (Harlequins), B Moore (Harlequins), J Probyn (Wasps), M Bayfield (Northampton), W Dooley (Preston Grasshoppers), M Skinner (Harlequins), P Winterbottom (Harlequins), T Rodber (Northampton & Army).

Scorers – *Tries:* Webb 2 (1,78), Morris (32), Guscott (36), Underwood (56), Halliday (69). *Conversions:* Webb 4 (1,32,36,78). *Penalty goals:* Webb 2 (13,41).

Ireland: J Staples (London Irish); R Wallace (Garryowen), B Mullin (Blackrock Coll), D Curtis (London Irish), S Geoghegan (London Irish); R Keyes (Cork Constitution), L Aherne (Lansdowne); N Popplewell (Greystones), S Smith (Ballymena), D Fitzgerald

(De La Salle), M Galwey (Shannon), N Francis (Blackrock Coll), P Matthews (Wanderers, capt), M Fitzgibbon (Shannon), B Robinson (Ballymena).

Scorer – *Try:* Keyes (10). *Conversion:* Keyes. *Penalty goal:* Keyes (23).

Referee: D Bevan (Wales).

Series score: Played 105, England 61, Ireland 36, Drawn 8.

Ireland (3) 10, Scotland (9) 18
Dublin, 15 February 1992

Ireland's enigmatic season takes another bizarre twist. Their heroic World Cup campaign is but a distant memory as they capitulate at the hands of their Gaelic counterparts. The Irish save their best for first, with Simon Geoghegan crossing for a try inside the opening minute only for referee Tony Spreadbury to chalk it off for an offside infringement. Scotland's riposte begins in the safe hands of Doddie Weir, whose textbook line-out catch on the right touchline paves the way for Tony Stanger to touch down his 14th International try on the left, his opposite wing. Ireland – flanker Michael Fitzgibbon excepted – quickly lose their way. Ralph Keyes, the World Cup's leading scorer, is a model of profligacy, though his persecution by the dissatisfied Dublin faithful hardly fits the crime. A bad day he might have had, but it is still only a game of rugby. Is winning becoming too important? Whatever the answer, it is Scotland who come out on top. Andy Nicol, Gary Armstrong's impressive deputy, hares up the touchline for the decisive Scottish try, although Richard Wallace keeps Irish hopes alive with a powerful solo score. Sean Lineen and Scott Hastings, chastised in some quarters for their failings against England, celebrate becoming the world's most capped centre pairing (24 times) with performances of a suitably high quality.

Ireland: K Murphy (Constitution); R Wallace (Garryowen), B Mullin (Blackrock Coll), P Danaher (Garryowen), S Geoghegan (London Irish); R Keyes (Cork Constitution), L Aherne (Lansdowne); N Popplewell (Greystones), S Smith (Ballymena), G Halpin (London Irish), M Galwey (Shannon), N Francis (Blackrock Coll), P Matthews (Wanderers, capt), M Fitzgibbon (Shannon), B Robinson (Ballymena). *Repl:* D Fitzgerald (DLSP) for Halpin, 28 mins; D Curtis (London Irish) for Geoghegan, 40 mins.

Scorers – *Try:* Wallace (70). *Penalty goals:* Keyes 2 (11,73).

Scotland: G Hastings (Watsonians); A Stanger (Hawick), S Hastings (Watsonians), S Lineen (Boroughmuir), I Tukalo (Selkirk); C Chalmers (Melrose), A Nicol (Dundee HSFP); D Sole (Edinburgh Acads, capt), K Milne (Heriot's FP), P Burnell (London Scottish), N Edwards (Harlequins), G Weir (Melrose), D McIvor (Edinburgh Acads), I Smith (Gloucester), D White (London Scottish). *Repl:* R Wainwright (Edinburgh Acads) for Edwards, 78 mins.

Scorers – *Tries:* Stanger (27), Nicol (45). *Conversions:* G Hastings 2. *Penalty goals:* G Hastings 2 (34,80).

Referee: A Spreadbury (England).

Series score: Played 104, Ireland 45, Scotland 54, Drawn 4, Abandoned 1.

France (4) 13, England (15) 31
Paris, 15 February 1992

The tabloids predict 'War', to the disapproval of the purists but, ultimately, England's rout of the French is indeed marred by foul play. Gregoire Lascube, a police detective, and Vincent Moscato, an amateur boxer, are sent off by Irish referee Stephen Hilditch for stamping and head-butting respectively. What shame for a side whose coach, Pierre Berbizier, had decreed, pre-match, that anyone perpetrating foul play would not play again for France. He could hardly have thought that such a warning would precede the first double dismissal for one team in Five Nations' history. England, with 11 survivors to France's 2 from the previous Five Nations' rout in Paris (1990), extend their mastery in the fixture with a fifth successive triumph. England's early lead, through Jonathan Webb's penalty, is quickly usurped when Sebastien Viars rounds off a French move which capitalises on the absence of injured Rob Andrew. David Pears replaces Andrew (face injury) for his Five Nations' debut. England, unimpressed by the Gallic retort, counter with two touchdowns before the interval: first a penalty try when Philippe Gimbert is adjudged to have collapsed a 5-metre scrummage, and then a score for Webb made possible by splendid decoy runs from his brothers-in-arms. Half-time cannot slow England's momentum. Rory Underwood claims his customary try, number 35, and his fourth in consecutive matches against France, after a French scissors movement backfires. So much so, in fact, that Jean-Luc Sadourny, who had only replaced injured skipper Philippe Sella 3 minutes earlier, is helped off to be replaced by debutant Pierre Montlaur. After Christophe Mougeot is again replaced by Olivier Roumat, the rudderless French opt for adding physical insults to their plethora of injuries. *Adieu* Gregoire, *adieu* Vincent (both handed seven-month bans) and, after Dewi Morris' third try in consecutive Five Nations' games, *au revoir* France.

France: J-B Lafond (Racing); P Saint-Andre (Montferrand); P Sella (Agen, capt), F Mesnel (Racing), S Viars (Brive); A Penaud (Brive), F Galthie (Colomiers); G Lascube (Agen), V Moscato (Begles-Bordeaux), C Mougeot (Begles-Bordeaux), C Mougeot (Begles-Bordeaux), M Cecillon (Bougoin Jallieu), J-F Tordo (Nice), L Cabannes (Racing), A van Heerden (Tarbes). *Repl:* J-L Sadourny (Colomiers) for Sella, 55 mins; O Roumat (Dax) for Mougeot, 64 mins; P Montlaur (Agen) for Sadourny, 64 mins.

Scorers – *Tries:* Viars (33), Penaud (68). *Penalty goal:* Viars (46). *Conversion:* Viars (68). *Sent off:* Lascube, Moscato.

England: J Webb (Bath); S Halliday (Harlequins), J Guscott (Bath), W Carling (Harlequins, capt), R Underwood (Leicester & RAF); R Andrew (Toulouse), D Morris (Orrell); J Leonard (Harlequins), B Moore (Harlequins), J Probyn (Wasps), M Bayfield (Northampton), W Dooley (Preston Grasshoppers), M Skinner (Harlequins), P Winterbottom (Harlequins), D Richards (Leicester). *Repl:* D Pears (Harlequins) for Andrew, 35 mins.

Scorers – *Tries:* penalty try (38), Webb (41), Underwood (63), Morris (81). *Conversions:* Webb 3 (38,41,63). *Penalty goals:* Webb 3 (5,56,72).

Referee: S Hilditch (Ireland).

Series score: Played 68, England 37, France 24, Drawn 7.

England (15) 24, Wales 0
Twickenham, 7 March 1992

The outcome that England desires, the world expects, and the record books have awaited. Yet, in spite of the scoreline, which confirms Wales' second heaviest defeat this century by their arch rivals, the boys from the Principality can take great heart from a valiant defensive effort which slows England's progress towards completion of the first back-to-back Grand Slams since 1924. Not that things begin well for the visitors, with Will Carling claiming Rob Andrew's garryowen to poach the first of England's three tries inside the opening minute. It is a fitting score for a man celebrating equalling Wilson Whineray's 22-match-winning run as captain. Other history makers are Rob Andrew, becoming the most-capped international outside-half of all time, and big Wade Dooley, who marks his 50th cap with the 77th minute try that, with conversion, seals Welsh fate. Jonathan Webb caps a marvellous season with 12 points which not only give him a Championship record haul of 67 points, but also lift him above Dusty Hare as England's leading points scorer with 246. England's 118 points scored also represent a Championship best, surpassing by 16 the previous best, established by Wales in 1976.

England: J Webb (Bath); S Halliday (Harlequins), J Guscott (Bath), W Carling (Harlequins, capt), R Underwood (Leicester & RAF); R Andrew (Toulouse), D Morris (Orrell); J Leonard (Harlequins), B Moore (Harlequins), J Probyn (Wasps), M Bayfield (Northampton), W Dooley (Preston Grasshoppers), M Skinner (Harlequins), P Winterbottom (Harlequins), D Richards (Leicester). **Repl**: N Heslop (Orrell) for Carling, 74 mins.

Scorers – *Tries:* Carling (1), Skinner (22), Dooley (77). *Conversions:* Webb 3. *Penalty goals:* Webb 2 (28,79).

Wales: A Clement (Swansea); I Evans (Llanelli, capt), S Gibbs (Neath), N Jenkins (Pontypridd), M Hall (Cardiff); C Stephens (Llanelli), R Jones (Swansea); M Griffiths (Cardiff), G Jenkins (Swansea), L Delaney (Llanelli), G O Llewellyn (Neath), T Copsey (Llanelli), M Morris (Neath), R Webster (Swansea), S Davies (Swansea). **Repl**: M Rayer (Cardiff) for Clement, 40 mins.

Referee: R Megson (Scotland).

Series score: Played 98, England 39, Wales 47, Drawn 12.

Scotland (4) 10, France (3) 6
Edinburgh, 7 March 1992

As Five Nations' spectacles go, this is a shocker, and not the ideal contest in which to celebrate becoming Scotland's most-capped wing. But wingers can't be choosers. Indeed, Iwan Tukalo can barely have touched the ball on his record-breaking 34th appearance. France, offensively hesitant to the point of being paranoid in the wake of the Paris shambles against England, lack the desire to bend down and pick up a win which is theirs for the taking in the Edinburgh rain. Scotland, who have reigned supreme over the French at Murrayfield since 1978, can scarcely believe their good fortune. Neil Edwards, Harlequins' Anglo-Scot, benefits more than anyone. He and his family have taken the 40-1 offered against him scoring the first try and they clean up when he soars above a 4th minute line-out and drives over the French line with the spoils. Two penalty goals by Jean-Baptiste Lafond flatter to deceive. Gavin Hastings quickly restores the home advantage with a brace of his own, and when Derek White produces a simply sensational tackle to cut down the marauding Franck Mesnel inches short of the line, the Scots are home and, if not dry, then mighty relieved.

Scotland: G Hastings (Watsonians); A Stanger (Hawick), S Hastings (Watsonians), S Lineen (Boroughmuir), I Tukalo (Selkirk); C Chalmers (Melrose), A Nicol (Dundee HSFP); D Sole (Edinburgh Acads, capt), K Milne (Heriot's FP), P Burnell (London

Scottish), N Edwards (Harlequins), G Weir (Melrose), D McIvor (Edinburgh Acads), R Wainwright (Edinburgh Acads), D White (London Scottish).

Scorers – *Try:* Edwards (4). *Penalty goals:* G Hastings 2 (56,71).

France: J-L Sadourny (Colomiers); J-B Lafond (Racing); P Sella (Agen, capt), F Mesnel (Racing), P Saint-Andre (Montferrand); A Penaud (Brive), F Galthie (Colomiers); L Armary (Lourdes), J-P Genet (Racing), P Gallart (Beziers), M Cecillon (Bourgoin), O Roumat (Dax), J-F Tordo (Nice), L Cabannes (Racing), A van Heerden (Tarbes)

Scorer – *Penalty goals:* Lafond 2 (11,54).

Referee: F Burger (South Africa).

Series score: Played 63, Scotland 30, France 30, Drawn 3.

France (18) 44, Ireland (6) 12
Paris, 21 March 1992

If Irish fears need any reinforcing before the summer tour to New Zealand then France oblige with a celebration of their own renaissance. After decidedly dodgy displays against the English and Scots, French fortunes take an upturn inspired by Sebastien Viars whose 24 points constitute a Championship record. Philip Danaher's first match as captain coincides with Ireland's worst ever defensive display. Never before have they conceded more than 38 points in an outing. The 32-point margin matches the previous highest – when England won 35-3 at Twickenham in 1988 – and defeat continues Ireland's unbroken run of failure in France dating back to 1972 and the home nation's pre-Parc des Princes era. France's 44 points represents their highest ever Championship score, and the highest in any Five Nations' match since they themselves lost 49-14 to Wales in Swansea 82 years ago. The only bright spot for Ireland is the debut performance of Derek McAleese, who lands four penalty goals from as many attempts.

France: J-L Sadourny (Colomiers); P Saint-Andre (Montferrand), P Sella (Agen, capt), F Mesnel (Racing), S Viars (Brive); A Penaud (Brive), A Hueber (Toulon); L Armary (Lourdes), J-P Genet (Racing), P Gallart (Beziers), J-M Cadieu (Toulouse), O Roumat (Dax), J-F Tordo (Nice), L Cabannes (Racing), M Cecillon (Bourgoin). **Repl**: J-B Lafond (Racing) for Saint-Andre, 70 mins.

Scorers – *Tries:* Penaud 2 (2,85), Viars 2 (40,47), Cecillon (60), Cabannes (62), Sadourny (75). *Conversions:* Viars 5 (40,47,60,62,75). *Penalty goals:* Viars 2 (23,29).

Ireland: K Murphy (Constitution); R Wallace (Garryowen), D Curtis (London Irish), P Danaher (Garryowen, capt), S Geoghegan (London Irish); D McAleese (Ballymena), F Aherne (Lansdowne); N Popplewell (Greystones), S Smith (Ballymena), G Halpin (London Irish), B Rigney (Greystones), M Galwey (Shannon), P Hogan (Garryowen), M Fitzgibbon (Shannon), B Robinson (Ballymena).

Scorer – *Penalty goals:* McAleese 4 (7,25,53,65).

Referee: F Burger (South Africa).

Series score: Played 65, France 35, Ireland 25, Drawn 5.

Wales (9) 15, Scotland (6) 12
Cardiff, 21 March 1992

The word is that Wales need to achieve something they have been unable to in three years of home matches if coach Alan Davies is not to be returned from whence he came. Victory is a must and Scotland, led for the last time in Five Nations' combat by David Sole, play a full and shabby part in ensuring the Welsh manager's continued survival. Arms Park matches have long been listed as Away Bankers – since England's unexpected demise in 1989 – but with Davies' neck apparently on the chopping block, Wales break with recent tradition. They believe they should have beaten France when the Championship show last rolled into town and now, with long-awaited debutant Roger Bidgood adding substance to their midfield, they possess the self-belief to make amends. Triumph they do, too, although the match serves only to highlight the dichotomy of standards between the haves (England) and the have-nots (the rest!). Eleven points from the boot of Neil Jenkins and an excellent try, created out of nothing by Hugh Williams-Jones, for the deserving Richard Webster, prove sufficient to undo a lacklustre Scottish challenge.

Wales: A Clement (Swansea); I Evans (Llanelli, capt), R Bidgood (Swansea), S Gibbs (Neath), M Hall (Cardiff); N Jenkins (Pontypridd), R Jones (Swansea); M Griffiths (Cardiff), G Jenkins (Swansea), H Williams-Jones (South Wales Police), G O Llewellyn (Neath), T Copsey (Llanelli), E Lewis (Llanelli), R Webster (Swansea), S Davies (Swansea).

Scorers – *Try:* Webster (22). *Conversion:* N Jenkins. *Penalty goals:* Jenkins 3 (7,48,71).

Scotland: G Hastings (Watsonians); A Stanger (Hawick), S Hastings (Watsonians), S Lineen (Boroughmuir), I Tukalo (Selkirk); C Chalmers (Melrose), A Nicol (Dundee HSFP); D Sole (Edinburgh Acads, capt), K Milne (Heriot's FP), P Burnell (London Scottish), N Edwards (Harlequins), G Weir (Melrose), D McIvor (Edinburgh Acads), I Smith (Gloucester), D White (London Scottish). **Repl**: P Jones (Gloucester) for Burnell, 55 mins.

Scorers – *Penalty goals:* G Hastings (13), Chalmers 2 (67,77). *Dropped goal:* Chalmers (20).

Referee: M Desclaux (France).

Series score: Played 96, Wales 53, Scotland 41, Drawn 2.

1991/92 FIVE NATIONS' CHAMPIONSHIP

1990/91 positions in brackets

		P	W	D	L	F	(t, c, p, dg)	A	(t, c, p, dg)	Pts
England	(1)	4	4	0	0	118	(15, 11, 11, 1)	29	(4, 2, 3, 0)	8
France	(2)	4	2	0	2	75	(10, 7, 6, 1)	62	(5, 3, 12, 0)	4
Scotland	(3)	4	2	0	2	47	(4, 2, 8, 1)	56	(4, 2, 11, 1)	4
Wales	(5)	4	2	0	2	40	(2, 1, 9, 1)	63	(5, 5, 9, 2)	4
Ireland	(4)	4	0	0	4	46	(3, 2, 10, 0)	116	(16, 11, 9, 1)	0

SCORERS: 67 – J Webb (England) 3t,11c,11p (Championship record). 36 – S Viars (France) 3t,6c,4p. 29 – N Jenkins (Wales) 1c,9p. 26 – R Keyes (Ireland) 1t,2c,6p. 22 – G Hastings (Scotland) 6p,2c. 15 – A Penaud (France) 3t,1dg. 12 – D McAleese (Ireland) 4p; D Morris (England) 3t; R Underwood (England) 3t. 9 – C Chalmers (Scotland) 2p,1dg. 8 – J-B Lafond (France) 1c,2p; R Wallace (Ireland) 2t. 7 – J Guscott (England)

1t,1dg. **4** – L Cabannes (France) 1t; W Carling (England) 1t; M Cecillon (France) 1t; S Davies (Wales) 1t; W Dooley (England) 1t; N Edwards (Scotland) 1t; S Halliday (England) 1t; A Nicol (Scotland) 1t; J-L Sadourny (France) 1t; P Saint-Andre (France) 1t; M Skinner (England) 1t; T Stanger (Scotland) 1t; R Webster (Wales) 1t; D White (Scotland) 1t; penalty try (England). **3** – C Stephens (Wales) 1dg. **TOTAL**: 326 (34t, 23c, 44p, 4dg).

Italy B (7) 10, England B (6) 16
Rome, 7 March 1992

England B complete their own Grand Slam by adding the scalp of Italy B to those of Spain, Ireland B and France B. The supposed Italian second string bears an uncanny resemblance to their World Cup XV, and lead at half-time, but superior English technique ultimately wins the day.

Italy B: L Troiani; P Vaccari, S Barba, S Bordon, Mar Cuttitta; D Dominguez, A Ghini; Mas Cuttitta, G Pivetta (capt), A Piazza, R Favoro, D Sasenna, A Bottacchiari, M Giovanelli, D Beratta. **Repl**: G Croci for Sasenna, 4 mins.

Scorers – *Try:* Croci. *Penalty goal:* Dominguez. *Dropped goal:* Dominguez.

England B: I Hunter (Northampton); T Underwood (Cambridge Univ), J Buckton (Saracens), P de Glanville (Bath), J Fallon (Bath); S Barnes (Bath, capt), S Bates (Wasps); G Baldwin (Northampton), G Dawe (Bath), A Mullins (Harlequins), D Sims (Gloucester), M Johnson (Leicester), N Back (Leicester), M Greenwood (Nottingham), B Clarke (Bath). **Repl**: D Scully (Wakefield) for Bates, 20 mins.

Scorers – *Tries:* Hunter, Scully. *Conversion:* Barnes. *Penalty goals:* Barnes 2.

Referee: R Yeman (Wales).

Series score: Played 6, Italy B 0, England B 5, Draw 1.

Cathay Pacific/Hong Kong Bank Invitation Sevens
Hong Kong, 4-5 April 1992

The Home Unions' presence in Hong Kong is informal, with neither Wales nor Scotland repeating previous precedents and sending offical representatives. The Irish Wolfhounds defeat only Papua New Guinea in failing to make the quarter-final stage where Dick Best's Barbarians bow out against South Korea. Fiji repeat their 1991 final triumph over New Zealand, this time 22-6.

Pool matches: **A** – Fiji 34, Sri Lanka 0; Japan 18, Sri Lanka 0; Fiji 38, Japan 0. **B** – France 22, Papua New Guinea 0; Irish Wolfhounds 28, Papua New Guinea 0; France 22, Irish Wolfhounds 6. **C** – Argentina 10, Germany 4; US Eagles 22, Germany 4; Argentina 12, US Eagles 0. **D** – Australia 42, Singapore 0; Tonga 20, Singapore 4; Australia 18, Tonga 0. **E** – Barbarians 36, Taipei 0; Romania 0, Taipei 24; Barbarians 22, Romania 0. **F** – Canada 50, Thailand 0; South Korea 30, Thailand 4; South Korea 16, Canada 12. **G** – Western Samoa 54, Arabian Gulf 0; Namibia 34, Arabian Gulf 0; Western Samoa 8, Namibia 0. **H** – New Zealand 54, Malaysia 0; Hong Kong 22, Malaysia 0; New Zealand 38, Hong Kong 0.

Quarter-finals: Fiji 22, France 6; Australia 28, Argentina 0; South Korea 16, Barbarians

10; New Zealand 18, Western Samoa 12. **Semi-finals**: Fiji 28, Australia 4; New Zealand 14, South Korea 0. **Final**: Fiji 22, New Zealand 6.

Plate final: Hong Kong 12, Tonga 8 (aet). **Bowl final**: Romania 18, Papua New Guinea 12.

TEAMS – Barbarians: G Hastings (Scotland), A Joubert (South Africa), D Stark (Scotland), H Thorneycroft (England), I Tukalo (Scotland), S Davies (Wales), A Nicol (Scotland), I Hunter (England), R Wainwright (Scotland), J Cassell (England). **Irish Wolfhounds**: D Beggy, V Cunningham, D Jackson, N Woods, J Garth, P Johns, W Mulcahy, D Cleary (England), G Townsend (Scotland).

Spain 6, Romania 0
Madrid, 4 April 1992
Spain score their first ever win over Romania, in more than 30 years of trying, playing in the FIRA Championship.

Scotland U-21 (3) 19, Wales U-21 (14) 28
Stirling, 18 April 1992
The Principality continues to reign over Scotland at U-21 age-level – Wales have now won all six contests since the series was inaugurated in 1987 – though they are less convincing than their assembled talent merits. Nevertheless, it is a case of selectorial eyes down at Stirling. History has taught the game's sages that mighty impressive oaks grow from the tiny acorns; or, in the case of 6ft 10in, 19st Llanelli lock Derwyn Jones, not so tiny. No fewer than 17 Welsh caps (Tony Clement, Richard Webster and Mike Hall, to name but three) have thus far graduated from the U-21 ranks.

Scotland U-21: M Thomson (Stewart's-Melville FP); K Milligan (Stewart's-Melville FP), W Tonkin (Currie), R Shepherd (Edinburgh Acads), J Newton (Dundee HSFP); G Townsend (Gala), B Redpath (Melrose); R McNulty (Stewart's-Melville FP), C Cowan (Dundee HSFP), R Hastings (West of Scotland), S Campbell (Dundee HSFP), M McVie (Edinburgh Acads), J Clinkenbeard (Currie), A Ness (Glasgow H/K, capt), G Flockhart (Stirling County).

Scorers – Try: Campbell. *Penalty goals*: Newton 5.

Wales U-21: J Westwood (Newport); P Harries (Pontypridd), J Redrup (Bristol), N Boobyer (Llanelli), W Proctor (Llanelli); M McCarthy (Neath), R Howley (Bridgend); M Davis (Newport), A Phillips (Bridgend Athletic), K Allen (Aberavon), S Williams (Neath, capt), D Jones (Llanelli), A Gibbs (Newbridge), O Lloyd (Bridgend), S Quinnell (Llanelli). **Repl**: J Williams (Abertillery) for Boobyer, 76 mins.

Scorers – Tries: Quinnell 2, Harries, Westwood, Redrup. *Conversion:* Westwood. *Penalty goals*: McCarthy, Westwood.

Referee: D Lamont (Ireland).

Series score: Played 6; Scotland 0, Wales 6.

WORLD XV TO NEW ZEALAND
(NZRU Centenary celebrations)

April 1992: P4 W2 D0 L2 F143 A97

It might be billed as something of a festival – a three-match celebratory series to mark the centenary of the New Zealand Rugby Union – but the All Blacks are not in a party mood. There is rebuilding work to be done in the light of the World Cup and the painful memory of semi-final elimination by arch-rivals Australia. Everyone loves to see the Mighty tumble and there is no shortage of talent (include Jeremy Guscott, Gavin Hastings and David Sole) prepared to help keep New Zealand down. The Blacks, in transitionary phase, experiment during the series (which they accord Test status) and, despite losing the opener, come back strongly to win the second and third games, orchestrated by centre-turned-outside half Walter Little. The series is marred only by the dismissal (for stamping) of Frenchman Olivier Roumat by David Bishop, the Kiwi referee who had been assaulted in the Parc des Princes tunnel after the France-England World Cup quarter-final. Roumat receives a four-week suspension.

PARTY: G Hastings (Scotland – 1R,2,3R,4), A Joubert (South Africa – 1,3), M Knoetze (South Africa – 1R,2,3R,4), P Hendrick (South Africa – 1,2,3,4), T Horan (Australia – 1R,2,4), J Little (Australia – 4R), J Claassen (South Africa – 1,3,4), J Guscott (England – 1,2,3), Y Yoshida (Japan – 1,3), D Camberabero (France – 1,2), N Botha (South Africa – 3,4), A Nicol (Scotland – 1,2,4R), N Farr-Jones (Australia – 3*,4*), D Sole (Scotland – 1*,2*,4), U Schmidt (South Africa – 1,3), P Fatialofa (Western Samoa – 1R,2,4), E McKenzie (Australia – 3), P Kearns (Australia – 1R,2,4), F Mendes (Argentina – 1,2R,3), O Roumat (France – 1,2,3), J Eales (Australia – 3), T Coker (Australia – 3R,4), G Whetton (New Zealand – 4), A Perelini (Western Samoa – 1R,3), M Cecillon (France – 1,2,3), B Nasser (Australia – 1,3), G Mackinnon (Canada – 1,2,4), P FitzSimons (Australia – 4R), W Ofahengaue (Australia – 1R,2,4), D White (Scotland – 1,2,4).

Fixtures: (1) Hanan Shield Select 3, World XV 74 (Timaru, 15 April); (2) first 'Test': **New Zealand 14, World XV 28** (Christchurch, 18 April); (3) second 'Test': **New Zealand 54, World XV 26** (Wellington, 22 April); (4) third 'Test': **New Zealand 26, World XV 15** (Auckland, 25 April).

Scorers: Camberabero 35 (13c,2p,1dg), Hendrick 20 (5t), Botha 17 (4c,3p), Joubert 12 (3t), Cecillon 8 (2t), Guscott 8 (2t), White 8 (2t), Hastings 7 (1t,1p), Eales 4 (1t), Fatialofa 4 (1t), Horan 4 (1t), Knoetze 4 (1t), Nicol 4 (1t), Ofahengaue 4 (1t), Yoshida 4 (1t).

New Zealand (3) 14, World XV (15) 28
first 'Test': Christchurch, 18 April 1992

New Zealand: G Cooper (Otago); J Kirwan (Auckland), F Bunce (North Harbour), W Little (North Harbour), V Tuigamala (Auckland); G Fox (Auckland), G Bachop (Canterbury); S McDowell (Auckland), S Fitzpatrick (Auckland, capt), R Loe (Waikato), I Jones (North Auckland), M Cooksley (Counties), M Jones (Auckland), P Henderson (Southland), R Turner (North Harbour).

Scorers – *Tries:* Turner, Tuigamala. *Penalty goals:* Fox 2.

World XV: Hastings; Knoetze, Horan, Guscott, Hendrick; Camberabero, Nicol; Sole (capt), Kearns, Fatialofa, Roumat, Cecillon, Mackinnon, Ofahengaue, White. **Repl**: Mendez for Fatialofa, 48 mins.

Scorers – *Tries:* Hendrick 2, Knoetze. *Conversions:* Camberabero 2. *Penalty goals:* Hastings, Camberabero 2. *Dropped goal:* Camberabero.

Referee: W D Bevan (Wales).

Series score: Played 1, New Zealand 0, World XV 1.

New Zealand (34) 54, World XV (6) 26
second 'Test': Wellington, 22 April 1992

New Zealand: G Cooper (Otago); J Timu (Otago), E Clarke (Auckland), F Bunce (North Harbour), V Tuigamala (Auckland); W Little (North Harbour), A Strachan (Auckland); S McDowell (Auckland), S Fitzpatrick (Auckland, capt), R Loe (Waikato), B Larsen (North Harbour), I Jones (North Auckland), J Joseph (Otago), P Henderson (Southland), A Pene (Otago). **Repls**: R Turner (North Harbour) for Henderson, 32 mins; G Fox (Auckland) for Little, 67 mins; J Kirwan (Auckland) for Cooper, 70 mins.

Scorers – *Tries:* Cooper 2, Loe 2, Pene, Clarke 2, Tuigamala, Larsen, Strachan. *Conversions:* Cooper 6, Fox.

World XV: Joubert; Yoshida, Claassen, Guscott, Hendrik; Botha, Farr-Jones (capt); McKenzie, Schmidt, Mendes, Roumat, Eales, Perelini, Nasser, Cecillon. **Repls**: Knoetze for Guscott, 40 mins; Coker for Eales, 59 mins; Hastings for Joubert, 66 mins. **Sent-off**: Roumat.

Scorers – *Tries:* Yoshida, Eales, Cecillon, Hendrik, Hastings. *Conversions:* Botha 3.

Referee: D Bishop (New Zealand).

Series score: Played 2, New Zealand 1, World XV 1.

New Zealand (9) 26, World XV (6) 15
third 'Test': Auckland, 25 April 1992

New Zealand: G Cooper (Otago); J Kirwan (Auckland), E Clarke (Auckland), F Bunce (North Harbour), V Tuigamala (Auckland); W Little (North Harbour), A Strachan (Auckland); S McDowell (Auckland), S Fitzpatrick (Auckland, capt), R Loe (Waikato), B Larsen (North Harbour), I Jones (North Auckland), M Jones (Auckland), P Henderson (Southland), A Pene (Otago). **Repl**: J Joseph (Otago) for Henderson, 19 mins.

Scorers – *Tries:* Pene, Kirwan, Loe, Clarke. *Conversions:* Cooper 2. *Penalty goals:* Cooper 2.

World XV: Hastings; Knoetze, Horan, Claassen, Hendrik; Botha, Farr-Jones (capt); Sole, Kearns, Fatialofa, Coker, Whetton, Ofahengaue, Mackinnon, White. **Repls**: Nicol for Farr-Jones, 64 mins; Little for Claassen, 65 mins; FitzSimons for Ofahengaue, 76 mins.

Scorers – *Try:* Fatialofa. *Conversion:* Botha. *Penalty goals:* Botha 3.

Referee: W D Bevan (Wales).

Series score: Played 3, New Zealand 2, World XV 1.

———————

England U-21 (9) 21, French Armed Forces (9) 21
Twickenham, 2 May 1992

Paul Grayson, the Preston Grasshopper who helped Lancashire upset the odds and beat Cornwall in the County Championship final, returns to Twickenham to ensure that England, despite losing 3-1 on the try-count, share the spoils with a French side featuring senior outside-half Alain Penaud. Grayson lands 17 points, including the conversion of Matt Dawson's try.

England U-21: M Mapletoft (Rugby); J Sleightholme (Wakefield), M Dawson (Northampton), S Ravenscroft (Saracens), R Bryce (Sale); P Grayson (Preston Grasshoppers), K Bracken (Bristol); C Clark (Swansea Univ), R Cockerill (Coventry), G Rowntree (Leicester), R Bramley (Wakefield), R West (Gloucester), I Desmond (Harlequins), G Adams (Bath, capt), M Rennell (Bedford).

Scorers – *Try:* Dawson. *Conversion:* Grayson. *Penalty goals:* Grayson 3. *Dropped goals*: Grayson 2.

F.A.F: G Bedouin (Montelimar); P-Y Soubira (Brive), J-L Pelaez (Racing), M Marfaing (Toulouse), J-V Bertrand (Valence); A Penaud (Brive), L Courbis (Romans); J-M Pinet (Romans), E Jamin (Toulouse), J-P Jean (Romans), A Paute (Perpignan), R Chamelot (Aurillac), D Violle (Paris Univ), S Filali (Brive), E Dalle (Racing, capt).

Scorers – *Tries:* Soubira, Marfaing, Bertrand. *Conversions*: Marfaing 3. *Penalty goal:* Marfaing.

Referee: C Thomas (Wales).

Series score: Played 3, England U-21 2, F. A. F 1.

Netherlands 12, England U-21 48
Leiden, 3 May 1992

England maintain their unblemished record against the Dutch senior team with win number three proving to be the most comprehensive yet. The Netherlands, with an inexperienced seam running through their line-up, are no match for Paul Flood's charges, conceding eight tries including a hat-trick from Leicester Tigers' wing Stephen Wills. Fullback Chris Thompson weighs in with 20 points, 16 by way of the boot.

Netherlands: M Marcker (Castricum); K Sanchez (HRC Den Haag), G Bos (DIOK Leiden), S Hadinogoro (HRC), M Nagtegaal (Hilversum); M Michelsen (DIOK), M Eeman (HRC); Y Kummer (DIOK, capt), R Koot (HRC), A N Other, E-J Berendsen (DIOK), R Wijnbergen (Hilversum), D Pace (Delft), M Magis (Delft), M Geelhoed (HRC).

Scorers – *Tries:* Michelsen, Nagtegaal. *Conversions:* Bos 2.

England U-21: C Thompson (Sheffield Univ); S Wills (Leicester), J Alexander (Harlequins), P Flood (Bridgend, capt), M Griffiths (Blackheath); T Hanley (DLSP), I Sanders (Bath); D Molloy (Wasps), R Kellam (Newbury), D Crompton (Essex), A Diprose (Loughborough Students), A Meadows (Newcastle Gosforth), D Blyth (Waterloo), C Millhouse (Bristol), L Dallaglio (Wasps).

Scorers – *Tries:* Wills 3, Meadows, Thompson, Sanders, Griffiths, penalty try. *Conversions:* Thompson 5. *Penalty goals*: Thompson 2.

Referee: B Smith (Ireland).

Series score: Played 3, Netherlands 0, England U-21 3

SUMMER TOUR SQUADS
(* denotes uncapped players)

IRELAND TO NEW ZEALAND
May-June 1992 – 7 games

PARTY – Backs: J Staples (London Irish), K Murphy (Constitution), R Wallace (Garryowen), *R Carey (Dungannon), P Danaher (Garryowen, capt), V Cunningham (St Mary's), *M Ridge (Blackrock), *M McCall (Bangor), *N Furlong (UCG), J Clarke (Dolphin), D McAleese (Ballymena), P Russell (Instonians), F Aherne (Lansdowne), M Bradley (Constitution). **Forwards**: N Popplewell (Greystones), T Clancy (London Irish), S Smith (Ballymena), T Kingston (Dolphin), G Halpin (London Irish), *P McCarthy (Constitution), *J Etheridge (Northampton), M Galwey (Shannon), B Rigney (Greystones), *R Costello (Garryowen), M Fitzgibbon (Shannon), D McBride (Malone), *K Leahy (Wanderers), B Robinson (Ballymena), N Mannion (Lansdowne), *P Johns (Dungannon).

Fixtures: (1) v South Canterbury (Timaru, 13 May); (2) v Canterbury (Christchurch, 16 May); (3) v Bay of Plenty (Rotorua, 20 May); (4) v Poverty Bay-East Coast (Gisborne, 23 May); (5) first Test: **v New Zealand** (Dunedin, 30 May); (6) v Manawatu (Palmerston North, 2 June); (7) second Test: **v New Zealand** (Wellington, 6 June).

See page 329 for results.

SCOTLAND TO AUSTRALIA
May-June 1992 – 8 games

PARTY – Backs: *D Bain (Melrose), C Chalmers (Melrose), P Dods (Gala), G Hastings (Watsonians), S Hastings (Watsonians), S Lineen (Boroughmuir), *K Logan (Stirling County), *D Millard (London Scottish), A Nicol (Dundee HSFP), G Shiel (Melrose), T Stanger (Hawick), *D Stark (Ayr), *G Townsend (Gala), I Tukalo (Selkirk). **Forwards**: *I Corcoran (Gala), D Cronin (London Scottish), N Edwards (Harlequins), C Gray (Nottingham), *C Hogg (Melrose), P Jones (Gloucester), D McIvor (Edinburgh Academicals), K Milne (Heriot's FP), *S Reid (Boroughmuir), *J Robertson (Heriot's FP), I Smith (Gloucester), D Sole (Edinburgh Academicals, capt), R Wainwright (Edinburgh Academicals), A Watt (Glasgow H/K), G Weir (Melrose), *P Wright (Boroughmuir).

Fixtures: (1) v Northern Territory (Darwin, 28 May); (2) v Queensland (Brisbane, 31 May); (3) v Emerging Wallabies (Hobart, 3 June); (4) v New South Wales (Sydney, 6 June); (5) v NSW Country (Newcastle, 9 June); (6) first Test: **v Australia** (Sydney, 13 June); (7) v Queensland County (Toowoomba, 17 June); (8) second Test: **v Australia** (Brisbane, 21 June).

See page 143 for results.

ENGLAND B TO NEW ZEALAND
June-July 1992 – 8 games

PARTY – Backs: *I Hunter (Northampton), *J Fallon (Bath), A Harriman (Harlequins),

*H Thorneycroft (Northampton), *T Underwood (Leicester), *G Childs (Wasps), *P de Glanville (Bath), *D Hopley (Wasps), *G Thompson (Harlequins), S Barnes (Bath, capt), *N Matthews (Gloucester), *J Steele (Northampton), *A Kardooni (Leicester), *D Scully (Wakefield). **Forwards:** *G Baldwin (Northampton), *M Hynes (Orrell), A Mullins (Harlequins), *V Ubogu (Bath), G Dawe (Bath), *K Dunn (Gloucester), M Bayfield (Northampton), *M Haag (Bath), *M Johnson (Leicester), *D Sims (Gloucester), *J Cassell (Saracens), *M Greenwood (Nottingham), D Ryan (Wasps), *N Back (Leicester), *B Clarke (Bath), *M Russell (Harlequins).

Fixtures: (1) v North Otago (Oamaru, 10 June); (2) v Southland (Invercargill, 13 June); (3) v NZ Universities (Wellington, 17 June); (4) v Wairarapa-Bush (Masterton, 20 June); (5) v Wanganui (Wanganui, 24 June); (6) v New Zealand XV (Hamilton, 28 June); (7) v North Auckland (Whangarei, 1 July); (8) v New Zealand XV (Pukekohe, 6 July).

See page 227 for results.

England scrum-half Dewi Morris slips the ball inside to Brian Moore during England's 25–7 Championship win over Scotland at Murrayfield

MAJOR FIXTURES FOR
SEASON 1992/93

NOTE: The following dates are subject to alteration. Check National Press
before setting out!

1992

SEPTEMBER
3 – South of Scotland v. Leinster
5 – Glasgow v. Leinster
– Heineken Welsh Club Championship (Round 1)
12 – Heineken Welsh Club Championship (Round 2)
19 – Pilkington Cup (Round 1)
– Heineken Welsh Club Championship (Round 3)
26 – Courage English Club Championship (Round 1)
– Heineken Welsh Club Championship (Round 4)
– McEwan's Scottish Club Championship (Round 1)

OCTOBER
3 – Courage English Club Championship (Round 2)
– Heineken Welsh Club Championship (Round 5)
– McEwan's Scottish Club Championship (Round 2)
7 – Wales XV v. Italy (Cardiff)
10 – Courage English Club Championship (Round 3)
– Insurance Corporation All-Ireland Club Championship (Round 1)
– Heineken Welsh Club Championship (Round 6)
– McEwan's Scottish Club Championship (Round 3)
14 – England U-21 v. Ireland U-21
– Wales B v. North of England (Pontypool)
17 – FRANCE v. SOUTH AFRICA (first Test)
– Leinster v. Australia (Dublin)
– Heineken Welsh Club Championship (Round 7)
– McEwan's Scottish Club Championship (Round 4)
21 – Munster v. Australia (Cork)
24 – FRANCE v. SOUTH AFRICA (second Test)
– Ulster v. Australia (Belfast)
– Courage English Club Championship (Round 4)
– Heineken Welsh Club Championship (Round 8)
– McEwan's Scottish Club Championship (Round 5)
27 – Connacht v. Australia (Galway)
28 – Ireland U-21 v. Wales U-21 (Dublin)

31   – IRELAND v. AUSTRALIA (Dublin)
       – French Barbarians v. South Africa (Tarbes)
       – Courage English Club Championship (Round 5)
       – Heineken Welsh Club Championship (Round 9)
       – McEwan's Scottish Club Championship (Round 6)

NOVEMBER
4   – Monmouthshire v. Australia (Ebbw Vale)
7   – Wales B v. Australia (Cardiff)
       – England B v. South Africa (Bristol)
       – Pilkington Cup (Round 2)
       – Insurance Corporation All-Ireland Club Championship (Round 2)
       – McEwan's Scottish Club Championship (Round 7)
11   – Neath v. Australia (The Gnoll)
14   – ENGLAND v. SOUTH AFRICA (Twickenham)
        (The Save & Prosper International)
       – FRANCE v. ARGENTINA (Nantes)
       – Llanelli v. Australia (Stradey Park)
       – Courage English Club Championship (Round 6)
       – Insurance Corporation All-Ireland Club Championship (Round 3)
       – McEwan's Scottish Club Championship (Round 8)
16   – Scottish Students v. Oxford University
17   – Wales Students v. Australia (Bridgend)
20   – Wales B v. Spain
21   – WALES v. AUSTRALIA (Cardiff)
       – McEwan's Inter-District Championship:
        Edinburgh v. Glasgow
        North & Midlands v. South of Scotland
       – Courage English Club Championship (Round 7)
       – Insurance Corporation All-Ireland Club Championship (Round 4)
24   – Swansea v. Australia
28   – BARBARIANS v. AUSTRALIA (Twickenham)
       – Pilkington Cup (Round 3)
       – McEwan's Inter-District Championship:
        North & Midlands v. Edinburgh
        Glasgow v. South of Scotland
       – Heineken Welsh Club Championship (Round 10)

DECEMBER
2   – McEwan's Inter-District Championship:
        Anglo Scots v. Glasgow
5   – McEwan's Inter-District Championship:
        South of Scotland v. Anglo Scots
        Glasgow v. North & Midlands
       – ADT English Divisional Championship (Round 1)
       – ADT English County Championship (1)
       – Heineken Welsh Club Championship (Round 11)

8	– Varsity match: Oxford v. Cambridge (Twickenham)
	(for The Bowring Bowl)
9	– McEwan's Inter-District Championship:
	Edinburgh v. Anglo Scots
12	– Colts County Championship final (Twickenham)
	– ADT English Divisional Championship (Round 2)
	– ADT English County Championship (2)
	– McEwan's Inter-District Championship:
	South of Scotland v. Edinburgh
	Anglo Scots v. North & Midlands
	– Heineken Welsh Club Championship (Round 12)
19	– Scotland A v. Spain A
	– French Schools v. Scottish Schools
	– ADT English Divisional Championship (Round 3)
	– ADT English County Championship (3)
26	– Ireland A v. Scotland A
28	– East Wales v. West Wales (Cardiff)

1993

JANUARY

2	– Scotland Trial (Edinburgh)
	– Heineken Welsh Club Championship (Round 13)
4	– Scottish Schools v. Welsh Schools
9	– Courage English Club Championship (Round 8)
	– Heineken Welsh Club Championship (Round 14)
	– McEwan's Scottish Club Championship (Round 9)
9/10	– Insurance Corporation All-Ireland Club Championship (Round 5)
15	– England B v. France B
	– Scotland U-21 v. Ireland U-21 (Edinburgh)
	– Scottish Students v. Irish Students
16	– ENGLAND v. FRANCE (Twickenham)
	(The Save & Prosper International)
	– SCOTLAND v. IRELAND (Edinburgh)
	(The Royal Bank of Scotland International)
	– Heineken Welsh Club Championship (Round 15)
17	– Scottish Schools B v. New Zealand Schools
20	– Scottish Schools v. New Zealand Schools (Edinburgh)
23	– Pilkington Cup (Round 4)
	– Insurance Corporation All-Ireland Club Championship (Round 6)
	– McEwan's Scottish Club Championship (Round 10)
30	– Insurance Corporation All-Ireland Club Championship (Round 7)
	– Heineken Welsh Club Championship (Round 16)

FEBRUARY

| 5 | – England B v. Italy B |
| | – France U-21 v. Scotland U-21 (Paris) |

	– French Students v. Scottish Students
6	– WALES v. ENGLAND (Cardiff)
	(The British Gas Challenge)
	– FRANCE v. SCOTLAND (Paris)
6/7	– Insurance Corporation All-Ireland Club Championship (Round 8)
7	– Netherlands v. Wales B
13	– Courage English Club Championship (Round 9)
	– Insurance Corporation All-Ireland Club Championship (Round 9)
	– Heineken Welsh Club Championship (Round 17)
	– McEwan's Scottish Club Championship (Round 11)
19	– Scotland U-21 v. Wales U-21 (Edinburgh)
	– Scottish Students v. Welsh Students
	– Scottish Universities v. Welsh Universities
20	– SCOTLAND v. WALES (Edinburgh)
	(The Royal Bank of Scotland International)
	– IRELAND v. FRANCE (Dublin)
	(The Digital International)
	– ADT English County Championship (semi-finals)
27	– Pilkington Cup (Quarter-finals)
	– McEwan's Scottish Club Championship (Round 12)

MARCH

5	– England B v. Spain
	– Wales B v. Ireland B (Newport)
	– England U-21 v. Scotland U-21 (London)
	– English Students v. Scottish Students
	– English Universities v. Scottish Universities
6	– ENGLAND v. SCOTLAND (Twickenham)
	(The Save & Prosper International)
	– WALES v. IRELAND (Cardiff)
13	– England Colts v. Italy Youth (US Portsmouth)
	– Royal Navy v. Army (Twickenham)
	– Courage English Club Championship (Round 10)
	– Heineken Welsh Club Championship (Round 18)
	– McEwan's Scottish Club Championship (Round 13)
17	– UAU Final (Twickenham)
19	– Ireland B v. England B
20	– IRELAND v. ENGLAND (Dublin)
	(The Digital International)
	– FRANCE v. WALES (Paris)
	– Scotland A v. France A
24	– Army v. Royal Air Force (Twickenham)
27	– England Colts v. Wales Youth (Bath)
	– Courage English Club Championship (Round 11)
31	– Royal Navy v. Royal Air Force (Twickenham)

APRIL
   3 – England 18-Group v. Scotland U-18 (Wolverhampton)
     – Scottish Schools v. Irish Schools
     – Courage English Club Championship (Round 12)
     – Heineken Welsh Club Championship (Round 19)
   4 – England 16-Group v. Spain U-16
   5 – Welsh Schools U-15 v. Scottish Schools U-15
   7 – England 18-Group v. France U-18 (Camborne)
     – English Schools v. Scottish Schools
  10 – Scotland U-19 v. England Colts
     – Italy U-16 v. England 16-Group
     – Scotland U-18 v. Ireland U-18
     – Provincial Insurance Cup final (Twickenham)
     – Pilkington Cup (Semi-finals)
     – Heineken Welsh Club Championship (Round 20)
  14 – Ireland U-18 v. England 18-Group (Belfast)
16–18 – Rugby World Cup Sevens (Edinburgh)
  17 – Italy v. Scotland A
     – Wales U-19 v. Scotland U-19
     – England 16-Group v. Welsh Schools U-16
     – ADT English County Championship final (Twickenham)
  24 – France Juniors v. England Colts
     – Courage English Club Championship (Round 13)
     – Heineken Welsh Club Championship (Round 21)

MAY
   1 – Pilkington Cup final (Twickenham)
     – Heineken Welsh Club Championship (Round 22)
   8 – Middlesex Seven-a-side finals (Twickenham)
       (sponsored by Save & Prosper)
  22 – North Auckland v. British Lions (Whangarei)
  26 – North Harbour v. British Lions (Auckland)
  29 – New Zealand Maoris v. British Lions (Wellington)

JUNE
   2 – Canterbury v. British Lions (Christchurch)
   5 – Otago v. British Lions (Dunedin)
   8 – Southland v. British Lions (Invercargill)
  12 – NEW ZEALAND v. BRITISH LIONS (first Test: Christchurch)
  16 – Taranaki v. British Lions (North Plymouth)
  19 – Auckland v. British Lions (Auckland)
  22 – Hawkes Bay v. British Lions (Napier)
  26 – NEW ZEALAND v. BRITISH LIONS (second Test: Wellington)
  29 – Waikato v. British Lions (Hamilton)

JULY
   3 – NEW ZEALAND v. BRITISH LIONS (third Test: Auckland)

383

FULL LIST OF ENTRIES

ENGLAND

Ackford, P.J. (Retiree)
Adebayo, A.A.
  (Appendix)
Adams, G.E.
Ainscough, G.C.
  (Appendix)
Alexander, J.
  (Appendix)
Andrew, C.R.
Back, N.A.
Baldwin, G.P.S.
Barnes, S.
Bates, S.M.
Bayfield, M.C.
Boyle, L.S.
Bramley, R.
  (Appendix)
Bromley, S.
  (Appendix)
Bryce, R. (Appendix)
Bullock, W.
  (Appendix)
Buckton, J.R.
Carling, W.D.C.
Cassell, J.P.S.
Childs, G.C.
  (Appendix)
Clark, C. (Appendix)
Clarke, B.B.
Cockerill, R.
  (Appendix)
Crompton, D.
  (Appendix)
Dallaglio, L.
  (Appendix)
Dawson, M.
  (Appendix)

Dawe, R.G.R.
Desmond, I.
  (Appendix)
De Glanville, P.R.
Diprose, A.
  (Appendix)
Dooley, W.A.
Douglas, S.M.
Dunn, K.A.
  (Appendix)
Fallon, J.A. (Retiree)
Flood, J.P. (Appendix)
Grayson, P.J.
  (Appendix)
Greenwood, M.
  (Appendix)
Griffiths, M.
  (Appendix)
Guscott, J.C.
Haag, M.
Halliday, S.J. (Retiree)
Harriman, A.T.
  (Appendix)
Heslop, N.J.
Hill, R.J.
Hodgkinson, S.D.
Hopley, D.P.
  (Appendix)
Hunter, I.
Hynes, M.P.
Johnson, M.O.
Kardooni, A.
  (Appendix)
Kellam, R. (Appendix)
Knight, S. (Appendix)
Leonard, J.
Liley, R.J. (Appendix)
Mapletoft, M.
  (Appendix)

Matthews, N.J.
Meadows, A.
  (Appendix)
Millhouse, C.
  (Appendix)
Molloy, D. (Appendix)
Moore, B.C.
Morris, C.D.
Mullins, A.R.
Olver, C.J.
Oti, C.
Pearson, J.T.V.P.
  (Appendix)
Pearce, G.S.
Pears, D.
Probyn, J.A.
Ravenscroft, S.
  (Appendix)
Rennell, M.I.
  (Appendix)
Redman, N.C.
Rees, G.W.
Rendall, P.A.G.
  (Retiree)
Richards, D.
Rodber, T.A.K.
Rowntree, G.C.
Russell, M. (Appendix)
Ryan, D. (Appendix)
Sanders, I. (Appendix)
Scully, D.A.
Sims, D.
Skinner, M.G.
Sleightholme, J.
  (Appendix)
Steele, J. (Appendix)
Teague, M.
Thompson, C.
  (Appendix)

Thompson, G.J.
(Appendix)
Thorneycroft, H.S.
(Appendix)
Ubogu, V.E.
(Appendix)
Underwood, R.
(Retiree)
Underwood, T.
West, R.J. (Appendix)
Webb, J.M.
Wills, S.R. (Appendix)
Winterbottom, P.J.

IRELAND

Aherne, L.F.P.
Barry, N.
Blair, A.G.
Bradley, M.T.
Carey, R. (Appendix)
Clancy, T.P.J.
(Appendix)
Clarke, J.D.
Costello, R.
(Appendix)
Coughlin, T.
(Appendix)
Costello, V.C.P.
Crossan, K.D.
Cunningham, V.J.G.
Curtis, D.M.
Danaher, P.P.A.
Etheridge, J.
(Appendix)
FitzGibbon, M.J.
Fitzgerald, D.C.
Fitzgerald, J.J.
Francis, N.P.
Fulcher, G.M.
(Appendix)
Furlong, N.
(Appendix)
Galwey, M.J.
Geoghegan, S.P.

Halpin, G.F.
Hamilton, G.F.
Hogan, N.A.
Hogan, P.J.
Hunter, R. (Appendix)
Johns, P.S.
Kernohan, M.
(Appendix)
Keyes, R.P.
Kingston, T.J.
Kiernan, M.J. (Retiree)
Lavin, G.J.
Lawlor, P.J.
Leahy, K.T.
Lenihan, D.G.
(Retiree)
Longwell, G.
(Appendix)
McAlesse, D.R.
McBride, W.D.
McCall, M.
(Appendix)
McCarthy, P.D.
McCartney, D.
(Appendix)
McCluskey, G.
(Appendix)
McDermott, M.
(Appendix)
Malone, N.G.
Mannion, N.P.S.
Matthews, P.M.
Millar, P. (Appendix)
Murphy, J. (Appendix)
Murphyy, L.
(Appendix)
Mullin, B.J. (Retiree)
Murphy, K.J.
O'Callaghan, U.
(Appendix)
O'Hara, P.T.
O'Mahony, B.G.
O'Shea, C.M.P.
O'Shea, W.J.
Potts, K. (Appendix)

Popplewell, N.J.
Ridge, M.P.
Rigney, B.J.
Robinson, B.F.
Rolland, A.C.P.
Rooney, S.V.J.
Russell, P. (Appendix)
Saunders, R.
Scott, P. (Appendix)
Smith, S.J.
Soden, P.J.
Staples, J.E.
Toland, L.T.
(Appendix)
Wallace, P. (Appendix)
Wallace, R.M.
Wilkinson, C.R.
Wilson, R.K.
Woods, N. (Appendix)

SCOTLAND

Adam, D.R.W.
(Appendix)
Allingham, M.J.De G.
(Appendix)
Allan, J.
Amos, J.P. (Appendix)
Appleson, M.E.
Armstrong, G.
Barrett, D. (Appendix)
Burns, G.G.
(Appendix)
Burnell, A.P.
Calder, F. (Retiree)
Chalmers, C.M.
Clinkenbeard, J.M.
(Appendix)
Corcoran, I.
(Appendix)
Cousar, G.S.
(Appendix)
Cowan, C.J.
(Appendix)
Cronin, D.F.

Dods, P.W.
Edwards, N.G.B.
Flockhart, G.N.
    (Appendix)
Fraser, A.M.
    (Appendix)
Glasgow, I.C.
    (Appendix)
Gray, C.A.
Hamilton, D.R.
    (Appendix)
Hastings, R.K.
    (Appendix)
Hay, J.A. (Appendix)
Harrold, F.R.
Hastings, A.G.
Hastings, S.
Hogg, C.D.
    (Appendix)
Isaac, G.R. (Appendix)
Jardine, I.C.
Jeffrey, J. (Retiree)
Jones, P.M.
Lineen, S.R.P.
Macdonald, A.E.D
Marshall, G.R.
McIntosh, D.L.M.
McIvor, D.J.
McNulty, R.
    (Appendix)
McVie, M.J.
    (Appendix)
Millard, D. (Appendix)
Milligan, K.R.
    (Appendix)
Milne, D.F.
Milne, I.G.
Milne, K.S.
Moncrieff, M.
Moore, A.
Newton, J. (Appendix)
Nichol, S.A.
    (Appendix)
Nicol, A.D.
Oliver, G.H.

Redpath, B.W.
Reid, S.J.
Robertson, G.B.
Scott, S. (Appendix)
Scott, M.W.
Scott, R.
Shepherd, R.J.S.
Shiel, A.G.
Smith, T.J. (Appendix)
Smith, I.R.
Sole, D.M.B. (Retiree)
Stanger, A.G.
Stark, D.A.
Thomson, M.M.
    (Appendix)
Tonkin, W.M.
    (Appendix)
Townsend, G.P.J.
Tukalo, I.
Turnbull, D.J.
Wainwright, R.I
Watt, A.G.J.
Weir, G.W.
White, D.B. (Retiree)
Wilson, G.D.
Wyllie, D.S.

WALES

Allen, K.W.
    (Appendix)
Arnold, P.
Bidgood, R.A.
Booth, A.H.
    (Appendix)
Boobyer, N.
Bridges, C.J.
Clement, A.
Collins, R.G.
Copsey, A.H.
Davies, G. (Appendix)
Davies, A.
Davies, P.T.
Davies, S.
Davis, M.E.

Delaney, L.
Emyr, A.
Evans, J. (Appendix)
Evans, D.W.
Evans, I.C.
Evans, I.L.
Ford, S.P.
Fox, D.C.
Gibbs, A. (Appendix)
Gibbs, I.S.
Goodey, R.
    (Appendix)
Goodwin, C.
    (Appendix)
Griffiths, M.
Hall, M.R.
Harries, P.T.
Hembrow, I.L.
    (Appendix)
Howley, R.
Jenkins, G.R.
Jenkins, N.R.
Jones, D. (Appendix)
Jones, I.W.
Jones, P. (Appendix)
Jones, R. (Appendix)
Jones, R.N.
Jones, R.J. (Appendix)
Joseph, D. (Dai).
    (Appendix)
Knight, P.
Langley, C.
    (Appendix)
Lewis, I. (Appendix)
Legge, S.
Lewis, E.W.
Lewis, S.L.
Lloyd, O.S.
    (Appendix)
Llewellyn, G.D.
Llewellyn, G.O.
May, P.S.
McCarthy, M.
    (Appendix)
Moon, R.H.St J.B.

Morris, M.S.
Moseley, K.
Orrell, T.
Phillips, A. (Appendix)
Phillips, K.H.
Proctor, W.T.
Quinnell, L.S.
Rayer, M.A.
Redrup, J. (Appendix)
Ring, M.G. (Retiree)
Roy, S. (Appendix)
Stephens, C.J.
Thomas, D.
   (Appendix)
Thorburn, P.H.
   (Retiree)
Waters, K.
Webster, R.E.
Westwood, J.
Williams, A.
   (Appendix)

Williams, J.A.
   (Appendix)
Williams, S.M.
Williams-Jones, H.

FRANCE

Armary, L.
Benazzi, A.
Benetton, P.
Blanco, S.
Cabannes, L.
Cadieu, J.- M.
Camberabero, D.
Cécillon, M.
Champ, E.
Courtiols, M.
Devergie, T.
Gallart, P.
Galthie, F.
Genet, J.- P.
Gimbert, P.
Hontas, P.

Hueber, A.
Lacroix, T.
Lafond, J.- B.
Lagisquet, P.
Lascube, G.
Marocco, P.
Melville, E.
Mesnel, F.
Montlaur, P.
Moscato, V
Mougeot, C.
Ondarts, P.
Penaud, A.
Roumat, O.
Sadourny, J.- L.
Saint-André, P.
Sanz, H.
Sella, P.
Simon, S.
Tordo, J.- F.
Van Heerden, A.
Viars, S.